Man in Ecological Perspective

Edited by
James F. Metress
University of Toledo

MSS EDUCATIONAL PUBLISHING COMPANY, INC.
19 EAST 48th STREET, NEW YORK, N. Y. 10017

H·L·

This is a custom-made book of readings prepared for the courses taught by the editor. For information about our program, please write to:

MSS Educational Publishing Company, Inc.
19 East 48th Street
New York, New York 10017

MSS wishes to express its appreciation to the authors of the articles in this collection for their cooperation in making their work available in this format.

CONTENTS

Preface
Man in Ecological Perspective

Ecology is the study of the interrelationships between living organisms and their biophysical environment. As a body knowledge it has been developed largely by investigators in the biological sciences.

Human ecology, on the other hand, places emphasis on one species and its place in nature. It considers the effects of man's biophysical environment upon him and the effects he has on his environment. The subject matter of human ecology is being developed by a coalescence of several disciplines. The anthropological, biological, geographic, medical and sociological approaches all contribute important principles and information to this interdisciplinary field.

The purpose of this collection is to introduce students in a variety of disciplines to human ecology. It makes no pretense that it is a complete introduction but it is representative and does not lean heavily toward one discipline or another.

The first section, Man in Ecological Perspective, introduces the student to the human animal in an ecological context. It touches on the biological and cultural aspects of human adaptation to environment.

Sections II and III, Ecology of Human Diseases and Nutritional Ecology, deal with two major areas of human ecological research. These two sections attempt to examine disease and nutrition from an ecological point of view in some depth.

The last two sections deal with man's role in upsetting the balance of nature due to overproduction of his species, and his pollution and degradation of his environment. It serves to introduce the student to problems of overpopulation, misuse of pesticides, radiation, air and water pollution and advancing technology.

This reader can be used as a basic text in a human ecology course or as an outside reading source in anthropology, geography, and biology courses with a variety of titles. The general reader can use the book to acquire an ecological view of man and his problems.

James F. Metress
The University of Toledo

The Biological Nature of Man

George Gaylord Simpson

It has often and confidently been asserted, that man's origin can never be known: but ignorance more frequently begets confidence than does knowledge: it is those who know little, and not those who know much, who so positively assert that this or that problem will never be solved by science. (1)

Those words were written by Charles Darwin nearly 100 years ago and were published in 1871 in the introduction to his book on The Descent of Man. In his even better known work on The Origin of Species (2), which had appeared 12 years earlier, he had been content to say (somewhat coyly) that by that work "light would be thrown on the origin of man and his history." Others soon indicated the nature of that light. Thomas Henry Huxley's classic Man's Place in Nature (3) was published in 1863, and by 1871 numerous other naturalists of the first rank had already accepted the evolutionary origin of the human species. Darwin's own contribution to the problem of man's origin firmly established two points: first, Homo sapiens, like all other organisms, has evolved from prior, extremely different species by natural means and under the directive influence of natural selection; and second, man is the descendant of apes or monkeys of the Old World.

Darwin's first point, that man is the product of evolution involving natural selection, has been attacked on emotional grounds, but it was not and is not now honestly questionable on strictly scientific grounds and by anyone really familiar with the facts. The second point, of man's descent from an Old World ape or monkey, was for some time more open to scientific dispute. However, here, too, the debate

The author is Alexander Agassiz Professor of Vertebrate Paleontology at Harvard University, Cambridge, Massachusetts.

was often more emotional than objective. In some pedagogic circles it became usual to maintain that man is not descended from an ape but from a common ancestor neither man nor ape nor, if one cared to go still further afield, monkey. Some went so far as to attempt to enlist Darwin posthumously in their own pussyfooting ranks by saying that he never maintained that man arose from an ape but only from a common ancestor . . . and so forth. In fact, although Darwin was slow to enter the dispute, when he did so he was more honest than those supposed defenders. He flatly said, "We must conclude, however much the conclusion may revolt our pride, that our early progenitors would have been properly . . . designated [as apes or monkeys]." The unscientific and really uncalled-for remark on pride does little to modify the forthrightness of the conclusion.

Darwin's conclusions in 1871 already covered what is most vital for consideration of man's biological status. Subsequent discovery and study have fully corroborated Darwin and have added an enormous amount of detail. That is interesting and important, and most of what I have to say here concerns it. At this point, however, the essential thing is that Darwin put the whole subject of the nature of man on a new and sound footing. To be sure, in the introduction of The Descent of Man, from which I have already quoted, Darwin went on to say that, "The conclusion that man is the co-descendant with other species of some ancient, lower, and extinct form, is not in any degree new." He then cited Lamarck, Wallace, Huxley, Lyell, Vogt, Lubbock, Büchner, Rolle, Haeckel, Canestrini, and Barrago as "having taken the same side of the question."

Science, April 22, 1966, Vol.152, No.3721, pp. 472-478.

In fact, as regards this particular point, Darwin was doing too much honor to those worthies, some still famous and some now forgotten. It is true that they had all discussed the descent of man before Darwin himself did so in an explicit way, but with the sole exception of Lamarck they had done so after publication of *The Origin of Species* and on the basis of that work by Darwin. As for the few who really had postulated an evolutionary origin for man before *The Origin of Species*, their views were largely philosophical speculations inadequately or not at all supported by objective evidence and sometimes, as in the case of Lamarck, reaching a conclusion only approximately correct on grounds that were flatly wrong (4).

What Is Man?

The question "What is man?" is probably the most profound that can be asked by man. It has always been central to any system of philosophy or of theology. We know that it was being asked by the most learned humans 2000 years ago, and it is just possible that it was being asked by the most brilliant australopithecines 2 million years ago. The point I want to make now is that all attempts to answer that question before 1859 are worthless and that we will be better off if we ignore them completely. The reason is that no answer had a solid, objective base until it was recognized that man is the product of evolution from primeval apes and before that through billions of years of gradual but protean change from some spontaneously, that is, naturally, generated primordial monad.

It is the biological nature of man, both in his evolutionary history and in his present condition, that presents us with our only fixed point of departure. These are the facts we can find out for ourselves, in great, ever-increas-

ing detail and soundness, open to all of us in irrefutable observations. Their interpretation is in some respects ambiguous and disputable, but interpretation at a given point becomes increasingly clear and undisputed as time goes on. Doubtfulness moves outward with the expanding frontier of knowledge.

I do not mean to say that the biological study of man or even that the scientific study of man in terms broader than biological can here and now—if ever—provide a satisfactorily complete answer to the question "What is man?" The other, older approaches through metaphysics, theology, art, and other nonbiological, nonscientific fields can still contribute, or can now contribute anew. But unless they accept, by specification or by implication, the nature of man as a biological organism, they are merely fictional fancies or falsities, however interesting they may be in those nonfactual categories. I am here concerned with man's biological nature in a rather broad sense, on the grounds that this is a necessary, even though it is not a completely sufficient, approach to comprehension of man's nature.

Already in Darwin's day it was clearly established that among living animals the great apes are anatomically most similar to man. Some anatomists, reluctant to acknowledge their poor relatives, stressed differences between man and any apes: the larger human brain, obviously; the longer and less divergent first toe of man; the absence or, more commonly, the only-sporadic presence in us of certain apish muscles and other structures. Such discussions completely missed the point. Of course men and apes differ. In itself, that means only that we belong to different species. The point at issue is not whether we differ, but in what way and how closely the different species are related.

All later study has corroborated the special relationship between men and apes and has made knowledge of it more precise. The evidence has lately been greatly increased in extent, in detail, and in its basic character. It now includes such fundamental points as the numbers and shapes of chromosomes, the exact molecular structure of hemoglobins, the resemblances and differences of serum proteins, and many others (5). All the evidence agrees and the conclusion is unequivocal. Man is not identical with apes in these or other respects. However, he is clearly related to the apes, and among the apes he is most particularly related to chimpanzees and gorillas, which are closely related between themselves. A necessary inference from this evidence is that the common ancestor of apes and men was itself a member of the ape family. Not only that; we had a common ancestor with gorilla and chimpanzee after their ancestry had become distinct from **that of the other living apes (orangutan and gibbons). Our relationships to gorilla and to chimpanzee are about equal, although gorillas may have become somewhat more specialized with respect to the common ancestry.**

Evidence from Fossils

More precise evidence as to relationships and as to the course of anatomical change in the human ancestry must come from fossils. There are special reasons why pertinent fossils are comparatively uncommon: Crucial stages apparently occurred in the tropics, where preservation and discovery of fossils are difficult and where exploration has generally lagged; populations of apes and of pre-humans were always small, not at all comparable with the great herds of grazing animals, for example, common as fossils; and the habits and abilities of apes and pre-humans were such as to reduce chances of natural burial and preservation as fossils.

Nevertheless, a great many fossils have been recovered and discovery is active at present. We are far from having the whole story, but parts of it are increasingly clear.

In Darwin's time only one really distinctive kind of fossil ape (*Dryopithecus*) and only one really distinctive kind of fossil man (Neandertal) were known. From the former, Darwin correctly inferred that by late Miocene, at least, the lineages of apes and monkeys had separated. He was not clear as to the possible implications for separation of the strictly human lineage, which he thought might have occurred much earlier. As regards Neandertal man Darwin could only express surprise that in spite of their antiquity the Neandertals had brain capacities probably greater than the average for modern man.

Now it is known that apes more or less similar to *Dryopithecus* were widespread and, as apes go, numerous through the Miocene and Pliocene of Europe, Asia, and Africa (6). Present estimates place the beginning of the Miocene at approximately 25 million years ago (7). The divergence of apes and Old World monkeys is thus at least that old. There is, in fact, some evidence that this divergence occurred in the Oligocene, which preceded the Miocene and began some 10 million **years earlier. Divergence of apes and monkeys was identical with divergence of the human ancestry and monkeys, because the earliest apes were also ancestral to man. The time of the final split of the specifically prehuman lineage from that leading to gorilla and chimpanzee has not yet been closely determined. On present evidence it seems most likely to have occurred during the Miocene, that is, quite roughly between 10 and 25 million years ago. The earliest known forms that may be definitely on a prehuman line as distinct from a pre-gorilla-chimpanzee line are *Ramapithecus* from India and the closely similar, indeed probably identical supposed genus *Kenyapithecus* from Africa (8). Un-**

fortunately those animals are known only from teeth and fragments of jaws, so that their affinities are somewhat uncertain and the anatomy of their skulls and skeletons is entirely unknown. The known specimens are approximately 10 million years old, give or take a few million.

The next significant group of fossils is that of the australopithecines, literally "southern monkeys" although they almost certainly were not exclusively southern and with complete certainty were not monkeys. They are surely and comparatively well known from East and South Africa, doubtfully and, at best, poorly known from elsewhere in Africa and from Eurasia. In Africa they are clearly divisible into two distinct groups. There is dispute as to whether those groups should not be subdivided still further and whether they should be called species or genera. Although the specialists can become enraged over those questions, they have no real importance for others, the important fact being simply that the two separate groups did exist, a point on which even the specialists now agree. Both groups resemble apes much more than we do now, but both are more nearly related to us than to the apes— another point on which the specialists have finally agreed after years of wrangling. They definitely belong to the human family, Hominidae.

One group, typified by *Australopithecus robustus* or, as it is also often called, *Paranthropus robustus*, retained some particularly primitive (more or less apelike) features and yet became somewhat aberrantly specialized. It cannot have been directly ancestral to modern man. The other group, typified by *Australopithecus africanus*, although also primitive within the human family, more closely resembles our own genus, *Homo*. Both groups are now believed to have appeared at least 2 million years ago. For a long time, perhaps 1½ million years, there were at least two distinct lineages of the human family living in

Africa and probably throughout the warmer parts of the Old World. One, more primitive and aberrant, showed little progress and finally became extinct. The other, more progressive, evolved into *Homo*. A matter still under sharp dispute is whether the latter lineage included *Australopithecus africanus* as our direct ancestor, or whether for a time there were not actually three distinct lines: the two kinds of australopithecines and still another more directly related to *Homo*. The latter suggestion arises from Leakey's discovery of what he calls *Homo habilis* (9). However, some authorities believe that supposed species not to be on a distinct lineage but to belong to the line leading from *Australopithecus africanus* eventually to *Homo sapiens*.

That dispute is interesting and we hope it may soon be settled, but it is far less important than the fact that our ancestry passed through a stage closely similar to *Australopithecus africanus* if it was not that group itself. Our ancestors were then fully bipedal, ground-living animals, using their hands for manipulation as we do but perhaps not quite so skillfully. Their teeth were so like ours as to be hard to distinguish, but their brains were little larger than those of apes, and if we could see them alive their physiognomy, while distinctive, would probably strike us as more apelike than manlike.

By a time probably not later than 500,000 years ago and perhaps earlier, gradual evolution from australopithecines had reached a stage that was human in a more restricted sense, belonging not only to the human family, Hominidae, but also to the same genus as ourselves, *Homo*. Doting and ambitious discoverers have given many different names to such early fossil men, including *Pithecanthropus* and *Sinanthropus*, but most of them are now usually placed in a single species, *Homo erectus*. Bodily anatomy and even physiognomy were now almost fully human, but to our eyes there was still a coarse or brutish cast of countenance because of heavy brow ridges over the eyes and a low, small brain case. The brain size was neatly intermediate between australopithecines (or modern apes) and modern man.

Finally, and still gradually, our own species, *Homo sapiens*, emerged. Although not entirely certain, it is now the usual opinion that the quite varied fossils known collectively as Neandertal men belonged to *Homo sapiens* and only represent ancient races that were at first primitive (not so far removed from *Homo erectus*) and later somewhat aberrant. The more aberrant late Neandertals became extinct as such, although it is probable that some of their genes survive.

So much for more or less direct knowledge of man's physical, anatomical origin. The main points are these:

1) Man evolved from apes also ancestral to chimpanzees and gorillas, but less specialized than the latter.

2) The divergence of man's ancestry from the apes was early marked by bipedalism and upright posture, with extensive correlations and implications in anatomy, habits, and capabilities.

3) Also early was divergent dental evolution, again with other implications, for example as to diet and means of defense. It is not known whether posture and dentition diverged from the apes simultaneously or in which order.

4) Only after evolution of human posture and dentition was essentially complete did man's brain begin to enlarge beyond that of the apes. (Intelligence depends not only on size of the brain but also on its internal anatomy, and we do not know the internal anatomy of our fossil ancestors' brains. However, it is fairly certain that a species with average brain size as in apes could not be as intelligent as *Homo sapiens*.)

Systematics of Modern Man

Now let us briefly consider the taxonomic, biological systematic nature of mankind as it exists today. First and most important is the fact that mankind *is* a kind, a definite and single species. A biological species is an evolutionary unit composed of continuing populations that regularly interchange genes by interbreeding and that do not or cannot have such regular interchange with other species (*10*). The definition clearly applies to mankind: all human populations can and, as opportunity occurs, do interbreed, producing fertile offspring and thus continuing the species and keeping it bound together as a unit. It is unlikely that, for example, a Greenland Eskimo has ever interbred with a South African Bushman, but since all intervening populations can and do interbreed they are nevertheless members of the same species. That species, *Homo sapiens*, is not connected with any other species by interbreeding.

Comparison of Eskimo and Bushman brings up the obvious (although occasionally denied) fact that the human species includes quite diverse races. A race is simply a population (or group of populations) that is genetically distinguished from others. The distinction is not absolute. It is unlikely that Negroes, for example, have any genes that do not occur in some white populations, or that whites have any genes absent in all Negro populations. The usual situation is that a race has certain genes and gene combinations that are more frequent in it than elsewhere, and therefore typical in that sense, but not confined to the race. Races always grade into each other without definite boundaries. There is not now and never has been such a thing as a pure race, biologically speaking. Any two human populations, no matter how small or how large, differ in some respects, so that there is no fixed number of races. One could count thousands or two, and no matter how many are counted, there will be

11

some populations and many individuals that do not clearly fit into one or another. Moreover, races are evanescent in the course of evolution. A given race may change, disappear by fusion with others, or die out altogether while the species as a whole simply continues its evolutionary course (11).

Races of man have, or perhaps one should say "had," exactly the same biological significance as the subspecies of other species of mammals. Widespread animals have local populations that live under diverse conditions and that may become temporarily and in part isolated from each other. They may then more or less accidentally have different proportions of genes (in stricter technical language, of alleles) from other such populations, and if the situation continues long enough, they will almost inevitably evolve somewhat different adaptations to local conditions. Primitive men were relatively few in number and relatively immobile, but they spread over enormous areas—the whole land area of the earth except for Antarctica and a few small islands. They evolved into races or, in better biological terms, into subspecies exactly as any other animal would have under those circumstances. Racial differentiation in man was originally geographic and, for the most part, adaptive.

That was the original biological significance of race. One must say that Negroes were biologically superior to whites, if reference is to prehistoric times, when the races were originating, and to African conditions, to which Negroes were biologically adapted and whites were not. At the present time race has virtually no strictly biological significance because of two crucial changes. First, human adaptation to different environments is now mostly cultural and is directly biological only in lesser part, so that the prehistoric biological adaptations have lost much of their importance. Second, tremendous increases in population size, in mobility, and in environmental changes brought about by man himself have the result that extremely few men are now living under the conditions to which their ancestors were racially adapted.

Evolution does not necessarily proceed at the same rate in different populations, so that among many groups of animals it is possible to find some species that have evolved more slowly, hence are now more primitive, as regards some particular trait or even over-all. It is natural to ask—as many have asked—whether among human races there may not similarly be some that are more primitive in one way or another or in general. It is indeed possible to find single characteristics that are probably more advanced or more primitive in one race than in another. For example, the full lips and kinky hair of some Negroes are almost certainly progressive traits in comparison with the more primitive, decidedly apelike thin lips and straight hair of most whites. However, that does not mean that whites in general are more primitive than Negroes or otherwise inferior to them. Overall primitiveness and progressiveness in comparison of different groups of animals is practically confined to cases in which the groups are of different species, so that genes of the more rapidly evolving species cannot be transferred to the lagging species. Human races all belong to the same species and have generally had enough interbreeding so that genetic progress, as distinct from local adaptation, could and evidently did spread through the entire species. Only if some race entirely ceased to interbreed with any other would it be likely for it to fall behind and become definitely inferior. Let us hope that will not happen.

Resemblances, Anatomical and Psychological

Regardless of the diversity of races, it is obvious that all men resemble one another much more than any of them differ from each other. They all share the basic qualities, anatomical, physiological and psychological, that make us human, *Homo sapiens,* and no other species that is or ever was. Something has already been said of anatomical peculiarities of *Homo sapiens* with respect to living apes and human ancestors. Here are some of the most striking human anatomical traits:

Normal posture is upright.

Legs are longer than arms.

Toes are short, the first toe frequently longest and not divergent.

The vertebral column has an *S* curve.

The hands are prehensile, with a large and strongly opposable thumb.

Most of the body is bare or has only short, sparse, inconspicuous hair.

The joint for the neck is in the middle of the base of the skull.

The brain is uniquely large in proportion to the body and has a particularly large and complex cerebrum.

The face is short, almost vertical under the front of the brain.

The jaws are short, with a rounded dental arch.

The canine teeth are usually no larger than the premolars, and there are normally no gaps in front of or behind the canines.

The first lower premolar is like the second, and the structure of the teeth in general is somewhat distinctive.

Given those characteristics, a museum curator could readily identify any specimen of *Homo sapiens* that was added to the collections, or that happened to walk into his office. However, we who are pondering the question "What is man?" must feel that these anatomical features, fully diagnostic as they are, yet do not amount to an answer adequate for our purposes. Even if we were defining, say, a species of mouse, the anatomical definition would not take us far toward understanding "What is mouse?" or, better, "What is mouseness?" unless we related the bodily mouse to the behaving mouse and the thinking mouse. Even thus, human anatomy reflects truly essential man-ness or human nature only to the extent that it is related to human activities and psychology. Already in *The Descent of Man (1)* Darwin discussed such traits in which man appears to be most distinctive.

His points, here greatly abbreviated and paraphrased, were as follows:

In proportion with his higher intelligence, man's behavior is more flexible, less reflex or instinctive.

Man shares such complex factors as curiosity, imitation, attention, memory, and imagination with other relatively advanced animals, but has them in higher degree and applies them in more intricate ways.

More, at least, than other animals, man reasons and improves the adaptive nature of his behavior in rational ways.

Man regularly both uses and makes tools in great variety.

Man is self-conscious; he reflects on his past, future, life, death, and so forth.

Man makes mental abstractions and develops a related symbolism; the most essential and complexly developed outcome of these capacities is language.

Some men have a sense of beauty.

Most men have a religious sense, taking that term broadly to include awe, superstition, belief in the animistic, supernatural, or spiritual.

Normal men have a moral sense; in later terms, man ethicizes.

Man is a cultural and social animal and has developed cultures and societies unique in kind and in complexity.

The last point, which some students now consider the most important of all, was least emphasized by Darwin, who was here mainly concerned with the relationship of social evolution to the origin of the moral sense. Darwin's general purpose was not to characterize *Homo sapiens* as the unique species that he is. The purpose was to show that the characteristics that make him unique are nevertheless foreshadowed in other animals, and that the evolution of man from other, earlier, quite distinct species is therefore plausible. We are no longer concerned with *whether* man

13

evolved, because we know that he did. We are still very much concerned with *how* he evolved, with what is most characteristically human about him and how those characteristics arose. The list of traits discussed by Darwin is still valid from this somewhat different point of view.

That list should not be taken as involving so many separate and distinct things. These are aspects of the behavior, capacities, and accomplishments of a species that is characterized by all of them together and not by each or any one separately. They interact and interlock not only with each other but also with the previously mentioned physical or anatomical characteristics of man. For example, complex human societies, especially the modern industrial civilization rapidly spreading to the whole world, require specialization of activities by different members of society further involving manipulation of complex machines. Such specialization, which is nongenetic, requires individual flexibility and could not occur in a mainly instinctive animal. The machines are tools and could only have been devised by a reasoning, tool-making animal. Invention also required manual deftness, which was provided by (and which also gave selective value to) the structure of the human hand, which required upright posture and could not have been acquired by a quadruped. Further evolution of the early cultural adaptations that led eventually to modern industry also had increased intelligence as a necessary concomitant, and that eventually required larger brains, which in turn involved change in skull structure and in stance —and so on. Even the changing pattern of the teeth can be related to this unitary complex.

The Major Evolutionary Changes

Because all the specifically human traits are integrated within the whole that is human, and because each of the traits as well as their integration must have arisen gradually, it is somewhat questionable to speak of definite milestones or even of particular critical phases in the evolution of man. Yet there are three among these slow and coordinated changes that seem particularly basic for the concept of human-ness. The most crucial single anatomical point is acquisition of upright posture and strictly bipedal locomotion. Most of the other main peculiarities of human anatomy either follow from that or are coadapted with it. The other two major factors are cultural, but are no less biological since both represent attainment and maintenance of biological adaptation by cultural means. They are tool making and language.

Extremely crude but unmistakable stone tools are found in the oldest rock strata containing indisputable members of the human family, nearly, if not quite, 2 million years old. It will be difficult to authenticate still older and more primitive stone tools, because they must have consisted of natural pebbles or rock fragments picked up and used with little or no modification. It has long been maintained that deliberate manufacture of a tool is the distinctive human trait, since many other animals, even including some insects, use natural objects as tools but do not make tools. Now it has been found that chimpanzees may trim and shorten twigs or straws for use as tools (*12*), and although that simple behavior is almost too primitive to be called tool making, it sufficiently demonstrates that the capacity for tool making is biologically ancient and prehuman. If one wants a more diagnostic statement, it probably is true that man is the only living animal that uses tools to make tools. However, that trait would follow soon and inevitably once tool making really got under way. A stone used to knock flakes off an incipient stone ax is already a machine tool.

Ancient tools more perishable than

stone are rarely preserved. Nevertheless, the course of increasing diversity and complication of tools can be followed well enough to demonstrate the gradual and inconstant but generally continual progress through prehistory. The tremendously accelerated progress in historic times is very well documented and is familiar to all of us in general outline, at least. The whole sweep from stone axes to electronic computers is a natural and comprehensible extension of the biological capacities of an unusual species. It is uniquely wonderful, and yet, lest we stand too much in awe of our own products, let us remember that a digital computer is merely a rapid and automated tool for what amounts to counting on fingers.

As posture is focal for consideration of man's anatomical nature and tools are for consideration of his material culture, so is language focal for his mental nature and his non-material culture (13). Language is also the most diagnostic single trait of man: all normal men have language; no other now-living organisms do. That real, incomparably important, and absolute distinction has been blurred by imprecise use of the word "language" not only in popular speech but also by some scientists who should know better, speaking, for example, of the "language of the bees" (14).

In any animal societies, and indeed in still simpler forms of aggregation among animals, there must be some kind of communication in the very broadest sense. One animal must receive some kind of information about another animal. That information may be conveyed by specific signals, which may be of extremely diverse kinds both as to form and as to modality, that is, the sensory mode by which it is received. The odor of an ant, the movements of a bee, the color pattern of a bird, the howl of a wolf, and many thousands of others are all signals that convey information to other animals and that, in these and many other examples, are essential adaptations for behavioral integration in the species involved.

Human language is also a system of interpersonal communication and a behavioral adaptation essential for the human form of socialization. Yet human language is absolutely distinct from any system of communication in other animals. That is made most clear by comparison with other animal utterances, which most nearly resemble human speech and are most often called "speech." Nonhuman vocables are, in effect, interjections. They reflect the individual's physical or, more frequently, emotional state. They do not, as true language does, name, discuss, abstract, or symbolize. They are what the psychologists call affective; such purely affective so-called languages are systems of emotional signals and not discourse. The difference between animal interjection and human language is the difference between saying "Ouch!" and saying "Fire is hot."

That example shows that the non-language of animal interjection is still present in man. In us it is in effect not a part of language, but the negative of language, something we use in place of speech. In part we even use the same signals as do the apes, a fact already explored to some depth by Darwin in another of his basic works, *The Expression of the Emotions in Man and Animals* (15). Much more is now known about such expressions in animals, and particularly in our closer relatives the apes and monkeys, and it is not surprising to find that the non-linguistic, affective system is particularly complicated in them and has not progressed but may even have retrogressed in man. Still we do retain that older system along with our wholly new and wholly distinct system of true language. It is amusing that the human affective interjectional reaction to a bad smell is practically the same as in all other primates, down even to the most primitive.

15

Attempts To Trace Language

Darwin's study and many later studies sought to trace the evolutionary origin of language from a prehuman source. They have not been successful. As a recent expert in the field (*16*) has said, "The more that is known about it [that is, communication in monkeys and apes], the less these systems seem to help in the understanding of human language."

Many other attempts have been made to determine the evolutionary origin of language, and all have failed. Because language is so important for any concept of man and because this is an interesting example of methodology and limitations, it is worthwhile to consider some of these futile attempts. One, fairly obvious once the idea of linguistic evolution had arisen, was by comparison of living languages. One result was a supposed genetic sequence: (i) isolating languages, like Chinese, which string together invariable word roots; (ii) agglutinating languages, like Mongolian, which modify roots by tacking on prefixes and suffixes; and (iii) flexional languages, like Latin, which modify by (partly) internal changes in words. The trouble is that these categories are not really distinct and, especially, that they did not historically occur in this sequence. For example, Chinese was probably flexional at one time and is now becoming agglutinating with a possibility of becoming flexional again. English was flexional until quite recently and is now mostly isolating with a strong dash of agglutination. Moreover at the present time no languages are primitive in the sense of being significantly close to the origin of language. Even the peoples with least complex cultures have highly sophisticated languages, with complex grammar and large vocabularies, capable of naming and discussing anything that occurs in the sphere occupied by their speakers. Tales of tribal natives who cannot count beyond 4 and who have vocabularies of only two or three hundred words betray the shortcomings of gullible travelers, not of the natives (*17*).

Another approach is to follow back directly historical records, which cover several thousand years for some European, Asiatic, and north African languages. It is then possible to project still further and to reconstruct, for example, a proto-Indo-European anterior to Sanskrit. But this still leaves us tens or hundreds of thousands of years—perhaps even more—from the origin of language. The oldest language that can reasonably be reconstructed is already modern, sophisticated, complete from an evolutionary point of view.

Still another attempt, which now seems very naive, is through the ontogeny of language, that is, the acquisition of language by children. This relies on the famous but, as it happens, quite erroneous saying that ontogeny repeats phylogeny. In fact the child is not evolving or inventing primitive language but is learning a particular modern language, already complete and unrecognizably different from any possible primitive language. Moreover, the child is doing this with a modern brain already genetically constructed (through the long, long action of natural selection) for the use of complete, wholly nonprimitive language.

It is a tempting hypothesis that the time, at least, of the origin of language might be determined by structural characteristics in fossils. One rather elaborate attempt departed from the fact that all linguistic phonetic systems, varied as they are, depend in part on the shape of the lower jaw and the hard palate, anatomically quite different in typical members of the human and the ape families. It was postulated that speech began when these anatomical parts reached human form, which was in the australopithecines or somewhat earlier. But the postulate is clearly wrong. Audible signals capable of expressing language do not require any particular phonetic apparatus, but only the ability to produce sound, any sound at all. Almost all mammals and a great number of other animals can do that. Moreover, a number of animals, not only birds but also some mammals, can produce sounds recognizably similar to those of human language, and yet their jaws and palates are radically non-human. A parrot is capable of articulating a human word but is completely incapable of understanding what the word means.

Given any method of sound production, the capacity for language depends not on characteristics of the sound apparatus but on the central nervous system. Speech is particularly connected with the left temporal lobe of the human brain, as shown, for example, by the fact that ability to speak is generally lost if that lobe is severely damaged. The gross development of the lobe can be seen in plaster casts of the insides of fossil skulls, and that, too, **has been proposed as a means of determining whether or not a given fossil individual could speak.** But all mammals have left temporal lobes, some smaller and some larger. Those with smaller lobes do not speak just a little and those with larger lobes more. There is no graded sequence: normal men speak completely; other animals, whatever the relative size of their temporal lobes, do not speak at all.

The essential anatomical and physiological basis of speech is nevertheless in the structure and function of the brain (*18*). That basis is not fully known, but it evidently involves not just a language center, such as might be localized in the temporal lobe, but an intricate and widespread system of associative connections throughout much of the brain. (The nature or presence of these connections cannot be determined in fossils.) Thus sensations of any kind derived from an external object or event can be generalized according to similarities with others. Each kind can then be associated with a distinctive symbol, which does not resemble the object or event at all but which arbitrarily stands for it. That symbol, a supreme element in the nature of man, is the word, and it is not surprising that words meaning "word," abstraction and symbolization on still another level, have acquired such mystical and philosophical overtones. ($\Lambda \acute{o} \gamma o \varsigma$!)

It is still possible but it is unlikely that we will ever know just when and how our ancestors began to speak. Yet it is certain that this ability depends on physical, structural, and chemical characteristics of the nervous system which evolved from our nonspeaking ancestors under the force of natural selection. The capacity for this unique kind of symbolization is quite general. It does not determine what symbol will be used for a given concept, but that any symbol can be associated with any concept. Thus we are all using exactly the same genetic capacity and symbolizing the same concept when various of us say "woman," "Weib," "femme," "mujer," "zhenshchina," or "imra," depending on whether we happen to have been raised in England, Germany, France, Spain, Russia, or Egypt. The words do not resemble each other and even less resemble the concept they stand for. Moreover, they can be written in different ways, as in Latin, Arabic, or Chinese characters, that do not resemble each other and that have no physical resemblance to the spoken words. They can even be associated with some symbol that is not verbal at all, as in this example with the simplified representation of Venus's mirror that biologists use to designate females: ♀.

Conclusion

Language has become far more than a means of communication in man. It is also one of the principal (although far from the only) means of thought, memory, introspection, problem-solving, and all other mental activities. The uniqueness and generality of human symbolization have given our mental activities not only a scope but also a quality far outside the range of other animals. It keeps us aware, to greater extent than can otherwise be, of past and future, of the continuity of existence and its extension beyond what is immediately sensed. Along with other peculiarly human capacities, it is involved in what I consider the most important human characteristic from an ethical point of view: foresight. It is the capacity to predict the outcome of our own actions that makes us responsible for them and that therefore makes ethical judgment of them both possible and necessary (*19*).

Above the individual level, language and related powers of symbolization make possible the acquisition, sharing, and preserving of knowledge far beyond what would be possible for any single individual. That is an indispensable element in all forms of human social organization and cultural accomplishment, even the most primitive.

It is obvious that I have by no means touched on all aspects of the biological nature of man. That would be impossible in one essay by one author. Those familiar with recent developments in biology may particularly miss reference to molecular biology and especially to the compound called DNA, now known to be largely involved in heredity and also in control of biochemical activities in cells. Those subjects are extremely fascinating at present and may be portentous for the future. However, in my opinion nothing that has so far been learned about DNA has helped significantly to understand the nature of man or of any other whole organism. It certainly is necessary for such understanding to examine what is inherited, how it is expressed in the developing individual, how it evolves in populations, and so on. Up to now the triumphs of DNA research have had virtually no effect on our understanding of those subjects. In due course molecular biology will undoubtedly become more firmly connected with the biology of whole organisms and with evolution, and then it will become of greater concern for those more interested in the nature of man than in the nature of molecules.

Finally, it should be pointed out that although man is a unique animal and although we properly consider his nature in the light of his peculiarities, he also has many non-peculiarities. Man is not *merely* an animal, that is, his essence is not simply in his shared animality. Nevertheless he *is* an animal and the nature of man includes and has arisen from the nature of all animals. Indeed if all the material characteristics of man could be enumerated, it would surely be found that the vast majority of them also occur in other animals. In fact at the level of molecular structure and interaction, information storage and transfer, energy transactions, and other defining characteristics of life, man is hardly significantly different from a bacterium—another illustration of the fact that that level of study is not particularly useful in considering the nature of man.

Like other animals, man develops, is born, grows, reproduces, and dies. Like other animals, he eats, digests, eliminates, respires, locomotes. He bends the qualities of nature to his own ends, but he is as fully subject to nature's laws as is any other animal and is no more capable of changing them. He lives in biological communities and has a niche and an ecology, just as do robins and earthworms. Let us not forget those aspects of man's nature. But let us also remember that man stands upright, builds and makes as never was built or wrought before, speaks and may speak truth or a lie, worships and may worship honestly or falsely, looks to the stars and into the mud, remembers his past and predicts his future, and writes (perhaps at too great length) about his own nature.

References and Notes

1. C. Darwin, *The Descent of Man, and Selection in Relation to Sex* (Murray, London, 1871).

2. ———, *On the Origin of Species by Means of Natural Selection, or The Preservation of Favoured Races in the Struggle for Life* (Murray, London, 1859).

3. T. H. Huxley, *Evidence as to Man's Place in Nature* (Williams and Norgate, London, 1863).

4. Lamarck's view (unknown to most Neo-Lamarckians) was that *all* organisms are evolving toward and will eventually become human, after which they will degenerate through the inorganic world and eventually be spontaneously generated as lowly organisms and start again on the path to man. Today's amoeba is tomorrow's man, day after tomorrow's mineral, and still another day's amoeba once more. In the state of knowledge and philosophy of Lamarck's day it would perhaps be too strong to label his views as absurd, but they were certainly less sensible and less progressive than has often been claimed.

5. These new data are well exemplified in S. L. Washburn, Ed., *Classification and Human Evolution* (Aldine, Chicago, 1963).

6. E. L. Simons and D. R. Pilbeam, *Folia Primatol.* No. 46 (1965).

7. On this and other absolute (year) dates see D. E. Savage, J. F. Everdnen. G. H. Curtis, G. T. James, *Am. J. Sci.* **262**, 145 (1964).

8. E. L. Simons, *Postilla* (Yale Peabody Museum) No. 57 (1961); *Proc. Nat. Acad. Sci. U.S.* **51**, 528 (1964).

9. L. S. B. Leakey, P. V. Tobias, M. D. Leakey, J. R. Napier, *Nature* **202**, 3 (1964); P. V. Tobias, *Science* **149**, 22 (1965). For discussion and dissent see P. L. DeVore, Ed., *The Origin of Man* (transcript of a symposium, Wenner-Gren Foundation, New York, 1965).

10. Age-long argument on the definition of species is perhaps sufficiently summarized in G. G. Simpson, *Principles of Animal Taxonomy* (Columbia Univ. Press, New York, 1961) and E. Mayr, *Animal Species and Evolution* (Harvard Univ. Press, Cambridge, 1963).

11. On animal races see especially Mayr (*10*). On the perennial, knotty problem of human races, a sensible general statement with many references is in Th. Dobzhansky, *Mankind Evolving* (Yale Univ. Press, New Haven, 1962).

12. J. Goodall, in *Primate Behavior*, I. DeVore, Ed. (Holt, Rinehart and Winston, New York, 1965), p. 425.

13. The literature on human culture and linguistics is as voluminous as that of any field of science. Some recent studies especially pertinent to my text are: A. L. Bryan, *Current Anthropol.* **4**, 297 (1965); M. Critchley, in *Evolution after Darwin*, S. Tax, Ed. (Univ. of Chicago Press, Chicago, 1960), vol. 2, p. 289; A. S. Diamond, *The History and Origin of Language* (Philosophical Library, New York, 1959); E. L. DuBrul, *Evolution of the Speech Apparatus* (Thomas, Springfield, Ill., 1958); B. R. Fink, *Perspectives Biol. Med.* **7**, 85 (1963); C. F. Hockett, in *The Evolution of Man's Capacity for Culture*, J. N. Spuhler, Ed. (Wayne State Univ. Press, Detroit, 1959), p. 32; C. F. Hockett and R. Ascher, *Current Anthropol.* **5**, 135 (1964); A. Kortlandt, *ibid.* **6**, 320 (1965). See also works cited in 16.

14. Misuses of the term "language" are too widely exemplified to need citation. The distinction is discussed by several of the authors cited in *13*, also (among other places) in J. B. S. Haldane and H. Spurway, *Insectes Sociaux* **1**, 247 (1954) and J. B. S. Haldane, *Sci. Progr.* No. 171, 385 (1955).

15. C. Darwin, *The Expression of the Emotions in Man and Animals* (Murray, London, 1872).

16. J. B. Lancaster, in *The Origin of Man*, P. L. DeVore, Ed. (transcript of a symposium, Wenner-Gren Foundation, New York, 1965). See also discussions by A. R. Diebold, Jr., T. A. Sebeok, D. Slobin in the same volume, and bibliography on pp. 149–150.

17. I first began to appreciate the richness and complexity of "primitive" languages when I visited the Kamarakotos of Venezuela in 1939, and I commented on it in G. G. Simpson, *Los Indios Kamarakotos* (Ministerio de Fomento, Caracas, 1940).

18. N. Geschwind, *Brain* **88**, 237 (1965).

19. G. G. Simpson, *Am. Psychologist* **21**, 27 (1966).

20. During 1965 varying versions of this essay were presented as lectures at Randolph Macon College, the University of Paris, and the University of Washington. I have profited by discussions on those occasions.

Biology, Society, and Culture in Human Ecology

Frederick Sargent, II, *University of Illinois*

Demitri B. Shimkin, *University of Illinois*

"All creatures have a specific nature. all represent wholes having the character of individuality." (From *The Organism*, by K. Goldstein, p. 476)

Human ecology seeks to understand man and his problems by studying individuals and populations as biological entities profoundly modified by human society and culture and by studying the effects of physical, biological, and cultural environments upon man and those of man upon his environments. The viewpoint of ecology is at once statistical and typological (8). The observational reality is always a set of tolerances pertinent to the physics and chemistry of an individual's metabolism and behavior and to those of his behavioral products. Yet this reality persists only through genetic and social mechanisms that transcend individual life sequences to provide the continuities, feedback stabilities, and progressive adaptations of biological and cultural evolution.

General concepts

Biologically, man has both generic and unique characteristics as an organism. Among the former, the phenomena of distinctiveness and of persistence over time, through physiological and morphological changes, are central.

By what processes is this constancy maintained? To answer this question we must have some concept of a free-living organism in its natural life-situations. Many biologists prefer to view organisms as systems of self-regulatory processes (13). By this view alone one cannot really understand organisms. Equilibrium and constancy are important, but a more fundamental organismic characteristic among free-living animals is direction (13). Direction arises both from the organism and the environment, for the survival of the organism depends upon its finding an environment which is adequate for it (13). To succeed in this search the organism must select, from all sorts of environmental stimuli that act upon it, only those events that are pertinent to it. This milieu is certainly not "definite and static"; rather it forms continuously as the active organism grows, matures, and ages (13). Thus organism and environment are in essence inseparable (1). It is this bond that gives rise to direction in organismic behavior and to selection in evolution.

In finding this adequate environment, the free-living animal organism exhibits preferred behavior (13). To determine whether a particular phenomenon which seems to be preferred behavior is essential and genuine, one must consider the entire organism. As Goldstein (13, p. 364) states it, "We are dealing with genuine attributes or constants if we find, by examining as many fields as possible, order and 'adequate performance' in the rest of the organism. . . . In this way we apprehend certain characteristics of the organism with which we are dealing, certain norms and constants of its nature."

Among these "constants" of the nature of the organism are ways of behaving; sensory and motor thresholds; intellectual characteristics; affectivity; psychic or mental and physical traits; physiological attributes such as temperature, respiration, pulse, blood pressure; chemical qualities of the blood; blood types; and reactivity to noxious and stressful circumstances. The living organism tends to approach these relative constants or the "average mean." Thus, Goldstein (13, pp. 364-365) remarks, "We are only in position to

Bioscience, 1965, Vol.15, pp. 512-516.

speak of one and the same organism, if, in spite of temporary changes, these constants become manifest."

There are two groups of "constants": those which express "the essential nature of the species" and the "individual constants." Goldstein (13, p. 365) emphasizes the fundamental significance of the "individual constants": "On the basis of the constants of the species, the life of the normal and especially of the defective individual cannot be sufficiently comprehended, notwithstanding certain congruencies between the individuals of the same species. For that objective, an acquaintance with the nature of the individual, that is with the *individual's normal constants*, is prerequisite."

Merely enumerating innumerable constants, however, does not define the essential nature of the organism. The constants themselves are equivocal because they are measured under isolating conditions. To determine which phenomena are biologically relevant and which are not, we need "a conception of the organism in its qualitative organization and holistic function" (13, p. 400). This conception is *"the capacity of the organism to become adequate to its environmental conditions. . . . Whenever we speak of . . .* the organism, we have in mind these essentials for the realization of adequacy between the organism and its environment. And these are the principles of composition of that picture which biology has to grasp. . . ."* (13, p. 403).

Species constants

Man is a species that has proved unique in its fitness to survive and multiply under extremely varying selective pressures (7). In the Pliocene, the protohominus appear to have been brachiating dwellers in tropical forests, a habitat which favored depth perception, color vision, sound production and hearing, and truly prehensile hands. Increasing drought in the late Pliocene and early Pleistocene forced adaption to a forest-edge and grasslands environment, in which both escape from predation and increasingly successful predation were basic elements of survival (18). During this period, the precursors of man (Australopithecenes) become effective runners, in consequence of mutations and selection leading to the human heel, the reduced jaw, and the S-shaped spine. In general, less robust and more juvenile body builds sacrificing strength for endurance were evidently favored. These factors, jointly with the direct advantages of better perception, memory, symbolization, cerebral inhibition, learning and communication, fostered the absolute and relative growth of the brain.

Over the past half-million years, man has adapted to a wide range of nontropical climates, as a consequence both of migrations and climatic fluctuations during the ice ages (17). These events must have been associated with periods of population growth and dispersal alternating with others of decline and concentration. Mechanisms such as these account, in fact, for the extraordinary combination of long-persistent geographical variability and full reproductive unity characterizing man (9, 20). Even more important have been the selective advantages of variability, role specialization, and cooperation in human society. These and other expressions of polygenesis even in small populations of man are undoubtedly related to the propensities toward out-breeding and mating stability ubiquitous in man. The prolonged mobility and self-sufficiency, in primitive conditions, of preadolescent children, in combination with taboos on parent-child and sibling intercourse and the continuous sexual receptivity of the human female, seen to have been the behaviors crucial to expressing these propensities.

The increasing range and effectiveness of taught behavior — culture — have vastly altered selective pressures during the past half-million years. It limited the restrictions of cold through fire, shelter, and clothing. Effective cooking ended

21

the limitations of unaided human diges-
tion. Thus, with seed-gathering and,
later, agriculture, hunger became less of
a control on human numbers. But sedentary life, land clearance, the elimination
of other potential pathogenic hosts, and
symbiosis with domestic animals made
disease immunity and behavioral safe-
guards against infection basic selection
mechanisms. The significance of this
later selection has been insufficiently
stressed. Larger populations made more
mutations possible, while group survival
became far less random than earlier.
On one hand, new technology in some
areas radically increased population-
bearing capacities. On the other, endemic diseases (parasitism, malaria,
tuberculosis) systematically induced
child-birth and infant mortality, while
epidemics carried off entire susceptible
populations (e.g., smallpox and measles
in North America and Oceania). Thus,
intense growth in favored areas — the
Near East, India, China, Middle America — and stagnation or decline elsewhere, have predominated since the rise
of agriculture (5).

Associated with the control of food
and the increasing size of human populations has been the increasing importance of management: the determination of goals, the discovery of
means, the organization of efforts, and
the distribution of gains — in human
societies (33). An allied process has
been the increasingly high evaluation of
play and symbolic expression as ever
more structured societies have repressed
wider areas of biological desire. At
the same time, the change from simple
face-to-face communities to stratified
states brought with it lessened capacity
to identify and harness individual variation. Social criteria, such as the accidents of conquest or defeat, urban
or rural residence, white skin or black,
have dominated role choices. The significance of complex individual variations in human adaptation has thus
been diminished through feedbacks
from history. This diminution has also
lowered man's evolutionary adaptability.

At his present stage of evolution, man
as a species has many distinctive characteristics. He matures slowly; some
25% of his life span is occupied with
maturing. This long period of maturing
is, however, merely an exaggeration of
a primate phenomenon. Bolk (19) has
called the slowing "foetalization." Another term is neoteny.

Neoteny has had several important
consequences. First, it is advantageous
for learning and social cooperation to
be taught while the organism is docile
and sexually nonaggressive (34). Second, neoteny may be the cause of
nakedness in man. According to Huxley (19, p. 13), "The distribution of
hair on man is extremely similar to
that on a late foetus of a chimpanzee,
and there can be little doubt that it
represents an extension of this temporary anthropoid phase into permanence." Hairlessness is, except for desert
inhabitants, unique among terrestrial
animals. The hairless state, Huxley
(19) speculates must have encouraged
humans to protect themselves against
their enemies and the elements and thus
have been a spur to intelligence.

Perhaps this hairless state has played
a role in man's dependence upon evaporative cooling as a method of heat
economy. This physiological regulation, of course, is not exclusively human, for many terrestrial animals em-
ploy evaporative cooling as a defense
against overheating. What is unique
about man in this respect is that he is
an "eccrine animal." He is probably
the only animal utilizing active sweat
secreted by the eccrine sweat gland as
a process of evaporative cooling (36).
Other animals sweat but their sweat
derives from apocrine glands.

One might speculate that the long
period of maturing of the young has
been genetically related to the post-
mature longevity characteristic of man.
The survival of animals beyond the
reproductive period is unusually brief.
In man, long survival allows the species
to utilize social benefits accruing from
speech and tradition (19). The meno-

pause of the human female is unusually complete and sudden, and her long postreproductive period is exceptional among mammals (4). Williams (37) suggests that these features may have developed in man because of the selective advantages offered to the slowly maturing offspring.

Man exhibits great reproductive variability (19). The differential fertility among men is enormous, ranging from infertility to families of 1 to 12 and even 20. This differential fertility is of greater selective advantage than differential mortality; it provides a basis for rapid changes in human gene pools.

The rapid and profound evolution of man's brain (primarily encephalization) allowed for plasticity and potential variety. This plasticity has had several different consequences. With encephalization and growing cortical dominance, man's power of attention has shifted to self-stimulative phenomena. As a result he experienced not only tensions, e.g., memory tensions of inhibition, but also symbolic satisfactions. These satisfactions have allowed survival and adaptation to stresses, e.g., through ascetism and celibacy, not withstood by animals. Because of the tensions, however, ". . . man is the only organism normally and inevitably subject to psychological conflict" (19, p. 22). While experimental neurosis can be produced, under natural conditions avoidance of conflict is the general rule. "Only the peculiarities of the human mind," according to Huxley (19, p. 23), "have forced its partial abandonment upon man." Association mechanisms bring into relation knowing, feeling, and willing. Both unified mental life and mental illness result. Repression is a device for resolving conflicting impulses, but this repressed input may become harmful and lead to mental disturbance (23).

Taraxis or disorder (27) has come to dominate the lives of men. Events appear to be overwhelming and incomprehensible; everything appears to be in disorder. We suffer confusion, defeat, frustration, failure, remorse, humiliation, grief, and so on. Richards writes (27, pp. 250-251):

If one looks . . . at biology and the biological species, it is curious that the human being should be so sensitive and subject to external events and tormented by things that do not physically hurt; that it cannot accept adversity with the same philosophy that rabbits, rats, and guinea pigs can. To be sure, experiments can be set to torture the rat, the dog, possibly even the rabbit in taraxic patterns, but they have to be most deviously contrived. With man these things happen daily by themselves.

Thus creativity and disorder, distress and sublimation, are complementary properties of man in society and culture (15).

Consequences and implications

Man's unique endosomatic, and particularly his exosomatic, evolution have brought him to a position as the dominant animal. In almost all environments, he dominates the ecosystem and holds much of his own evolution in his own hands (10, 22). Cultural evolution — so inexorably interwoven with man's unique psychoneurological traits — has brought him to this position of power. He not only dominates but also consciously manipulates ecosystems (35). By virtue of this power he has created a biological revolution directed primarily toward the immediate enhancement of human welfare at the expense of competing species and often with reckless disregard for long-range consequences. Only in recent decades has there developed a broad awareness of the need for a continuing strategy of resource management (6).

A few examples will illustrate the problems man now faces. He has created what Rostlund (28) appropriately terms "the domesticated landscape," that panorama of domesticated plants and animals, cultivated fields and pas-

23

tures, and monosystem reforestations. This domesticated landscape (*anthroposere* may be suggested as a technical term) comprises a series of artificial ecosystems designed to assure man of plentiful food and raw materials to meet his domestic and industrial requirements. The domesticated plants and animals selectively bred to inhabit these ecosystems depend upon the continuing intervention of man for their survival. Because of competition with other organisms which continually invade these ecosystems man has been forced to institute control measures. These measures have been chemical more often than biological. The use and misuse of the biocides, moreover, have often complicated the problems of management, for not only do these chemicals have their intended effects but also unintended ones, ofttimes remote. Through his actions man tends to create a negative balance in the nutrient cycles of ecosystems. He extracts more than he returns. For example, he has caused a definite species reduction. Furthermore, since his artificial ecosystems are most susceptible to erosion through the agencies of water, wind, and fire, he must treat his fields and pastures with concentrated chemicals — the fertilizers. These fertilizers must be applied with care else more undesirable reactions accrue. There has resulted what in essence is a continuing managerial struggle to maintain the artificiality of the domesticated landscape.

The capture of energy is another problem for resource management strategy. It can be argued, for instance, that cultural advance is directly dependent upon an increased ability to capture energy. In the United States today, man's consumption of energy outside of the food chain exceeds that used directly and indirectly in food by some 25 times. While this energy has been vital in the support of man's technological establishment, there have resulted two profound consequences. In the first place, the disposal of technological wastes has become an increasing prob-

lem. Water and air have provided ready vehicles for discharge. The exponential increase in man's domestic and industrial use of energy has now demonstrated that the vital natural resources are not unlimited in their capacity to dilute and degrade his wastes. Water pollution and air pollution have become central problems of our times and there is ample evidence accumulating that these pollutants exert diverse and profound disturbances throughout ecosystems.

In the second place, this capture of energy has brought to him enormous power, power with which man can destroy himself as well as all other forms of life. This power will necessitate a drastic revision of his mode of thinking. He must turn from traditional views of ingroup survival to concern for the survival of mankind. Chisholm (3, p. 319) states the matter precisely:

> The whole method of survival by groups in competition to the death with other groups has broken down. The survival group, for the first time in human experience, has become the human race itself. From now on we will survive as members of the human race or not at all, but we have no previous experience of this situation and no traditional concern or education for survival of the human race. The occasion for such concern had not arisen until about fifteen years ago and was not foreseen or provided for by our parents or ancestors. Now we are all threatened with extinction by our own traditional survival patterns, a position which most of us still find impossible to accept as real, because we have been taught from infancy to depend upon our "conscious" values, and even to consider changes in them is commonly felt to be immoral and disloyal.

This same view was eloquently expressed by Lord Brain (2, p. 194) in a recent article entitled "Science and Antiscience":

> The evolution of the human race

24

is now threatened by a failure of integration. [By "integration" Lord Brain means bringing man into *adequate* relation with the ecosystem.] That integration is a social function, necessary both within individual national societies and, in the interest of our common humanity, between those societies.

The magnitude, speed, and imbalance of cultural advances over the past century have created other problems. New levels of anticipation have spread more rapidly than productive skills and technology. The control of epidemic diseases has had insufficient returns, too often in work opportunities for a growing, healthier labor force. More unemployment and more pressure on resources have been the tragic results. In addition, the world's population is already so large and the rates of growth are seemingly so rapid that the prospect of Malthusian limits has become real (25). Vast increases in productivity, better systems of international exchange, and drastic increases in birth control are essential. These problems involve complex moral as well as technical issues. In a world of prejudice, the problems of eugenics, except for overwhelming diseases, can scarcely be broached. This is especially true since traits of selective value in some environments, such as the sickle-cell gene and perhaps diabetes (21, 26), are very deleterious in others.

Individual constants

A basic question in human ecology is thus a clarification of relationships and values. What is "health?" How does one measure health? No one really knows the answer to either question. Why must we understand health so that we can measure it? As man more and more rapidly disturbs his ecosystem, he makes it increasingly difficult for each individual to find an adequate environment. The rapidity of environmental changes may soon exceed the norm of reaction, the adaptability, of the human organism. Thus

it becomes urgent that we gain some insight into the limits of the adaptability of individual organisms (29).

The disturbances which man has created in the ecosystem are manifold. He has polluted the water and the air and has contaminated his food. His gregariousness has led him to live in congested urban agglomerations where, if he is well off, his private quarters and place of work are air-conditioned. His physician administers to him an increasing array of chemicals designed fundamentally to assist him in coping with illness but which take their toll in iatrogenic diseases.

Problems such as these have led to an increasing concern about "environmental health" (14). Attention is now turning to controlling the environment so that it will not become inadequate. Questions that now confront those working on problems of environmental health include: (1) What are the long-term effects on human health of low levels of toxic chemicals such as biocides and water and air pollutants? (2) What are the long-term effects of living in atmospheres with closely regulated temperatures and humidities? (3) What effects accrue from such labor-saving devices as the automobile which eliminate the necessity of walking? (4) What impact do these man-made changes have on the ecosystem and how do these impacts affect the health of man?

To provide answers to these questions we must be able to measure health with sufficient precision to detect deviations from the healthy state before there is morbidity and mortality. To do this means a radical reorientation of our thinking, for health has heretofore been defined in terms of lack of evident morbidity and mortality. To arrive at a productive model of health we must begin with the individual's normal constants, needs, and requirements (29).

Several features of individuality must be integrated in this model. One particularly characteristic constant of individuality is "the constant in the temporal course of processes." Goldstein writes (13, p. 366):

Every human being has a rhythm of his own, which manifests itself in various performances. . . . A performance is normal when an individual can accomplish it in a rhythm which is his adequate rhythm for this performance. Just as for physiological processes, like heartbeating and respiration, this is valid for physico-chemical processes. The time constant indicates a particular characteristic of the personality.

In addition, there is a relation between biochemical and physiological individuality and sensitivity to noxious environmental influences and susceptibility to illness. Individuality is largely quantitative rather than qualitative (16, 38); each individual mobilizes different configurations or patterns of component homeostatic processes in making adjustments to environmental change. This diversity is probably polymorphic (30). Through systematic study of the diversity will emerge knowledge of the individual's adaptive capacity, which is required to deal constructively with the problems of environmental health (29).

Some examples may be given to illustrate these general points. Without a doubt, air pollution is a serious problem. The acute disasters serve to emphasize the grim prospects. Low levels of air pollution are now present in many urban centers. How do these low levels affect the health of the population? The individuals we should be most concerned about are those most sensitive to air pollution (12). If attention is devoted only to the "individual at the mean," many persons will be severely incapacitated or dead before the group within the "normal range" are affected. The most susceptible persons must be identified, for their individuality is a matter of fundamental importance in establishing criteria for air quality and other environmental standards.

The human being has a propensity to store excess energy as fat (24). This propensity creates significant health problems for a segment of the population identified as obese. Obesity predisposes to a variety of illnesses—for instance, diabetes mellitus, hypertension, and coronary artery disease. There is an individuality in the matter of fat storage (24). The ectomorph stores fat more readily than the endomorph. This fact suggests that the configuration of the component physiological regulations of the ectomorph differs from that of the endomorph. The needs and requirements of these types are not the same. That these types exist suggest that there are probably polymorphisms of physiological regulations in the population. These polymorphisms can only be elucidated through systematic studies of individuality. Such studies should contribute to an explanation of why some people have a high frequency of illness and others have a low frequency, why some persons are successful in finding an adequate environment and others are not (15).

Epilogue

Human ecology is, above all, a way of asking questions that may. be productive in understanding man's evolution, nature, and problems of adaptation. It recognizes that, in man, biology, society, and culture are deeply interrelated. Culture and society have transformed man's environment but, in doing so, have changed rather than eliminated the selective pressures to which he must adapt effectively if he is to survive.

The problems posed by human ecology are very difficult. In fact, until the theoretical structure of operations research (11) and the modern armament of instrument and data processing had become available, few of these problems could be effectively attacked. Today, both the necessity for, and possibility of, effective human ecological research present great challenges for the biological and behavioral sciences. It is to be hoped that such forthcoming scientific undertakings as the International Biological Programme will meet these challenges (31, 32).

REFERENCES

1. Bernard, C. 1949. *Introduction to the Study of Experimental Medicine.* Trans. by H. C. Greene. Schuman, Inc., New York.
2. Brain, W. R. 1965. Science and antiscience. *Science,* **148:** 192-198.
3. Chisholm, B. 1963. Future of the Mind. In *Man and His Future* (G. Wolstenholme, ed.). Little, Brown & Co., Boston, p. 315-321.
4. Comfort, A. 1964. *Ageing. The Biology of Senescence.* Revised ed. Holt, Rinehart, Winston, New York.
5. Committee on Human Ecology. 1964. *Introduction to Human Ecology. Syllabus.* University of Illinois, Urbana. Lecture 32.
6. Committee on Natural Resources. 1962. *Natural Resources.* National Academy of Sciences–Natural Research Council, Publ. No. 1000, Washington, D.C.
7. Dobzhansky, T. 1962. *Mankind Evolving. The Evolution of the Human Species.* Yale University Press, New Haven.
8. Dobzhansky, T. 1963. Evolutionary and population genetics. *Science,* **142:** 1131-1135.
9. Dobzhansky, T. 1963. Genetic entities in hominid evolution. In *Classification and Human Evolution* (S. L. Washburn, ed.) Aldine, Chicago, p. 347-362.
10. Dubos, R. 1961. *Mirage of Health.* Anchor Book (A258). Doubleday & Co., New York.
11. Flagle, C. D., W. H. Huggins, and R. H. Roy. 1960. *Operations Research and Systems Engineering.* The Johns Hopkins Press, Baltimore.
12. Goldsmith, J. R. 1962. Effects of air pollution on humans. In *Air Pollution* (Stern, A. C., ed.) Academic Press, Inc., New York, Vol. I, p. 335-386.
13. Goldstein, K. 1963. *The Organism.* Beacon Press (BP 165), Boston.
14. Gross, P. M. 1962. *Report of the Committee on Environmental Health Problems to the Surgeon General.* Public Health Service Publication No. 908. U.S. Government Printing Office, Washington, D.C.
15. Hinkle, L. E., Jr., and H. G. Wolf. 1957. The nature of man's adaptation to his total environment and the relation of this to illness. *A.M.A. Arch. Internal Med.,* **99:** 442-460.
16. Hirsch, J. 1962. Individual differences in behavior and their genetic basis. In *Roots of Behavior* (E. L. Bliss, ed.) Harper & Bros., Inc., New York. p. 3-23.
17. Howell, F. C. 1952. Pleistocene glacial ecology and the evolution of "classic Neanderthal" man. *Southwestern J. Anthropol.,* **8:** 377-410.
18. Howell, F. C., and F. Bourliere (eds). 1963. *African Ecology and Evolution.* Aldine, Chicago.
19. Huxley, J. S. 1941. *Man Stands Alone.* Harper & Bros., Inc., New York.
20. Johnston, F. E. 1964. Racial taxonomics from an evolutionary perspective. *Am. Anthropol.,* **66:** 822-828.
21. Livingstone, F. B. 1958. Anthropological implications of sickle cell gene distribution in West Africa. *Am. Anthropol.,* **60:** 553-562.
22. Medawar, P. B. 1957. *The Uniqueness of the Individual.* Methuen & Co., Ltd., London.
23. Menninger, K. 1963. *The Vital Balance. The Life Process in Mental Health and Illness.* Viking Press, New York.
24. Mitchell, H. H. 1962. *Comparative Nutrition of Man and Domestic Animals.* Vol. 1. Academic Press, Inc., New York.
25. Mudd, S. (ed.). 1964. *The Population Crisis and the Use of World Resources.* Indiana University Press, Bloomington.

27

26. Neel, J. V. 1962. Diabetes mellitus: a "thrifty" genotype rendered detrimental by "progress"? *Am. J. Human Genet.*, **14**: 353-362.

27. Richards, D. W. 1960. Homeostasis: its dislocations and perturbations. *Perspectives Biol. Med.*, **3**: 238-251.

28. Rostlund, E. 1961. Taming trees. *Bull. At. Scientists*, **17**: 326-330.

29. Sargent, F. II, and D. M. Barr. 1964. Health and Fitness of the Ecosystem. Mimeograph. (To be published by Travelers Research Center, Hartford, Conn., 1965.)

30. Sargent, F. II, and K. P. Weinman. 1965. Physiological individuality. In *Conference on Biology of Human Variation* (J. E. Brozek, ed.) New York Academy of Sciences. In Press.

31. Special Committee for International Biological Programme. 1965. IBP News No. 2. International Council of Scientific Unions. (IBP Secretariat, 2 via Sebenico, Rome, Italy.)

32. Stebbins, G. L. 1962. International horizons in the life sciences. *AIBS Bull.*, **12**: 13-19.

33. Steward, J. H., and D. B. Shimkin. 1961. Some mechanisms of sociocultural evolution. *Daedalus* (Summer), p. 477-497.

34. Tanner, J. M. 1955. *Growth at Adolescence*. C. C Thomas, Springfield, Illinois.

35. Thomas, W. L., Jr., ed. 1956. *Man's Role in Changing the Face of the Earth*. University of Chicago Press, Chicago.

36. Weiner, J. S., and K. Hellman. 1960. The sweat glands. *Biol. Rev.*, **35**: 141-186.

37. Williams, G. C. 1957. Pleiotropy, natural selection, and the evolution of senescence. *Evolution*, **11**: 398-411.

38. Williams, R. J. 1956. *Biochemical Individuality. The Basis of the Genetotropic Concept*. John Wiley & Sons, Inc., New York. (Also available in paperback edition, 1963.)

HUMAN BIOLOGICAL VARIATION AS AN ADAPTIVE RESPONSE TO THE ENVIRONMENT

PAUL T. BAKER
Department of Sociology and Anthropology
The Pennsylvania State University

Man, as any other animal species that still survives, is adapted to his environment. This statement only signifies that at this point in time, as measured by numbers and energy exchange, man is a successful animal on this planet with no immediate prospects of extinction. Of course, the statement implies much more, since the parameters of the physical and biological environments within which we exist are greater than for any other animal; and if we logically add that distillate of human behavior called culture to the environmental parameters, then the varieties of environment to which groups of men are adapted is truly prodigious compared to other species.

When we inquire into the sources of the great adaptability of our species, two concepts are generally evoked—culture and race. Both of these represent gross generalizations in the semantic sense and consequently represent the poorest of scientific exploratory tools.

Culture can be a useful abstraction when employed for the broad categorization of nonbiologically transmitted human information, but it can never serve as a complete explanation for any unit of human behavior inasmuch as it is biological organisms that are behaving. Thus the accumulated information on how to sew an Eskimo parka is a product of Eskimo culture, but the adaptive value of the parka in arctic cold also depends on the motor skill of the maker and the physiological responses of the wearer.

Race is an equally unsatisfactory conceptual tool. I would not disagree with Dobzhansky's contention that there exist conglomerates of morphological and genetic traits that permit a valid taxonomic subdivision of man (Dobzhansky, 1962).

Such a classification, however, has limited research use and is often badly abused when the results of a study on one small segment of a race is extrapolated to the whole group without a known basis in physiological functioning. To exemplify valid use and abuse of race as a research tool, cases from environmental physiology may be cited. It has been shown that because of more melanin in the skin of an American Negro, it absorbs more solar radiation than does white skin (Baker, 1958). Since in most classification systems "Negro" always means a high skin melanin, we may generalize that Negroes in a nude condition will absorb more heat from the sun than whites. On the other hand, to cite a possible abuse, it has been found by several investigators that the fingers of American Negro soldiers are, with all other conditions constant, "colder" in ice water than are the fingers of American white soldiers (Adams and Covino, 1958; Iampietro et al., 1959). This appears to be the result of lower warm blood circulation in the Negro hands; but since the causes of this circulatory difference are unknown and may be unrelated to the traits associated with race, it is pure speculation to say that most classificatory "Negroes" would have colder fingers in ice water. Also, since the mechanisms are unknown and no such studies have been performed on

Eugenics Quarterly, June, 1966, Vol.13, No.2, pp. 81-91.

U.S. Negro females, it cannot even be stated with more than a low degree of probability that American Negro females would test lower than American white females.

From these considerations it appears to me that if we wish to understand how man has adapted to his varied environments and what role his biological variability has played in this adaptation, we must deal in specifics rather than in abstractions such as culture and race.

THE SOURCES OF MAN'S ADAPTATION TO THE ENVIRONMENT

Man owes his adaptive structure to the evolutionary process, but in many ways it seems to have exceeded in complexity that of any other animal. He, as all other animals, may adapt to a new form of environmental stress by mutational change acted upon by selection with subsequent changes in gene frequency. Indeed, as recent studies have shown, this has probably been more common than had been assumed. However, the enormous range of adaptive mechanisms that man has available are primarily the consequence of the increasing somatic and behavioral plasticity that seems to have occurred throughout the mammalian evolutionary process, culminating at the moment in man.

One of the secular trends in mammalian evolution was the rise in adaptive phenotypic plasticity that increasingly allowed animals to vary their pattern of functioning and behavior in response to the information provided by the environment in which they developed. Man's culture-creating capacity might be considered the inevitable end product of this increasing plasticity. The most apparent aspect of increasing plasticity was the increasing ability to learn, and the most important single attribute for the development of culture is man's enormous learning capacity. In biological terms this capacity might simply be conceived of as his great ability to pattern his behavior in response to environmental challenges. Of equal consequence for adaptation to diverse environments is man's functional and morphological adaptive plasticity. The functional and morphological plasticity of man is probably most familiar to us in its short-term manifestations. For example, temperature and altitude acclimatization are well-documented examples of modification in the functioning of man that increase his performance capability in the face of new environmental stress. Other examples would be the increase in muscle fibre size that accompanies exercise or the psychological process of accustomization that allows the organism to ignore distracting stimuli in the environment. Perhaps of similar import, but less well studied, are the long-term adaptive changes that occur in human beings when they develop under particular types of environmental stress. For example, children, when they must exist in a caloric deficient environment, can do so for prolonged periods of time by a cessation of growth which, if the deprivation period is not of excessive length, will later be recouped (McCance and Widdowson, 1951). In the same vein, man has the capacity to store calories in the form of fat when he has available "more than adequate" calories. Those stored calories can later be used during periods of short calorie supply. Other examples include the increased size of the lungs and the heart that occurs in individuals who grow up in a high-altitude environment with its low oxygen pressure (Monge, 1948).

Less is known of the possibilities of long-term improvements in physiological function, but possible examples include the increased tolerance for certain drugs over long exposure.

Thus, if we look closely at the problem of studying human adaptability, we see that man has such a large variety of environmental stresses to which he adapts and such a large variety of mechanisms available to him for adaptation that we are probably dealing with a fairly unique set of interactions in each human population that is studied. More than with any other animal, we must take great care to identify properly the stresses to which a given human population has been exposed and to consider all of the parameters of adaptation man has available to solve the problem of survival in a given environment.

Given the uniqueness of each adaptive pattern, we may still believe that the limitations of the human germ plasm are such that similar partial solutions to adaptive needs will be found over broad population isolates. That such is indeed the case for cultural adaptation seems to be demonstrated by the independent inventions of such material culture items as house forms and agriculture. Biologically, the instances are even more impressive, since the existence of morphological and genetic traits that are clustered enough to permit racial classification indicates a common genetic response to selection. Even the fact that man conforms as well as any species to Allen and Bergman's rules suggests that he has responded to similar environmental stresses by similar adaptive responses (Harrison et al., 1964).

In the remainder of this paper, we will overview some small part of the knowledge so far available on man's adaptive responses. Because our knowledge is more precise in this area, the discussion will be limited primarily to physical and biological environmental stresses; and since our primary goal is to examine the role of man's biological variation in his adaptive structure, the discussion will also be strongly oriented to the biological responses even though these must always be considered in the cultural context.

While the sources of cultural adaptation to stresses remain obscure in the problems of understanding human learning and culture transmission, the sources of biological adaptation can be conceived even though we still do not have available the methods required to partition the biological components of adaptation precisely. As implied earlier in the paper, the sources of biological adaptation may be arbitrarily categorized into at least four interrelated types: psychological accommodation, physiological acclimatization, developmental acclimatization, and genetic adaptation. The functional differentiation between genetic and the other types of adaptation are apparent. However, the psychological accommodation, physical acclimatization, and developmental acclimatization are more arbitrary, since all are part of adaptive plasticity. The differentiation is based on the length of time involved and the discipline differences in perspective.

THEORIES OF GENETIC ADAPTATION

The problem of the relationship between the variability in the genetic structure of human populations and their adaptive significance may be approached from two perspectives: (1) the theoretical relationship established by genetic evolutionary theories, and (2) the demonstrable adaptive value of specific genetic variation in man. Until the end of the 1940's most anthropologists were concerned with the search for nonadaptive inherited traits even though they recognized that many traits might be functional. Indeed, the old goal was to establish a taxonomy of man based on nonfunctional morphological variation so that migration and population admixture could be reconstructed much as the archaeologist reconstructs culture history from pottery designs.

Since this era the geneticist has forcefully pointed out that the body of evolutionary theory derived from genetic studies on other animals does not permit such an interpretation of human variation. Thus, studies of the way human genetic variability relates to human adaptation are essentially confined to the past 15 years.

As will be seen, the well-established relationships remain meager; and it is possible that if the accumulated genetic theories were less conclusive, a majority of human biologists might still hold the view that most genetic variation in man is and was without adaptive significance. Let us, therefore, examine first the nature and strength of this theoretical structure.

EVOLUTIONARY THEORY AND GENETIC ADAPTATION

At the base lies the simple mathematical theorem generally referred to as the Hardy-Weinberg theorem that points out that the gene randomization process that occurs in bisexually reproducing higher animals will not within itself change the frequency of genes in a population. Of course, as Sewall Wright showed mathematically, the size of the population and the frequency of a gene in a finite population is related to the gene's chances of survival (Wright, 1943). Thus, in very small populations pure chance can lead to the loss of a gene with a fairly low frequency, while a gene with a very high frequency may completely replace its heterozygous partner. Since this is a purely statistical concept, the probability of these occurrences is strictly determined by population numbers and gene frequencies.

Aside from these statistical models the only possibilities for modifying gene frequencies in a population are (1) mutation and chromosomal abberations; (2) gene flow (in or out of the population); and (3) selection (any nonchance phenomena that lead to the greater or lesser reproduction of a gene). Mutational and chromosomal abberations cannot be evoked as an explanation for the major part of genetic variation in human populations since they are at least similar in kind and frequency for all groups. Without selection or drift to fix variants, no population variation would develop.

Gene flow is meaningless in the overall problem since we are asking the question, "How did differentiation in genetic structure occur within our species?," which, by definition, is or was a breeding unit. Coon (1962) argues that modern man has a history of racial variation that precedes the *sapiens* form, but even if this proves true, there was genetic overlap. Furthermore, the reasons for the initial variation in genotype must fit into our scheme of genetic evolutionary theory.

Thus, only two explanations remain— the Sewall Wright genetic drift explanation, or selection. Drift first presented an attractive explanation since man in his hunting and gathering days was a thinly spread animal in very small bands. If we assume that he was then endogamous, there existed a perfect situation for drift effects. Undoubtedly, drift did have some effect. It has been demonstrated, fairly conclusively, to be the cause for some of the variation in other species, and at least one example has been presented with strong evidence for man (Giles, 1965). However, drift is a very unsatisfactory explanation for the major variations in human population genotypes. For one thing, if early man was endogamous, he should have rapidly formed different species as other endogamous animal populations did. More importantly, the genetic drift theory is a probability theory; so that while the probability of two populations' developing a difference in the frequency in one gene due to drift is fairly high, the statistical probability of developing multiple gene differences is progressively lower. Indeed, on the basis of this theorem, the probability of two populations' developing a high frequency difference in even 100 genes over the period of time that our species existed as hunters and gatherers is so low that it may be classified as bordering on the impossible. Even the few major morphological characteristics on which broad racial classifications are based seem to relate to quite a large number of genotype differences, so that one must at the present state of knowledge conclude that drift is an unsatisfactory explanation for most of the genetic differences between human populations.

By a process of elimination we are, therefore, left with the conclusion that most group differences in population genotypes are the result of selection. Since selection acts by increasing the frequency of those genes that improve adaptation while it decreases those which lower adaptation, one is further forced to the conclusion that genotypic differences in human populations represent adaptive responses to the environment.

This does not mean that the genotype of a group is adapted to the environment in which it is now found. Because of the long generation time for man and the rapid changes he has produced in some aspects of his environment through culture formation, a given present-day gene may not have had any adaptive value to a population for even thousands of years. Once the environment to which a gene has adapted is modified, the persistence of that gene is governed purely by the intensity of selection against it and its dominance characteristics. The sicklemia gene found among U.S. Negroes is an excellent example. Although it is quite clearly maladaptive in the recent environment of the U.S. Negro, selection has not yet eliminated this gene, which was quite adaptive in the malarial environment from which many U.S. Negro genes were derived (Allison, 1955).

The conclusion that population differences in genotypes arose through selection also must not be viewed as proof that any given phenotypic characteristic of a group is or has been adaptive to an environment. As pointed out earlier, the phenotype is for man almost always subject to environmental patterning through the various forms of genetic plasticity. Equally important, most genes affect multiple phenotypic products, while most phenotypic characteristics have multiple gene determinants. Therefore, even when a close relationship exists between genetic inheritance and phenotypic characteristics, the adaptive value of the gene need not be related to any one aspect of the phenotype. As an example, eye color may be cited. The exact inheritance pattern is not known, but it appears to be quite closely related to the genes involved in skin color variation. In such a situation the variation in eye color and skin color may both have adaptive value, but it is equally possible that only variation in one provides adaptive value while the other tags along as a product of the pleiotropic effects of the gene.

The net product of the widely accepted theories that have been outlined is a scientific posture quite different from the two widely popular views. These views assume either (1) that variation in the genetic structure of human populations (race) is of prime importance to a group's ability to function in modern culture, or (2) that it has no significance to man's ability to live in any given culture. Instead, we are inclined to accept the following as a set of hypotheses to be tested:

1. Population differences in genotype including gene frequency differences are the product of environmental adaptation (including culture as a part of the environment).
2. The longer a population has lived in a set environment, the greater the probability that their genotypic eccentricities are a product of adaptation to that environment.

   Subhypothesis
   A. Ecologically stable populations will be more likely to show genetic adaptation than ecologically unstable units.
   B. Genetic differences are more likely to be related to the stable stresses of the environment such as climate and disease than to the more changeable stresses such as those produced by culture.
3. Many phenotypic variations in man are not the product of genetic adaptation.

EVIDENCE FOR GENETIC ADAPTATION

When we turn from theory to the demonstrable evidence for population differences in genetic adaptation, the findings are thin. This does not necessarily imply a poor theory. Instead, it may at this time be attributed to (1) the relatively small number of studies that have been undertaken with the preceding hypotheses, and (2) our lack of knowledge concerning man's genetic system and the degree to which it is involved in man's enormous structural, functional, and behavioral diversity.

Each year a considerable number of new genes are identified in man, and very often they are found to be unequally distributed in human populations. This immediately suggests that they have some adaptive value in those populations where a high frequency exists. Occasionally, such an assumption is supported by strong presumptive evidence, such as the sicklemia-malaria chain (Allison, 1955). In other instances, such as the many links between the abnormal hemoglobins and infectious disease, a direction for future research is indicated (Motulsky, 1960). However, for the majority of identified genes, even those such as the long-known genes underlying the ABO blood types, it has not been possible to even suggest an acceptable adaptive explanation for frequency differences. Perhaps the most striking fact is that biochemical investigators have demonstrated such a wide genetic diversity in man without more than lightly touching on the wide morphological diversity in human populations that was known to have some major genetic determinants before the biochemistry of blood was considered.

At the opposite side of the problem the newly rekindled interest in the sensory and physiological functioning of non-Western groups is also demonstrating an increasingly large variety of differences in human populations. True, these differences are not of the magnitude that the 19th century scientist conceived or the 20th century "racist" imagines, but the number is great and the differences are often of significant adaptive value to populations in their present or recently past environments. For this increasing list of traits, one of the major problems is the differentiation between the responses related to genetic variation and those produced by adaptive plasticity. For example, it is quite clear that the warmer temperatures of the Eskimo hand when exposed to cold enhanced his adaptation to the environment in which he lived (Coffee, 1955). On the other hand, the extent of genetic causation in the warmer hand temperatures is not clear. Despite a prodigious literature, the degree to which the different sources of biological adaptation are involved is not clear. It has been demonstrated that psychological accommodation to cold increases the temperature of the fingers when exposed to cold (Fox, 1963). Presumably, this is because anxiety is reduced by repeated exposures. It has also been shown that an acclimatization or training effect occurs, which further produces warmer hands by greater blood flow in most subjects (Egan, 1963). This still does not appear to account for most of the variation. Yoshimura's and Iida's work (1952) showed that northern and southern Japanese have a difference in response after training, so probably there is a developmental factor. It has also been suggested that there is a genetic factor, since U.S. Negro and white soldiers manifest vastly different responses even though they both came from the south (Iampietro et al., 1959). Also, Meehan (1955) showed a striking similarity in twins. Thus, one is inclined to assume a genetic component even though no specific genes have been identified.

It would be most surprising if any specific genes were found associated with the differences in hand temperature upon extreme cold exposures. From what is known of the mechanisms involved, gene action would be indirect, involving such links as hand size, the size of arterial anastomoses, forearm size and insulation, neural pathways, and even brain functions. When attempts at genetic analysis have been made on these possible intermediates, they have consistently yielded the same type of partial genotype causation answer. This is easily explainable by the multiple genes involved in each of these phenotypic characteristics, plus, of course, all the levels of plasticity.

As the preceding discussion has emphasized, evidence for genetic adaptation has been emanating from two sources, but the two sources are at this point not making a great deal of contact. The geneticist wishing to test the hypothesis that genetic variation is the product of adaptation, must trace the known gene through the almost impossible chain that ties it to morphology, function, and behavior; while the psychophysiologist or environmental physiologist has the equally difficult task of tracking the behavior or function with demonstrable adaptive value through the chain of its environmental determinants to the genetic core. In these two lines of inquiry it is not surprising that the most conclusive cases have contained the simplest links. Thus, the adaptive nature of genotype and gene frequency variation have been best demonstrated between simply inherited hemoglobin types and the diseases that attack hemoglobin, and the best case for demonstrating a genetic component in adaptive behavior or function is where the function is closely associated with morphology, such as climate tolerance and body morphology (Hammel, 1964).

Probably the greatest danger to the understanding of human adaptation comes from the fact that these simple relationships are the easiest to establish and, therefore, lead to the conclusion that they are the most important ones. Indeed, this has happened with geneticists concentrating their efforts on the study of infectious disease while the environmental physiologist has concentrated on temperature. In such important environmental stress areas as nutrition, culture, sensory and motor requirements, altitude and radiation very few attempts have been made to link adaptive behavior and function to genetic factors. Yet, there is no theoretical reason to doubt that selection due to these forms of stress was at least as significant in producing genetic variation as was temperature and infectious disease.

BEHAVIORAL AND SOMATIC PLASTICITY AS ADAPTATION

It is surprising to find that despite an extensive literature on man's adaptative capacity in the presence of stress there does not exist a commonly accepted terminology that differentiates the nature or the types of adaptive responses. If for the moment we ignore the vast literature that deals with intelligence as an adaptive response and deal only with the more specific functions studied by the physiologist, we find that the areas of terminological agreement are still too few. If we use Prosser (1964) as a guide, physiologists would accept the concept of a stress and a response to it on the part of the organism. The responses that enhance the organism's functioning in the presence of stress are *adaptive responses;* these are divided into genetically determined *adaptive variations* and environmentally induced responses called *acclimation,* or *acclimatization.* The geneticists would also point out that acclimatization responses are built into the genetic structure; or, as Prosser states it, "the genotype determines the 'capacity' of an organism to adapt." To the physiologist the concept of acclimatization appears adequate to cover all of the non-genetic changes in man that enhance adaptation. However, the terminological problem may very well prevent the physiologist, psychologist, medical scientist, geneticist, anthropologist, etc. from realizing that they often are involved in the study of very closely related facets of the same problem.

In the majority of psychological studies, for example, an improvement in the human organism's adaptation to the environment is called adjustment, accommodation, or perhaps adaptation. If the word "acclimatization" appears, it must be rare, indeed. In the field of human growth and development the language of the evolutionary geneticist or physiologist is even more alien. The studies of psychological development use the language of psychology, while in the area of physical growth the concept of growth as an adaptive process is so alien that almost no terminology exists. It was with the terminological confusion in mind that a three-way breakdown in adaptive phenotypic plasticity was suggested earlier in this paper.

It may be logically argued that there is no essential difference in the mechanisms that enhance adaptation through psychological accommodation, physiological acclimatization, and developmental acclimatization. All are based on the inherited plasticity of man; and all depend upon environmental stress, which feeds back through the human nervous system to enhance the functioning of the organism in the presence of a given stress. There is, perhaps, a time factor difference, since the three categories of adaptation require progressively longer developmental time. However, the major point is the reminder that whether one is studying the changes in pain threshold or the effect of altitude on the growth of human lungs, all may be viewed as part of man's enormous adaptive capacity and may be profitably considered within the framework of evolutionary adaptational theory.

Perhaps the most difficult aspect of studying phenotypic plasticity is the process of distinguishing between adaptive and maladaptive responses to stress. In most cases the critical question is, "adaptive to what?" The physiologist often has no problem. If he has exposed individuals to a high heat stress, then any response that reduces the strain on the temperature regulation system and enhances work performance is adaptive. On the other hand, it is not so clear to the psychologist that a reduction in the pain sensation with chronic exposure represents a reduction of strain, and the situations in which it would enhance performance must be carefully defined.

For this reason, the psychologist has been quite sparing with the label "adaptive," and in sensory systems such as hearing a considerable difference of opinion is found on whether a given change in response to a sound should be called "masking," "fatigue," or "adaptation." Most of this problem is not meaningful when the researcher is considering adaptive responses in relation to a specific stress. For a hungry hunter in the woods, identification of the sounds of a food animal among the myriad sounds of the forest is adaptive and would be fixed by evolution whether it conforms to the psychologist's definition of fatigue, masking, or adaptation. Indeed, it appears that the precise reason why the terminology of adaptation is so confused is the lack of evolutionary and selection concepts in its usage by the psychophysiologist and even most other physiologists. Until very recent years, the search has always been for the universal changes that improved performance or function. Individual differences were ignored when encountered, and the testing of different human populations was seldom attempted. This contrasts strangely with the psychology of tests and measurements where consideration of the individual and group variation has been paramount, while the

hopes of establishing the underlying reasons for the variation were minimal.

POPULATION VARIATION IN ADAPTIVE RESPONSES

As noted in the section on genetic adaptation, two methods are available for the discovery of population differences in adaptive capacity. The one involves relating known gene frequency variations to the adaptive requirements of the environment. The second involves the actual measurement and comparison of the functional capacities of human populations in the presence of a given stress. Once a population difference has been established in functional capacity, the difficult problem of sorting out the genetic from the different forms of plasticity sources-of-adaptation begins. But first there must be the test for functional differences. In those cases where functional differences have been investigated, the population differences have usually proven more substantial than anticipated. Thus, Motulsky (1960) showed that different populations show enormous differences in death rates from common infectious diseases. The environmental physiologist has also discovered a quite broad variation in population responses to physical environmental stresses such as temperature and altitude. Even in the area of nutrition it is now widely accepted that the nutritional needs of different human populations are not uniform (Grande, 1964).

Of course, knowledge in these areas is quite fragmentary, and often the adaptive significance of population variation is not apparent. Hopefully, the Human Adaptability Project of the International Biological Program will provide the stimulus for a rapid expansion of information in these areas. I would, therefore, like to end this brief overview with a special emphasis on the study of population differences in sensory and motor capabilities. The historical and travel literature is replete with comments on the special sensory and motor skills of primitive popoulations. Yet, our scientific knowledge on the subject is negligible. The few studies that have been made have suggested that there may be dramatic differences in the visual (Mann, 1966) and auditory (Rosen et al., 1962) characteristics of different populations. We have essentially no knowledge about the possibilities of other sensory differences or motor skills. I would not presume at this time to suggest whether there exist population genetic differences, but I would be surprised if there did not exist significant population variations in most of the sensory and motor characteristics. Certainly, the testing of populations would be an important contribution to our knowledge of how human biological variability contributes to adaptation.

CONCLUSIONS

Many readers of this article may at this point feel that they have been exposed to a great deal of theory and generalities about how man's biological variation is related to his adaptive capacity but to very little firm data. The author is sympathetic to this view and refers the reader to *The Biology of Human Adaptability* (Baker and Weiner, 1966) for a survey of factual knowledge on this subject as viewed by geneticists and human biologists. *The Handbook of Physiology* section entitled "Adaptation to the Environment" (Dill et al., 1964) provides a comprehensive coverage from the viewpoint of physiology.

I have not attempted a summarization of this information for two major reasons: (1) the mass of material is too great for an article of this length; and (2) the information is too fragmentary to construct an overall pattern at this time. The purpose, therefore, has been, not factual summary, but, instead, to provide a progress report on the scientific productivity of studying human biological variability as the product of adaptation in the evolutionary sense.

Viewed in terms of an interim report, what conclusions can be reached? In my opinion, the following seem justified.

1. The concept that most genotypic differences in human populations is the result of adaptation to differing environments has emerged as a dominant theory.

2. The phenotypic variation in the behavior, physiological function, and morphology of human populations may very often be "caused" by adaptation. Thus the search for the causes of racial variation, differences in the physiological and psychological functioning of groups, as well as cultural variations can be profitably pursued from the framework of evolutionary adaptation.

3. The phenotypic adaptations of man contain a high environmental patterning component. Thus, geneticists would do well to broaden the base from which they search for genetic adaptation, while psychophysiologists and environmental physiologists would profit in their understanding of the sources of human adaptability by the design of studies that would allow the demonstration of developmental acclimatization and genetic adaptation.

Finally, I must note that popular questions such as whether race differences in intelligence exist, and if so, are they cultural or genetic in origin, are not meaningful questions at the present state of adaptational theory or evidence. At this time we cannot even state with certainty the degree of genetic versus environmental patterning involved in the presumably adaptive variation in hand temperature; therefore, to debate seriously the genetic versus environmental patterning involved in man's total adaptive behavioral capacity (a common definition of intelligence) in a variety of environmental settings is inappropriate as a scientific endeavor.

REFERENCES

ADAMS, T., and B. G. COVINO, 1958. Racial variations to a standardized cold stress. *J. Appl. Physiol.*, **12**: 9–12.

ALLISON, A. C., 1955. Aspects of polymorphism in man. Cold Spring Harbor Symposium, *Quant. Biol.*, **20**: 239–252.

BAKER, P. T., 1958. Racial differences in heat tolerance. *Amer. J. Phys. Anthrop.*, **16**: 287–305.

—— and J. S. WEINER (eds.), 1966. *The Biology of Human Adaptability.* Oxford University Press, Oxford and New York.

COFFEE, M. F., 1955. "A Comparative Study of Young Eskimo and Indian Males with Acclimatized White Males." *In* Ferrer (ed.), *Cold Injury.* J. Macy Foundation, New York.

COON, C. S., 1962. *The Origin of Races.* Alfred A. Knopf, New York.

DILL, D. B., E. F. ADOLPH, and C. G. WILBUR (eds.), 1964. *Handbook of Physiology*, Sect. 4, "Adaptation to the Environment." American Physiological Society, Washington, D.C.

DOBZHANSKY, T. H., 1962. *Mankind Evolving.* Yale University Press, New Haven and London.

EGAN, C. J., 1963. Local vascular adaptations to cold in man. *Fed. Proc.*, **22**: 547–551.

FOX, R. H., 1963. Comment following "Local vascular adaptations to cold in man" by C. J. Egan. *Fed. Proc.*, **22**: 952.

GILES, EUGENE, 1965. Anthropological significance of recent New Guinea genetic studies. *Amer. J. Phys. Anthrop.*, **23**: 326.

GRANDE, FRANCISCO, 1964. "Man Under Caloric Deficiency." *In* D. B. Dill et al. (eds.), *Handbook of Physiology*, Sect. 4, "Adaptation to the Environment." American Physiological Society, Washington, D.C.

HAMMEL, T. H., 1964. "Terrestrial Animals in Cold: Recent Studies of Primitive Man." *In* D. B. Dill et al. (eds.), *Handbook of Physiology*, Sect. 4, "Adaptation to the Environment." American Physiological Society, Washington, D.C.

HARRISON, G. A., J. S. WEINER, J. M. TANNER, and N. A. BARNICOT, 1964. *Human Biology.* Oxford University Press, New York and Oxford.

IAMPIETRO, P. F., R. F. GOLDMAN, E. R. BUSKIRK, and D. E. BASS, 1959. Responses of Negro and white males to cold. *J. Appl. Physiol.*, **14**: 798–800.

MANN, IDA, 1966. *Culture, Race, Climate and Eye Disease.* Charles C Thomas, Springfield, Ill.

McCANCE, R. A., and W. M. B. WIDDOWSON, 1951. The German background studies of undernutrition, Wuppertal, 1946–49. *Med. Res. Counc. Spec. Rep.* (London) **275**: 1–20.

MEEHAN, J. P., 1955. Individual and racial variation in a vascular response to a cold stimulus. *Milit. Med.*, **116**: 330–334.

MONGE, CARLOS, 1948. *Acclimatization in the Andes: Historical Confirmation of "Climate Aggression" in the Development of Andean Man.* Johns Hopkins Press, Baltimore.

MOTULSKY, A. G., 1960. "Metabolic Polymorphisms and the Role of Infectious Diseases in Human Evolution." *In* G. W. Lasker (ed.), *The Processes of Ongoing Human Evolution.* Wayne State University Press, Detroit.

PROSSER, C. L., 1964. "Perspectives of Adaptation: Theoretical Aspects." *In* Dill et al. (eds.), *Handbook of Physiology*, Sect. 4, "Adaptation to the Environment." American Physiological Society, Washington, D.C.

ROSEN, SAMUEL, M. BERGMAN, D. PLESTER, A. EL. MOFTY, and M. H. SATTI, 1962. Presbycusis study of a relatively noise-free population in the Sudan. *Ann. Otol.*, **71**: 727–743.

WRIGHT, SEWALL, 1943. Isolation by distance. *Genetics*, **28**: 114.

YOSHIMURA, H., and T. IIDA, 1952. Studies on the reactivity of the skin vessels to extreme cold, Part 2: Factors governing individual reactivity on the resistance to frostbite. *Jap. J. Physiol.*, **2**: 177–185.

The Cultural Basis for Our Environmental Crisis

Judeo-Christian tradition is only one of many cultural factors contributing to the environmental crisis.

Lewis W. Moncrief

One hundred years ago at almost any location in the United States, potable water was no farther away than the closest brook or stream. Today there are hardly any streams in the United States, except in a few high mountainous reaches, that can safely satisfy human thirst without chemical treatment. An oft-mentioned satisfaction in the lives of urbanites in an earlier era was a leisurely stroll in late afternoon to get a breath of fresh air in a neighborhood park or along a quiet street. Today in many of our major metropolitan areas it is difficult to find a quiet, peaceful place to take a leisurely stroll and sometimes impossible to get a breath of

The author is assistant professor in the department of recreation resources administration of the School of Forest Resources, and he holds an associate faculty appointment with the department of sociology and anthropology, both at North Carolina State University, Raleigh 27607. This article is based on an address given at a Man and Environment Conference at Arizona State University on 16 April 1970.

Science, October 30, 1970, Vol.170, pp. 508-512.

fresh air. These contrasts point up the dramatic changes that have occurred in the quality of our environment.

It is not my intent in this article, however, to document the existence of an environmental crisis but rather to discuss the cultural basis for such a crisis. Particular attention will be given to the institutional structures as expressions of our culture.

Social Organization

In her book entitled *Social Institutions* (*1*), J. O. Hertzler classified all social institutions into nine functional categories: (i) economic and industrial, (ii) matrimonial and domestic, (iii) political, (iv) religious, (v) ethical, (vi) educational, (vii) communications, (viii) esthetic, and (ix) health. Institutions exist to carry on each of these functions in all cultures, regardless of their location or relative complexity. Thus, it is not surprising that one of the analytical criteria used by anthropologists in the study of various cultures is the comparison and contrast of the various social institutions as to form and relative importance (*2*).

A number of attempts have been made to explain attitudes and behavior that are commonly associated with one institutional function as the result of influence from a presumably independent institutional factor. The classic example of such an analysis is *The Protestant Ethic and the Spirit of Capitalism* by Max Weber (*3*). In this significant work Weber attributes much of the economic and industrial growth in Western Europe and North America to capitalism, which, he argued, was an economic form that developed as a result of the religious teachings of Calvin, particularly spiritual determinism.

Social scientists have been particularly active in attempting to assess the influence of religious teaching and practice and of economic motivation on other institutional forms and behavior

and on each other. In this connection, L. White (*4*) suggested that the exploitative attitude that has prompted much of the environmental crisis in Western Europe and North America is a result of the teachings of the Judeo-Christian tradition, which conceives of man as superior to all other creation and of everything else as created for his use and enjoyment. He goes on to contend that the only way to reduce the ecologic crisis which we are now facing is to "reject the Christian axiom that nature has no reason for existence save to serve man." As with other ideas that appear to be new and novel, Professor White's observations have begun to be widely circulated and accepted in scholarly circles, as witness the article by religious writer E. B. Fiske in the *New York Times* earlier this year (*5*). In this article, note is taken of the fact that several prominent theologians and theological groups have accepted this basic premise that Judeo-Christian doctrine regarding man's relation to the rest of creation is at the root of the West's environmental crisis. I would suggest that the wide acceptance of such a simplistic explanation is at this point based more on fad than on fact.

Certainly, no fault can be found with White's statement that "Human ecology is deeply conditioned by beliefs about our nature and destiny—that is, by religion." However, to argue that it is the primary conditioner of human behavior toward the environment is much more than the data that he cites to support this proposition will bear. For example, White himself notes very early in his article that there is evidence for the idea that man has been dramatically altering his environment since antiquity. If this be true, and there is evidence that it is, then this mediates against the idea that the Judeo-Christian religion uniquely predisposes cultures within which it thrives to exploit their natural resources with indiscretion. White's own examples weaken his argument considerably. He points out that human intervention in the periodic flooding of the Nile River basin and the fire-drive method of hunting by prehistoric man have both probably wrought significant "unnatural" changes in man's environment. The absence of Judeo-Christian influence in these cases is obvious.

It seems tenable to affirm that the role played by religion in man-to-man and man-to-environment relationships is one of establishing a very broad system of allowable beliefs and behavior and of articulating and invoking a system of social and spiritual rewards for those who conform and of negative sanctions for individuals or groups who approach or cross the pale of the religiously unacceptable. In other words, it defines the ball park in which the game is played, and, by the very nature of the park, some types of games cannot be played. However, the kind of game that ultimately evolves is not itself defined by the ball park. For example, where animism is practiced, it is not likely that the believers will indiscriminately destroy objects of nature because such activity would incur the danger of spiritual and social sanctions. However, the fact that another culture does not associate spiritual beings with natural objects does not mean that such a culture will invariably ruthlessly exploit its resources. It simply means that there are fewer social and psychological constraints against such action.

In the remainder of this article, I present an alternative set of hypotheses based on cultural variables which, it seems to me, are more plausible and more defensible as an explanation of the environmental crisis that is now confronting us.

No culture has been able to completely screen out the egocentric tendencies of human beings. There also exists in all cultures a status hierarchy of positions and values, with certain groups partially or totally excluded from access to these normatively desirable goals. Historically, the differences in most cultures between the "rich"

and the "poor" have been great. The many very poor have often produced the wealth for the few who controlled the means of production. There may have been no alternative where scarcity of supply and unsatiated demand were economic reality. Still, the desire for a "better life" is universal; that is, the desire for higher status positions and the achievement of culturally defined desirable goals is common to all societies.

The Experience in the Western World

In the West two significant revolutions that occurred in the 18th and 19th centuries completely redirected its political, social, and economic destiny (6). These two types of revolutions were unique to the West until very recently. The French revolution marked the beginnings of widespread democratization. In specific terms, this revolution involved a redistribution of the means of production and a reallocation of the natural and human resources that are an integral part of the production process. In effect new channels of social mobility were created, which theoretically made more wealth accessible to more people. Even though the revolution was partially perpetrated in the guise of overthrowing the control of presumably Christian institutions and of destroying the influence of God over the minds of men, still it would be superficial to argue that Christianity did not influence this revolution. After all, biblical teaching is one of the strongest of all pronouncements concerning human dignity and individual worth.

At about the same time but over a more extended period, another kind of revolution was taking place, primarily in England. As White points out very well, this phenomenon, which began with a number of technological innovations, eventually consummated a marriage with natural science and began to take on the character that it has retained until today (7). With this revolution the productive capacity of each worker was amplified by several times his potential prior to the revolution. It also became feasible to produce goods that were not previously producible on a commercial scale.

Later, with the integration of the democratic and the technological ideals, the increased wealth began to be distributed more equitably among the population. In addition, as the capital to land ratio increased in the production process and the demand grew for labor to work in the factories, large populations from the agrarian hinterlands began to concentrate in the emerging industrial cities. The stage was set for the development of the conditions that now exist in the Western world.

With growing affluence for an increasingly large segment of the population, there generally develops an increased demand for goods and services. The usual by-product of this affluence is waste from both the production and consumption processes. The disposal of that waste is further complicated by the high concentration of heavy waste producers in urban areas. Under these conditions the maxim that "Dilution is the solution to pollution" does not withstand the test of time, because the volume of such wastes is greater than the system can absorb and purify through natural means. With increasing population, increasing production, increasing urban concentrations, and increasing real median incomes for well over a hundred years, it is not surprising that our environment has taken a terrible beating in absorbing our filth and refuse.

The American Situation

The North American colonies of England and France were quick to pick up the technical and social innovations that were taking place in their motherlands. Thus, it is not surprising that the inclination to develop an industrial and manufacturing base is observable rather early in the colonies. A strong trend toward democratization also evidenced itself very early in the struggle for nationhood. In fact, Thistlewaite notes the significance of the concept of democracy as embodied in French thought to the framers of constitutional government in the colonies (8, pp. 33–34, 60).

From the time of the dissolution of the Roman Empire, resource ownership in the Western world was vested primarily with the monarchy or the Roman Catholic Church, which in turn bestowed control of the land resources on vassals who pledged fealty to the sovereign. Very slowly the concept of private ownership developed during the Middle Ages in Europe, until it finally developed into the fee simple concept.

In America, however, national policy from the outset was designed to convey ownership of the land and other natural resources into the hands of the citizenry. Thomas Jefferson was perhaps more influential in crystallizing this philosophy in the new nation than anyone else. It was his conviction that an agrarian society made up of small landowners would furnish the most stable foundation for building the nation (8, pp. 59–68). This concept has received support up to the present and, against growing economic pressures in recent years, through government programs that have encouraged the conventional family farm. This point is clearly relevant to the subject of this article because it explains how the natural resources of the nation came to be controlled not by a few aristocrats but by many citizens. It explains how decisions that ultimately degrade the environment are made not only by corporation boards and city engineers but by millions of owners of our natural resources. This is democracy exemplified!

Challenge of the Frontier

Perhaps the most significant interpretation of American history has been Fredrick Jackson Turner's much criticized thesis that the western frontier was the prime force in shaping our society (9). In his own words,

If one would understand why we are today one nation, rather than a collection of isolated states, he must study this economic and social consolidation of the country. . . . The effect of the Indian frontier as a consolidating agent in our history is important.

He further postulated that the nation experienced a series of frontier challenges that moved across the continent in waves. These included the explorers' and traders' frontier, the Indian frontier, the cattle frontier, and three distinct agrarian frontiers. His thesis can be extended to interpret the expansionist period of our history in Panama, in Cuba, and in the Philippines as a need for a continued frontier challenge.

Turner's insights furnish a starting point for suggesting a second variable in analyzing the cultural basis of the United States' environmental crisis. As the nation began to expand westward, the settlers faced many obstacles, including a primitive transportation system, hostile Indians, and the absence of physical and social security. To many frontiersmen, particularly small farmers, many of the natural resources that are now highly valued were originally perceived more as obstacles than as assets. Forests needed to be cleared to permit farming. Marshes needed to be drained. Rivers needed to be controlled. Wildlife often represented a competitive threat in addition to being a source of food. Sod was considered a nuisance—to be burned, plowed, or otherwise destroyed to permit "desirable" use of the land.

Undoubtedly, part of this attitude was the product of perceiving these resources as inexhaustible. After all, if a section of timber was put to the torch to clear it for farming, it made little difference because there was still plenty to be had very easily. It is no coincidence that the "First Conservation Movement" began to develop about 1890. At that point settlement of the frontier was almost complete. With the passing of the frontier era of American history, it began to dawn on people that our resources were indeed exhaustible. This realization ushered in a new philosophy of our national government toward natural resources management under the guidance of Theodore Roosevelt and Gifford Pinchot. Samuel Hays (10) has characterized this movement as the appearance of a new "Gospel of Efficiency" in the management and utilization of our natural resources.

The Present American Scene

America is the archetype of what happens when democracy, technology, urbanization, capitalistic mission, and antagonism (or apathy) toward natural environment are blended together. The present situation is characterized by three dominant features that mediate against quick solution to this impending crisis: (i) an absence of personal moral direction concerning our treatment of our natural resources, (ii) an inability on the part of our social institutions to make adjustments to this stress, and (iii) an abiding faith in technology.

The first characteristic is the absence of personal moral direction. There is moral disparity when a corporation executive can receive a prison sentence for embezzlement but be congratulated for increasing profits by ignoring pollution abatement laws. That the absolute cost to society of the second act may be infinitely greater than the first is often not even considered.

The moral principle that we are to treat others as we would want to be treated seems as appropriate a guide as it ever has been. The rarity of such teaching and the even more uncommon instance of its being practiced help to explain how one municipality can, without scruple, dump its effluent into a stream even though it may do irreparable damage to the resource and add tremendously to the cost incurred by downstream municipalities that use the same water. Such attitudes are not restricted to any one culture. There appears to be an almost universal tendency to maximize self-interests and a widespread willingness to shift production costs to society to promote individual ends.

Undoubtedly, much of this behavior is the result of ignorance. If our accounting systems were more efficient in computing the cost of such irresponsibility both to the present generation and to those who will inherit the environment we are creating, steps would undoubtedly be taken to enforce compliance with measures designed to conserve resources and protect the environment. And perhaps if the total costs were known, we might optimistically speculate that more voluntary compliance would result.

A second characteristic of our current situation involves institutional inadequacies. It has been said that "what belongs to everyone belongs to no one." This maxim seems particularly appropriate to the problem we are discussing. So much of our environment is so apparently abundant that it is considered a free commodity. Air and water are particularly good examples. Great liberties have been permitted in the use and abuse of these resources for at least two reasons. First, these resources have typically been considered of less economic value than other natural resources except when conditions of extreme scarcity impose limiting factors. Second, the right of use is more difficult to establish for resources that are not associated with a fixed location.

Government, as the institution representing the corporate interests of all its citizens, has responded to date with dozens of legislative acts and numerous court decisions which give it authority to regulate the use of natural resources. However, the decisiveness to act has thus far been generally lacking. This indecisiveness cannot be understood without noting that the simplistic models that depict the conflict as that of a few powerful special interests versus "The People" are altogether inadequate. A very large proportion of the total citizenry is implicated in environmental degradation; the responsibility ranges from that of the board and executives of a utility company who might wish to thermally pollute a river with impunity to that of the average citizen who votes against a bond issue to improve the efficiency of a municipal sanitation system in order to keep his taxes from being raised. The magnitude of irresponsibility among individuals and institutions might be characterized as falling along a continuum from highly irresponsible to indirectly responsible. With such a broad base of interests being threatened with every change in resource policy direction, it is not surprising, although regrettable, that government has been so indecisive.

A third characteristic of the present American scene is an abiding faith in technology. It is very evident that the idea that technology can overcome almost any problem is widespread in Western society. This optimism exists in the face of strong evidence that much of man's technology, when misused, has produced harmful results, particularly in the long run. The reasoning goes something like this: "After all, we have gone to the moon. All we need to do is allocate enough money and brainpower and we can solve any problem."

It is both interesting and alarming that many people view technology almost as something beyond human control. Rickover put it this way (*11*):

It troubles me that we are so easily pressured by purveyors of technology into permitting so-called "progress" to alter our lives without attempting to control it—as if technology were an irrepressible force of nature to which we must meekly submit.

He goes on to add:

It is important to maintain a humanistic attitude toward technology; to recognize clearly that since it is the product of human effort, technology can have no legitimate purpose but to serve man—man in general, not merely some men; future generations, not merely those who currently wish to gain advantage for themselves; man in the totality of his humanity, encompassing all his manifold interests and needs, not merely some one particular concern of his. When viewed humanistically, technology is seen not as an end in itself but a means to an end, the end being determined by man himself in accordance with the laws prevailing in his society.

In short, it is one thing to appreciate the value of technology; it is something else entirely to view it as our environmental savior—which will save us in spite of ourselves.

Conclusion

The forces of democracy, technology, urbanization, increasing individual wealth, and an aggressive attitude toward nature seem to be directly related to the environmental crisis now being confronted in the Western world. The Judeo-Christian tradition has probably influenced the character of each of these forces. However, to isolate religious tradition as a cultural component and to contend that it is the "historical root of our ecological crisis" is a bold affirmation for which there is little historical or scientific support.

To assert that the primary cultural condition that has created our environmental crisis is Judeo-Christian teaching avoids several hard questions. For example: Is there less tendency for those who control the resources in non-Christian cultures to live in extravagant affluence with attendant high levels of waste and inefficient consumption? If non-Judeo-Christian cultures had the same levels of economic productivity, urbanization, and high average household incomes, is there evidence to indicate that these cultures would not exploit or disregard nature as our culture does?

If our environmental crisis is a "religious problem," why are other parts of the world experiencing in various degrees the same environmental problems that we are so well acquainted with in the Western world? It is readily observable that the science and technology that developed on a large scale first in the West have been adopted elsewhere. Judeo-Christian tradition has not been adopted as a predecessor to science and technology on a comparable scale. Thus, all White can defensibly argue is that the West developed modern science and technology *first*. This says nothing about the origin or existence of a particular ethic toward our environment.

In essence, White has proposed this simple model:

I	II	III
Judeo-Christian tradition	→ Science and technology →	Environmental degradation

I have suggested here that, at best, Judeo-Christian teaching has had only an indirect effect on the treatment of our environment. The model could be characterized as follows:

I	II	III	IV
Judeo-Christian tradition	1) Capitalism (with the attendant development of science and technology) 2) Democratization	1) Urbanization 2) Increased wealth → 3) Increased population 4) Individual resource ownership	Environmental degradation

Even here, the link between Judeo-Christian tradition and the proposed dependent variables certainly have the least empirical support. One need only look at the veritable mountain of criticism of Weber's conclusions in *The Protestant Ethic and the Spirit of Capitalism* to sense the tenuous nature of this link. The second and third phases of this model are common to many parts of the world. Phase I is not.

Jean Mayer (*12*), the eminent food scientist, gave an appropriate conclusion about the cultural basis for our environmental crisis:

It might be bad in China with 700 million poor people but 700 million rich Chinese would wreck China in no time. . . . It's the rich who wreck the environment . . . occupy much more space, consume more of each natural resource, disturb ecology more, litter the landscape . . . and create more pollution.

References and Notes

1. J. O. Hertzler, *Social Institutions* (McGraw-Hill, New York, 1929), pp. 47–64.
2. L. A. White, *The Science of Culture* (Farrar, Straus & Young, New York, 1949), pp. 121–145.
3. M. Weber, *The Protestant Ethic and the Spirit of Capitalism*, translated by T. Parsons (Scribner's, New York, 1958).
4. L. White, Jr., *Science* **155**, 1203 (1967).
5. E. B. Fiske, "The link between faith and ecology," *New York Times* (4 January 1970), section 4, p. 5.
6. R. A. Nisbet, *The Sociological Tradition* (Basic Books, New York, 1966), pp. 21–44. Nisbet gives here a perceptive discourse on the social and political implications of the democratic and industrial revolutions to the Western world.
7. It should be noted that a slower and less dramatic process of democratization was evident in English history at a much earlier date than the French revolution. Thus, the concept of democracy was probably a much more pervasive influence in English than in French life. However, a rich body of philosophic literature regarding the rationale for democracy resulted from the French revolution. Its counterpart in English literature is much less conspicuous. It is an interesting aside to suggest that perhaps the industrial revolution would not have been possible except for the more broad-based ownership of the means of production that resulted from the long-standing process of democratization in England.
8. F. Thistlewaite, *The Great Experiment* (Cambridge Univ. Press, London, 1955).
9. F. J. Turner, *The Frontier in American History* (Henry Holt, New York, 1920 and 1947).
10. S. P. Hays, *Conservation and the Gospel of Efficiency* (Harvard Univ. Press, Cambridge, Mass., 1959).
11. H. G. Rickover, *Amer. Forests* **75**, 13 (August 1969).
12. J. Mayer and T. G. Harris, *Psychol. Today* **3**, 46 and 48 (January 1970).

MAN'S ECOSYSTEM

LaMont C. Cole, *Cornell University*

Introduction

My survey here will be superficial by scientific standards, will almost entirely neglect the very important sociological environments in which modern man lives, and will touch on areas in which I am dependent, at best, on second-hand sources of information. I make the effort less for ecologists than in the hope that the message will eventually reach an audience that has forgotten, or has never learned, that man is a part of nature.

The earth's atmosphere, hydrosphere, biosphere, and the superficial layers of its lithosphere all together constitute a vast ecosphere within which a change in any one component evokes changes in all the others. Man's survival will ultimately depend upon an understanding of the functioning of the ecosphere, and I here present my conception of how all these things reached their present state and of where they may go in the future.

Early history of the earth

We must start by referring to some astronomical accidents. First, the earth originated in, or settled into, an orbit at a distance from the sun such that, after it evolved its definitive atmosphere, temperatures permitted water to be present in the liquid state over most of the surface, most of the time. This must be a cosmic rarity but was vitally important to the origin of life as we know it. Second, the earth's axis of rotation turned out to be tipped away from normal to the plane of its revolution about the sun. This accident, of course, is responsible for the existence of seasons and thus greatly accentuated the diversity between regions in different latitudes. Another astronomical accident of some sort provided the earth with a moon which, after the oceans developed, was responsible for the existence of an intertidal zone where, eventually, organisms adapted to life in the sea could become tolerant of life out of water and so be prepared to colonize the land.

However the earth may have originated, some 4.5 billion (4.5 x 10^9) years ago by present estimates, all theories with which I am familiar agree that at one time it was at too high a temperature to retain an atmosphere composed of the gases that are now present. Oxygen was probably bound in hydrated silicates and metallic oxides, and nitrogen, carbon, and phosphorus may have been bound as nitrides, carbides, and phosphides which occur today in meteorites but which are unstable in an atmosphere containing oxygen and water vapor.

The oldest known rocks show evidence of volcanic activity, and I accept the conclusion of Rubey (1951) that the atmosphere and hydrosphere originated from the degassing of rocks in the earth's interior after the surface had cooled sufficiently for its gravitational field to retain water vapor and other light gasses. I also see no reason to doubt that the primeval atmosphere was a reducing atmosphere lacking free oxygen, because we know that today there are enough reduced compounds of iron and magnesium alone in superficial layers of the lithosphere to extract all of the oxygen from the atmosphere in a geologically very short

Bioscience, April, 1966, Vol.16, No.4, pp. 243-248.

time, were it not for photosynthesis.

Whether the primeval atmosphere was a strongly reducing one consisting of ammonia, hydrogen, methane, and water, as postulated by Oparin (1936), and supported by observations on the atmospheres of the outer planets (Kniper, 1951), and by the experiments of Miller (1953), or whether it was only weakly reducing as postulated by Rubey (1955) need not concern us here. Abelson (1957) has shown experimentally that electrical discharges can induce the synthesis of amino acids in weakly reducing gaseous mixtures containing oxidized carbon compounds so long as free hydrogen is present. In the more strongly reducing atmosphere, Miller obtained a complex mixture of amino acids, aldehydes, organic acids, and urea.

Electrical discharges doubtless occurred in the primeval atmosphere and, more important, ultraviolet radiation of high energy content per quantum would reach the earth's surface in the absence of atmospheric oxygen and drive unfamiliar chemical reactions. Whether or not carbides, nitrides, and phosphides existed in the primitive solid material of the earth, they must have arrived in meteorites and reacted with water to produce hydrocarbons and other compounds of biological interest.

So the primeval sea gradually became a dilute soup of organic compounds which Urey (1952) postulates may have reached a concentration of 1%. Amino acids polymerize readily and, given as much time as we care to postulate, it is not difficult to conceive of polypeptides or even primitive proteins arising under these conditions. A number of authors (Oparin, 1936) have discussed the possible origin of larger organic complexes through such mechanisms as adsorption on clay particles and there is no need to repeat these speculations here. In this complex primeval soup there may have arisen transient forms exhibiting some of the properties we associate with life; for example, scavenging molecules building large aggregates by ingesting other molecules and perhaps metabolizing them in some simple manner. It is even possible that some primitive photosynthetic process may have arisen because, at wavelengths shorter than 200 nanometers, photons have enough energy to reduce CO_2 and H_2O to carbohydrate as a one-step photochemical reaction. Such a process, however, would be self-defeating because some of the evolved oxygen would be ionized by sunlight to ozone which is responsible in our present atmosphere for limiting the short wavelength end of the solar spectrum to 300 nm where photons lack sufficient energy to drive photosynthesis in a single step. In any case, a single-step photosynthetic process would have had to be a transient phenomenon because the photochemical lysis of water vapor in the thin upper atmosphere would result in the loss of hydrogen to space and the addition of some oxygen to the atmosphere.

Whatever protoliving processes may have occurred in the primitive seas, nothing that we would today be willing to call "life" could exist until some organic system acquired the means of producing replicates of itself — the process of reproduction. It is clear that the formation of a nucleic acid was the key step. Once this step was taken, life in the primitive soup could expand rapidly. This, however, was an exploitive form of life, using up the non-renewable resources of organic matter that had been accumulating for millions of years. Natural selection and speciation doubtless began to operate with different living forms competing for the energy in the organic compounds and with some forms adopting new modes of life as predators and parasites of other forms. Physico-chemical conditions, then as now, varied with differences of latitude and depth and some of these early living forms doubtless became specialists adapted to particular environmental conditions where they were competitively superior in acquiring the stored energy.

This primitive biosphere would have been destined to eat its way to extinction by virtue of its exploitive economy had there not been another large energy source in the form of solar radiation that could be tapped. As Lotka (1925) describes the situation: " . . . so long as there is an abundant surplus of available energy running 'to waste' over the sides of the mill wheel, so to speak, so long will a marked advantage be gained by any species that may develop talents to utilize this 'lost portion of the stream.' Such a species will therefore, other things equal, tend to grow in extent (numbers). . . . "

Pyrrole rings may have appeared as metabolic by-products and complete porphyrins may have been present. It was therefore not too tremendous a step to develop the talent of photosynthesis (Granick, 1957) and, with this process established, the atmosphere necessarily became oxidizing, if it was not so already, as a result of the photolysis of water. At this point life acquired the potential for a balanced nonexploitive economy — one not based on the destruction of nonrenewable resources.

All this took place in early pre-Cambrian time, for which, to speak generously, the geological and paleontological record is miserably poor. Possible fossils of photosynthetic organisms from rocks 2.7 billion years old have recently been reported (Cloud et al., 1965) and there is considerable evidence for crude oils and other hydrocarbons of biological origin in rocks 1-2 billion years old (Banghoorn et al., 1965). The deposition of such "fossil fuels," which are potential sources of energy for organisms living in an oxidizing environment, indicates that the biosphere did not at this time achieve the potentially permanent state represented by the legendary "balanced aquarium," but the advent of photosynthesis, employing visible light, certainly made life much less exploitive and gave it a much greater expected duration than had previously been the case.

Despite the poor fossil record we know that a major part of all organic evolution must have occurred in the pre-Cambrian because, immediately after a geological revolution of vulcanism and diastrophism ushered in the Cambrian some 600 million years ago, many modern phyla and even some modern classes of animals were already distinct.

Thus the earth entered the Paleozoic era with a great variety of genetically diverse organisms ready to compete for occupancy of its diverse habitats. At first, no doubt, great quantities of mineral nutrients were washed into the seas by runoff of water from land areas of rough topography that had been elevated in the geological revolution. As erosion of the bare surface proceeded to level mountains and hills, the transport of minerals to the seas decreased and the earth gradually settled down into what Brooks (1949) calls "the normal state of affairs on this our earth." This is a state of low relief of the land with great arms of the sea extending far into the interiors of the continents, with warm ocean currents able to reach high latitudes, and with greatly reduced climatic contrasts between different latitudes. It is a state of arid conditions on land and with freezing temperatures unusual or nonexistent.

By Silurian times plants colonized the land and they evolved greatly during the Devonian, at which time animals began to follow them out of the water. It is tempting to suggest that the great deposits of fossil fuels laid down in Carboniferous times were a result of the fact that biotic communities on land were incomplete — that animals and other heterotrophs had not perfected the talent of land life to the point where they could radiate into all available ecological niches (roles in the economy of nature) and use up the organic matter from plants as rapidly as it was produced. In any case, production of these great unoxidized organic deposits probably brought the oxygen in the atmosphere close to its present concentration of 23.2% by weight. It is a sobering thought that if all of the fossil fuels on earth could be extracted and burned, the process would virtually exhaust the oxygen of the atmosphere.

The Paleozoic ended with another great geological revolution of mountain-building, vulcanism, and glaciation some 200 million years ago and with the wholesale extermination of plants and animals which, under the pressure of competition and natural selection, had become highly efficient by becoming highly specialized for exploiting environments that were wiped out in the geological revolution. Every plant species that became extinct probably took with it specialized herbivores and the specialized predators, parasites, and other dependents of these herbivores.

The same pattern repeated in the Mesozoic with gradual leveling of the land and assumption of the normal geological state of affairs, but this time the predominant organisms were different. Of particular interest to us is the fact that the amniote vertebrates and the flowering plants now came into their own. After some 130 million years of base-leveling of the land and specialization of the biota to outcontend competitors for the various ecological niches, the Mesozoic also ended with a geological revolution and the massive extinction of prominent plants and animals. At this point the geological record is clearer (Newell, 1962), and we know that the wave of extinction involved not just such conspicuous forms as the "ruling reptiles" and the ammonites but also even the marine plankton — a phenomenon which Bramlette (1965) has recently suggested may have been associated with the reduced supply of nutrients reaching the seas from land.

The Cenozoic era again repeated the geological story and, with the start of the Pleistocene, the earth may have entered a new geological revolution. Certainly, mountain-building, vulcanism, and glaciation today are far in excess of the geological norm. But in this particular highly abnormal instant of geological time, a new species, *Homo sapiens*, has risen to prominence.

Ecosystems

It is the nature of ecosystems that they tend toward a steady state in which the organic matter produced by autotrophs is all broken down by heterotrophs and other oxidative processes. We have indicated that there are exceptions and that the 1.2×10^{21} gm of oxygen in the atmosphere plus 1% of this amount dissolved in the oceans all represents organic matter that has not been used up and which is what we refer to as "fossil fuels." This is really a small quantity. Green plant photosynthesis releases one gram of oxygen in storing 3.5 kcal of energy, so the oxygen in the atmosphere represents 4.2×10^{21} kcal stored. I have estimated elsewhere (Cole, 1958) the net annual production of organic matter by plants at 5×10^{17} kcal, so the unused potential energy from all of geological time corresponds to about 8400 years of plant production which has gone unutilized in at least two billion years of photosynthesis. This figure is too small if, as Dr. John Cantlon has tried to persuade me, a major part of the earth's oxygen was originally bound as water. In that case, much of the oxygen now bound in oxides of iron and aluminum and in limestones also represents fossil fuel. Putnam (1953), employing such assumptions, has given a maximum estimate 18 times my figure, but even this corresponds to well under 1/100 of 1% of the total organic carbon fixation which has gone unutilized. The approximation to a steady state is evidently very close.

Implicit in the tendency of ecosystems to attain a steady state is the fact that an environmental situation to which it is difficult to adapt will have relatively few species present but that those that do adapt successfully will maintain the largest possible numbers and tend to maximize the energy flux through the system. We recognize this situation, for example, in the large populations of relatively few species living in arctic regions or in difficult habitats, such as salt lakes. On the other hand, an equitable environment where many forms can tolerate the physical and chemical features acquires a great variety of species, most of which become specialists at utilizing some very limited ecological niche within which they are superior to potential competitors. We meet the extreme of this situation in the tropical rain forest or on coral reefs where the energy flux is divided among many species and the mean number of individuals per species is accordingly relatively small. We have learned empirically that complex ecosystems tend toward stability in time while simpler systems are subject to numerical fluctuations often of violent proportions.

Whether simple or complex, just about all of the conceivable niches in any ecosystem tend to be filled be· cause, so long as there remains a way to seize a share of the available energy, natural selection will favor any form that may develop the talent for doing so. Thus, selection pressure tends to produce similar ecosystems in separated regions of similar environment. The tropical rain forests of Africa, South America, and the Pacific area have similar organizations but different origins, and therefore different species (Richards, 1952), and many of the marsupial mammals of Australia are startlingly close ecological counterparts of placental mammals on other continents.

A mature ecosystem has autotrophic organisms producing organic matter, usually a variety of primary consumers, including grazers and decomposers, parasites and predators of these, and a complement of "opportunistic" species with a special talent for finding and colonizing the temporary habitats that appear following events such as fires, landslides, or geological revolutions, and then moving on when exposed to the pressure of competition from more efficient but more specialized forms. There is a balance between energy income and energy output, and a new species can only invade or rise to prominence by displacing forms that are already present.

Primitive man subsisted by hunting, fishing, and gathering wild foods. Of course, we shall never know for certain what forms may have had to suffer reduction of numbers or been brought to extinction to make room for man; or perhaps he appeared at a time when biotic communities were incomplete as a result of wholesale extinctions brought on by glacial periods and merely had to establish himself in a niche from which no competitor could displace him.

Human history

Primitive food gatherers had to learn something about ecology; they had to learn what forms were edible and when and where and how to find these. Early hunters probably used fire to drive game, and perhaps they noticed that this had a subsequent effect on the vegetation as, for example, by increasing berry crops and later by concentrating grazing ungulates. Something like this may have been man's first accomplishment in controlling the other species in his ecosystem for his own advantage.

By more than 10,000 years ago man had domesticated both plants and animals, and some of his accomplishments still merit admiration; for example, he did such a job with the corn (maize) plant that authorities are still not in complete agreement as to what wild species he started with. On the other hand, some species probably practically

52

domesticated themselves. I would expect this of wild canids, and Helbaek (1959) interprets barley as originally a weed of wheat fields which, when man tried growing wheat with an admixture of barley seed in new environments, may have proved hardier than the wheat and have replaced it in some regions. Rye and oats may have had a similar history.

Food-gathering man probably had to make annual migrations to obtain food at all seasons, but early agricultural man could settle by the river flood plains that were easiest to farm and build permanent settlements that would grow into villages and cities. At this stage, if not before, man must have differentiated his activities into distinct professions comparable to ecological niches. Farming, production of meat and milk products, mining, and trading all seem to be about equally ancient ways of life. By selection of seed and breeding stock man "improved" his domestic forms and continued to bring other species under domestication. With the advent of trade, and probably growing populations, he expanded his agricultural activities and discovered that water shortage often limits plant growth and that he could circumvent this by irrigation.

In places, this type of agriculture was a spectacular success. The annual flood of the Nile was dependable both in time of occurrence and depth attained, and it brought to the flood plain not only water but also an alluvium rich in plant nutrients. Irrigation in Egypt goes back to at least 2000 B.C. and, after continuous use of the land, that country was still the principal granary of the Roman Empire.

Results were less happy in some other regions. At this stage man could hardly have been expected to anticipate that irrigation without adequate drainage would cause the water table to rise and produce waterlogged soils inimical to agriculture, or that evaporation of water moving upward would deposit a crust of salts on the surface, or that insidious erosion by wind and water, so slow as to be barely perceptible, could eliminate the fertile topsoil, ruin the plant cover, and end in violent erosion and gullying. These things had to be learned empirically and at great cost, for they were probably the principal factors causing the collapse of the great Babylonian Empire and other civilizations of the Middle East and Mediterranean regions.

By Plato's time (347 B.C.) a reflective scholar could write of deforestation and grazing as causing the drying up of springs and the destruction of the most fertile soils by causing water to "run from naked earth into the sea" so that lands "resemble the bones of a diseased body; such of the earth as was soft and fat being washed away, and a thin body of the country alone remaining." Virgil (30 B.C.) recommended crop rotation with wheat following a legume (or vetch or lupine), leaving land fallow on alternate years, dressing exhausted soils with manure or ashes, weeding, repelling birds, and selecting by hand the best quality seed for planting. A century later Pliny (77 A.D.) told of man altering climates by changing river courses and draining a lake with the result that olives and grapes in the region were killed by frost. So, by the beginning of the Christian era, man had acquired a good deal of practical ecological knowledge. But, despite the eminence of these authors, this knowledge failed to enter the mainstream of Western thought.

Meanwhile, agriculture along somewhat different lines had developed under other types of climates. In forested regions the "slash and burn" technique, then as now, was the method of choice. After killing the trees, the land was burned over and crops grown for as long as profitable — then the process was repeated in a new location, giving the exhausted area a chance to recover. Land can often be cultivated less than 10% of the time in tropical regions where humus decomposes rapidly and accumulates little, so a large ratio of land to population is necessary.

Thus man achieved his dominance over the face of the earth, and there is no accurate way of estimating the number of extinctions and displacements that he may have caused by altering and eliminating distinctive habitats and increasing his numbers in an already saturated ecosphere. At the same time he created some new problems for himself. As he crowded into villages and later cities he created ideal conditions for the spread of pathogens and other parasites, and he thus became subject to devastation by frightful epidemics. As populations exhausted or outgrew the resources of their own territories, they came to covet the resources of their neighbors and developed the almost uniquely human institution of war. Man's agricultural technique of simplifying ecosystems to favor a crop plant of his choice also favored the opportunistic species that are present in all ecosystems but usually as a minor element capable of inhabiting temporary habitats by virtue of their hardiness, adaptability, great reproductive potential, and powers of dispersal. The tendency toward monoculture agriculture, often employing annual plants, was as if designed to favor these forms which do not compete successfully in a mature, diverse ecosystem, and they remain today as our important "pest" species.

Just as the crowding of man predisposed him to epidemics, so fields crowded with a single variety of plant provided ideal conditions for the spread of pathogenic fungi and the multiplication of larger consumers, such as insects and rodents. So man at this stage was also subject to mass destruction by famine caused sometimes by pests and sometimes by unfortunate long runs of unfavorable weather.

Despite these occasional setbacks, human numbers gradually increased, and this growth was eventually assisted by the exploitation of new lands, especially in the new world. Then, 300 years ago, the industrial revolution started and initiated a new cycle of population growth that has not yet ended.

Mankind today

The most significant feature of the industrial world is its dependence on the fossil fuels. In the early stages wood, charcoal, water, wind, and animal power could supply much of the necessary energy, but we are far past that point now; and it is doubtless true that half of all the fuel ever burned by man has been burned in the past 50 years. But the fossil fuels are nonrenewable resources so, for the second time in the history of life, it is running on an exploitive economy that will destroy itself if continued long enough.

As soon as the rate at which fuel is burned comes to exceed the rate of photosynthesis, the oxygen content of the atmosphere must start to decrease. I wish I could estimate how near we are to that frightening compensation point but I have found no reasonably satisfying way of doing so. For the United States, Putnam estimated in 1953 that: "If all the carbon fixed in one year . . . was burnt and the energy recovered, it would amount to about one and one-half times the present requirements of the national energy system."

If he was approximately correct, this country and some other industrial nations may by now have passed the compensation point. Fortunately, there remain vast areas, such as the Amazonian rain forest, that have not even started on this hazardous path, but we hear every year of exploitive interests bent on promoting "progress" that are casting covetous eyes on these "undeveloped" areas.

Even modern agriculture is industrialized. We boast of our efficiency in raising more food on less land with the labor of fewer people, but we are deceiving ourselves. If we were to deduct from the food calories that a farmer produces the calories consumed by his machinery, the calories used to build and transport that machinery, to mine raw materials, to process, transport, and apply fertilizers and pesticides, and to process and distribute the food, we would see that modern agriculture is largely a device for exchanging the calories in fossil fuels for calories in food.

The modern world is divided up into a series of nations, each operating under the curious unecological assumption that it is beneficial to export each year more of its resources (including food which represents a portion of its soil fertility) than it receives in return. It is also considered desirable to maximize the rate at which resources such as minerals leave the ground, enter into products, and pass to the scrap heap. The creation of accelerated absolescence, which some of us took to be a joke when we first heard of it, appears now to be a serious economic policy without concern for the renewability of resources.

I cannot remember at what age or in what young people's magazine I first encountered an arithmetic problem concerning a bowl containing an amoeba which every hour divided into two amoebae the size of the original, and where each descendant continued the process. The computations, of course, led to the ludicrous conclusion that the mass or volume of amoebae would soon exceed that of the earth. The actual human population today, like the hypothetical amoeba, is reproducing in a manner that, if continued, would cause it to double in every generation. The hypothetical consequences in this case are ludicrous also, but this is no hypothetical problem. Man has some other very serious problems to face but, unless he achieves a rational solution of the problem of his own population growth instead of leaving its control to wars, epidemics, and famine, I see little hope that he will be able to solve the technologically more difficult problems.

Man is damaging the earth in various ways, not the least of which is through environmental pollution. Products of erosion, sewage, and industrial wastes have been polluting environments for a long time, but the problem has become more acute as the population pressure increases. Agriculture has recently embraced the theory that the way to avoid damage from pest organisms is to make the environment poisonous. Naturally poisonous environments often teem with tremendous populations of the few opportunistic species that can adapt to them, and I think it is an ecologically sound prediction that long continued use of toxins with residual action will produce similar effects on agricultural land. After all, bacteria have recently evolved strains that require antibiotics for growth, and we can expect fungi and insects to be only a little slower in evolving. Some pesticides, notably DDT, have become virtually a normal constituent of the world environment and have turned up even in the fat of penguins from Antarctica, where, of course, agricultural chemicals are ridiculous. The frightening thing is that man brought this about in just a few years with an irresponsible disregard for possible effects on ecosystems. He did damage wildlife, but apparently he was lucky this time and did not upset any vital process, such as the activities of the various bacteria involved in the nitrogen cycle, without which man could not survive.

Contamination with radioisotopes is another modern problem that is not being approached with the intelligence or candor it merits. A committee of prominent scientists (Commoner, 1965) has recently called attention to the fact that millions of curies of radioactive fallout have dropped on the earth over the last 20 years, while, as late as 1962, the scientists responsible were "apparently unaware that iodine-131 constitutes the most severe immediate hazard." The finding (Weiss and Shipman, 1957) of high concentrations of the radioisotope cobalt-60 in clams 2 years after contamination of the water by fallout is instructive for two reasons. First, cobalt-60 is not a product of nuclear fission, so this shows the necessity for considering all of the possible interactions of radioactive materials with other components of the environment. Second, this illustrates the ability of an organism to take an unnatural chemical from an almost infinitely dilute medium and concentrate it to hazardous levels. This biological concentration of novel materials has also often been a factor in the killing of wildlife by pesticides (Cottam, 1965) and it shows the necessity for a full understanding of the food chains in ecosystems before subjecting them to contamination.

Mankind must outgrow its ancient illusion that the atmosphere and hydrosphere represent waste receptacles of infinite capacity. In this country we are beginning to be disillusioned about this for rivers and lakes, and a few local areas are even beginning to try to do something about the pollution of the atmosphere and of harbors. However, the predominating attitude was illustrated less than 2 years ago by a leading news magazine (Time) which, in reporting a proposal to dig a new Panama canal with nuclear explosives, explained that the amount of radioactivity that would get into the water cannot be estimated, "but the strong current that will run through the canal should carry most of it away." And so it should, at the risk of making seafood from the Atlantic Ocean unsafe to eat!

I have been given to understand that solid-fuel rocket engines release beryllium into the atmosphere but, despite some inquiries, I know absolutely nothing about the quantities involved. I do know that there have been a number of reports of beryllium toxicity to vertebrate animals and that the 1938 USDA Yearbook of Agriculture reports that very low concentrations of beryllium are toxic to citrus cuttings in solution culture (McMurtrey and Robinson, 1938). I should like to feel confident that due consideration was given to this, and appropriate experiments performed, prior to the decision to test such rocket engines at ground level in southern California, but I do not expect such reassurance to be forthcoming. I offer this as a fairly typical example of the things that make ecologists distrustful of many of the decisions being made by society.[1]

I could go on listing things that, from an ecological viewpoint, man is clearly doing wrong, such as depleting the supply of fresh water and developing increased reliance on monoculture agriculture and animal husbandry, and I could draw up a long list of man-made changes I deplore. I regret that I can never expect to see a wild wolverine in the eastern United States, but I recognize that the wolverine's requirements and habits are incompatible with man's. I regret that the same processes that have made it possible for me to live in a house built of cypress have brought America's largest woodpecker, the ivory-bill, to the verge of extinction, but I recognize that some such displacements are inevitable when any species greatly expands its sphere of activity. However, I can see no excuse for the extinction, through reckless overexploitation, of species man values. One would think that the most primitive savage could understand that a species once gone cannot be restored, and that his greatest harvest in the long run depends upon always preserving a breeding stock. Yet today, whaling ships from scientifically and technologically advanced nations are threatening the existence of the largest animal that has ever lived on earth.

---

[1]Since this was written the toxicity of beryllium has been explicitly acknowledged (Glassman, 1965) and it is noted that ". . . currently, Be is under active investigation."

Conclusion

If the picture I have painted of man and his ecosystem appears to be a gloomy one, let me state that the situation is not hopeless. Man has the necessary technology to regulate his population size; what is needed is a consensus as to how many people should be allowed to inhabit the earth at one time. Because our present economy is exploitive, we are in need of a breakthrough comparable in significance to the discovery of photosynthesis. Atomic energy does not quite represent such a breakthrough because it depends on a nonrenewable resource, but I think it can take us quite a way into the future if man will use it responsibly. Also, a large amount of deuterium is found in the oceans, and future technology may include a way to use that source of potential energy. And, finally, there is solar radiation, which must ultimately become man's energy source if the species persists long enough.

With an adequate energy supply assured, man can solve many of his other problems by methods that are shunned today as too expensive. He can distill sea water and transport the distillate to regions of shortage; the scrap heaps and junk yards of today can become mines tomorrow, and it will almost certainly become necessary to mine the ocean bottoms, at least for phosphorus fertilizer.

The problems I have dealt with here are all essentially ecological. I have not ventured to suggest what the world we are developing may do to man's mental health, nor have I discussed the factors that have given man the capacity to render the earth uninhabitable almost instantaneously, nor the social factors that make it a real possibility that man will use that destructive capacity. The ecological problems are serious enough and, unfortunately, the most prestigious bodies of scientists, the ones that administrators listen to most intently, are woefully ignorant of ecology. I am encouraged that a prominent committee of scientists (Commoner, 1965), including no ecologists, has surveyed the current status of "the integrity of science" and has caught a glimpse of the fundamental role of ecology. I hope that this news will spread quickly.

References

Abelson, P. H. 1957. Some aspects of paleobiochemistry. *Ann. N.Y. Acad. Sci.,* **69**: 176-285.

Banghoorn, E. S., W. G. Meinschein, and J. W. Schopf. 1965. Paleobiology of a Pre-Cambrian shale. *Science,* **148**: 461-472.

Banghoorn, E. S. 1957. Origin of life. *Mem. Geol. Soc. Am.,* **67**: 75-86.

Bramlette, M. N. 1965. Massive extinctions in biota at the end of Mesozoic time. *Science,* **148**: 1696-1699.

Brooks, C. E. P. 1949. *Climate through the Ages.* Rev. ed. McGraw-Hill Book Co., New York.

Cloud, P. E., J. W. Gruner, and H. Hagen. 1965. Carbonaceous rocks of the Soudan iron formation (early pre-Cambrian). *Science,* **148**: 1713-1716.

Cole, L. C. 1958. The ecosphere. *Sci. Am.,* **198**: 83-92.

Commoner, B. (Chairman). 1965. The integrity of science. A report by the AAAS Committee on Science in the Promotion of Human Welfare. *Am. Scientist,* **53**: 174-198.

Cf. Cottam, C. 1965. The ecologists' role in problems of pesticide pollution. *BioScience,* **15**: 457-463.

Glassman, I. 1965. The Chemistry of Propellants. *Am. Scientist,* **53**: 508-524.

Cf. Granick, S. 1957. Speculations on the origins and evolutions of photosynthesis. *Ann. N.Y. Acad. Sci.,* **69**: 292-308.

Helbaek, H. 1959. Domestication of food plants in the old world. *Science,* **130**: 365-372.

Kuiper, G. P. (ed.) 1951. *The Atmospheres of the Earth and Planets.* University of Chicago Press, Chicago.

Lotka, A. J. 1925. *Elements of Physical Biology.* Williams & Wilkins Co., Baltimore, p. 190.

McMurtrey, J. E., Jr., and W. O. Robinson. 1938. Neglected soil constituents that affect plant and animal development, in: Soils and man. *USDA Yearbook of Agriculture.* Govt. Printing Office, Washington, D.C., pp. 807-829.

Miller, S. L. 1953. A production of amino acids under possible primitive earth conditions. *Science,* 117: 528-529.

Miller, S. L. 1955. Production of some organic compounds under possible primitive earth conditions. *J. Am. Chem. Soc.,* 77: 2351-2361.

Newell, N. D., 1962. Paleontological gaps and geochronology, **J. Paleontol.,** 36: 592-610.

Oparin, A. I. 1936. *The Origin of Life.* (English translation, 1938.) Macmillan Co., New York.

Oro, J., D. W. Nooner, A. Zlatkis, S. A. Wikström, and E. S. Banghoorn. 1965. Hydrocarbons of biological origin in sediments about two billion years old. *Science,* 148: 77-79.

Plato. ca. 347 B.C. Critias. in: *The Timaeus and The Critias or Atlanticus.* The Thomas Taylor translation. Pantheon Books, New York, 1944.

Pliny the Elder. ca. 77 A.D. *Natural History.*

Putnam, P. C. 1953. *Energy in the Future.* D. Van Nostrand Co., Inc., New York, p. 117.

Richards, P. W. 1952. *The Tropical Rain Forest.* Cambridge University Press, New York.

Rubey, W. W. 1951. Geological history of sea water. *Bull. Geol. Soc. Am.,* 62: 1111-1148.

Rubey, W. W. 1955. Development of the hydrosphere and atmosphere with special reference to the probable composition of the early atmosphere. *Spec. Papers, Geol. Soc. Am.,* 62: 631-650.

Time Magazine, January 21, 1964, p. 36.

Urey, H. C. 1952. On the early chemical history of the earth and the origin of life. *Proc. Natl. Acad. Sci. U.S.,* 38: 351-363.

Virgil. ca. 30 B.C. *First Georgics.*

Wald, G. 1954. The origin of life. *Sci. Am.,* 191: 44-53.

Weiss, H. V. and W. H. Shipman. 1957. Biological concentration by killer clams of cobalt-60 from radioactive fallout. *Science,* 125: 695.

FRANCIS C. EVANS
Institute of Human Biology,
University of Michigan, Ann Arbor

Ecosystem as the Basic Unit in Ecology

The term *ecosystem* was proposed by Tansley (*1*) as a name for the interaction system comprising living things together with their nonliving habitat. Tansley regarded the ecosystem as including "not only the organism-complex, but also the whole complex of physical factors forming what we call the environment." He thus applied the term specifically to that level of biological organization represented by such units as the community and the biome. I here suggest that it is logically appropriate and desirable to extend the application of the concept and the term to include organization levels other than that of the community.

In its fundamental aspects, an ecosystem involves the circulation, transformation, and accumulation of energy and matter through the medium of living things and their activities. Photosynthesis, decomposition, herbivory, predation, parasitism, and other symbiotic activities are among the principal biological processes responsible for the transport and storage of materials and energy, and the interactions of the organisms engaged in these activities provide the pathways of distribution. The food-chain is an example of such a pathway. In the nonliving part of the ecosystem, circulation of energy and matter is completed by such physical processes as evaporation and precipitation, erosion and deposition. The ecologist, then, is primarily concerned with the quantities of matter and energy that pass through a given ecosystem and with the rates at which they do so. Of almost equal importance, however, are the kinds of organisms that are present in any particular ecosystem and the roles that they occupy in its structure and organization. Thus, both quantitative and qualitative aspects need to be considered in the description and comparison of ecosystems.

Ecosystems are further characterized by a multiplicity of regulatory mechanisms, which, in limiting the numbers of organisms present and in influencing their physiology and behavior, control the quantities and rates of movement of both matter and energy. Processes of growth and reproduction, agencies of mortality (physical as well as biological), patterns of immigration and emigration, and habits of adaptive significance are among the more important groups of regulatory mechanisms. In the absence of such mechanisms, no ecosystem could continue to persist and maintain its identity.

The assemblage of plants and animals visualized by Tansley as an integral part of the ecosystem usually consists of numerous species, each represented by a population of individual organisms. However, each population can be regarded as an entity in its own right, interacting with its environment (which may include other organisms as well as physical features of the habitat) to form a system of lower rank that likewise involves the distribution of matter and energy. In turn, each individual animal or plant, together with its particular microenvironment, constitutes a system of still lower rank. Or we may wish to take a world view of life and look upon the biosphere with its total environment as a gigantic ecosystem. Regardless of the level on which life is examined, the ecosystem concept

Science, June, 1956, Vol.23, No.3208, pp. 1127-1128.

can appropriately be applied. The ecosystem thus stands as a basic unit of ecology, a unit that is as important to this field of natural science as the species is to taxonomy and systematics. In any given case, the particular level on which the ecosystem is being studied can be specified with a qualifying adjective—for example, community ecosystem, population ecosystem, and so forth.

All ranks of ecosystems are open systems, not closed ones. Energy and matter continually escape from them in the course of the processes of life, and they must be replaced if the system is to continue to function. The pathways of loss and replacement of matter and energy frequently connect one ecosystem with another, and therefore it is often difficult to determine the limits of a given ecosystem. This has led some ecologists to reject the ecosystem concept as unrealistic and of little use in description or analysis. One is reminded, however, of the fact that it is also difficult, if not impossible, to delimit a species from its ancestral or derivative species or from both; yet this does not destroy the value of the concept. The ecosystem concept may indeed be more useful when it is employed in relation to the community than to the population or individual, for its limits may be more easily determined on that level. Nevertheless, its application to all levels seems fully justified.

The concept of the ecosystem has been described under many names, among them those of *microcosm* (2), *naturkomplex* (3), *holocoen* (4) and *biosystem* (5). Tansley's term seems most successfully to convey its meaning and has in fact been accepted by a large number of present-day ecologists. I hope that it will eventually be adopted universally and that its application will be expanded beyond its original use to include other levels of biological organization. Recognition of the ecosystem as the basic unit in ecology would be helpful in focussing attention upon the truly fundamental aspects of this rapidly developing science.

References

1. A. G. Tansley, *Ecology* 16, 296 (1935).
2. S. A. Forbes, *Bull. Peoria Sci. Assoc.* (1887).
3. E. Markus, *Sitzber. Naturforsch. Ges. Univ. Tartu* 32, 79 (1926).
4. K. Friederichs, *Die Grundfragen und Gesetzmässigkeiten der land-und forstwirtschaftlichen Zoologie.* (Parey, Berlin, 1930).
5. K. Thienemann, *Arch. Hydrobiol.* 35, 267 (1939).

30 January 1956

The Ecology of Man, the Animal

S. Charles Kendeigh

University of Illinois

The fundamental and basic concepts of animal ecology are also the fundamental and basic concepts of human ecology. Primitive man had few, if any, characteristics not also found in animals. Modern man is certainly more highly developed and specialized psychologically than any animal, but specialization of one sort or another is found in every animal species. Specialization is a product of evolution, and those characteristics or traits of man often considered to be unique can all be traced back to primitive characteristics, traits, or potentialities found also in animals. Many analogous traits not in direct line of descent to man have been evolved in other organisms. Let us enumerate a few.

Erect bipedal locomotion occurs in birds. A squirrel will use its hands to manipulate a nut, or a monkey a banana, as expertly as man. Laughter in man appears as an exaggeration of facial expressions and specific behavior indicating pleasure found among mammals at play. Sticks are used as a tool by a Galapagos finch to pry insect larvae out of holes in dead wood; spiders set a web net to capture food from the air as a fisherman does from the water; and hermit crabs use empty shells as homes and shields against predation by enemies.

Many tropical species maintain sexual and reproductive activities throughout the year as does man who comes from tropical ancestors. Parental care of young is perhaps more complex and highly developed in birds than in any other animal, including man. Intercommunication between individuals is well evolved within animal species, not by use of a vocabulary or the written word it is true but by a great variety of scent stimuli — color displays, sounds, call-notes, and songs — each conveying a special meaning. It may not be entirely coincidental that the songs of birds have an esthetic appeal to man; perhaps they have also to birds themselves who have evolved specific song patterns, melodies, and qualities of tone through a long period of natural and sexual selection. Social hierarchies exist among many gregarious species of animals and territorial behavior is evidenced among solitary nesting ones, equivalent to similar behavior in the human species. The leaf-cutting ants of the tropics practice agriculture when they bring leaves into their nest-mounds on which they cultivate a mold used as food. They likewise practice sanitation by systematically removing and depositing feces and wastes at some distance from their nests. The organized industry of ants, termites, and some birds is well shown in the construction of colonial nests. Division of labor is expressed at various levels in the animal kingdom, beginning with separation of reproductive and somatic cells in the colonial protozoans and the differentiation of tissues and organs in the lower invertebrates and attaining complex dimensions among the social insects where different individuals are adapted for special functions. Division of labor is also evident in the biotic community where various species play special roles in the cycling of nutrients, the capture and transmission of energy, the regulation of popu-

Bioscience, August, 1956, Vol.15, No.8, pp. 521-523.

lation balances, the creation of microclimates, etc., analogous to the role of different trades or vocations in the human community. Animals may even have a primitive type of culture and ethics, if we mean a mores or behavior that is beneficial and traditional for the species and which is handed down to succeeding generations in large part by learning of the young.

Man's chief claim to uniqueness lies in the highly specialized development and functioning of his brain. His morphological and physiological capacities to do things are very limited, likewise his innate tolerance of even moderately rugged climatic conditions. However, his highly evolved intelligence has enabled him to circumvent many of his limitations: he has invented complex tools to do his tasks, he uses fire and air-conditioning to keep his shelter comfortable, his manufactured clothing allows him to invade microclimates for which otherwise he is not physiologically adapted, and his industrial skill has enabled him more completely to exploit natural resources. Conceptual thought, capacity for abstraction and synthesis, the use of symbols in speech and writing, ability to reason and anticipate events, self-consciousness, and the spiritual and esthetic values seen in religion and art were doubtless latent in primitive man and had to be developed through effort and practice to reach the fruition seen in modern man. This cultural evolution has gone on mostly independently of biological evolution, and the mind of modern civilized man is the latest step in an evolutionary process that began only about 40,000 to 50,000 years ago and reached explosive proportions only within the last 5000 years. This specialization, although unique to man, is actually no more unique in evolution than specializations of other sorts found in many other animals. Man still requires food, water, and space; a favorable microclimate; protection from enemies; and reproduction. To obtain these requirements for life he must fit into an ecosystem as do other animal species, even through the ecosystem is a highly modified one of his own creation.

If one looks at the geological time table, one sees that during the last billion or so years life has evolved from single celled plants and animals living in the sea to more complex invertebrates and primitive fish, invasion of freshwater and land habitats, and evolution of insects, amphibians, reptiles, birds, and mammals. Man did not come physically into this succession until a million or so years ago. There can be no prediction nor certainty but that in the next million years — or billion years — many new types of animal life will appear; and man, as we know him today, will either be exterminated or greatly altered in appearance, form, and function.

Man probably originated, as did most groups of vertebrate animals, in the Old World tropics and dispersed as shifting climates, vegetation, and land bridges permitted, into Europe, northern Asia, North and South America. Australia, and southern Africa. In these different areas, populations of man became isolated for many thousands of years and were prevented from interbreeding with other populations by physiographic, climatic, or biotic barriers. As is common with animals, this geographic isolation allowed genetic variations to occur and become established, involving color of skin, texture of hair, and other characteristics. Variations in tribal customs evolved. Occupancy of new environments and contacts with different biota exposed populations in different areas to different selection pressures and they came to occupy somewhat different ecological niches. If this geographic isolation had persisted a few more thousand years, doubtlessly reproductive isolating mechanisms, already partially formed, would have become fully established, and *Homo sapiens* would have differentiated into a number of new species. The evolution of civilization, however, interrupted this process of speciation.

Artificial means of transportation encouraged world-wide travel, and this brought the bypassing of geographical barriers, the breaking down of ecological and ethological evolving reproductive isolating mechanisms, and the fusing of the races and their cultures again into one, so that the species was preserved in its biological unity.

The population density and distribution of primitive man varied in relation to natural conditions according to the normal or Gaussian curve, reaching a peak under optimum conditions and tailing off toward both maximum and minimum limits of physiological tolerance for environmental extremes. Shelford's law of tolerance is a generalization of these relations between abundance, physiological comfort, and environmental factors applicable to all organisms. Modern man has skewed the curve somewhat by this fabrication of artificial home and working environments but the law still applies.

Liebig's law of the minimum and Blackman's limiting factors state that the growth, activity, or even existence of an organism is determined or regulated by that essential factor or condition in shortest supply. Modern man has developed methods of distributing essential elements or products to alleviate local deficiencies, but when his transport system breaks down or in areas where it has not been perfected, the working of this law is apparent.

Primitive man was certainly a constituent member of the biotic community. He was dependent upon the vegetation for shelter from the weather, as protection against enemies, as a source of food, and for use in other ways. His niche in the community has been compared with that of one of the larger carnivores. He had to compete with other carnivores and the larger herbivores for the essentials of life, and his role in the community was determined by his successes and failures in establishing favorable interrelations. When primitive man changed into modern man with the perfection of his intelligence and his invention of new tools, he changed from an ordinary member of the community to an ecological dominant. By building a home of his own that gave shelter from both weather and enemy and the development of agriculture, he was no longer dependent on the community as it was originally constituted. He modified the community to suit his own needs, determined to a large extent what other species he would permit to associate with him, and established the rules and conditions for their doing so. During geological time there have been a long series of organisms that have assumed dominance for periods of time, and often by no less drastic changes in the habitat and community. Man, in fact, has not yet obtained complete dominance in the arctic tundra, the desert, the tropical rain forest, or the ocean. Even in temperate regions, whenever man relaxes his dominance or mismanages the habitat, there is reversion of the region to dominance by other native species.

Civilized man, as primitive man, is still dependent on plants for nutrition and energy. Civilized man, however, has created an ecosystem where the kinds of nutrients that he likes and the energy that he needs can be obtained more efficiently than in ecosystems which he does not dominate. Crops have been developed through selective breeding and have been cultivated by special methods to give high yields. Competition for food from other species has been greatly reduced by use of fences, guns, pesticides, and the hoe. Plant crops are either consumed directly or fed to domesticated animals in a higher trophic level, so that meat as well as vegetables are eaten. In removing this harvest from his ecosystem he removes nutrient elements that in natural ecosystems circulate continuously, first through plants, then animals, then to the transformers in the soil that render them available for reabsorption by plants. Man acknowledges the important role of nutrient cycles in the ecosystem when he returns the nutrients that he has taken for food in the form of fertilizers unsuitable for his direct assimilation.

In natural ecosystems, food chains start with green plants because of their unique ability to capture solar energy and to synthesize nutrients from raw materials. With each additional link in the food chain through which energy and nutrients are transmitted there is a loss of some 80 or 90%. Each trophic level uses energy for maintaining its own existence and activities and there is wastage through prey not eaten, non-predatory deaths, excreta, and heat. Consequently, with addition of links in the food chain, there is decrease in number of individuals or biomass that can be supported and in variety of species. The biomass of herbivores is always greater than the biomass of carnivores. In densely populated parts of the human world, man has largely given up the luxury of eating beef, pork, fowl, and lamb and depends instead on wheat, rice, or corn, thereby eliminating one trophic level and taking fuller advantage of the productivity of the land. If man could reduce the length of the food chain still further through bypassing plants and using solar radiation directly for the manufacture of food and for other uses, he would have a supply of energy several hundred times greater than is now captured by plants.

The sigmoid growth curve represents approximately the manner and rate by which cells, organs, individuals, populations, and communities increase in size and complexity. In the lower part of the curve, conditions for growth are very favorable and growth proceeds at an ever accelerating pace. However, inhibiting factors come to exert an increasingly important role and beyond the point of inflection they gradually bring the growth curve to an asymptote. With animals, the size of the asymptotic population is determined by available space, suitable food, and favorable climate. Factors that may ultimately stabilize the population at the asymptote are density-dependent, that is, they vary in intensity of their action with the density of the population. These factors consist of predation, disease, emigration, competition, and fecundity. Some species, certain insects and perhaps Arctic rodents and grouse among others, never attain stabilized populations. Their populations continue to increase to the limit of space or food supply or until unfavorable weather occurs. Then there is a crash and the few scattered survivors start the growth process over again.

Modern man has largely eliminated predation as a mortality factor, he has conquered many diseases and may conceivably subdue the rest, and he has emigrated to all favorable parts of the world even though he has not settled in large numbers as yet in some parts of it. With the harnessing of solar energy and intelligent use of minerals, man may be able to produce a superabundance of food through a sort of artificial photosynthesis as well as apply this energy industrially. Likewise, he may obtain control over the weather. Space is limited, however, at least on earth, and it is difficult to see what he can do about it aside from building megalopoli, skyscrapers, underground burrows, sea platforms, or vast air chambers underwater. Space may be the limiting factor ultimately setting the limit to the size of the human population on earth. The amount of space reduction that the human animal will tolerate may not be just space to stand on but space in which he can carry on a comfortable existence. Competition will continue to be a potent factor, as it is in regulating all animal populations. War may someday be eliminated and the world someday may function as a single economic unit, but it is difficult to conceive how competition between individuals can be significantly reduced as the limits of space are approached; more likely it will become accentuated in the final struggles for existence.

With the advent of civilization and modern industrialization, all efforts to date have been to reduce mortality rates and expand available resources. This has thrown the stabilized populations of primitive man out of balance and brought on a new accelerating phase in the growth curve. Populations will not again be brought into stabilization until birth rate and mortality rates again balance. This means that the birth rate must be reduced in proportion to the reduction of mortality rate. This occurs in populations of wild animals more or less automatically through changes in physiology and behavior. Man's biggest challenge in the present age is whether his great intellect will give him the self-discipline and skill to regulate his own population growth to the level best suited for the perpetuation of the culture that he has evolved as well as for his physical existence.

The laws of Nature apply to man as they do to animals. There are no exceptions. If he can come to understand what they are and how they work, he will know better what to anticipate concerning their effects on himself. He cannot ignore the dynamic forces of the environment with impunity, but being blessed with an intelligence far above that of other animals, he can guard against them or alleviate their effects to his own advantage.

CAN THE WORLD BE SAVED?

Lamont C. Cole

My title here is not my first choice, but a year or so ago a physicist discussing some of the same subjects (Berkner, 1966) beat me to the use of the title I would have preferred: "Is There Intelligent Life on Earth?" However, the present title may have merit if it attracts just a few persons who are looking for something about either religion or warfare — because such persons constitute an audience I would like to reach.

In recent years we have heard much discussion of distinct and nearly independent cultures within our society that fail to communicate with each other. This strikes me forcibly, for example, almost every time I hear natural scientists attempting to communicate with social scientists, and we surely have many more than two cultures with such difficulties of communication.

The dichotomy I am concerned with here is that between ecologists and their fellow thinkers on the one hand and, on the other, persons who consider continuous growth desirable — growth of population, of government, industry, trade, and even agriculture. This is also, in part, a dichotomy between the thinkers and the doers — those who insist that man should try to know the consequences of his actions before he takes them versus those who want to get on with the building of dams and canals, with the straightening of river channels, with the firing of nuclear explosives, and with the industrialization of backward countries simply because they know how to do these things.

Paper presented at the 134th meeting of the American Association for the Advancement of Science, December 27, 1967.
The author is a professor in the Section of Ecology and Systematics, Division of Biological Sciences, Cornell University, Ithaca, N.Y.

[1] Several investigators have concluded that the atmosphere is very slowly losing its oxygen to these processes despite photosynthesis.

Bioscience, 1968, Vol.18, No.7, pp. 679-684.

The Background

To develop my theme, I shall have to start far back in time. When the world was young, it did not have an atmosphere of the gases that are now present. The water that now fills the oceans and furnishes our precipitation and the nitrogen that makes up most of the present atmosphere originated from rocks in the earth's interior by a degassing process (Rubey, 1955).

The amount of oxygen in the atmosphere was negligible before the origin of living organisms that could carry on photosynthesis of the type characterizing green plants (Urey, 1959, Berkner and Marshall, 1965), and oxygen would disappear from the atmosphere now through natural geological processes if all the green plants should be killed (Clarke, 1920).[1] In the early days of photosynthesis, oxygen was used as rapidly as it was produced so there was virtually no accumulation of a reservoir in the atmosphere. But, very gradually, some of the compounds produced by organisms began to pass out of circulation by being deposited in sedimentary rocks in such forms as crude oil. With these compounds protected from oxidation, a small percentage of oxygen became a regular constituent of the atmosphere. Eventually, perhaps not until Carboniferous times only three or four hundred million years ago, the deposition of unoxidized organic matter, partly in the form of what we call the fossil fuels, coal, petroleum, and natural gas brought the oxygen content of the atmosphere to approximately its present level of slightly over 20%.

The combination of green plants and oxidizing organisms, including animals, apparently became very efficient at taking oxygen from the atmosphere and returning it at equal rates so that the amount present has remained virtually constant. Photosynthesis stops, of course, during the hours of darkness, and on land areas in high latitudes it practically stops during the winter. It continues, however, in low latitudes (although often greatly reduced by seasonal drought) and in the oceans and, fortunately, atmospheric circulation patterns are such that we have not yet had to be concerned that man would run out of oxygen to breathe at night or in winter.

The atmosphere and the bodies of organisms are the earth's only important reservoirs of the nitrogen which all organisms require for building proteins, and in this case also the totality of life was able to balance the rates of use and return so that the percentage of nitrogen in the atmosphere remains constant. This, however, is a much more complex process than the maintenance of oxygen.

Certain bacteria and primitive algae absorb nitrogen and convert it to ammonia. Others convert the ammonia to nitrate. Green plants use both ammonia and nitrate to build their proteins, and animals and microorganisms build all of their proteins from the constituents of plant proteins. Then a variety of decay organisms degrade the nitrogen compounds of dead plants and animals to simpler compounds, and additional kinds of microrganisms regenerate the molecular nitrogen in the atmosphere. If any one of the numerous steps in this nitrogen cycle were to be disrupted, disaster would ensue for life on earth. Depending upon which step broke down, the nitrogen in the atmosphere might disappear, it might be replaced by poisonous ammonia, or it might remain in the atmosphere with life disappearing for want of a way to use it in building proteins.

There are many other chemical elements in addition to oxygen and nitrogen which are required by organisms.

Some of these also undergo fascinating cycles and a few, notably phosphorous and potassium, are gradually washing into the oceans to remain there in sediments until major geological upheavals, or possibly human ingenuity, can retrieve them and so perpetuate life on earth.

Here I shall mention only one additional cyclic chemical element, carbon, which is the distinctive constituent of all organic compounds. Its great reservoir is in the oceans which dissolve carbon dioxide from the atmosphere and precipitate it as limestone. This, however, is a slow process depending, in part, on the rate of turnover of deep ocean water (Bolin and Eriksson, 1959). Plants use carbon dioxide to build their organic compounds and animals combine the organic compounds with oxygen to obtain the energy for their activities. And this is possible only because, millions of years ago, the deposition of organic matter in sedimentary rocks created a reservoir of oxygen in the atmosphere.

The Impact of Man

Man existed on earth before the Pleistocene ice ages, but his numbers then were certainly negligible. Primitive hunters and food gatherers probably used fire to drive game and in so doing altered much of the earth's vegetation. Many of our major grassland areas have climates that would permit the growth of forests were it not for recurring fires and, more recently, heavy grazing and cultivation by man. These earlier grasslands included much of what has become the world's best agricultural land; therefore these early hunting cultures set the stage for the next phase in man's development — pastoral life and agriculture.

Early agricultural man concentrated his efforts on the flood plains of rivers where the soil was fertile and well watered and easy to cultivate with simple tools. It was discovered that certain types of food could be stored so that the produce of the growing season could support man and his domestic animals throughout the year. Then man started to build towns and cities and to expand his numbers. Crowding predisposed man to epidemics and these, together with wars and famines, took a frightful toll of human life. Nevertheless, the total human population continued to increase and to discover and exploit new lands.

I am referring here to times many centuries before the industrial revolution and the population explosion which are the forces behind our present world crisis. Plato knew that deforestation and overgrazing could cause soil erosion that would ruin fertile land and, at least a millennium before his time, great civilizations had destroyed themselves by means of what turned out to be unsound agricultural practices. But our present troubles stem from the time when man began serious exploitation of the fossil fuels. First it was coal that was important and now it is petroleum, but inexorably man is extracting the fossil fuels and recombining their carbon with oxygen. And this exploitive way of life permits, for the moment, so many more people to exist on earth simultaneously than has ever been possible before that man seems unwilling to consider what he is really doing to the earth.

"Backward Countries"

We hear a lot today about "underdeveloped" and "developing" nations, but these actually tend to be overdeveloped nations (Borgstrom, 1965).

The valleys of the Tigris and Euphrates supported the Sumerian civilization in 3500 B.C. A great irrigation complex was based on these rivers by 2000 B.C., and this was the granary of the great Babylonian Empire. Pliny tells of their harvesting two annual crops of grain and grazing sheep on the land between crops. But less than 20% of the land in modern Iraq is cultivated and more than half of the national income is from oil. The landscape is dotted with mounds representing forgotten towns, the ancient irrigation works are filled with silt, the end product of soil erosion, and the ancient seaport of Ur is now 150 miles from the sea with its buildings buried under as much as 35 feet of silt.

Similar conditions prevail in Iran which was once the seat of the great Persian Empire and where Darius I was the "King of Kings" 2400 years ago. The present Shah is making a determined effort to rejuvenate this land, and this may be the test case of what the industrial world can do in repairing the ravages of the past.

The valley of the Nile was another cradle of civilization. Every year the river overflowed its banks at a predictable time, bringing water to the land and depositing a layer of silt rich in mineral nutrients for plants. Crops could be grown for 7 months each year. Extensive irrigation systems were established before 2000 B.C. This land was the granary of the Roman Empire, and this type of agriculture flourished for another 2000 years. But the population has continued to grow and economic considerations have diverted land from growing food to cash crops such as cotton. Then, in 1902 a dam was built at Aswan to prevent the spring flood and permit year-round irrigation. Since then the soils have been deteriorating through salinization, and productivity has decreased. The new Aswan high dam is designed to bring another million acres of land under irrigation, and it may well prove to be the ultimate disaster for Egypt. Meanwhile, population growth has virtually destroyed any possibility that the new agricultural land can significantly raise the average level of nutrition.

Sorry stories like this could be told for country after country. The glories of ancient Mali and Ghana in west Africa were legends in medieval Europe.

Ancient Greece had forested hills, ample water, and productive soils. In the land that once exported the cedars of Lebanon to Egypt, the old Roman roads which have prevented erosion of the soil beneath them now stand several feet above the rock desert. But in a church yard that had been protected from goats for 300 years, the cedars were found about 1940 to be flourishing as in ancient times (Lowdermilk, 1948). Where there is soil left, this country could evidently be rehabilitated. In China and India, ancient irrigation systems stand abandoned and filled with silt. When the British assumed the rule of India two centuries ago, the population was about 60 million. Today, it is about 500 million and most of its land problems have been created in the past century through deforestation and plowing and the resulting erosion and siltation, all stemming from efforts to support this fantastic population growth.

In southern and eastern Asia there is a tendency to blame destruction of the land on invaders, in particular, Genghis Khan in the 13th Century and Tamerlane in the 14th. But engineering works can be rebuilt if it is worth doing so. The Romans cultivated mountain slopes and thus caused erosion that clogged streams and produced marshes which, as sources of malaria, are thought by some to have had more than a little to do with the decline of the Empire. But these lands have been reclaimed, as have comparable areas in France where Napoleon's engineers succeeded in reclaiming land from swamps and sand dunes which were created when the Vandals burned forests in the 5th Century.

Overdevelopment by man is not confined to the classical world. Gambia, with 96% of its income from peanuts, has very little left to develop. Archaeologists have long wondered how the Mayas managed to support what was obviously a high civilization on the now unproductive soils of Guatemala and Yucatan. Evidently, they exploited their land as intensively as possible until both its fertility and their civilization collapsed. In parts of Mexico the water table has fallen so that towns originally located to take advantage of superior springs now must carry in water from distant sites. As recently as the present decade, aerial reconnaissance has revealed ancient ridged fields on flood plains, the remnants of "a specialized system of agriculture that physically reshaped large parts of the South American continent" (Parsons and Denevan, 1967), and, even more recently, the same system of constructing ridges on seasonal swamps to permit agriculture free from either waterlogged soils or seasonal drought has been described from Tanzania in Africa (Deshler, 1967). The South American ridges occur in areas that have been considered unfit for agriculture and, indeed, salinization, the ancient curse of irrigation systems, has ruined the potential of at least some of these areas. In Africa, this practice of mounding or ridging soil to grow root crops is known to accelerate erosion (Nye and Greenland, 1960).

Even our own young country is not immune to deterioration. We have lost many thousands of acres to erosion and gullying, and many thousands more to strip mining. It has been estimated that the agricultural value of Iowa farmland, which is about as good land as we have, is declining by 1% per year. In our irrigated lands of the West, there is the constant danger of salinization from rising water tables while, elsewhere, from Long Island to Southern California, we have lowered water tables so greatly that in coastal regions salt water is seeping into the aquifers. Meanwhile, an estimated 2000 irrigation dams in the United States are now useless impoundments of silt, sand, and gravel.

So this is the heritage of man's past. Do we know better today? Two recent publications sponsored by the Federal government (Pres. Sci. Advis. Com., 1965; Linton, 1967) have examined, in detail our damage to our environment, especially by pollution. I do not wish to cover the same ground here except to the extent that some current practices and proposals are relevant to the question of whether or not we can mend our ways while, and if, there is still time to save our civilization. I shall not deal here with direct hazards of pollution to man and his domesticated plants and animals. These are very serious problems but less alarming, in my opinion, than some of the larger and less obvious threats.

Hazards of Environmental Deterioration

Every year we are destroying fossil fuels at a greater rate than in the preceding year while, in this country alone, we are annually removing, largely by paving, a million acres from the cycle of photosynthetic productivity. We do not know to what extent we are inhibiting photosynthesis in either freshwater or marine environments. Thus, while we are accelerating the recombination of fossil carbon with oxygen, we are reducing the rate at which the oxygen in the atmosphere is regenerated.

When, and if, we reach the point where the rate of combustion exceeds the rate of photosynthesis, we shall not only have to worry about running out of oxygen at night and in winter, but the oxygen content of the atmosphere will actually decrease. If this occurred gradually, its effect would be approximately the same as moving everyone to higher altitudes, a change that might help to alleviate the population crisis by raising death rates. I am told, however, that the late Lloyd Berkner (1966) was less optimistic and thought that atmospheric depletion might occur suddenly and disastrously.

It is true that 70% or more of the total oxygen production by photosynthesis occurs in the oceans and is largely produced by planktonic diatoms. It is also true that we are dumping into the oceans vast quantities of pollutants consisting, according to one estimate by the U.S. Food and Drug Administration (Linton, 1967), of as many as a half-million substances. Many of these are of recent origin and are biologically active materials such as pesticides, radioisotopes, and detergents to which the earth's living forms have never before had to try to adapt. No more than a minute fraction of these substances and combinations of them has been tested for toxicity to marine diatoms or, for that matter, to the equally vital forms involved in the cycles of nitrogen and other essential elements. I do not think we are in a position to assert right now that we are not poisoning the marine diatoms and thus bringing disaster upon ourselves. If the tanker *Torrey Canyon* had been carrying a concentrated herbicide instead of petroleum, could photosynthesis in the North Sea have been stopped? Berkner is said to have considered that a very few such disasters occurring close enough together in time might cause the ultimate disaster. We must have our green plants both on land and in the sea, and I am happy that, so far, schemes such as a UNESCO plan of 20 years ago to "develop" the Amazon basin have been judged impracticable. Surely man's influence on earth is now so predominant that he must stop trusting to luck that he will not upset any of the indispensable biogeochemical cycles.

Another aspect of the combustion of fossil fuel is that we are adding carbon dioxide to the atmosphere more rapidly than the oceans can assimilate it (Bolen and Eriksson, 1959). Both carbon dioxide and water vapor in the atmosphere are more transparent to shortwave solar radiation than to the

70

longwave heat radiation from the earth to space. They tend to raise the surface temperature and they have the potentiality for altering the earth's climates in ways that are still highly controversial, but which, everyone agrees, are undesirable.

Industrial plants, automobiles, and private homes are the big consumers of fossil fuels. To appreciate the magnitude of the problem, however, let us consider very briefly a still minor source of atmospheric pollution, the airplane. It may have disproportionate importance because much of its carbon dioxide and water are released at high altitudes where they can take a long time to be removed from the atmosphere. When you burn a ton of hydrocarbon, you obtain as by-products about one and one-third tons of water and about twice this amount of carbon dioxide. A Boeing 707 in flight does this roughly every 10 minutes. I read in the papers that 10,000 airplanes per week land in New York City alone, and this does not include military planes. If we assume very crudely that the 707 is typical of airliners and that its average flight takes 4 hours, this amounts to an annual release into the atmosphere of about 18 million tons of water and twice that amount of carbon dioxide. And not all flights terminate in New York! How long can this go on or how much can it be expanded before we seriously alter the radiation balance of the earth and atmosphere?

In any case, if we do not destroy ourselves first, we are going to run out of fossil fuels, and this prospect is surely not many generations away. Then, presumably, we shall have to turn to atomic energy and face agonizing problems of environmental pollution. One would think that the present custodians of this vital resource for the future, which is also a nonrenewable resource, could think of better things to do with it than creating explosions.

I am aware that reactors to produce electricity are in use and under development, but I am apprehensive of what I know of the present generation of reactors and of those proposed for the future. The fuel for present reactors has to be reprocessed periodically. This yields long-lived and biologically hazardous isotopes such as ^{90}Strontium and ^{137}Cesium that should be stored where they cannot contaminate the environment for at least 1000 years; but a fair proportion of the storage tanks employed so far are leaking after only about 20 years (Snow, 1967; Belter and Pearce, 1965). This process also releases ^{85}Krypton into the atmosphere to add to the radiation exposure of the earth's biota including man, and I do not think that anyone knows a practicable way to prevent this. We are glibly offered the prospect of "clean" bombs and thermonuclear power plants which would not produce these isotopes, but, to the best of my knowledge, no one yet knows how this is to be accomplished. And, if development is successful, these reactors will produce new contaminants, among others tritium (^{3}Hydrogen) which becomes a constituent of water, in this case long-lived radioactive water, which will contaminate all environments and living things (Parker, 1968).[2] Even in an official publication of the Atomic Energy Commission it is suggested that for certain mining operations it may be better to use fission (i.e., "dirty") devices instead of fusion (i.e., "clean") devices "to avoid ground water contamination or ventilation problems" (Frank, 1964).

As a final example of what we may irresponsibly do to the world environment, let me mention the proposed new sea-level canal across Central

---

[2] Since this was originally written, it has been calculated that the amount of tritium released from fusion reactors, if these were to replace our other electrical generators, "would result in unacceptable worldwide dosages by the year 2000." (See Parker, 1968.) Even more recently this statement has been hedged and confidence expressed that a solution can be found. (See Parker and Rose, 1968.)

71

America. In that latitude the Pacific Ocean stands higher than the Atlantic by a disputed amount which I believe to average 6 feet. The tides are out of phase on the two sides of the Isthmus of Panama so the maximum difference in level can be as great as 18 feet. Also, the Pacific is much colder than the Atlantic as a result of current patterns and the upwelling of cold water. If the new canal should move a mass of very cold water into the Caribbean, what might this do to climates, or to sea food industries? Nobody has the information to give an authoritative answer, but I have heard suggestions of a new hurricane center, or even diversion of the Gulf Stream with a resultant drastic effect on the climates of all regions bordering the North Atlantic.

We know that the sea-level Suez Canal permitted the exchange of many species between the Red Sea and the Mediterranean, and we know that the Welland Canal let sea lampreys and alewives enter the upper Great Lakes with disastrous effects on fisheries and, more recently, on bathing beaches. What will a tropical sea-level connection between the Atlantic and Pacific cause? Nobody knows.

Even more alarming to me is the prospect that nuclear explosives might be used to dig the canal because, in terms of immediate costs, this is evidently the most economical way. If 170 megatons of nuclear charges will do the job, as has been estimated by the Corps of Engineers which apparently wants to do the job (Graves, 1964), we can again take figures from an official Atomic Energy Commission publication (Stead, 1964) and see what this means in terms of environmental contamination with radioisotopes, assuming the explosions to take place in average materials of the earth's crust. For ^{137}Cesium alone there would be produced 2.72×10^5 curies and, since the permissible whole-body human exposure to this isotope is set at 3×10^{-6} cu-

ries, this amounts to 26.5 limiting doses for every one of the 3.4×10^9 persons on earth. Cesium behaves as a gas in a cratering explosion and prevailing winds in the region are from East to West, so the Pacific would presumably be contaminated first. And cesium behaves like potassium in biological food chains, so we could anticipate its rapid dissemination among living things.

Our Multiple Cultures

This brings me back to our multiple subcultures and their failure of intercommunication. I do not want to comment on the advertising executive who asserts that billboards are "the art gallery of the public" or the spokesman of industry who said that "the ability of a river to absorb sewage is one of our great natural resources and should be utilized to the utmost." And I feel a little sorry for many of my friends who try to promote conservation on esthetic grounds, because I have come to suspect that those of us who care about open spaces and natural beauty are an incomprehensible minority. Are we selecting for genotypes those who can satisfy their esthetic needs in big city slums? Are the Davy Crockett's and Kit Carson's who are born today destined for asylums, jail, or suicide? I am afraid this depressing thought may contain an element of truth. However, it is clear to me that the fundamental problem in the world today is simply too many people multiplying too rapidly and placing demands on the world's resources that cannot be sustained.

It alarms me to read almost daily suggestions as to how food production can be increased "to keep up with the growing population," but only infrequently, and usually in obscure places, to come across authors who recognize the obvious fact that it is impossible to provide food for a population that continues to grow exponentially as ours is now doing at a rate of 1.7% per year. Recently, I have been hearing suggestions for using bacteria, fungi, or yeasts to convert petroleum directly into food for man. This is superficially attractive because it appears to be more efficient than first feeding the petroleum to a refinery and then to tractors and other machines which eventually deliver food to us. It is a melancholy fact that the metabolism of bacteria, fungi, and yeasts does not generate oxygen.

Population Regulation

There appears to be no way for us to escape our dependence on green plants and no way for us to survive except to halt population growth completely or even to undergo a period of population decrease if, as I anticipate, definitive studies show our population to be already beyond what the earth can support on a continuous basis. In order to accomplish this, natural scientists, social scientists, and political leaders will have to learn to communicate with each other and with the general public. This is a large order, but I have learned in recent years that intercommunication is possible with social scientists who are concerned with population problems, and I am now hopeful that these subcultures can come to understand each others' problems and to appreciate efforts to solve them. Even some of the extreme optimists, who believe that it would be possible for some time to make world food production increase more rapidly than the human population, agree that population limitation is necessary to prevent other forms of environmental deterioration (Mayer, 1967).

As a natural scientist it would not occur to me that in many cultures it is important to save face and prove virility by producing a child, as soon after marriage as possible. As a result of this, population planners must evidently aim at delaying the age of marriage or spreading out the production of children after the first. After it is brought to one's attention, it is easy to see that a tradition to produce many children would develop under conditions where one wants descendants and where few children survive to reach maturity (Sheps and Ridley, 1965).

In a Moslem country like Pakistan where women will not be examined by a male physician, birth control by such measures as the intra-uterine device (IUD) is impracticable, and it is difficult to convey a monthly schedule of pill-taking to the poorly educated. However, just as the reproductive cycles of cattle can be synchronized by hormone treatments so that many cows can undergo simultaneous artificial insemination, so the menstrual cycles of populations of women can be synchronized. Then the instructions for contraception can take such a simple form as: "take a pill every night the moon shines." But in a country like Puerto Rico, the efforts of an aroused clergy to instill guilt feelings about the decision a woman must make each day can render the Pill ineffective. Here, the IUD, which requires only one decision, is more practicable.

In any case, there is ample evidence that people the world over want fertility control. Voluntary sterilization is popular in India, Japan, and Latin America. In Japan and western European countries that have made legal abortion available upon request, the birth rates have fallen dramatically. With such recent techniques as the Pill and the IUD, and the impending availability of antimeiotic drugs which inhibit sperm production in the male, and anti-implantation drugs which can prevent pregnancy when taken as much as 3 days after exposure, practicable fertility control is at last available.

Prospects

I shall try to end on a note of optimism. Japan has shown that a determined people can in one generation bring the problem of excessive population growth under control. Japan's population is still growing slowly but they know how to stop it and, as the age distribution of her population adjusts to the new schedule of fertility, there may be no need for further deliberate actions.

Kingsley Davis (1967) has recently expressed skepticism about schemes for family planning on the grounds that they do not actually represent population policy but merely permit couples to determine their family size voluntarily. This is certainly true, but the evidence is overwhelming that a large percentage of the children born into the world today are unwanted. I think we must start by preventing these unwanted births and then take stock of what additional measures such as negative dependency allowances may be called for.

In the meantime, I consider it urgent that social and natural scientists get together and try to decide what an optimum size for the human population of the earth would be. If this can be achieved before some miscalculation, or noncalculation, sends the earth's environment into an irreversible decline, there is hope that the world can be saved. It is encouraging that the Soviet Union seems finally to have abandoned the dogma that overpopulation problems are by-products of capitalism and could not exist in a socialist country (Cook, 1967). It is to be hoped that this will open the door to true international cooperation, possibly even within the United Nations, to try to solve man's most desperate problem.

References

Belter, W. G., and D. W. Pearce. 1965. Radioactive waste management. *Reactor Tech.* (AEC), Jan. 1965, p. 203.

Berkner, L. V. 1966. Man versus technology. *Population Bull.,* 22: 83-94.

Berkner, L. V., and L. C. Marshall. 1965. On the origin and rise of oxygen concentration in the earth's atmosphere. *J. Atmos. Sci.,* 22: 225-261.

Bolin, B., and E. Eriksson. 1959. Changes in the carbon dioxide content of the atmosphere and sea due to fossil fuel consumption. In: *The Atmosphere and the Sea in Motion.* B. Bolin, Ed. The Rockefeller Institute Press, New York.

Borgstrom, G. 1965. *The Hungry Planet.* Macmillan, New York.

Clarke, F. W. 1920. The data of geochemistry. *U.S. Geol. Surv. Bull.,* 695.

Cook, R. C. 1967. Soviet population theory from Marx to Kosygin. *Population Bull.,* 23: 85-115.

Davis, K. 1967. Population policy: will current programs succeed? *Science,* 158: 730-739.

Deshler, W. 1967. *Sci. Am.,* 217 (4): 8.

Frank, W. J. 1964. Characteristics of nuclear explosives. In: *Engineering with Nuclear Explosives.* U.S. Atomic Energy Commission. TID-7695.

Graves, E. 1964. Nuclear excavation of a sea-level, Isthmian canal. In: *Engineering with Nuclear Explosives.* U.S. Atomic Energy Commission. TID-7695.

Linton, R. M. (Chairman). 1967. A strategy for a livable environment. Report of The Task Force on Environmental Health and Related Problems. U.S. Dept. H.E.W. Govt. Printing Office, Washington, D.C.

Lowdermilk, W. C. 1948. Conquest of the land through seven thousand years. USDA, Soil Cons. Serv. MP-32.

Mayer, J. 1967. Nutrition and civilization. *Trans. N.Y. Acad. Sci.,* 29: 1014-1032.

Nye, P. H., and D. J. Greenland. 1960. The soil under shifting cultivation. Commonwealth Ag. Bur. Farnham Royal, Bucks, England. Tech. Comm. 51.

Parker, F. L. 1968. Wastes from fusion reactors. *Science,* 159: 83.

Parker, F. L., and D. J. Rose. 1968. Wastes from fusion reactors. *Science,* 159: 1376.

Parsons, J. J., and W. M. Denevan. 1967. Pre-Columbian ridged fields. *Sci. Am.,* 217(1): 92-100.

Rubey, W. W. 1955. Development of the hydrosphere and atmosphere, with special reference to probable composition of the early atmosphere. Geol. Soc. Am., Spec. Paper 62, Crust of the earth, 631-650.

Sheps, M. C., and J. C. Ridley (Eds.), 1965. *Public Health and Population Change.* University of Pittsburgh Press.

Snow, J. A. 1967. Radioactive waste from reactors. *Scientist and Citizen,* 9: 89-96.

Stead, F. W. 1964. Distribution in groundwater of radionuclides from underground nuclear explosions. In: *Engineering with Nuclear Explosives.* U.S. Atomic Energy Commission. TID-7695.

Tukey, J. W. (Chairman). 1965. Restoring the quality of our environment. Report of the President's Scientific Advisory Committee. Govt. Printing Office, Washington, D.C.

Urey, H. C. 1959. Primitive planetary atmospheres and the origin of life. In: *The Origin of Life on the Earth*. Macmillan, New York.

EVOLUTIONARY RESPONSE TO HUMAN INFECTIOUS DISEASES

George J. Armelagos and John R. Dewey

The study of the evolution of man seldom takes into consideration the role of disease in this development. This is understandable since the evidence available is essentially inferential and consequently open to interpretation. These inferences are based on the actual paleontological record with additional information provided by the historical accounts of disease. We are also able to speculate on the occurrence of disease in prehistoric populations from the disease patterns in contemporary *Homo sapiens* and nonhominid populations. This study is an attempt to discuss infectious diseases in human evolution.

There are three variables which we must consider in the study of infectious diseases—the host, the pathogen, and the environment (Cockburn, 1963). The study of diseases in man, then, would involve the interrelationship of these variables. Although there have been changes in the host (in this case, man) and the pathogen, some of the most significant changes are those in the environment (Armelagos, 1967). It is important to note that the environment of man includes not only biotic, climatic, geologic, and geographic elements, but also all aspects of his culture (Bates, 1953). This presents somewhat of a dilemma, since man has used culture as his major mode of adaptation in an attempt to control the other aspects of his environment. The study of man's culture—his technology, social system, and even his idealogy—must be considered if we are to understand the disease patterns of man.

The role of culture is so significant in understanding the disease process that May (1960) has constructed a model in which culture is dealt with as a separate factor, as are the environment (which includes the pathogen) and the host. May illustrates the role of culture with particular disease patterns in North Vietnam. North Vietnam has two relevant geomorphological features: fertile delta and the fertile hills. Although rice is grown in the hills, the major area of rice cultivation is in the delta. The rice growers in the delta build houses on the ground, with a stable on one side and a kitchen on the other. The hill people, on the other hand, build houses on stilts with living rooms about 8 to 10 ft above the ground. The animals are kept underneath the houses, while the cooking is done in the living room.

The vector for malaria, *Anopheles minimus,* occurs in the hills, but the flight ceiling of this vector is about 8 or 9 ft and, consequently, the *Anopheles* encounter only the animals under the house. If the vector were to stray to the living room, fumes from the cooking would tend to drive it away. The malaria vector does not occur in the delta.

Some people have been forced to move to the hills under pressure of overpopulation in the delta. Typically, movement of the delta people to the hills has not resulted in the acceptance of the culture of the hill people. The delta tribes still build their houses on the ground, with the animals kept in the stables on the side. Food is cooked outside and brought into the house to be eaten in the smoke-free living room. This results in the *Anopheles minimus* feeding on the humans, whom they prefer to the nonhuman animals. This transfer results in the transmission of malaria to the new inhabitants. According

Dr. Armelagos is a member of the department of anthropology, University of Massachusetts and Dr. Dewey is at the Chico State College, Chico, California.
This is the fourth paper in the symposium "Pleistocene Man—Environmental Relationships."

Bioscience, March, 1970, Vol.20, No.5, pp. 271-275.

to May, the people of the delta have been discouraged from relocating, feeling that the evil spirits in the hills do not like them. The intimate relationship between disease and culture noted by May is not unique; others (Hackett, 1937; Livingstone, 1958; Lambrecht, 1964; Alland, 1967; and Hudson, 1965) have presented similar interactions.

The Cultural Adaptation

The beginning of the cultural adaptation began about 2 million years ago with the emergence of man. During the Paleolithic, which lasted for 99% of human history, man was essentially a hunter and gatherer. Cultural development was excruciatingly slow. Pebble tools of the Oldowan culture persisted over a million years. The more refined hand axes and flake tools of the Abbevillian and Acheulian periods lasted another half-million years. There were other changes during the Lower Paleolithic which are relevant. The Australopithecines, the original hominids, were restricted to the tropical grasslands and exploited only a small portion of the available habitat. Although the diet of the Australopithecines, according to Howell (1964), consisted of a small amount of meat from fish, amphibians, reptiles, small mammals, and moderate-sized herbivorous ungulates, the major proportion was made up of gathered vegetal material.

During the latter part of the Lower Paleolithic, a period in which the hominids reached the *Homo erectus* stage of development, there was an increase in hunting ability. There are archeological sites which indicate preferential hunting. Seventy per cent of a large sample of bones found at Choukoutien, near Peking, China, belong to two species of deer (Howell, 1964). It is from this same site that the first evidence of fire is found. The major consequence of the cultural adaptation was an expansion of populations into the temperate zone. It is important to note that in our model we emphasize an expansion, rather than a migration, of population.

The changes during the latter part of the Lower Paleolithic, the Middle Paleolithic (130,000-40,000 B.P.), and Upper Paleolithic (40,000-12,000 B.P.) were variations of the same theme. The adaptation of intensive hunting persists, with specialization in the Upper Paleolithic to differing environments. Again expansion is noted, this time into the tundra zone. It is during this period that we have the arrival of the first hominids into the New World (Griffin, 1964).

The close of the Pleistocene was marked by significant climatic changes in both the Old and New Worlds. The disappearance of the last glacier and a general warming trend caused significant changes in the distribution of large animals. Added to the apparent migration, the efficiency of Upper Paleolithic hunters led to the disappearance of many of the large animals in many areas. The hunting continued, but fishing and collecting became more important. Regional specialization continued in this period, the Mesolithic (12,800-8,000 B.P.).

In the Near East, these changes were responsible for an increased dependence on wild cereal which eventually led to semi-sedentary adaptation. This increased sedentarism, diversification of food sources, and decreased dependency on large animals were prerequisite to the domestication of plants and animals (Adams, 1964).

Although Neolithic development in the New World and Old World were independent, the consequences were similar. Sedentary villages were built to protect and care for the fields. There was a substantial increase in the size of residential units and total population. Increased food supply and the economic importance of children were causal factors for these increases. The agricultural adaptation led quickly to the development of sedentary villages in the Near East (4200 B.C.), urban centers (3100 B.C.), and preindustrial cities and industrial cities (1800 A.D.).

Neolithic development resulted in drastic shifts in the ecological balance. Prior to the Neolithic, man had little observable effect on the environment (Sears, 1956).

The utilization of fire (Stewart, 1956) represents one cultural practice which could have altered the landscape. In addition, the improvement of hunting techniques late in the Lower Paleolithic may have led to the extinction of the megafauna (Martin, 1967).

The adaptation we have been talking about is better reflected in population figures computed by Deevey (1960). By the end of the Lower Paleolithic, total population was 125,000 with a density of $0.00425/km^2$. This increased to 1,000,000 (density $0.012/km^2$) in the Middle Paleolithic and to 5,320,000 (0.04 people/km^2) in the Mesolithic. Following the Neolithic Revolution, there was nearly a sixteenfold increase over the Mesolithic population to 86,500,000 (1.4 people/km^2). The increase in population, it is sad to say, continues.

Another factor which is relevant is the size of the social unit. A group of hunters and gatherers is not likely to increase much over 100 people and a more likely figure is 50-75 before fission occurs. The early agricultural villages at Jarmo, which were quite small, had over 150 people. Other agricultural villages would likely have had 300 or 400 people, but urban centers which followed far outshadowed this. Ur, according to Woolley (1965), had a population of 350,000, while Sjoberg (1965) estimates a population of 100,000 people for the Valley of Mexico. By 1600 A.D. only 1.6 of the total European population was living in centers of 100,000 or more people. By 1700 A.D. this increased to 1.9%, and by 1800 A.D., to 2.2%. Following the Industrial Revolution, in Great Britain alone 10% of the population was living in centers of over 100,000. By 1990, Davis (1965) estimates that half the world will be living in urban areas of this size or larger.

The changes in cultural adaptation, with the resulting increases in population size, population density, and changes in the ecological balance, altered the disease pattern of man. Polgar (1964) suggests five stages in the disease history of mankind: hunting and gathering, settled villages, preindustrial cities, industrial cities, and the present. Our discussion of infectious disease in human evolution will utilize Polgar's description of these stages.

The Hunting and Gathering Stage

For almost 2 million years man has subsisted on the animals he could hunt and on the edible plants he could gather. As one would expect, populations adapted to a hunting and gathering subsistence are small and are distributed over a wide area. In addition to their low density, these groups would have led a semi-nomadic existence. Small population size and low density would restrict the types of infectious disease which would have plagued them. Contagious diseases, for example, would not have had a large enough population base to have an impact on the evolution of these populations. Polgar suggests that the hunters and gatherers would have been afflicted with two types of disease—those which had adapted to the prehominids and persisted to infest them after speciation of the hominids, and those (zoonoses) which did not have human hosts but were accidentally transmitted to man. Such parasites as the head and body louse (*Pediculus humanus*), pinworms, yaws, and malaria would fall into the first category. Cockburn (1967b) would add that most of the internal protozoa found in modern man and bacteria such as *Salmonella typhi* and staphylococci would have been present. It is interesting to note that Livingstone (1958) would argue against malarial infections in early man. The small population size and bipedalism indicating a savannah adaptation would preclude the presence of malaria.

The second type of disease is that which has adapted to another host and is transmitted to man accidentally by insect bite, wounds, or from consuming meat of the infected animal. Sleeping sickness, scrub typhus, relapsing fever, tetanus, trichinosis, tularemia, leptospirosis, and schistosomiasis are examples of diseases which, Polgar speculates, may have been transmitted accidentally to man.

The range of the hunters and gatherers

is a limiting factor for the kinds of parasites which would have been present. During the earlier period of the hunting and gathering stage, the hominids were restricted to the tropical zone. With an expansion of hominids into the temperate zone (by the time of *Homo erectus*), new and different parasites would have been present. It is important to note that by this time some food was being cooked, a process which would kill some of the parasites present.

Missing from the list of diseases which would have involved man prior to the Neolithic are contagious community diseases such as measles, influenza, smallpox, and mumps (Polgar, 1964). Burnet (1962) goes further and suggests that few viruses would have infected early man. Cockburn (1967a) disagrees strongly, since there are a number of viral infections found in monkeys. Although it is possible that monkeys studied may have contracted the viruses in captivity, the differences in the form of these viruses, according to Cockburn, are enough to argue against this.

The Settled Village Stage

The semi-sedentary encampments of the Mesolithic and sedentary villages of the Neolithic resulted in the concentration of populations in relatively small areas. As one could expect, this would create new and different problems. In hunting and gathering societies, the disposal of human excrement presents no great problem since nomadic travel would preclude the accumulation of human waste (Heinz, 1961). It should be pointed out that in some cases, hunters and gatherers living in caves were forced to abandon them as the debris accumulated.

The sedentarism which is characteristic of the Mesolithic and Neolithic would provide new breeding places for many forms of life which harbor disease. In addition, domestication would have led to the herding of animals near the areas of habitation. Prior to this time, the dog was the only domesticated animal. *Salmonella* and *Ascaris* are carried by domesticated

animals such as pigs, sheep, cattle, and fowl. C. A. Hoare (1957) has suggested that the trypanosomes were spread beyond the range of the normal host by domesticated animals. Polgar (1964) also suggests that the products of domesticated animals (milk, skin, hair) and the dust raised by the animals provide for the transmission of anthrax, Q Fever, brucellosis, and tuberculosis.

The expansion of agricultural societies into new environments created other problems. Audy (1961) has demonstrated that as new ground is broken for cultivation, scrub typhus increases. In this case, the agriculturalists exposed themselves to the bites of insects as they toiled in the fields. Livingstone (1958) has impressively illustrated the relationship between the spread of agriculture, malaria, and sickle cell anemia. As the West African agriculturalists expanded into the forest and destroyed the trees in the preparation of ground for cultivation, they encroached on the environment of the pongids. The pongids, which were the primary host of the *Plasmodium falciparum* carried by *Anopheles gambiae*, were exterminated or forced further into the forest. The mosquitoes quickly transferred to the hominids for their meals. Livingstone points out that agricultural activity, which provides new breeding areas for mosquitoes and provides a large population for the mosquitoes to feed, led to malaria becoming an endemic disease. Populations in this area have developed a genetic polymorphism—sickle cell trait—which gives those individual heterozygotes for the trait immunity to malaria. In other words, as the agriculturalists expanded, malaria would increase. In response to the increase in malaria, the **frequency of the abnormal sickle cell hemoglobin would increase.**

Preindustrial Cities

The expansion of the population which began in the Neolithic continued with the development of large urban centers in the preindustrial cities. The problem which faced the settled communities of the Neolithic are present but are significantly more difficult to control. The concentration of a large population in a small area creates problems in supplying food and water and removing human waste. Since many cities dispose of waste via their water supply, serious health hazards developed Cholera, for example, was transmitted by polluted water. Even with our advanced technology, pollution is still a serious concern.

The increased frequency of contact between members of the population resulted in the transmission of disease by contact. Typhus was transmitted by lice which moved from person to person. Plague bacillus which was originally spread by rodents could, with the high population density, be transmitted by inhalation. During the preindustrial stage, viral diseases such as measles, mumps, chickenpox, and smallpox were also transmitted by contact.

Social change resulting from urbanization was responsible for alteration in the expression of some of the diseases. Prior to urbanization, syphilis was a nonvenereal disease, but with the changes in family structure, crowding, and sexual promiscuity, syphilis became a venereal disease (Hudson, 1965).

It was during this period that exploration resulted in the introduction of disease into new areas.

Population during this period approached a size for the maintenance of diseases in an endemic form. Cockburn (1967b) has suggested that a population of about one million is necessary for measles to be maintained as an endemic disease.

Industrial Cities

Increase in population size and density was again a consequence of the cultural advances of the industrial revolution. The social and environmental changes were important. Industrial wastes increased pollution of water and air. Unsanitary conditions in the slums were ideal focal points for the spread of infectious diseases, and imperialistic expansion transported disease into new areas.

Epidemics also created havoc in the industrial populations. Typhus, typhoid, smallpox, diphtheria, measles, malaria, and yellow fever epidemics are well documented for the late 18th and early 19th centuries (Polgar, 1964). Tuberculosis and respiratory diseases such as pneumonia and bronchitis were enhanced by the crowding and harsh working conditions.

Perhaps the saddest consequence of the industrial period was the spread of epidemic diseases to populations which had not developed an immunity to them. Although contact had occurred earlier, in the preindustrial period, the impact was greater during the industrial period.

Present

The advances that have been made in recent times have been quite remarkable; our understanding of the relevant features of infectious diseases has allowed us to make significant strides in preventing and controlling some infectious diseases. Even with these advances, infectious diseases are still prevalent in many areas. Attempts to control disease are more difficult with rapid transportation. Infectious diseases may be transmitted in hours to populations which, 50 years ago, were 2 weeks distant.

The Evolutionary Response

The study of infectious diseases and their impact on human development is the host and the parasite (Motulsky, 1960). The duration of a human generation is much longer than that of the parasites which feed on man. This would favor evolutionary changes in the parasites leading to less severe manifestations of the disease. This is understandable since a parasite which causes the death of the host can then die from lack of a host.

The responses in the host were also significant. Haldane (1949) suggests that infectious diseases have been the most important selective factor in human evolution. Since the factors (i.e., large, dense population) which led to epidemic infectious diseases arose rapidly following the Neolithic revolution, the genetic factors

80

would not have been present to provide immunity against these infectious diseases. In other words, the genotypes that were selected during the hunting and gathering stage would have provided little protection against the infectious diseases, but the genetic heterogeneity of the population would have been adequate to protect some individuals from the diseases. Lederberg (1963) disagrees, since many of the diseases which have animal reservoirs would be important in an epidemic sense. Instead of rapid selection acting on a large population, Lederberg suggests that the persistent application of small differentials over a long period of time, as characteristic of "reservoir disease," could have developed factors of genetic immunity.

Motulsky (1963) states that there are three areas of concern in disease-susceptibility and resistance: (1) factors of immunity in the conventional antigen-antibody reaction; (2) generalized host factors; and (3) highly specific gene-determined factors which provide resistance.

Motulsky points out that there may be a genetic potential for antibody production, but it would be difficult to demonstrate in man. Lederberg (1959) has provided other data which would suggest a possible genetic variation in the response to antibody protection. Although not much is known about the inheritance of the nonspecific host factors in the response to infectious disease, they do appear to have a genetic basis. Efficiency of phagocytosis, levels of complements, antimicrobial factors in tissue, and serum inhibitors of microbial growth may have been important in providing immunity to diseases (Motulsky, 1963).

The highly specific genetic factors may have had a key role in the evolutionary response to infectious diseases. Although it would be impossible to demonstrate the genetic factors involved, populations appear to have developed a genetic immunity to disease. Motulsky (1960) states that when tuberculosis strikes a population which was not previously exposed to the disease, the mortality is high and the

infection is acute. The individuals which are most susceptible to the disease would perish, while those with genetic characteristics which provide some resistance would survive. In subsequent episodes, the mortality is lower and infection is less severe. The differential susceptibility in different populations could result from a genetic difference. For example, American Indians and Eskimos developed a more acute tubercular infection. The evidence for genetic immunity is suggestive, however, since environmental differences in nutrition and sanitation may explain some of the population differences.

The evidence for highly specific genetic factors is more convincing in the metabolic polymorphisms which have evolved in response to disease (Motulsky, 1960). For example, the sickle cell trait, which provides resistance to malaria, has been discussed. Other polymorphisms have evolved in areas where malaria is endemic. The hemoglobinopathy thalassemia and glucose-6-phosphate dehydrogenase deficiency also appear to provide protection against malaria (Motulsky, 1963).

The evolution of genetic protection against infectious disease would have been essential for the survival of population, since epidemic diseases could destroy large segments of the population. In some instances, infectious diseases may act as a factor inhibiting population growth. In those populations in which epidemic diseases are still an important factor, increases in population are evidence. Cultural practices tend to maintain population size. As cultural groups are better able to prevent and control infectious diseases, the population increases at an alarming rate. In order to combat this increase in population, Polgar (1964) suggests that public health programs which are designed to control and prevent infectious diseases in countries with high fertility rates should include programs to limit population increase.

In addition to the problem of the exploding population, the control of infectious diseases has helped to increase life expectancy. The increase in longevity would have created new problems for the older segments of the population; increase in degenerative disease would have been a consequence. In a population in which the oldest individuals live to 60 years of age, degenerative diseases are relatively unimportant. Neel (1958) states that in the state of Michigan, of the deaths in 1953 from arteriosclerotic, hypertensive, or degenerative heart disease (which constituted 33.1% of all deaths), 7.4% occurred prior to age 50. By the 60th year, approximately 25% have died of degenerative heart disease. The remaining 75% of deaths due to degenerative heart disease occur after 60 years of age.

Recently, we were able to demonstrate that osteoporosis (loss of bone mass with age) occurs earlier and is more severe in prehistoric Nubian populations when compared to bone loss in a modern population. In the prehistoric Nubian population, the frequency of fractures due to severe bone loss was not evident. An examination of the mortality pattern would indicate why this should be the case. Approximately 40% of the population die before their 40th year. Only 15% live past 40 years and all are dead before age 60. In the United States, 91% live past their 40th year, 75% past their 60th, 29% past their 80th, and 6% past their 90th year. Since many individuals live past age 60 and osteoporosis continues, the decrease in bone mass becomes great enough to predispose the neck of the femur to pathological fracture. It should be pointed out that since these degenerative conditions occur in that segment of the population which is past reproductive age, selective responses to degenerative conditions could not occur.

With the possibility that we may be able to control infectious diseases in some populations, concern with degenerative conditions (Spiegelman, 1956) and population control should be two areas of future research.

Acknowledgment

Partial support was received from a grant (H. D. AM02771-01) from the National Institute of Child Health and Human Development, United States Public Health Service.

References

Adams, R. M. 1964. The origin of agriculture. In: *Horizons in Anthropology*, S. Tax (ed.). The Johns Hopkins Press, Baltimore, Md., p. 120-131.

Alland, A., Jr. 1967. War and disease: An anthropological perspective. *Natur. Hist.*, 76: 58-61.

Armelagos, C. J. 1967. Man's changing environment. In: *Infectious Diseases: Their Evolution and Eradication*, A. Cockburn (ed.). Charles C Thomas, Springfield, Ill., p. 66-83.

Audy, J. R. 1961. The ecology of scrub typhus. In: *Studies in Disease Ecology*, J. M. May (ed.). Hafner Publishing Co., New York, p. 387-433.

Bates, M. 1953. Human ecology. In: *Anthropology Today*, A. L. Kroeber (ed.). University of Chicago Press, Chicago, Ill., p. 700-713.

Burnet, Sir F. M. 1962. *Natural History of Infectious Disease*. Cambridge University Press, England.

Cockburn, T. A. 1963. *The Evolution and Eradication of Diseases*. The Johns Hopkins Press, Baltimore, Md.

———— 1967a. Infections of the order Primates. In: *Infectious Diseases: Their Evolution and Eradication*, T. A. Cockburn (ed.). Charles C Thomas, Springfield, Ill., p. 38-107.

———— 1967b. The evolution of human infectious diseases. In: *Infectious Diseases: Their Evolution and Eradication*, T. A. Cockburn (ed.). Charles C Thomas, Springfield, Ill., p. 84-107.

Davis, K. 1965. The urbanization of human population. *Sci. Amer.*, 213: 40-54.

Deevey, E. W., Jr. 1960. The human population. *Sci. Amer.*, 208: 48, 194-198.

Griffin, J. B. 1960. Some connections between Siberia and America. *Science*, 131: 801-812.

Hackett, L. W. 1937. *Malaria in Europe*. Oxford University Press, London.

Haldane, J. B. S. 1949. Disease and evolution. Supplement to *La Ricerca Scientifica*, 19: 68-76.

Heinz, H. J. 1961. Factors governing the survival of bushmen worm parasites in the Kalahari. *S. Afr. J. Sci.*, 8: 207-213.

Hoare, C. A. 1957. The spread of African trypanosomes beyond their natural range. *Z. Tropenmed. Parasitol.*, 8: 1-6.

Howell, F. C. 1964. The hominization process. In: *Horizons of Anthropology*, S. Tax (ed.). Aldine Publishing Co., Chicago, Ill., p. 49-59.

Hudson, E. H. 1965. Treponematosis and man's social evolution. *Amer. Anthropol.*, **67**: 885-902.

Lambrecht, F. L. 1964. Aspects of evolution and ecology of tsetse flies and trypanosomiasis in prehistoric African environments. *J. Afr. Hist.*, **5**: 1-24.

Lederberg, J. 1959. Genes and antibodies. *Science*, **129**: 1649-1653.

———. 1963. Comments on A. Motulsky's *Genetic Systems in Disease Susceptibility in Mammals.* In: *Genetic Selection in Man*, W. J. Schull (ed.). University of Michigan Press, Ann Arbor, p. 112-260. (The comments are interspersed with motulhoup text).

Livingstone, F. B. 1958. Anthropological implication of sickle cell gene distribution in West Africa. *Amer. Anthropol.*, **60**: 533-562.

Martin, P. S. 1967. Pleistocene overkill. In: *Pleistocene Extinctions: The Search for a Cause*, P. S. Martin and H. E. Wright (eds.). Yale University Press, New Haven & London, p. 75-120.

May, J. M. 1960. The ecology of human disease. *Ann. N. Y. Acad. Sci.*, **84**: 789-794.

Motulsky, A. G. 1960. Metabolic polymorphism and the role of infectious diseases. *Hum. Biol.*, **32**: 28-63.

———. 1963. Genetic systems involved in disease susceptibility in mammals. In: *Genetic Selection in Man*, W. J. Schull (ed.). University of Michigan Press, Ann Arbor, p. 112-260.

Neel, J. V. 1958. The study of natural selection in primitive and civilized human populations. *Amer. Anthropol. Assoc. Mem.*, **86**: 43-72.

Polgar, S. 1964. Evolution and the ills of mankind. In: *Horizons of Anthropology*, S. Tax (ed.). Aldine Publishing Co., Chicago, Ill., p. 200-211.

Sears, P. B. 1956. The processes of environmental changes by man. In: *Man's Role in Changing the Face of the Earth*, W. L. Thomas (ed.). University of Chicago Press, Chicago, Ill., p. 471-484.

Sjoberg, G. 1965. The origin and evolution of cities. *Sci. Amer.*, **213**: 55-63.

Spiegelman, M. 1956. Recent trends and determinants of mortality in highly developed countries. In: *Trends and Differentials in Mortality*, F. C. Boudreau and C. V. Kiser (eds.). Milbank Memorial Fund, New York, p. 51-60

Stewart, O. C. 1956. Fire as the first great force employed by man. In: *Man's Role in Changing the Face of the Earth*, W. C. Thomas (ed.). University of Chicago Press, Chicago, Ill.

Woolley, L. 1965. *Beginnings of Civilization, History of Mankind.* Vol. 1, Part II. The New American Library. Mentor Books, New York & Toronto.

Medical Problems of the Developing Countries

Roy E. Brown

Although developing countries vary in geographic size, population pressures, and natural resources, a number of generalizations can be applied to them. Their economies are based on subsistence agriculture, and average incomes are low. In almost all fields there is a lack of trained technicians. Despite the governmental premium on education and massive education programs, the literacy rates are very low, a fact related to the lack of trained teachers.

By Western standards the populations are young, with almost half the people less than 15 years of age, and up to one quarter below school age (1). Approximately 90 percent of the population of developing countries is rural, with a definite trend toward urbanization (2). Vital statistics are either unreliable or nonexistent, but childhood mortality rate is known to be extremely high. Infant mortality is 3 to 10 times that of developed countries, the mortality among pre-school children is as much as 30 to 50 times as great, and about 40 percent of the total mortality occurs in children under the age of 5 years. Approximately half of the children born never reach their fifth birthdays (1) (see Table 1).

Fertility rates are so high that, in spite of large losses among children and the resultant shortened life expectancy, there is a population increase which is estimated to approach 3 percent annually (3). The population explosion causes land hunger, which is directly related to physical hunger. Thus medical prevention of death from disease may merely add to the numbers dying from starvation.

Population has often been equated with power, and curtailing the growth of population is synonymous to some minds with inhibiting the growth of power. Birth control programs may meet resistance, as government agencies reject certain plans or render them ineffectual through indifference.

As a result of mass migrations, the annual growth of the population in cities and towns is even greater than the growth of the population in general. Associated with the drift to the towns is a rapid dissolution of rural familial and social structure which is inaugurating major changes away from the traditional mode of living. Juvenile delinquency, alcoholism, and promiscuity will predictably increase along with those diseases of overcrowding, poliomyelitis, typhoid fever, and tuberculosis.

Education is being sought by the young as a means by which to escape the closed agricultural life of their ancestors, and it is ironic, if understandable, that at a time when food production is becoming more critical the departments of agriculture in the universities of these countries have very few applicants. The consequences of limitations in educational progress are obvious. Although the governments are concerned with education, the shortage of trained teachers and adequate buildings and the ever-present shortage of funds must limit the eventual supply of professional people, technicians, teachers, and administrators.

The author is an Honorary Lecturer in the Department of Paediatrics and Child Health at Makerere Medical School, University of East Africa, P.O. Box 2072, Kampala, Uganda.

Science, July, 1966, Vol.152, No.3733, pp. 271-275.

Medical Services Are Deficient

In the presence of population pressure, high childhood mortality, limited educational facilities, and the failure of rapid development of agriculture, there are gross deficiencies in quantity of medical services (see Tables 2 and 3). Governmental expenditures in the field of health are low in relation to the need (4). The doctor-patient ratio ranges from 1 to 20,000 to 1 to 100,000, compared to a ratio of 1 to 1000 in many developed countries (5). For various reasons most of the available doctors are found working in larger towns, and so the situation in rural areas is even more acute than these figures indicate.

There are correspondingly few trained nurses, midwives, and other medical personnel, in addition to shortages of hospital beds, clinics, and health centers (6). With a limited national budget, there are many urgent problems, and very little money is available for solving those related to health. Medical expenditures may range from one-twentieth to one-tenth of the amounts designated in developed countries for each person annually (5, 7).

Characteristic Disease Pattern

To understand the medical problems of the developing countries, it is important to appreciate the background of the complex interrelationships among health, economics, political considerations, and sociological parameters. Despite many variable factors, the disease pattern is surprisingly similar in all developing countries. There are certain common childhood diseases, most if not all of which are preventable. Leading the list invariably are malnutrition, diarrhea, and respiratory illnesses, often interrelated. The pediatric list continues with malaria, tuberculosis, intestinal parasites (especially hookworm and roundworm infections), and the so-called childhood infectious diseases (particularly measles

and whooping cough), followed by accidents such as kerosene poisoning and burns.

Among adults are found various types of anemia and deficiency diseases, tuberculosis and leprosy, such parasitic diseases as malaria, schistosomiasis, filariasis, and others caused by locally prevalent parasites, trachoma, venereal diseases, mental illnesses, dys-

Table 1. Life expectancies, at birth, for people (both sexes) in some developing countries and the United States. Adapted from (16).

Country	Life expectancy (years)
Mali	20.3
Guinea—rural areas	30.5
urban areas	35.8
Central African Republic	32.3
Senegal	36.9
Rhodesia and Nyasaland	48.0
Mozambique	45.0
Zanzibar	42.8
U.S.A.	Over 70

entery, and cholera. Also present are all the other medical conditions which are found throughout the rest of the world. There are, of course, a number of unusual diseases peculiar to one region or another, but these usually do not constitute significant problems.

The major difference in the pattern of disease is that rarely is a single condition present alone. The salient feature is the superimposition of a particular disease on a malnourished, anemic, and parasite-burdened individual. The underlying problems will weaken the person, undermine his resistance, create a far more serious medical problem of management, and most likely increase the complications and militate against survival. As can be imagined, chronic diseases of elderly persons, the so-called degenerative diseases, are not a significant public health problem.

A limited health budget, few hospital beds, and shortages of medical and technical staff, added to the weakened and disease-ridden population,

85

create major medical problems for administrator and clinician. The criterion for hospital admission is often the basic consideration of survival. Hospital treatments are aimed not necessarily at cure, but at lightening the burden or tipping the balance in favor of the patient so that he can be discharged from the hospital and free the bed for the next admission. In many instances this approaches what could be classified as first aid.

Most patients admitted to modern hospitals in developing countries have already been seen and treated by a local practitioner or healer. Despite this tendency, modern facilities have gained popularity and are constantly hard-pressed to keep up with the demands for service.

Many of the medical conditions described are preventable. This is a valid statement in theory, but in actuality prevention is hampered by many factors. Far less costly than therapy in terms of personnel and money, prevention remains difficult in places where there is inadequate education, general illiteracy, and ignorance. Health is affected by various superstitions, taboos, and erroneous beliefs about the causes and cures of illnesses. Fatalistic acceptance of death is very common and presents a major obstacle.

It is extremely important for workers in the health fields to attempt to understand indigenous beliefs and practices concerning health and disease. The field knowledge of anthropologists and sociologists can and should be of great importance in the solution of what appear to be overwhelming medical problems. Arensberg and Niehoff recently commented that, although it might appear that a superior technique for growing crops or for healing the sick or for educating the young would automatically be accepted by those lacking these techniques, any technician who has worked in the developing countries can tell of **superior techniques that failed to be accepted only because the habits and**

Table 2. Number of patients per doctor, and health expenditure per capita, in various countries. Data from (*17*).

Country	Ratio	Health expenditure ($)
Soviet Union	529	
United States	710	30
Argentina	770	
Japan	916	
England and Wales	1,060	39
Brazil	2,420	0.65
Dominican Republic	3,000	
Turkey	3,500	
Ceylon	4,700	2.50
India	5,040	0.46
Madagascar	11,100	1.95
North Borneo	12,279	2.80
New Guinea	13,000	
Uganda	13,100	1.40
Congo (Brazzaville)	14,000	5.50
Angola	14,820	1.40
Tanzania	18,000	0.56
Basutoland	21,000	1.20
Ghana	21,000	
Sierra Leone	21,200	1.50
Colombia	23,000	
Indonesia	31,000	
Afghanistan	33,000	
Nigeria	33,000	0.70
Mauretania	36,000	
Central African Republic	39,000	
Togo	46,875	
Chad	61,000	0.95
Nepal	72,000	0.42

customs of the local people were not taken into consideration by those proposing them (*8*).

Some local customs are excellent and necessary; these should be encouraged and protected. Other traditions are harmful and often can be dislodged only by circuitous means and with the combined efforts of doctors, nurses, health educators, social scientists, and politicians (*9*). Typical of the harmful customs are those which impose dietary restrictions, such as reverence for cows in India, refusal to eat fish or chicken or eggs in certain regions, and taboos limiting the use of foods during pregnancy and lactation. The health worker must use great skill and ingenuity to counteract these harmful customs.

The general conditions of health in developing countries today are not dissimilar from conditions existing in Europe and the United States 50 or 100 years ago. Chaudhuri observed that "masses of children in India, especially in the slums of large cities, know nothing of life but the pain and lassitude of hunger. Children do not die only of hunger, but also of lack of care and unhygienic conditions. Many children have no home or shelter at all. Many live in the streets of the town and sleep on the pavement" (*10*).

Table 3. The number of hospital beds per 1000 population in various countries (1957–60). Data from (*17*).

Country	Beds per 1000
Canada	10.6
United States	9.1
Gabon	6.6
Colombia	4.9
Congo (Brazzaville)	4.5
Jamaica	4.2
Uruguay	3.9
South Africa	3.6
Chile	3.5
Ceylon	3.1
Bechuanaland	2.9
Ecuador	2.2
Angola	2.1
El Salvador	2.0
Togo	1.8
Ruanda	1.53
Central African Republic	1.5
Basutoland	1.4
Uganda	1.4
Tanzania	1.36
Kenya	1.3
Indonesia	0.84
Thailand	0.84
Mozambique	0.8
Ghana	0.79
Burma	0.58
Nigeria	0.47
Niger	0.43
India	0.24

General living conditions and diet were described by a Joint UNICEF-WHO Committee on Health Policy: "Probably three-fourths of the World's population drink unsafe water, dispose of human excreta recklessly, prepare milk and food dangerously, are constantly exposed to insect and rodent enemies, and live in unfit dwellings" (*11*). These factors, whose adequacy is often taken completely for granted in advanced societies, are responsible for many common medical problems which could be controlled simply by improved environment.

Malnutrition a Principal Problem

Undernutrition and malnutrition constitute perhaps the most serious deterrents to progress in the developing nations. Nutritional defects can limit the physical and mental development of individuals, which in turn will limit their contribution to social and economic progress (*12*). Malnutrition is the major public health problem in the world today. In areas where protein deficiency is the most significant nutritional disorder, there is often, curiously, an abundance of protein. Those people who are malnourished are not aware that they lack protein, and unfortunately protein foods may be available only in a form which is either unacceptable to their customary food pattern or too dear for their normal household budgets.

Since malnutrition retards economic development and interferes with educational progress, it is not only a medical but also a political and social problem. Half the world's population suffers from hunger, defined as insufficient quantity of food, or from malnutrition, which is inadequate quality of diet, or from both. Recent figures indicate that the population increase is outstripping the food supply so that available food per capita is decreasing despite improvements in food production. It must be appreciated that the natural balance of selection which at present functions in many countries is gradually being interfered with by developing preventive medicine and curative services which add to the population explosion.

It is apparent that the answer to many of these problems must involve long-range planning in fields beyond that of the traditional healer. Education of farmers, mechanization of agriculture, use of fertilizers, and improvement of crops and animal varieties must be combined with intelligent programs of birth control and family planning. If malnutrition does not directly or indirectly cause death in the developing countries, it may cause physical and mental stunting and make individuals listless and incapable of vigorous activity.

Birth rates tend to fall whenever standards of living rise. Impairment of social and economic growth is related to nutritional problems, and with the passage of time one can add to the other in a vicious circle. The solution, therefore, must be broadly based, with the knowledge that nutrition may very well be the key factor.

Those most susceptible to protein deficiency are infants, pre-school children, and lactating and pregnant women. The amount of protein necessary for growth and development of body tissues at these critical periods is very great. Emphasis must be placed on the cultural patterns which determine what foods are available, how they are prepared, and who may eat them.

Protein quality is assayed on a scale of biological value, the perfect protein food being given a value of 100. Milk, eggs, fish, and beef have very high values. Although cereal grain, oil seeds, and legumes have somewhat lower values, these can be upgraded by means of processing and proper mixing with other foods.

In many countries high-value proteins are generally not available or too costly for people with low incomes. The usual diet is composed of cereal grains or starchy foods, which may provide enough calories but which contain less than 15 percent protein. It would require an impossibly large intake of these foods to fulfill daily requirements. It is urgent that the poor, uneducated person be assisted in appreciating the fact that he and his children are malnourished and be given information on the utilization of his existing food resources. Local governments must similarly first recognize that this constitutes a major problem before they seek a solution.

Overseas Financial Support
Is Not the Solution

Developing countries of Africa, Asia, and Latin America at present lack the technical and financial resources to achieve the level of social and economic advancement they desire. The advanced countries must recognize both humanitarian and international obligations toward the less-favored countries. These obligations are not simply a matter of introducing financial aid from abroad.

The management of medical problems involves a consideration of nature's delicate balance and an understanding of the social-economic-political structures of nations embued with the desire to advance, as well as an awareness of the problems of altering fundamental traditional structures. The ultimate answer lies in the field of education, which will be developed with the passage of time.

The world is divided into countries that are rich and countries that are poor, and the medical problems in each of these categories are distinctly different. The rich countries have more than enough doctors, nurses, and technicians; there are drugs, hospital beds, food, and equipment in abundance, reliable sources of water and milk, good sanitation, high standards of general education, adequate transportation and communication, and a reasonable per-capita income to insure a high standard of living. These factors represent a historical development of gradually improved socio-economic conditions, in the course of which medical problems were systematically approached and solved. While medical facilities were being improved in the developed countries and adequate personnel trained, environmental improvements independently alleviated many of the public health problems.

In the countries of Africa, Asia, and Latin America the present situation can be described in completely contrasting terms. The discrepancy between the two worlds is only in part a matter of finances. Money alone will not completely solve these complex problems. In the developing countries an improvement is needed in the general attitude toward health and disease, which ultimately is a factor of education. Long-standing customs and superstition govern much of what is currently thought and practiced in health matters. As standards of living improve, the bases for many medical problems will be eradicated. As the numbers of trained medical workers increase and the general level of education improves, the problems here described will be altered.

Is There a Solution?

The basic problems of medicine can be approached with simple, effective, scientifically guided modern methods, predominantly preventive, applied in spite of adverse circumstances. At the moment the health problems facing a surprisingly small number of workers with drastically limited facilities are staggering. There are simply too many extremely ill patients to be managed under conditions far removed from the ideal. There is no prospect of an early solution. The application of available modern methods would save many lives, especially in early infancy and childhood. But, unless the trend is modified by careful planning, birth rates will continue to be high, and total numbers in the population will consume available food supplies and add to the already crowded schools and hospitals.

Increasing urbanization will create more unemployment and extend the un-healthy conditions in and around the towns and cities. Until mechanization is introduced in force, agricultural production cannot be developed, and food shortages will persist or become worse. It can be predicted that the numbers of trained teachers and schools will continue to be insufficient to cope with the population's growing concern with education, and there will be an increase in the number of discontented people. Training facilities are inadequate at all levels of medical education as well.

There is a need for trained individuals in every field—teachers, lawyers, agriculturalists, administrators, and so forth. Within governments various ministries are competing for limited funds, and within educational structures various departments are competing for the few well-qualified people available. Time will provide many of the solutions, but the interim growth pains and developmental processes will be plagued by difficulties.

Paradoxically, the highly developed nations are ill prepared to provide the developing countries with needed assistance in health matters (13). Medical graduates from advanced countries are often poorly qualified to assist in the development of health services in these other countries because, in their training, curative medicine has been stressed to the neglect of preventive and public health medicine. Ultimately, all mankind will benefit from modern medical advances, but present-day research is distant from such urgent considerations as the prevention of severe childhood malnutrition or the control of endemic bilharzia.

Conclusions and Summary

There can be no immediate solution to the medical problems of the developing countries. Priorities are demanded, and it must be acknowledged that in allocation of medical priorities certain compromises are required. It can be hoped that the least detrimental compromises will be selected. Careful planning of health services and also of training programs for various medical personnel must not rely on what exists in developed countries, because those facilities and programs may be completely inappropriate to other situations.

At the same time as inroads are made into the preventable conditions which now claim thousands of young lives, programs of birth control and improvement of agricultural methods must be emphasized. The reduced morbidity and mortality which results from immunization against childhood infectious diseases, smallpox, and tuberculosis must be borne in mind in overall planning for schools and general health services. Inexpensive and practical programs that could be managed by medical personnel who are not highly trained should be considered.

As the benefits of technical development gradually reach the urbanizing population living under poor social and hygienic conditions, changes in the disease picture must be anticipated. Those involved with planning and training must understand various cultural influences so that the transiticn period can be made as painless as possible. Certain seemingly attractive Western **procedures should be guarded against if they are not practical. For instance,** a common tendency is to build large modern hospitals throughout the land with disregard for the fact that these hospitals cannot possibly be staffed, equipped, or maintained because of shortages of trained people and available funds (14). This has been called an "edifice complex" and is unfortunately found in many developing regions, stimulated often by ill-considered advice from overseas experts.

At the same time as medical services are being improved, it is extremely important to document the improvements by means of carefully recorded statistics. Guidance in necessary methods for documentation should be sought early in the development of medical care (15). Obviously it is vital to determine what and where the major medical problems are so that programs will be designed to attack them. Once the problems are sorted out, available resources can be allocated and preventive measures and health education can be aimed at specific aspects of public health.

Many general statements have been made to describe the medical problems in the developing countries of the world. There is a need to particularize the problems and approach the specific manifestations of disease with knowledge of local conditions and resources. Accepted textbook solutions no longer apply in the field, and the ultimate solution may be along lines which are completely unique and nontraditional. **To break the usual rules may be the only practical means to solve the problem at hand, and modified common sense must often replace modern technology. The practical variations on the general theme described here make medical work in developing countries interesting, exciting, and rewarding.**

References and Notes

1. D. B. Jelliffe, *Lancet* **1965-II**, 229 (1965).
2. L. K. Musoke, *Arch. Disease Childhood* **36**, 305 (1961).
3. S. Mudd, Ed., *The Population Crisis and the Use of World Resources* (Indiana Univ. Press, Bloomington, 1964).
4. N. R. E. Fendall, *Public Health Rept. U.S.* **78**, 979 (1963).
5. D. S. H. Cannon and V. J. Hartfield, *J. Obstet. Gynaecol. Brit. Commonwealth* **71**, 940 (1964); N. R. E. Fendall, *J. Trop. Med. Hyg.* **68**, 12 (1965).
6. N. R. E. Fendall, *E. African Med. J.* **37**, 171 (1960).
7. M. H. King, Ed., "Medical Care in Developing Countries" (Makerere Univ. Press, Kampala, Uganda, 1966).
8. C. M. Arensberg and A. H. Niehoff, "Technical Cooperation and Cultural Reality" (Agency for International Development, U.S. Dept. of State, Washington, D.C., 1963).
9. D. B. Jelliffe, *Pediatrics* **16**, 398 (1955).
10. K. C. Chaudhuri, *Indian J. Pediat.* **18**, 54 (1951).
11. UNICEF-WHO Joint Committee on Health Policy, 6th Session, May 1953.
12. R. E. Brown, *E. African Med. J.* **42**, 584 (1965); A. N. Davison and J. Dobbing, *Brit. Med. Bull.* **22**, 40 (1966).
13. T. H. Weller, *W. Indian Med. J.* **10**, 73 (1961).
14. M. G. Candau, *World Health Org. Chron.* **19**, 423 (1965).
15. R. F. A. Dean, *J. Trop. Med. Hyg.* **57**, 283 (1954).
16. E. C. Long "Health problems in Africa with particular reference to East Africa" (mimeograph, 1965).
17. *World Health Situation, 2nd Report, 1957–1960* (World Health Organization Official Records No. 122, Geneva, 1963).
18. I thank R. Wellingham of the Medical Illustration Department, Mulago Hospital, for his photographs and for assisting in the reproduction of the photographs which were provided by Professor D. B. Jelliffe through the courtesy of the UNICEF files. Reference has also been made in the preparation of this article to E. C. Long (*16*). The author is supported by NIH grant AI-16764-01.

Eradication of Infectious Diseases

"Control" is an unending operation. After
"eradication," no further effort is required.

T. Aidan Cockburn

"Eradication" of infectious disease as a concept in public health has been advanced only within the past two decades, yet it is replacing "control" as an objective. The meaning of the term varies with the user, and the difficulties of achieving eradication, in any form, are usually underestimated. In this article (1) my own definition of eradication is offered, the difficulties common to all schemes of eradication are discussed, the significance of animal parasites in this connection is outlined, and brief comments are offered on selected eradication schemes.

Definition

In my definition, eradication is the extinction of the pathogen that causes the infectious disease in question; so long as a single member of the species survives, then eradication has not been accomplished. The definition implies action on a world-wide scale, but world eradication has not yet been achieved for any infection. "Regional eradication" implies a basically unstable situation, because at any time the infection may be reintroduced by carriers or vectors from outside. The

The author is Assistant Commissioner of Health, City Hall, Cincinnati, Ohio.

occurrence of occasional small episodes of infection in a cleared area does not invalidate the claim that regional eradication has been achieved in that area, provided the infection was imported. For areas where vectors are present but without the parasite, one may still claim eradication—as, for example, in Sardinia where there are anopheles without the *Plasmodium*, and in the United States where there are *Aedes aegypti* without the yellow fever virus. In South America, yellow fever virus cannot be eradicated, since it is endemic in the monkey population of the forest; however, eradication of the domestic vector *A. aegypti* from the continent is under way, and this situation could be defined as "urban" eradication of yellow fever, and "regional" eradication of the mosquito.

Even if world-wide eradication of an infection is achieved, there is the possibility that a similar infection may evolve from related organisms still existing in nature after measures of eradication have been halted.

There is an essential difference between the concepts of eradication and control. Once eradication is achieved, the infection is gone forever, and the costly burden of recurring control measures may be dropped. Eradication can, therefore, be regarded as that state in which the infection does not return

Science, April 7, 1961, Vol.133, No.3457, pp. 1050-1058.

from infected areas after control measures have been abandoned. If procedures have to be continued to prevent return of the infection, then the state is one of control and not eradication.

Some pathogens persist in the body for long periods of time, and, strictly speaking, eradication has not been accomplished until the last parasite has died. However, in regional eradication, the practical definition can be used, and each infection can be judged independently. For example, in Brill's disease the rickettsiae persist in the body for very many years; in the United States, there must be people who became infected abroad and who are still carrying the pathogen, yet the infection must not be regarded as established here, since the chances of transmission are remote. Similarly, in malaria the parasite can persist in the body for years; many people in the United States are infected, but because the likelihood of transmission is very small, even without control measures, eradication can be claimed. The situation is different in an area where conditions favor the transmission of malaria; should eradication measures based on mosquito control be abandoned while the parasite still persists in the human host, then, even though the disease has not been reported for some time, there is a possibility of a recurrence of transmission, and the claim of eradication is not justified. In world eradication programs, the strictest adherence to the definition should be maintained; thus, in the case of smallpox virus, which can live for many months on infected clothing, a time allowance on this scale should be made after all other signs of the infection have disappeared. In malaria, before eradication as defined here can be claimed, there must be many years' surveillance after the last case has been diagnosed.

The definition given above is in general agreement with the World Health Organization's definition for malaria eradication. In its original form the World Health Organization definition was interpreted (2) as meaning "the ending of the transmission of malaria and the elimination of the reservoir of infective cases in a campaign limited in time and carried to such a degree of perfection that, when it comes to an end, there is no resumption of transmission." The criteria of malaria eradication to be adopted included adequately demonstrated absence of transmission and endemicity for a period of at least three years, in at least the last two of which no specific general measures of anopheline control and no routine chemtherapy had been applied (3). The World Health Organization definition was modified still further to give more precision to the surveillance requirements (4), but it still does not go so far as to include the final elimination of the last parasite and does not mention related infections in animals or the theoretical possibility that the infection may evolve again.

History

Deliberate attempts to stamp out infectious diseases began in the closing years of the last century. In 1892, an animal infection, contagious pleuropneumonia of cattle, was declared eradicated from the United States after a campaign that lasted five years and cost nearly two million dollars (5). In England, in 1896, rabies was eradicated successfully by enforcing a muzzling order for all dogs for one year and enforcing a six months' quarantine for all dogs and cats. In 1917, the decision was made to eradicate bovine tuberculosis in the United States, under the Federal-State Cooperative Plan for Eradication of Bovine Tuberculosis. The program called for the testing of all cattle in the United States and the killing of the reactors, and it was extremely costly both in money and in animals. The campaign was not pushed to the extreme required for eradication, and it was unsuccessful in that bovine tuberculosis still exists in this country (5). Yellow fever was eliminated from Cuba in the first decade of this century by antimosquito measures, and this gave rise to such high hopes that in 1914 Gorgas could state that world eradication of the disease not only was practical but could be achieved at a reasonable cost (6). With the discovery of forest yellow fever, these hopes were disappointed and the idea of eradication was discredited.

Modern ideas on eradication begin with the work of Soper and his colleagues in South America. In 1930, some dangerous African mosquitoes, *Anopheles gambiae*, were discovered in Brazil by Shannon, and in a few years these had spread and were the vectors responsible for a disastrous epidemic of malaria in the northeast section of the country. A program to eradicate every single specimen was begun in 1939, and by 1941 the task had been completed (7). Side by side with this program, the control of *Aedes aegypti* mosquitoes had progressed so well that in 1942 Soper was encouraged to propose eradication instead of control. The following year, Bolivia was the first country to proclaim that this goal had been reached (6). Since that time the countries of South America have joined forces, aiming for complete continental eradication. By 1959, substantial areas had been cleared (8) (Fig. 1).

These successes with mosquito eradication made *eradication* a respectable term once more, so that world eradication of smallpox and malaria are now proclaimed aims of the World Health Organization, in programs supported by many countries and backed financially by the United States. At present, eradication is described as the aim in many other infectious-disease projects.

Basic Program Needs

All eradication programs have many needs in common. These include the need for political stability, for popular support, for adequate organization, for logistic and technical backing, and usually for an efficient quarantine system to prevent reinfection of the cleared area. Most important of all, the efforts must be pushed to the limit until the last parasite has been eliminated. The last 5 percent is as important as the first 95 percent. Anything less than 100 percent is not eradication.

Political stability. Eradication programs are usually long-term, often requiring international cooperation. Obviously, nations work together better if they are at peace and friendly. Political upheaval and war usually disrupt such projects, and in countries like Tibet, where fighting is in progress, eradication programs are not likely to succeed. However, the recent collaboration of so many countries on issues such as malaria and smallpox has shown that much can be done even in a troubled world.

Popular support. Obviously, a program of eradication, with all its costs and inconvenience, will not be successful if it does not have popular support, even in a small country. On a world scale, this task of insuring popular support might well daunt the most fervid supporter of the principle were it not for the United Nations. It is only through the United Nations that the two programs of smallpox and malaria control have been adopted by the majority of people, and even then it is clear that some of the nations involved have only a lukewarm interest in the project, while mainland China, biggest of all countries, with its 600 million people, is not even in the United Nations.

Great difficulty arises in areas where an infection of global or continental significance is of no particular public health importance locally. It is difficult to persuade a community to put up the funds and make the effort required for something that causes little local inconvenience. For example, a few countries joined in malaria eradication only after some hesitation; for them, malaria was simply not a public health problem, and there was no public pressure to organize expensive measures to benefit neighboring countries.

The costly and time-consuming efforts made to eradicate *Aedes aegypti* mosquitoes in urban areas have been substantially successful in South America (8), but as there is no yellow fever in the United States, there is no public pressure to get rid of *Aedes aegypti* mosquitoes there (Fig. 1). None the less, the United States has an international obligation to eradicate this species of mosquito, for its representatives supported and voted for the resolution in the first meeting of the Directing Council of the Pan American Sanitary Organization, a meeting in which it was resolved that *Aedes aegypti* mosquitoes must be eradicated from the Americas (9). As long as there are *Aedes aegypti* mosquitoes in North America, there will always be a likelihood that they will reinfect the areas in South America that have been cleared.

Syphilis might be eradicated from the United States by means of antibiotics and technical services already available, but it is unlikely that the public would accept an eradication program.

Technology. Eradication in any particular country may be impractical because the government lacks the funds or the personnel or the equipment or the organization. In certain nations of Africa, Southeast Asia, and other parts of the tropics, the number of physicians and other trained personnel may be too small even for routine tasks, let alone the difficult and burdensome techniques of eradication. When the total national budget is inadequate, the proportion allotted for health purposes is usually small.

Equipment may be scarce, not to mention spare parts and repair technicians. Transport is frequently difficult because of a scarcity of vehicles and drivers and even of passable roads. For eradication it is not enough to reach most places; one must reach all places. Usually 95 percent are reasonably accessible, but the remaining 5 percent are equally important.

The administrative organization of the national health department in the country undertaking eradication procedures must be strong enough to take the load. Usually, in underdeveloped countries, the department is so small that one man does work that should be done by ten. Frequently major duties are left to clerks, since no one else is available. To expect these overworked people to take on responsibility for a large additional program is to be overoptimistic.

It might be expected that foreign aid would supply the needed technicians, administrators, equipment, and supplies. This it can do to a large extent, but there is a crucial service that can be performed only by the host nation itself. For example, the first stages of a program are usually easy enough, with teams of workers, imported or trained by foreign technicians, spraying the countryside with insecticides, giving injections or vaccinations, or handing out pills, and with everyone pleased as the disease in question recedes. But when the foreign teams depart, the task of finishing the job and of continuing surveillance falls to the host government. Then the government needs an efficient health service, with trained doctors who, in the course of their duties, will spot and report any recurrence of the disease. This program of surveillance has to be carried on for years in order that recurrences may be promptly discovered and stamped out in time. This task may be beyond the scope of any foreign aid, and all too often the national health department simply cannot carry it out. The final results over a ten-year period might well be especially disappointing if the program had started

95

off well.

Reintroduction of a pathogen is an obvious danger where the operation is limited to a country or a continent, with infection remaining in regions outside. The usual method is to enforce quarantine measures, but the volume and nature of travel nowadays, especially by air, is making quarantine increasingly ineffective.

Biologic Factors in Eradication

On the basis of modern evolutionary theory it may be assumed that all human infections are derived from ancestral animal infections, since man himself was once a nonhuman animal. *All human infections have related pathogens still existing in animal hosts, and the nature of these animal pathogens to a large extent decides whether or not an infection can be eradicated.* Man belongs to the order Primates, and his relations the apes, the monkeys, and other primates share with him parasites that have been handed from one generation to another from their common primate ancestor. Elsewhere it has been suggested that these parasites include the intestinal protozoa, pinworms, herpes virus, malaria parasites, and so on (*10*, theory 2). In addition, there is a sharing of parasites among animals in intimate contact in the same ecology, as, for example, between man and his domestic animals. Sometimes this sharing is continued without change in the form of the parasite, and a new form of zoonoses is established, while in other instances a newly parasitized species of host will convey the parasite within its own population and in time a new strain will be selected that is largely specific to that host. Elsewhere it has been suggested that this is the way in which the pox viruses evolved among the animals brought together into man's ecology when man settled down and domesticated animals (*10*, theory 6).

Some of these relationships are close indeed; others are not so close, and some are fairly distant. When any eradication of an infection is contemplated, it is essential that the evolution of the agent be studied to determine the nature of these relationships and the effect they will have on the final result of the program. Related animal infections can be grouped as follows.

1) *Identical.* These infections are the zoonoses. From the point of view of eradication they can be subdivided into infections of wild animals and infections of domestic animals. If wild animals are involved (as in rabies, yellow fever, plague, rickettsial infections, or salmonella infections), then eradication will be difficult if not impossible. If only domestic animals are involved (as in *Mycobacterium bovis* infections, brucellosis, and glanders), then "regional" eradication is easy, for all that is necessary is to test the animals and kill the reactors, or else immunize the stock. However, research may show that most infections in domestic animals occur also in wild animals, and that world eradication may be impossible.

2) *Closely related.* In nature, closely related species sharing the same ecologies compete with one another, and this must happen with parasites also. Possibly the distribution of each species is to a certain extent dependent on this interspecific competition. A zoonosis like yellow fever is related to a wide range of other arbor viruses and almost certainly is affected by them. This is the explanation sometimes proposed for the absence of yellow fever in India, where the facilities for spreading have existed for at least 2000 years. If yellow fever virus were completely eradicated from Africa, it might well be that related, competing viruses would emerge prominently in that area.

Parasites similar to malaria parasites of man exist in apes and monkeys. The question as to whether they are identical is a matter of urgent research at the moment, but in any event there is no

96

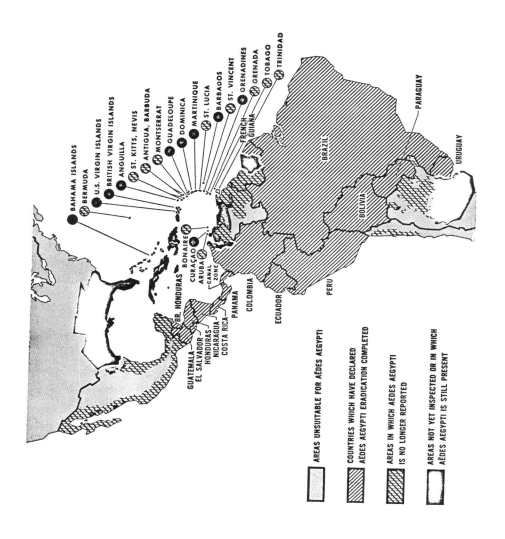

Fig. 1. Status of the *Aedes aegypti* eradication campaign in the Western Hemisphere in December 1960. "*Aedes aegypti* eradication completed" signifies that eradication has been verified in accordance with the standards established by the Pan American Sanitary Bureau. (Pan American Health Organization)

question but that man can be infected with these parasites (4). Should the human malaria parasites be eradicated but not the vectors, then, after the eradication measures had been halted, man would be reinfected from the primates, if these have identical parasites, or if they have not, over a period of decades human parasites might re-evolve from parasites of the primate reservoirs. In either case, human malaria would be likely to reappear.

As to treponemal infections, the various species are probably mere variants of one basic organism (11). Interspecific competition may partially determine whether a population contracts yaws or syphilis. Eradication of yaws will probably result in an increase in syphilis.

3) *Substantially different.* An infection such as smallpox is closely related to infections in other animals in man's immediate ecology—animals such as mice, cows, horses, sheep, or chickens. It is possible that all of these infections derive from a radiation of a single organism that occurred at the time man first settled down and domesticated animals (10, theory 6). These organisms are now so highly adapted to their hosts, and conditions have so changed from those under which they evolved, that the possibility that smallpox would re-evolve appears to be remote. The chances, therefore, of permanent eradication of the infection seem good.

4) *Very remote relationships.* Organisms like the leprosy bacillus have probably been symbiotes of man and his predecessors over many millions of years, are closely adapted to man, and have no close relations in other animals. Once eradicated, the chance of their re-evolving is extremely small.

It is becoming increasingly recognized that an organism that has radiated into many species is more capable biologically of surviving than one which has only a few species (12). A large organismal group is well equipped to withstand the adversities of changing environments and to adapt to new conditions as they arise. This strength arises from the variety of genetic mechanisms present in the radiation, in contrast to the limited range of mechanisms for organismal groups with only a few species. In general, wide radiations are found mainly in the locations of origin of the ancestral organism, and only single species or narrow radiations are found in areas where the organism has been newly introduced, for it takes considerable time for new species to appear. Eradication procedures will therefore be easier to complete and more successful, in long-term effects, when employed against species of parasite or insect vector that have colonized the area in recent times than when employed against species that have been established there perhaps for millions of years.

The program to eradicate *Anopheles gambiae* in Brazil was a success, possibly because the mosquito was an introduced species, while a similar program against *A. labranchiae* in Sardinia was a failure in the sense that the mosquito species was not completely eliminated, because the anopheles in Sardinia were indigenous to the island and probably had been there many thousands or even millions of years (13). In addition to the mosquitoes which have become adapted to feeding on man within recent times, there was the original native stock, still feeding on wild animals. These mosquitoes of the original stock were not greatly affected by the eradication program and, presumably, form a reservoir from which fresh strains of domestic mosquitoes will evolve now that the program has terminated. Similarly, eradication of *Aedes aegypti* is proceeding very well in South America, where it probably is a newcomer of only some 400 years' standing, and where wild strains in the forest are as yet unknown. The story would be different should a similar program be attempted in East Africa, where wild strains are well established in the forest.

It is sometimes said that when an organism has been reduced to very small numbers it cannot survive and will die out spontaneously. This idea is of practical importance in eradication programs, for the last few sources of infection are difficult to reach. It is probably often true as applied to animals that are genetically diploid, but not necessarily so with microorganisms that are haploid. For example, the whooping cranes are probably doomed to extinction merely because there are only about 40 of them left alive. Deleterious or lethal mutations will occur occasionally in them; since most will be recessive, those that do not result in death will be stored away without expressing themselves. The close inbreeding that occurs in so small a population as 40 will result in these recessive deleterious mutations becoming demonstrated in the phenotype, so that the birds will become increasingly unfit to survive. They will be saved only if the environment changes substantially in their favor.

With haploid organisms, this is not the case, for any mutation is likely to be expressed immediately in the phenotype, and if the mutation is sufficiently deleterious, the individual organism will fail to survive. The future population of the haploid organism will consist only of the descendants of those without the mutation, so that small numbers do not necessarily indicate that the population is doomed to become extinct.

In a vector-borne infection, the pathogen will die out if the density of the vector is too low. This is a well-recognized phenomenon in malaria, yellow fever, plague, and filaria, and usually in control programs there are indices, such as the *aegypti* or the *cheopis* indices, of the permissible levels of vector densities for control of the infections. Should the numbers of these vectors be kept permanently below the threshold levels, then in time the pathogens will be eradicated. However, in any large country there may be small local pockets where high density levels of the vectors may persist, even though the general level for the area is low, and in an eradication program these must be sought for diligently. These pockets will not be so important in an infection like yellow fever, where the infectious process in the host is brief and the host population soon becomes immune to the pathogen, but they can be extremely important in malaria and filaria, where the host can carry the parasites for years.

Certain infections have been known to dwindle to small numbers and then disappear spontaneously. The extinction, however, was not due to the parasite population's falling below a hypothetical numerical threshold but to the parasites' having lost their fitness to survive in the environment. "Fitness" can be defined as an organism's capacity to produce regularly as many viable members in one generation as in the preceding generation, for if it produces fewer in each succeeding generation it will become extinct. Changes in environment and in behavior in places such as England and the United States in the past hundred years have tipped the balance against many parasites such as lice, the malaria parasite, the cholera vibrio, bubonic plague bacilli, and tubercle bacilli, and these infections, if they have not completely disappeared, are becoming less and less frequent. This process is clearly due to environmental changes and not to mere smallness in numbers of the parasites; the paucity of the organisms in the closing stages is merely the final step in a continuing process.

In a country where conditions favor the parasite, the elimination of this last trace of the infection can be extremely troublesome; yet until it has been accomplished, the campaign will not be a success. If the operating procedures are stopped prematurely, the infection will return, and either the program will have to be recommenced or else all the effort will have been wasted. In Ceylon, antimosquito measures were commenced in 1945 with the then newly available residual insecticide DDT, and the results exceeded expectations, for within one year there had been a dramatic fall in the incidence of malaria. After a while the general spraying was stopped because of the increasing resistance of the mosquitoes, and reliance was placed on a surveillance system, with spraying of local infected areas. However, the malaria did not dwindle and vanish as expected but continued, and at the end of ten years it was still present in certain small foci (*14*). Malaria had been controlled but not eradicated. More vigorous measures are now being taken to discover and deal with these small foci.

The story has been much the same in Haiti, where yaws eradication is being attempted (Fig. 2). There had been 45,356 cases of yaws reported in 1949 in the island; in 1950 the general population had been given penicillin, and in 1953 only about 400 cases of yaws could be found. Every year since then the program has continued, and the early eradication of yaws has been eagerly expected, but each year up to 1959 there continued to be a hard core of about 300 cases (*8, 15*). In nearby Jamaica, the yaws eradication program had made considerable progress when the teams for checking and surveillance were withdrawn prematurely. In 1959, 415 new cases of infectious yaws were reported, and the program is to be resumed (*8*).

This kind of experience underlines the difficulties in the later stages of an eradication program. Once the first enthusiasm for the program has dwindled **and the disease to a large extent has disappeared, it is difficult to keep the teams in the field and at a high level of efficiency.** The mode of transmission may be difficult to see, so that cases pop up in unexpected places, and often supreme efforts are necessary to bring the transmitting agent to light. Soper has called this level of infectivity the "threshold of visibility" below which the mode of transmission of the infection cannot be seen with routine methods (*16*), and it is this that causes campaigns to drag on year after year when, according to all expectations, they should have been completed.

Eradication in Practice

Small islands are obviously the places where eradication efforts can best be made, for there the problems are clearcut and quarantine measures are easiest to enforce. In England, several infections have been deliberately eliminated, including smallpox, rabies, and glanders, while typhus, plague, relapsing fever, malaria, cholera, and possibly leprosy have vanished, probably as a result of changing environments and habits. Smallpox was everywhere in England in the 18th century, but in 1867 vaccination was made compulsory. By 1871 the annual death rate per million people was down to 1012, and in the ten-year period 1911–1920, not a single death was reported. However, a very mild form was common during the 1920's (*17*). Vaccination is no longer compulsory, and the immunity status of the nation is no longer so high, so that introduced infections every few years cause small outbreaks, but smallpox still is not an endemic disease.

Glanders in England was eliminated by slaughtering all horses with the infection.

There has been almost no plague in England since the 17th century, partially as a result of the change in the species of rats in the island, and partially because of the vigorous campaigns at ports to keep out foreign rats. However, in the early 1900's, sylvatic plague was discovered in East Anglia, where a handful of human cases was diagnosed, and this persisted for a few years until it died out spontaneously. Presumably it had been introduced at a nearby port.

Higher standards of living and greater cleanliness were responsible for the disappearance of typhus and relapsing fever, for body-lice infestations are uncommon, although infestation with head lice still is found. Cholera has not been seen since the 1860's as a consequence of improvements in sewage disposal and management of water supply. Malaria has disappeared, partially because of the draining of the marshes and partially because its foothold in the country was always precarious as a result of the low summer temperatures. Also, the vector mosquitoes prefer feeding on animals to feeding on human beings.

Ceylon is another island with a good record of eradication of infections. Within the past 20 years, smallpox, plague, and cholera have all been wiped out, although each is likely to be reintroduced from time to time from India, which is only 18 miles away, across the Palk Strait. Smallpox was dealt with by maintaining high levels of vaccination immunity. Cholera and plague were both introduced infections which responded well to orthodox public health measures. The plague-carrying fleas had been imported from India and were limited to the port area of Colombo and to one or two small sites on the coast; rat-control measures have caused the infection to die out (18).

As for eradication on a regional scale, in America north of Mexico, several infections have disappeared. The last reported case of smallpox authenticated by isolation of the virus was in 1949 in Hidalgo County, Texas (19). Malaria dwindled with drainage of swamps and mosquito-proofing of homes. Control projects such as those of the Tennessee Valley Authority and the Malaria Control in War Areas were also effective, so that by the end of World War II the surprising discovery was made that, without widespread use of DDT, malaria as an indigenous infection had practically ceased to exist, although it is continually being imported (20).

Yellow fever was easily eradicated in the United States, once the mosquito vector had been identified, and so far it

has not been reintroduced. The last cases of yellow fever were in New Orleans in 1905, when about 1000 deaths occurred (6). There has been no cholera for nearly 100 years.

Smallpox

Smallpox is the ideal target for an eradication program on a world scale. Since the layman, terrified by its threat, can see·that it is infectious, control and eradication measures usually receive full backing, even in primitive areas. Vaccination gives a solid immunity for about three to five years and a modified immunity for life. The vaccine is easy to make on a mass scale, even under field conditions, and remains potent for seven to ten days, without refrigeration, in the "wet" form and for six months to a year in the "dry" form. Little in the way of highly skilled technical help is required, except for overall direction and evaluation, for the techniques of vaccination are simple (21) (Fig. 3). The chances of the infection's evolving again are small.

Malaria

Malaria has often been described as man's number one killer. The discovery of residual insecticides gave rise to the hope that at long last a way had been found to deal with the menace. The subsequent appearance of resistance to insecticides led to the belief that, if this new weapon was to be effective, it had to be used once and for all, before its edge was blunted by this resistance. The objective of world eradication has been proclaimed by the World Health Organization, supported by the United States, and agreed to by many nations, and programs are now in progress in a number of countries. No one envisioned the task as being easy, but unexpected difficulties are arising. Where transport, communications, health services, and supplies are poor or ineffective, especially in the less developed areas, the campaigns suffer.

The practical difficulties of malaria eradication are so formidable that the time for completing the program with current weapons must be measured in decades rather than in years. At least 20 years will be required and perhaps many more.

This period will be shortened drastically only if research produces new and more efficient techniques of killing insects or eliminating plasmodia on a mass scale. In any country a minimum of ten years' surveillance is necessary to insure that the last parasite has been killed. This was illustrated recently in the United States when a small pocket of infection was found in Oklahoma, several years after the indigenous infection was supposed to have disappeared (22). If this can happen in the United States it is even more likely to occur in countries with primitive health services.

If and when the last plasmodium parasite in a human being has been killed, and eradication on a world scale has apparently been achieved, the next question will be how to deal with similar parasites in animals, particularly monkeys and apes. Elsewhere it has been proposed that human and simian malaria are variants of the one ancestral parasite (10), the ape and monkey plasmodia being closely related to, or even identical to, the human parasites. Recently, natural transmission of simian malaria to human beings has been reported (4), and this opens up the disturbing possibility that malaria is a zoonosis, somewhat like yellow fever. Obviously this matter needs further research. If a simian reservoir does indeed exist, then eradication of malaria as presently contemplated will not be possible.

Poliomyelitis

Eradication of poliomyelitis virus is also being discussed. Production of live attenuated virus for use as an immunizing agent gives some hope that, through oral vaccination of large numbers of individuals, the wild virulent strains will be replaced by harmless strains. What is being suggested is a practical test of a bitterly fought theoretical problem, known to biologists as Gause's principle or the "competitive exclusion" principle of Hardin (23). In its simplest form this can be stated as follows: "Two related species of the same ecology cannot live together in the same place," for one species will have an advantage over the other and in time will replace it. The question in poliomyelitis will be, which species will survive, the virulent wild virus or the vaccine? If it is proposed merely to release doses of the vaccine in the hope that it will spread under its own agency and replace the other virus, then the effort is almost certainly doomed to failure, for the wild strains have been selected under intensely competitive conditions over long periods and presumably are far better adapted to life under natural conditions than is any "hothouse" laboratory strain that is liberated. The all-important capacity to resist adverse circumstances while being transmitted from host to host in nature has been ignored during the passage procedures in the laboratory, for passive transfer by syringe or pipet is not likely to have encouraged the selection of strains resistant to adverse conditions outside the body. As a result, the vaccine virus can be expected to have relatively little capacity to move to new hosts, as compared with the wild strains, and is unlikely to become established as a self-perpetuating organism. The experience of the Russians has shown that about 50 percent of protected persons excrete live vaccine within three to five months after vaccination (24), but in contrast it is well known that during epidemics of the wild strains, almost everyone in a small, intimate community is infected. Experience in the United States indicates that the vaccine virus spreads poorly and does not establish itself as a permanent infection (25). The differences in spread in the U.S.S.R. and in the United States may be related to variations in sanitary conditions.

Elsewhere it has been proposed that for every infection and set of circumstances there is a minimum host population that is necessary to support the infection on a permanent endemic basis (10). The fact that poliomyelitis infection dies out in small communities has been recognized (26). In a large human population, the number of individuals susceptible to the virulent poliomyelitis infection can be reduced below this threshold level by repeated feedings of the competing attenuated and immunizing live virus. When this threshold is passed, the virulent wild virus will automatically die out. The percentage of susceptible individuals in the community that form this threshold population will vary from one population to another, being lower where the chance of person-to-person contact is high, as in areas with, say, 1000 persons per square mile, and high in areas with only five or ten persons per square mile. To state this another way, it may be necessary to immunize 90 percent of the people in a town and only 75 percent in a rural area to reach the threshold level at which the wild virus disappears.

In eradication programs confined to a continent, there will be no means of keeping out reinfecting imported strains, for there is no practical way of detecting carriers of poliovirus. This means that occasional cases of poliomyelitis will occur, but that, at the worst, any epidemic resulting will be small and sharply limited. It does not follow that, if the whole world were brought up to the required level of immunity and the wild strains of virulent virus became extinct, these strains would have been eradicated for good and all further efforts could be abandoned. The circumstances that led to the evolution of the wild strains will presumably still be operative, and natural selection would quickly produce new strains from the vaccine virus, so that the immunizing procedures would have to be maintained indefinitely. By practical definition, this situation would be one of control and not eradication.

Cholera

Cholera as an endemic infection is now confined to small areas of Southeast Asia, principally the Bengal area of India and East Pakistan. Elsewhere it has been suggested that the infection is basically a rural one and is due to the fact that the only sources of water in the dry hot months are the highly polluted "tanks" or ponds of surface water (27). If these tanks were replaced by water supplies from unpolluted sources, then there is a good possibility that cholera would disappear from the world. Of course, Bengal is not unique in having such a situation, and similar choleraic-disease-causing vibrios might evolve in pond water in other parts of the world. Such a situation seems to occur in Indonesia, where repeated outbreaks of "paracholera," due to a different vibrio, are reported. Steps are now being taken to provide the people of Bengal with clean water; if these are successful, cholera may well disappear completely, although paracholera may persist.

Discussion

Eradication has been demonstrated many times to be entirely practical within certain limits, even with the techniques of today. Modern research is proceeding so quickly that many tasks that now seem impossible or extremely tedious and time-consuming may tomorrow be quite simple and quite rapidly performed. Most of the practical difficulties listed earlier in this article may be resolved in one or two decades.

103

Presumably, there will be rapid improvement in such areas as transport, logistics, and the strengthening of health services. Tasks such as the inoculation of people by the tens of millions will be speeded up by machines such as the hypospray jet injector (28). The dosing of people with drugs through additions to food or drink will make mass chemotherapy a practical matter. The development of live vaccines that can be given orally to babies soon after birth may immunize the populations of the world against many viruses. Such techniques, which are emerging in the laboratory today, may be available for use in the field in the near future.

Therefore, we can look forward with confidence to a considerable degree of freedom from infectious diseases at a time not too far in the future. Indeed, if the present pace of research and the present increase in the world's wealth continue, and if we suffer no major calamities such as an atomic war or an uncontrolled population explosion, then it seems reasonable to anticipate that within some measurable time, such as 100 years, all the major infections will have disappeared. This desirable goal will not be easily reached, for the difficulties are many, and unpleasant surprises are inevitable. Most of all there must be very much more research. And even as we are successfully eliminating one set of infections, new ones will almost certainly appear, for we live in a world swarming with potential pathogens in many forms. Evolution is not merely something that happened in the past; it is an essential part of both the present and the future, so that out of all the microorganisms that are continually seeking to invade our bodies, one that is favored by changing conditions will occasionally succeed. Always we will have to be on our guard, watching for signs of danger among the potential pathogens and stamping out the latest comer among them in the small focus in which it is evolving, and before it has the opportunity to spread across the world.

References and Notes

1. This article was prepared while I was in residence at the School of Hygiene and Public Health, Johns Hopkins University, Baltimore, Md., on an epidemiological traineeship provided by the National Institutes of Health, U.S. Public Health Service.
2. *World Health Organization Tech. Rept. Ser. No. 123* (1957).
3. *World Health Organization Tech. Rept. Ser. No. 162* (1959).
4. *World Health Organization Tech. Rept.* (1960).
5. W. A. Hagan, *Ann. Rev. Microbiol.* 12, 127 (1958).
6. G. K. Strode, *Yellow Fever* (McGraw-Hill, New York, 1951).
7. F. L. Soper and D. B. Wilson, *Anopheles gambiae in Brazil 1930–1940* (Rockefeller Foundation, New York, 1943).
8. Director, Pan American Sanitary Bureau, *Annual Report* (Washington, D.C., 1959).
9. Final reports of the first, second, and third meetings of the Directing Council, Pan American Sanitary Organization, *Pan American Sanitary Bureau Publication No. 247* (1950), p. 3.
10. T. A. Cockburn, *Intern. Rec. Med.* 172, 493 (1959).
11. ———, *Bull. World Health Organization*, in press.
12. M. Bates, in *Evolution after Darwin*, S. Tax, Ed. (Univ. of Chicago Press, Chicago, 1960), p. 565.
13. J. A. Logan, *The Sardinian Project* (Johns Hopkins Press, Baltimore, 1953).
14. W. A. Karunaratne, *The Influence of Malaria Control on Vital Statistics in Ceylon* (1959), vol. 62, pp. 79–85.
15. Director, Pan American Sanitary Bureau, annual reports (Washington, D.C., 1950 to 1958).
16. F. L. Soper, *Am. J. Trop. Med. Hyg.* 9, 357 (1960).
17. Report of the Committee on Vaccination, Ministry of Health (His Majesty's Stationery Office, London, 1928).
18. L. F. Hirst, *The Conquest of Plague* (Clarendon, Oxford, 1953).
19. J. V. Irons, T. D. Sullivan, E. B. M. Cook, G. W. Cox, R. A. Hale, *Am. J. Public Health* 43, 25 (1953).
20. L. L. Williams, *Am. J. Trop. Med. Hyg.* 7, 259 (1958).
21. T. A. Cockburn, *Public Health Repts. (U.S.)* 75, 26 (1960).
22. R. L. Kaiser, "Malaria surveillance in the United States," *Proc. World Health Organization Expert Committee on Malaria, Geneva* (1960).
23. G. Hardin, *Science* 131, 1292 (1960).
24. *Chronicle World Health Organization* 14, 137 (1960).
25. H. M. Gelfand, R. LeBlanc, L. Potash, D. L. Clemmer, J. P. Fox, *Am. J. Public Hyg.* 5, 767 (1960).
26. D. Bodian, *Science* 122, 105 (1955).
27. T. A. Cockburn, *Public Health Repts. (U.S.)* 75, 793 (1960).
28. R. Towle, *ibid.* 75, 471 (1960).

THE ECOLOGY OF HUMAN DISEASE

Jacques M. May

American Geographical Society, New York, N. Y.

A famous French playwright once quipped: "A healthy person is nothing but an unrevealed patient." I have a great fondness for this definition, and I think there is much more to it than meets the eye. I like it because it stresses the fact that what we call health is nothing but a struggle between mysterious forces that occur below the horizon. Nothing happens in the visible field that does not stem from deep, invisible, and unknown roots. It has been said that one of the traits that distinguishes man from animals is that man suspects there is another value to the appearance of what he observes. A second reason I like this definition is that it mentions the hidden traits that the challenges of the environment may cause to be revealed in a person when he becomes a patient. We shall see a little later that these hidden traits that really stem from the genetic make-up of the patient are of great importance in our understanding of the ecology of disease and have been far too often neglected in the past in favor of what is merely visible. Thus the French playwright's remark implies that some day the challenges of the environment will reveal the strength and the weakness of the person and give us a measure of his ability to adjust to this environment.

The adjustment of man to the world around him is the study that should interest physicians more than it has in the past. If only patients were to read this paper there would be no need for me to give a definition of disease. However, readers will include physicians also, and I know that physicians are in great need of such a definition.

Disease is that alteration of living cells or tissues that jeopardizes survival in their environment. I like this definition not only because I think I have coined it but also because it introduces the idea of the *environment* in any concept of disease. Indeed the environment is extremely important since one phenomenon that may appear to be disease in one place is not the case in another place. When we find eight or nine million red cells per cubic millimeter in the people living on the highest plateaus of the Andes, we do not consider this pathological because it helps them to survive in that particular environment. If we should make the same observation at sea level, however, we might worry whether this would not overburden the tissues with oxygen, and it might be considered pathological. In the same way an aggressive, mentally ill patient would be more readily acceptable in the environment of a large farm of the Midwest than in a two-and-one-half room apartment on the east side of Manhattan.

This definition stresses as its criterion *survival*, which is, of course, the basic dynamic force of any living thing. I believe it is better to define disease in terms of survival than to define it in terms of health, since health is also a very relative concept. Finally, I think this definition is an opportune reminder that there is no function without structure. It places the phenomenon of

Annals of the New York Academy of Science, 1960, Vol.84, pp. 789-794.

disease in the tissues, where it belongs. We have heard so much in the past 50 years of so-called purely functional diseases, and much time has been wasted in discussing this without referring to the indispensable basis for any function, which is structure. A structure may be nothing more than a cell built around a few molecules, but it is a structure nevertheless. If we remind ourselves that there is no function without structure, most of the discussions about dysfunctions become idle if they are not supported by careful scrutiny of the underlying structure.

Having now defined disease let us explore a bit further and try to find out how disease occurs. This should seem to be a rather simple undertaking. While everybody believes he has a good conception of disease and how it occurs, I do not think our thoughts are as clear on the subject as they ought to be.

Disease, any disease—and let me remind you that by disease I mean maladjustment to the environment—can never occur without the combination of three orders of factors converging in time and space, that is, there must be stimuli from the environment, there must be responses from a host, and there must be the conglomeration of thoughts and traits that we call culture. In order to understand disease and maladjustment, let us review these three orders of factors in succession.

The stimuli from the environment can be classified into physical stimuli, biological stimuli, and emotional stimuli. Of course these three classes of stimuli interpenetrate each other, and this is only a convenient way of presenting the subject. Strangely enough we know very little of the real effect of physical stimuli on man. It has always been extremely difficult in the past to dissociate what is really the action of climate from the action of the biotics that occur in these climates. Some time ago Douglas Lee built up an interesting curve showing the combinations of temperature and humidity that result in comfort and well-being in most human individuals. Below or beyond certain areas on the curve, physical stress occurs that may eventually lead to death. Except for these computations little else is known. We can assume only that unchartered forces occur that are specific to certain areas on the surface of the earth that must have an enormous importance in eliciting survival-worthy responses from, or on the contrary, cause the detrimental alteration of living tissues. For example the so-called solar flares that we know can disturb electronic communications on the surface of the earth are probably not ineffective in disturbing electronic communication inside the tissues. At least it seems to me that it would be improvident on our part not to give them some credit and to explore these new stimuli from the point of view of their action on man. We know very little about the forces that combine to create the climate at any given point of the earth and about their effect on living things, man, and the surrounding biotics upon which man is so very dependent in so many ways.

If we now consider the action of these biotics, their challenges are numerous and, of course, much better known. I go as far as to say that my generation has been quite guilty in giving them primordial importance in our concept of disease. I think that we have been very near to committing the major sin in

106

disease etiology, that is, to consider that what we call disease may have a single cause. There is no such thing. A multiplicity of causes are always needed to produce that alteration of tissues creating maladjustment. These biotics, many of them more or less harmful parasites of our tissues, live in very definite environments of which we know little; their ecology is of great importance in our understanding of transmissible diseases. Last but not least we must always remember that these biotics live in societies like all living things, and that this social structure of very small or very large living objects dominates the picture. An example of this could be given by a study of what happens when we introduce *Penicillium notatum* or streptomycin into a society of bacteria.

In the same way that I gave to physicians my definition of disease, I think I should give to social scientists my concept of society. From the ecologist's point of view society is an organization of living things based on a pattern of mutual tolerance that occurs for a brief period of time after the dynamism of reciprocal exclusion has been temporarily exhausted. If we accept the idea that this is at least one aspect of what we call society, it is no wonder that every single unit living under such a climate will experience considerable stresses. By this I mean that stressful situations will occur and that, depending upon the host, these stressful situations may or may not translate themselves into actual physiological stress. Thus we have a brief sketch of the environmental stimuli that make up one third of the factors needed to produce that alteration of tissues that we call disease.

The second term of this equation is the host. I stress that I think this subject is the field of the future. Our forefathers had a good awareness of the importance of the individual, which they called "the terrain," in shaping the clinical forms of disease. Following the enlightening Pasteurian discoveries we have been mesmerized by the action of a single stimulus to produce disease, and have forgotten completely to explore the reasons that make the host respond in the way he does.

One of the fondest memories I have of my early days at medical school is that of my bewilderment when a professor of bacteriology told us that it was impossible to inoculate leprosy into animals and, vice versa, that certain bacteria that found themselves quite at home with animals could not, if inoculated into the human system, produce the symptoms that were observable in animals. Although I did not realize it at that time, this introduced the very potent idea of the genetic make-up of the host, and its importance in the kind of responses offered to environmental stimuli by the host. It is as though I had on a table three dolls, one of glass, another of celluloid, and a third of steel, and I chose to hit the three dolls with a hammer, using equal strength. The first doll would break, the second would scar, and the third would emit a pleasant musical sound.

This concept should never be forgotten (1) when we study the occurrence of transmissible diseases and the response of populations to the biological stimuli mentioned above; (2) when we study degenerative diseases and the response of individuals to the absorption of certain foods and poisons; and (3) when we study the so-called field of behavioral disorders in which we have had such a great tendency in the past to limit our investigations to stimuli, completely neglecting the more important host and the reasons for his responses.

In recent years we have learned to recognize the importance of certain blood groups, meaning certain genes, in increasing or diminishing our susceptibility to such diseases as duodenal peptic ulcer or carcinoma of the colon. We have learned the importance of the type of hemoglobin possessed by certain persons in relation to their susceptibility to malaria. We have begun to understand, as L. C. Dunn points out in his "Introductory Remarks," the role played in evolutionary processes by these genetic susceptibilities. We must now forge ahead in this field and try to map the various susceptibilities of the human host to the long list of known environmental challenges. This seems to me to be one of the most fascinating fields of the future.

The third order of factors that plays an important role in shaping disease patterns is, of course, culture. In the same way that I felt I should give a definition of disease to physicians and of society to social scientists, I owe to the anthropologists my definition of culture. Culture to me, as a disease ecologist, is the sum total of the concepts and techniques used by individuals or populations to control the environment in which they live. Of course, a culture trait may not always be survival-worthy, that is, may not promote survival. It may be erroneously conceived. It may have been received traditionally from ancient generations who had conceived it at a time when it had a purpose in a different environment, and may have been carried over faithfully throughout the centuries. Be that as it may it is useful for the disease ecologist and the public health worker to consider cultural traits observed in different populations as either promoting or preventing the survival of these populations. The sanitarian does not find it necessary to pass on the historical origin of these traits. He merely has to say whether the trait brings together the stimulus and the host or whether it keeps them apart. There are traits that do both, and they can be considered ambivalent. The revolting habit of smoking, now deeply ingrained in our society, may on the one hand precipitate death by cancer of a significant number of our population, while at the same time promoting survival if it soothes peoples' nerves to the point where it prevents them from rushing at each other's throats under the social emotional stresses alluded to previously. This role of culture as either a link between stimulus and host or a wall between them is, I think, a capital one.

A small Chinese village that I knew three decades ago may illustrate this linkage. To the epidemiologist, a puzzling problem was offered. One half of the inhabitants of this village were literally decimated by a very heavy hookworm infestation, while the other half enjoyed good health, at least from that point of view. An exploration of the local cultures revealed that almost all the patients were rice growers, while the healthy people bought their rice and had nothing to do with its cultivation. It was further found that the rice growers spent all their working days knee deep in mud thoroughly mixed with night soil which, of course, explained the introduction through skin penetration of the hookworm larvae. The healthy part of the population was engaged in silkworm farming, and spent their working days on ladders tending the mulberry trees.

In northern Vietnam many interesting situations, illustrating the role of culture in the disease patterns, occur. The country, from a geomorphological point of view, may be considered as composed of two parts: (1) a very fertile delta and (2) a much less fertile hill region. In the delta rice is grown. In the hill region some rice is grown, but there is considerable forest cover, and lumber is abundant. These are not the only two reasons for the differences in culture, but they are important nevertheless. As a result of these two situations the people of the delta build their houses on the ground. They have their stables on one side of the house and their kitchen on the other. Meals are brought into the house after they are cooked. The people in the hills, on the other hand, build their houses on stilts, and their living rooms usually are located about eight to ten feet above the ground. They keep their animals under the houses, and they do their cooking in the living rooms, which are usually full of smoke.

It happens that a very fierce malaria vector, *Anopheles minimus*, is found in the hill region, but the flight ceiling of this vector seldom exceeds nine to ten feet of elevation, so that during its flight it encounters only the animals under the houses. The fumes that emanate from the living rooms, where the people congregate, play a role in driving away any mosquitoes that might find themselves up there.

In the delta, on the contrary, there is no such malaria vector. When the people from the delta, under the economic pressure of overpopulation of the fertile land, seek relocation in the hills where space is more abundant, they take with them their delta culture. They build their houses on the ground floor, keep their animals outside, and see that their living rooms are free of smoke by cooking their food outdoors. As a result *Anopheles minimus*, which prefers human blood when it has a choice, becomes an active transmitter of malaria, and the people of the delta have become discouraged from participating in relocation schemes, feeling that there are evil spirits in the hills that do not like the delta people.

In the Vietnam delta itself we are confronted with three dominating factors: (1) the waters; (2) the aquatic life the waters cause to exist; and (3) the rice the waters help to grow. The water, represented chiefly by the Red River, is an important factor in the local culture. The mighty river not only has deposited its alluvial soil on the fields but continues pouring it deep into the China Sea. As a result the coastal population has developed no interest in sea fishing, the sea waters being too shallow and there being no fish along the coast. The Red River, fed by the snows and the rains of the eastern ranges of the Himalayas, has a shifty course, and it is very hard to predict its location for the next year. In addition to this it is subject to sudden rises, and the problem of flood control has been a major one in the area for centuries. Dams have been built for the triple purpose of protection, irrigation, and drainage. This has resulted in two important phenomena. The harvest does not occur at the same time in all parts of the delta, and repairs to the dams cause the necessity for a migrant labor force to rush where needed to keep the waters under control.

These dams have created conditions in which aquatic vegetation, snails, crayfish, and other biotics abound. Crayfish form an important item in the diet of the people.

From the waters the people also get their water-borne diseases, such as cholera, the dysenteries, and the typhoid fevers. From the migration of the labor force they get the pattern of these diseases that are transmitted from one point to the other by the migrant worker moving around wherever the need for his labor arises. From the snails they get their *Schistosoma japonicum*; from the aquatic vegetation, crayfish, and other biotics, they get their paragonimiasis and clonorchiasis.

However, from these soils and waters they also get their rice, which they prefer white and well polished. The polishing of the rice is done by machines in the more advanced villages. In the more backward villages it is done by mortar and pestle. As a result, the advanced villages get more beri-beri, while the backward villages get less, since hand polishing removes less of the thiamin-rich husk than does machine polishing.

All over the world numerous examples of the close interrelationship of culture and disease patterns could be given. As a result of the above I may say that the old art of reading symptoms and treating them by what appears to control them best is disappearing fast. The ancient formula of one ill, one pill, one bill, which seems to have been the credo of physicians for many generations, should be abandoned. Disease is a biological expression of maladjustment. This is what should be taught to our students in medical school, and this phenomenon against which they are going to fight all their lives cannot be understood without an ecological study in depth that should give equal importance to the three approaches: the environment, the host, and the culture.

Ecology and Nutritional Stress in Man

MARSHALL T. NEWMAN

Division of Physical Anthropology, U. S. National Museum

BEYOND the quite considerable metabolic tolerance of man to dietary inadequacies lie extreme conditions of nutritional stress where health and physical status may be affected from prenatal life onward. Through either starvation or acute shortage of essential nutrients, severe nutritional stress may result in death, especially in the young. When less severe, it retards physical development, reduces vitality, and increases susceptibility to most infectious diseases. Nutritional stresses in man are clearly a reflection of his ecology, culture, and biology. The ecological factors of particular importance in this regard are the direct effect of climate upon dietary needs, the disease environment that must be endured, and the food producing potential of the living area. Cultural factors are reflected principally in food producing technologies, food preparation, differential distribution to the people, and food habits. Biological factors of major import are population dynamics and the degree of acclimatization and adaptation to stress conditions. All these factors focus upon man's food intake, which in fair measure determine who thrives and propagates and who does not in this rapidly changing world.

CLIMATE AND NUTRITIONAL REQUIREMENTS

Quite apart from matters of food supply, the climate where humans reside has a direct bearing on their nutritional requirements. In cold climates, as Mitchell and Edman (1951:17–20) have shown, caloric needs are increased to help keep the body warm and allow for extra energy expenditures such as imposed by the hobbling effect of heavy clothing. In man there is a linear increase of resting metabolic rates below the critical level 78°–81° F. air temperature, although this is partly mitigated by well-designed clothing and built-in biological adaptations. There is, nevertheless, a highly significant average increase in basal metabolic rates with decreasing ambient temperatures, as Roberts (1952:174) has shown. In addition to enhanced caloric needs in cold climates, an increase in fat intake is also advantageous in helping preserve body temperatures at tolerable levels. The clinical consequences of inadequate fat intake in the Arctic is the sort of "rabbit hunger" described by Stefansson (1956:31).

Vitamin-wise there is incomplete evidence, drawn partly from animal experiments, that cold climates slightly decrease the need for niacin and increase it for ascorbic acid (Mitchell and Edman 1951:32–33; Dugal and Fortier 1952:146). Increased requirements for dietary Vitamin D also characterize cold climate living, since clothing and cloudy skies reduce the amount of ultraviolet radiation received by the body.

Caloric needs decrease in warm climates, partly because of the smaller body mass that must be sustained and partly because extra dietary calories are not needed for body heating. There is, however, a slight increase in protein needs in the heat, possibly 5–10 gm. per day (Mitchell and Edman 1951:94). This may be wholly cancelled by smaller body mass and by other adjustments to a hypoprotein intake. There are usually small vitamin losses through sweating in hot climate people, but these losses are mostly inconsequential except in the face of decidedly low intake for a particular vitamin. There is, of course, an increase in water needs and a great increase in salt requirements, although fully adapted or acclimated peoples possess special physiological mechanisms fostering water and salt economy. Increased sweat and fecal losses in hot climate peoples also call for increased iron and, less certainly, calcium needs. Increased fat intakes in hot dry climates and other areas of marked atmospheric aridity may also be indicated.

NUTRITION AND DISEASE

The bearing of disease upon nutritional status is summed up in the historic relationship of famine and pestilence. The diet-and-disease experiments on man and other animals clearly show that inadequate food intake increases the frequency and severity of most infections (Scrimshaw et al. 1959). There are only a few diseases such as malaria where inadequate diets serve some alleviative function (Scrimshaw et al. 1959:380–82). As Allison (n.d.) has indicated, malarial parasites do not thrive in human systems when hemoglobin levels are low because of grossly inadequate iron intake. Yet in such deficient hosts even a low parasite count may result in active malaria. But since dietary deficiencies are synergistic to many diseases in man, the actual cause of death in a poorly nourished individual may be in doubt. Unless special studies are made of the usual mortality records, credit is often given to some respiratory or gastroenteric disease that may in fact have only administered the coup de grâce.

112

The food producing potential of a living area depends basically upon the fertility of its soils, whether used for cultivation or pasturage. Soil fertility depends upon the available macro- and micro-nutrient elements and their interbalances, interacting with the climatic factors of rainfall, temperature, and their seasonal qualities. It is quite impossible to make broad generalizations by world zone on soil fertility. Large-scale detailed maps are needed to show nutritionally meaningful differences in soils. Phillips (1960) was only able to reduce the soils of subsaharan Africa to some 40 type-regions on the basis of climate and vegetation associations. Each type-region has its own particular problem in agricultural technology.

In general, however, the vast tropical zone within the 64° F. coldest month isotherm and the <30″ annual rainfall isohyet has the poorest agricultural soils. Due to extensive leaching by heavy rainfall the tropics has many areas of very poor soils, although some more fortunate areas have very fertile soils. The best agricultural lands, on the other hand, are in the middle latitudes of temperate climate. In this broad zone the soils of only moderate development by a medium and seasonally well distributed rainfall are superior. Other temperate zone soils are less satisfactory, being either drought-prone as in the mineral-rich prairie areas or overdeveloped as in the formerly heavily forested areas. Drought-prone areas are susceptible to crop failure and famine; areas of overdeveloped soils have problems akin to those in the extremely leached tropical soils.

It seems likely that within the broad framework of agricultural land use, proper solutions of the technological problems are more important to human welfare than soil fertility per se. In terms of technology, many of the New World and African cultivators in the tropics practice the extensive methods of shifting agriculture that exploit but a small portion of the arable land. These practices have low output in terms of harvest per unit area and low productivity viewed as yield per man-day. As Gourou (1956:343) indicates, these techniques limit slash-and-burn cultivators to the poorer lands such as the lighter soils of terraces and plateaus. Although he urges use of the swampy and heavy soils of the valley bottoms, they may have been avoided by shifting cultivators for epidemiological as well as technological reasons. In contrast, the Asian cultivators in the tropics use intensive methods on even the poorest soils and achieve a quite high proportion of land use, a high output, but a low productivity that is prodigal of human labor. Many of the temperate zone countries cultivate a high 40 to 60 percent of their total arable land, much more than in most of the tropics. Output is mostly high as well. Excepting the special hand techniques such as required in wet rice culture, productivity in the temperate zone is only high where advanced mechanized technologies are used.

NUTRITION AND HUMAN ADAPTATION

It is clear that the bulk of the world's population today is principally dependent upon agriculture for its sustenance, and that this dependence came only with the Neolithic Revolution less than 8,000 years ago. Thus, agricultural man anywhere has had only 150 to 400 generations to adapt himself to new dietaries, principally the grain and root crops that now support the world. Moreover, man has also been faced with adapting to different varieties of the same crop that have quite distinct nutritional properties and, indeed, have their own evolution. In this regard, Scrimshaw (1953) has emphasized that the variation is great enough in corn consumed in Central America to have important nutritional consequences. Increased yield and disease resistance in these corns may do damage to protein and oil content, and the amount of protein may bear no direct relationship to the content of tryptophan, methionine, and lysine.

In the long evolutionary view, 150 to 400 generations have been insufficient time for man wholly to adapt himself to new and changing foods. The degree of adaptation to shortages of different nutrients may vary considerably in human populations. Some of these differences may be regional and could reflect the length of time that adaptations to specific nutrient deficiencies have been necessary. For example, there is a possibility that the generally salutary adaptations of Negro Africans to low calcium and ascorbic acid intake (Scientific Council for Africa 1956:79) reflect a longer evolution than do their manifest and clinically expressed difficulties with protein and niacin shortages. The study of human responses to changing dietaries engendered by ecological and technological alterations is, in my opinion, equal in importance to researches on man's reactions to changing disease environments. Adjustments to dietary and disease hazards, themselves closely related, are rarely adequate over the present-day world except with the intervention of advanced food technologies and costly public health services. Neither biological nor cultural evolution have fully kept pace with rapidly shifting total environments. Yet in the fairly immediate past, the major racial blocks of mankind—Whites, Mongoloids, and Negroes—achieved salutary enough adaptations to their separate and distinct environments to undergo population explosions (cf. Hulse 1955:190).

NUTRITION AND POPULATION

In terms of the numbers of mankind, the world areas where intensive agricultural technologies are practiced are also the areas of the greatest population densities. Indeed, man's reproductive success can be seen to be pressing his food supply in almost all populous areas of the world. Food surpluses are a rarity among nations. Population increases move at such a rate that strong outmovement, such as from Italy to the United States around the turn of the century, only offers temporary relief before the gap is closed again. It would appear that man's biological success vis-à-vis reproduction is fully sufficient to strain his food resources and thus create a nutritional stress situation. As Spengler (1960:1499) recently put it, "Much of Asia, Africa, and Latin America—perhaps two-thirds of the world's population—is caught in a Malthusian trap, in a quasi-stable equilibrium system in which forces making for

114

increase in income evoke counter-balancing income-depressing forces, among them a high rate of population growth."

UNDERNUTRITION IN MAN

It is the nutritional consequences of this stress situation that are to be examined here. The observable aspects of nutritional stress lie in diet-connected mortality and morbidity rates, and in the residues of the latter. These residues are most readily observable in the altered growth and maturation rates of the children surviving these dietary crises, their disease susceptibilities, and in the vitality of the adults.

On a gross world basis the American Geographical Society (1953) maps show that the areas of undernutrition and malnutrition closely coincide with the tropical and warmer temperate regions of backward food producing technologies. Undernutrition in a hypocaloric sense and malnutrition in terms of vitamin and mineral deficiencies usually go along together, aiding and abetting each other, as it were, in creating human misery. The effects of famine and qualitative deficiencies in diet are therefore hard to separate. Where famine strikes, as in war disasters, the civilian mortality is quite selective, bearing down as it does on the very young and the old as well as the lower socio-economic strata. The effect of severe maternal undernutrition on the developing fetus is buffered to a considerable extent by a sort of homeostasis. In experiments where maternal nutrition has been carefully measured, intakes were never low enough to influence significantly the condition of the newborn. In the less well controlled war-time food crises, striking diminutions in birth size have been observed. For example, the undernutrition in northwest Holland during the war winter of 1944–45 was severe enough to interfere with the prenatal growth of infants born during that period (Smith 1954). Congenital malformations, which appear irregularly in normal times, were so slightly increased as to be inconclusive in the few conceptions occurring at the worst stage of the undernutrition. With this degree of famine the frequent intervention of amenorrhea, as a protective device, makes it virtually impossible to collect useful data on fetal anomalies.

When severely undernourished women go into labor, it may be prolonged by as much as five hours. This constitutes a well recognized hazard for both mother and newborn. Very poor nutrition can also affect lactation and cause sharp rises in infant mortality. This is especially the case in societies having no ready milk substitutes and no inter-family cooperation in wet nursing. Such was the case among Okinawans after the 1945 invasion of their island (see Emory 1946:616).

There is a vast literature on the influence of dietary deprivations on child growth. One of the most interesting of these reports concerns Howe and Schiller's (1952) unique 40-year record spanning the two World Wars for statures and weights of school children in Stuttgart, Germany. These cross-sectionally presented data show extreme sensitivity to economic conditions bearing upon nutritional status. Thus, there were dips in the stature and

115

weight curves during World War I, the 1922–23 inflation, the 1932 unemployment crisis, World War II, and the 1946–47 food shortage due to drought. For these German children, as well as those from Belgium, France, England, and Japan, Howe (n.d.) believes that, unless the undernutrition is of long duration, growth simply slows down and, as it were, waits for better times. When they arrive, growth takes place with unusual rapidity until the bulk of the children approach their genetically-determined growth tracks, along which they proceed as before. Viewing Howe's thesis critically, one significant consequence of a belated recuperative cycle lies in the timing of growth and its allometric effect upon somatotype. Another consequence of chronic undernutrition is reduced resistance to disease. Both consequences are well illustrated in Lewit's (1947) study of 4,000 Czech children at the end of World War II. In these children the pre-pubertal growth spurt in leg length was stated to be greater than the trunk height increases, resulting in a thin ectomorphic body build with weak musculature. Some 10 to 15 percent of the children were tested as tuberculin-positive, with the percentage increasing in each succeeding age-grade. Telltale enlargement of cervical glands was found in almost every child.

Another consequence of chronic undernutrition is the delay in skeletal maturation, which not only involves belated appearance of ossification centers and their slow subsequent development, but also a noteworthy increase in osseous anomalies (Snodgrasse et al. 1955; Dreizen et al. 1958). Studies thus far on non-Western children show them to average one to four years behind Greulich-Pyle (1959) and other standards for skeletal maturation, and for the gap to widen with increasing age. And there may also be, as Keys (1950:372) has suggested, far more critical residues of undernutrition and malnutrition expressed in lowered work capacities, reduced disease resistance, and various psychological traumata.

The classic study on the effect of famine upon physique was done by Ivanovsky (1923) during the long starvation period in post-Revolutionary Russia. In 16 populations of varying ethnic origins within the Soviet, adult statures decreased on average 3.8–6.6 cm. in men, 3.6–4.8 cm. in women, on a longitudinal basis. Weight losses of 30 percent occurred in a great number, and other bodily measures showed gross decreases. Organic and psychological traumata were common. A milder laboratory version of Ivanovsky's study was carried out on 34 U. S. White volunteers who were put on a semi-starvation diet for 24 weeks (Lasker 1947). They averaged a 24 percent weight loss and showed a 66 percent increase in ectomorphy.

The biological and psychological effects of seasonal shortages in food supply constitute another aspect of undernutrition. The effect of the "hungry months" from January to March upon social interactions is one of Richard's (1939) principal cultural themes for the Bemba of northeastern Rhodesia. Brock and Autret (1952:48) indicate that seasonal fluctuations in food supply are marked in subsaharan Africa, and the birth weights of infants are significantly less there during the "hungry months." Vitamin-deficiency states and kwashiorkor are also more prevalent during these lean times. These lean times

116

occur elsewhere in the world. For the Vicos Quechua in the northern Peruvian Sierra, the rainy season from December to February or March includes a period of food shortages for families without emergency stores. Kuczynski-Godard (1945:35–38) indicates that among the Aymará of Ichu the diet is particularly low in energy producing foods at just the time that the hardest harvesting labor is needed.

MALNUTRITION IN MAN

To a considerable extent the nutritional deficiency diseases are distributed by climate zones, are often worse at certain seasons, and are sometimes related to specific food crops. When these deficiency diseases reach epidemic proportions, they appear to represent the worst lags in man's adaptation to his nutritional environment. Rickets and osteomalacia are typically the nutritional deficiency diseases of cold climates. In the higher latitudes with more cloud cover, ultraviolet radiation is reduced, especially in the winter. In the United States wintertime, the percentage of total possible sunshine varies from 20 to 40 percent around the Great Lakes and the Pacific Northwest to 70 to 90 percent in the Southwest. Moreover, use of heavy clothing as a protection against cold blocks out most of the solar radiation reaching near-ground level. Bodily absorption of ultraviolet radiation makes possible the production of irradiated ergosterol which goes through a series of reactions to form vitamin D (Clark 1953:23). But where solar radiation is slight and blocked off, dietary vitamin D must take its place or deficiency diseases will result. It is in the dietarily acculturated cold climate peoples that rickets and osteomalacia are the greatest problems. Among the Labrador Eskimo who have largely abandoned their native dietary, rickets, scurvy, and combinations of these two deficiency diseases are said to be universal (Anonymous 1943:207). In Swedish Lapps who had also shifted their diet, almost one-half of the children had rickets. The severity of rickets was notably greater during the winter. Rickets and osteomalacia are also prevalent in the poorest socio-economic classes in the colder urbanized areas where intake of the so-called protective foods is very low. Neither rickets nor osteomalacia are likely to be killers of the very young, but they retard and deform and in so doing affect work capacity and disease resistance.

The present world distribution of scurvy shows no strong distributional patterning. Two centuries or more ago, however, it was a wide-spread disease throughout the northern part of the Western World and in other regions where antiscorbutic vitamin C was largely omitted from the dietary. Thus, we may think of scurvy as a wind sailor's disease and associate its ravages with Stefansson's (1956) "Pemmican War" between the Hudson Bay and the Northwest Companies. But scurvy used to be so common during the English winter months that it was known as the "London Disease." Lack of fruits and lightly cooked vegetables in the diets of all people at that time rendered all socio-economic classes scurvy-prone. Infantile scurvy can be a real killer, and very low vitamin C intake at any age can bring on the classic symptoms of joint pain, hemorrhage, gum softening, and tooth loss.

The iodine deficiency disease of goiter has an interrupted distribution in the mountainous parts of the world as well as the northern continental segment of North America (Amer. Geog. Soc., 1953:map 1). While more unsightly than serious in moderate form, strong iodine deficiencies in combination with other shortages can lead to severe degenerative syndromes such as D. C. Gajdusek (personal communication) found in the Mulia of the Central Highlands of Netherlands New Guinea.

Pellagra, due principally to niacin deficiency, is much more prevalent in the world's temperate zones than elsewhere and is more severe during the warmer months' maxima of solar radiation (Gillman and Gillman 1951:33). Moreover, pellagra is likely to be endemic in those areas where maize is a principal food crop, although the nature of this association is in some dispute (Gillman and Gillman 1951:40–41). Pellagra reached epidemic proportions during the 19th century in European countries such as France, Italy, and Rumania. After ameliorative measures reduced its morbidity and mortality rates in Europe, pellagra became the scourge of the southern part of the United States. Between 1890 and 1909, some 22 percent of those afflicted with pellagra in the South did not survive (Thompson-McFadden Commission 1913), and since that time the death rate has risen to 40 to 60 percent during epidemics. After an intensive campaign of agrarian and industrial reforms in the Southern States, pellagra became a much less serious public health problem. But in South Africa Gillman and Gillman (1951:64) tell us that the steep increase in pellagra " . . . is a reflection of the economic deterioration of the African. While at the moment [over 10 years ago] the disease in South Africa is not virulent, the history of pellagra in other countries has shown that the mortality rate can become very great, claiming as much as 60 percent of the afflicted." Pellagra is quite variable in the forms it takes, but often involves severe dermatoses, hepatic derangements, and severe alimentary and neurological disorders. It is a killer at all ages, from prenatal life onward. The growth and maturational disturbances and loss of vitality residual in the survivors is such that Africans recruited from pellagroid areas for work in the mines are said to be routinely "fed up" before they are expected to do the full day's work required of them.

What pellagra is to the maize consumers, so is beri-beri to the eaters of rice. The thiamine deficiency associated with diets based largely upon milled rice is the undeniable cause of beri-beri. Accordingly, this deficiency disease is largely restricted to Southeast Asia, but it is also present to some extent in Venezuela, the Minas Gerais area of Brazil, the former Cameroons, and Madagascar (Amer. Geogr. Soc. 1953). Beri-beri takes various forms in which a polyneuritis strongly affecting the lower extremities is an almost constant feature. This is "dry" beri-beri. "Wet" beri-beri also involves edema and the collecting of fluid in the body cavities. "Cardiac" beri-beri has the obvious association with heart failure. Infantile beri-beri can be a real killer. This used to be the case among lower class Burmese in Mandalay, where food restrictions imposed upon pregnant and lactating women and upon their ailing offspring caused high mortality in the latter (D. C. Sharma, personal communication). The East Indians and Chinese then resident in Mandalay imposed no such deprivations of thiamine-rich foods and had little infantile beri-beri. This is but one of the many instances where nutritional stresses are both class-structured and culture-conditioned.

The protein deficiency syndrome known as kwashiorkor has a broad distributional sweep of the lower latitudes from Mexico south to many parts of northern South America, throughout subsaharan Africa except for the cattle-raising eastern portion, and in India and much of China. Notably these are the countries of low agricultural productivity in terms of yield per man-day. Kwashiorkor, which means "red boy," is most serious in infants but also leaves perceptible residues in the children and adults who survive. The trouble may start with a poor prenatal and immediately postnatal nutritional environment. In Central America, Scrimshaw et al. (1957) found that partial starvation during the first year of life from insufficient maternal milk is more likely to result in marasmus (progressive wasting of the body) than kwashiorkor. For most children, however, the critical time for onset of kwashiorkor is toward the end of the first year when maternal milk fails to supply enough protein, and supplementary foods—if given at all—are principally carbohydrates. The clinical changes involved in active kwashiorkor include grossly retarded growth and maturation, apathy and anorexia, edema, depigmentation and other changes in the hair (hence "red boy"), diarrhea, and anemia. According to researches cited by Brock and Autret (1952:56–58) for subsaharan Africa, protein requirements per given caloric intake are perceptibly higher in children under five years of age than they are later on in life. The progressive decline in body weight for large numbers of Kampala infants and children, as viewed cross-sectionally in comparison with European standards, is but one of the observable symptoms of kwashiorkor in that area.

The mortality rate attributable to kwashiorkor is impossible to determine without special studies. Such studies were made, however, by Scrimshaw and his colleagues (1957) in four Guatemalan towns totaling 7,000 in population. In Guatemala as a whole the leading cause of death in children is listed as "gastroenteritis and diarrheal disease," yet a careful study of the four towns indicated that at least one-quarter of all deaths under five years of age was due to kwashiorkor or some other nutritional deficiency. Excepting the first year of life, at least half the deaths in one to four year-olds appeared to be a direct consequence of malnutrition. These death rates are highly class-structured in Guatemala and are race-conditioned as well, since the lowest socio-economic class and the most Indian are usually one and the same.

Even when protein deficiencies were not strongly expressed clinically, Scrimshaw et al. (1957) felt that the poorly nourished Guatemalan children were an easier prey to other diseases and might die as a direct consequence of pneumonia, measles, whooping cough, infectious diarrhea, or tuberculosis.

119

Moreover, extra stresses of any kind could result in the expression of frank clinical symptoms of kwashiorkor. Thus, if a child developed a heavy parasite load, it might lapse into severe kwashiorkor.

In subsaharan Africa, Brock and Autret (1952:24) report that mortality among kwashiorkor sufferers was high, especially in cases with edema. Until the advent of modern treatment the reported mortality rates never went below 30 percent. In the absence of such treatment, death was a 100 percent certainty in kwashiorkor-afflicted Congolese children. Closely associated with kwashiorkor in Africa are apparently irreversible fatty changes in the liver, hence the frequently used synonym of "fatty liver disease." There is a strong seasonal association of kwashiorkor outbreaks in Africa with the "hungry months."

Mention must be made of other nutritional deficiency diseases of less dramatic but nevertheless significant stress in man. There are the pro-vitamin A and vitamin A deficiencies associated with retarded growth rates in experimental animals and perhaps man (Clark 1953:12–13), as well as with dermal hyperkeratosis and impaired night vision. Ariboflavinosis is also associated with skin and visual disturbances. Then there are the various minerals that are often deficient in the soils or in the diets selected from them. Of the so-called macronutrients, calcium and phosphorus appear to be the most important to human welfare, but in part this is because they have been the best studied. Marett (1936:226–27) claims a strong ecological correlation between tropical rainforests and soils deficient in calcium and phosphorus and hypothecated that pygmy body size represented an advantageous economy in these macronutrient elements. There is fair evidence that other human populations have successfully adapted themselves to low calcium intakes by slow growth and maturation and small adult body size (Nichols and Nimalasuriya 1939; Schraer and Newman 1958). In the micronutrient group—iron, copper, zinc, and manganese—iron-deficiency anemias are widespread in man and have clear ecological and epidemiological correlates. One rather curious ecological association in Alaska Eskimos is the widespread but usually mild anemia (Scott et al. 1955) with heavy consumption of fish (Margaret Lantis, personal communication). Comparable anemias are not found in the caribou and sea mammal hunters.

CONCLUSIONS

Undernutrition and malnutrition often go together in man to provide gross and general stressing of a nutritional nature. Qualitative deficiencies are often multiple because of the metabolic interactions of the various nutrients. Where deficiency diseases principally attributable to a single nutrient are apparent, these diseases have strong ecological associations—rickets and osteomalacia with cold climates; scurvy and pellagra with, respectively, the more northerly and more southerly portions of the world's temperate zones; and beri-beri and kwashiorkor with warmer temperate and hot climates. Moreover, pellagra is associated in some way with maize cultivation, while beri-beri has a more direct relationship to heavy dietary use of milled rice. Most of these deficiency

120

uiseases have strong seasonal associations—rickets, osteomalacia, and scurvy with the winter months, pellagra with the summer months, and kwashiorkor with the "hungry months" whenever they occur.

Mortality attributable to dietary shortages is therefore frequently differential in its effect upon human populations, by region, socio-economic class, and age-grade. So are the biological and psychological residues in those who survive these diseases. In terms of mortality and morbidity rates, the greatest nutritional stresses are present in the underdeveloped countries of the world, especially where agricultural output and/or productivity are low. These are principally the countries of the tropics and warmer temperate zone, where the vectors of disease seem to be most strongly entrenched. Disease often goes along with poor nutrition, and the two are largely synergistic in relationship.

In terms of the histories of diseases, the underdeveloped countries are currently plagued by many of the nutritional deficiency and other diseases common less than several centuries ago in the more advanced countries. As Gordon's (1952:49) data suggest, the technologically more advanced countries have proceeded apace to develop new mortality patterns, with the degenerative diseases such as atherosclerosis and cancer now high on the list of killers. Atherosclerosis, for example, has a quite clear association with high intake of saturated fat and with reduced physical exercise, and hence has very obvious ecological and cultural connotations.

As a whole, then, nutritional stress in man has very strong ecological and cultural correlates. It should be equally apparent that the nutritional stresses that play such a potent role in human malaise must also impose their stamp upon the forms and functions of many aspects of man's culture as well.

REFERENCES CITED

AMERICAN GEOGRAPHICAL SOCIETY OF NEW YORK
    1953   Study in human starvation (Two sets of annotated maps).
ANONYMOUS
    1943   Food and health of Eskimo and Lapps. British Medical Journal ii:207.
ALLISON, A. C.
    1960   Genetic factors in resistance to malaria. Annals of the New York Academy of Sciences. N. Y. 91: (3): 710–29.
BROCK, J. F. and M. AUTRET
    1952   Kwashiorkor in Africa. World Health Organization Monograph Series No. 8.
CLARK, G. W.
    1953   A vitamin digest. Springfield, Charles C Thomas.
DREIZEN, S., R. M. SNODGRASSE, H. WEBB-PEPLOE, and T. D. SPIES
    1958   The retarding effect of protracted undernutrition on the appearance of the postnatal ossification centers in the hand and wrist. Human Biology 30:253–64.
DUGAL, L-P and G. FORTIER
    1952   Ascorbic acid and acclimatization to cold in monkeys. Journal of Applied Physiology 5:(3):143–46
EMORY, H. L.
    1946   Soybean milk-substitute as used on Okinawa. U. S. Navy Medical Bulletin 46:(4): 616–18.
GILLMAN, J. and T. GILLMAN
    1951   Perspectives in human malnutrition. New York, Grune and Stratton.

GORDON, J. E.
    1952   Ecological investigation of disease. New York, Milbank Memorial Fund.
GOUROU, P.
    1956   The quality of land use by tropical cultivators. *In* Man's role in changing the face of the earth, W. L. Thomas, ed. University Chicago Press.
GREULICH, W. W. and S. I. PYLE
    1959   Radiographic atlas of skeletal development of the hand and wrist. Stanford University Press.
HOWE, P. E.
    n.d.   Growth of the adolescent child as affected by restricted nutrition (Manuscript).
HOWE, P. E. and M. SCHILLER
    1952   Growth responses of the school child to changes in diet and environmental factors. Journal of Applied Physiology 5(2):51–61.
HULSE, F. S.
    1955   Technological advance and major racial stocks. Human Biology, 27:(3):184–92.
IVANOVSKY, A.
    1923   Physical modifications of the population of Russia under famine. American Journal of Physical Anthropology 6:(4):331–53.
KEYS, A.
    1950   The residues of malnutrition and starvation. Science 112:2909, pp. 371–73.
KUCZYNSKI-GODARD, M. H.
    1945   Estudio familiar demografico-ecologico en estancias Indias de la Altiplano del Titicaca (Ichupampa). Lima, Peru, Ministerio de Sálud Publica.
LASKER, G. W.
    1947   The effects of partial starvation on somatotype. An analysis of material from the Minnesota Starvation Experiment. American Journal of Physical Anthropology 5:(3):323–33.
LEWIT, E.
    1947   A preliminary report on a study of 4,000 Czechoslovakian children. Medical Women's International Journal, London. 54:(1):41–44.
MARETT, J. DE LA R.
    1936   Race, sex, and environment. London, Hutchinson's Scientific and Technical Publitions.
MITCHELL, H. H. and E. EDMAN
    1951   Nutrition and climatic stress. Springfield, Charles C Thomas.
NICHOLS, L. and A. NIMALASURIYA
    1939   Adaptation to a low calcium intake in reference to the calcium requirements of a tropical population. Journal of Nutrition 18:(6):563–77.
PHILLIPS, J.
    1960   Agriculture and ecology in Africa. New York, Praeger.
RICHARDS, A. I.
    1939   Land, labour, and diet in Northern Rhodesia. Oxford University Press.
ROBERTS, D. F.
    1952   An ecological approach to physical anthropology: environmental temperatures and physiological features. Actes du IVᵉ Congrés International des Sciences Anthropologiques et Ethnologiques, Vienne, Tome I: 145–48.
SCHRAER, H. and M. T. NEWMAN
    1958   Quantitative roentgenography of skeletal mineralization in malnourished Quechua Indian boys. Science 128:3322, pp. 476–77.
SCIENTIFIC COUNCIL FOR AFRICA SOUTH OF THE SAHARA (CSA)
    1956   Nutritional research in Africa south of the Sahara. London, CCTZ/CSA Pub. No. 19.

SCRIMSHAW, N. S.
 1953 Excerpt from address published in Proceedings Food and Nutrition Board, 12:24 (May), 1952, Journal American Dietetic Association 29:(2):133 (Feb.).
SCRIMSHAW, N. W., M. BÉHAR, F. VITERI, G. ARROYAVE, and C. TEJADA
 1957 Epidemiology and prevention of severe protein malnutrition (kwashiokor) in Central America. American Journal of Public Health 47:(1):53–62.
SCRIMSHAW, N. S., C. E. TAYLOR, and J. E. GORDON
 1959 Interactions of nutrition and infection. American Journal of the Medical Sciences 237:(3):367–403.
SCOTT, E. M., R. C. WEIGHT, and B. T. HANAN
 1955 Anemia in Alaskan Eskimo. Journal of Nutrition 55:(1):137–49.
SMITH, C. A.
 1954 Effects of maternal undernutrition upon the newborn infant in Holland (1944–45). Journal of Pediatrics 30:229–43.
SNODGRASSE, R. M., S. DREIZEN, C. CURRIE, G. S. PARKER, and T. D. SPIES
 1955 The association between anomalous ossification centers in the hand and wrist, nutritional status and rate of skeletal maturation in children five to fourteen years of age. American Journal of Roentgenology, Radium Therapy, and Nuclear Medicine 74:1037–48.
SPENGLER, J. L.
 1960 Population and world economic development. Science 131, 3412, 20 May, pp. 1497–1502.
STEFANSSON, V.
 1956 The fat of the land. New York, The Macmillan Co.
THOMPSON-MCFADDEN PELLAGRA COMMISSION
 1913 First progress report. American Journal of the Medical Sciences 191.

123

Nutritional Problems as Part of the Total Economy

HERBERT POLLACK, M.D., PH.D.[*]

IT WAS only thirty-one years ago that the principles of international mutual aid in the field of health were originally developed. Lord Bruce of Melbourne, who addressed the assembly of the League of Nations in 1935, declared that the marriage between health, nutrition and agriculture should now take place. This was the origin of two great international organizations, the World Health Organization and the Food and Agriculture Organization, which were born during the immediate postwar turmoil of international optimism. They succeeded in surviving and growing in the difficult years which followed, and we can now see the profound continuity of international efforts in an evolving world.

It has been learned from many sources that the nutritional problems most frequently encountered in the various parts of the world are calorie and protein malnutrition, marginal intakes of thiamine, riboflavin, vitamin A and vitamin C, in addition to the focal points of iodine deficiency. Thiamine intake can be controlled by the type of rice processing and the refinement of wheat flour. Thus, adjustments in these milling processes will take care of thiamine deficiencies. Riboflavin deficiency, however, is a much more difficult and, indeed, more common problem since it is extremely difficult to

From the George Washington University, and the Institute of Defense Analyses, Arlington, Virginia.
* Clinical Professor of Medicine.

provide adequate amounts of riboflavin in diets low in animal products. To overcome this problem, it may be necessary to enrich the basic rice or wheat diets with riboflavin. This process would be inexpensive and stable, and such products have proved acceptable to many peoples. The vitamin A and vitamin C inadequacies can be eradicated by employing educational technics and by encouraging increased consumption of fresh fruits and vegetables. However, the vitamin A problem is a bit more involved than would appear on the surface; one of the difficulties in providing adequate physiologic availability of this vitamin is the low fat content which interferes with its proper absorption.

The problem of the nutritional anemias is a difficult one to solve without further research.

The source of protein has been a subject of discussion for many years. There is no particular magic in animal proteins such as milk, meat and eggs. The fact that they provide a complete complement of the essential amino acids along with nonessential amino acids and, in general, have a high degree of digestibility gives them the great virtues that have been ascribed to them. Their amino acid content of vegetable proteins, on the other hand, is not always as complete. However, by proper admixture of vegetable proteins, the optimum aminogram can be obtained at lower cost and with greater availability. This area must be developed ex-

TABLE I

Distribution of Important Diseases in the Various Tropical and Subtropical Countries

Disease	Thailand	Viet Nam	Cambodia	Laos	Iran	Iraq	Yemen	Nepal
Enteric								
Bacillary	++++	++++	++++	++++	++++	++++	++++	+++
Cholera		±	++	++	±	−	++	++
Helminths								
Schistosomiasis		−	+	±	±	++	++	+++
Hookworm	+++++	+++++	+++	+++++	+++++	+++++	±	+++++
Ascariasis	+++++	+++++	+++++	+++++	+++++	+++++	+++++	+++++
Trichuriasis	+++++	+++++	+++++	+++++	+++++	+++++	+++++	+++++
Tuberculosis	+++++	+	+	+	++	++	+++	+++++
Leprosy	+++++	++++	++	++++	+	+++	+	+++++
Malaria	+++	+++	++	+++	+++	+++	+++	+++++
Filariasis	+++	++	+	+++	±	+	+++	+++++
Dengue	+++	+	+++	+++	+++	−	+++	+++++
Venereal diseases	+++	+	+++	+++	+++	+++	±	+
Yaws	+++	−	+++	+++	±	+++	++	
Respiratory diseases	++++	+++	++	+++	+++	++	+++	+++
Rabies	++	++	+	+++	+++	++	±	+++
Smallpox	−	+++++			++	+++	+++	+++
Yellow fever								
Trachoma	++++	+	++	+++	+++	+++	+++++	+++
Onyongnyong fever								
Hepatitis	+++	+++	++	++	+	+++	++	++
Leishmaniasis		++		++	++++	++++		+
Relapsing fever						++		
Tetanus	++	++				++++	++	
Trypanosomiasis								
Meningitis	+++++	+++++	+++++		++++	+++++	+++++	++++
Diphtheria	++++	+++++	+++++		++	+++++	+++	++++
Measles			++					
Mumps			++					
Chicken pox								
Dermatological	++++	+	+	+++	+++	+	++	
Typhus								
Scrub	++	+++	+++	+++	+++	−	−	+++
Murine	++	+++	++		+++	±	+	±
Epidemic			++			±	++	++

125

TABLE I (*continued*)

Distribution of Important Diseases in the Various Tropical and Subtropical Countries

Disease	Tanganyika	Ghana	Nigeria	Angola	Ethiopia	Fed. of Rhodesia and Nyasaland	Liberia	Basutoland	Bechuanaland
Enteric									
Bacillary	++++	++	++++	++	++++	+++	++++		
Cholera	–	–	–		–				
Helminths									
Schistosomiasis	++++	++++	+++	++++	++	++	++		+++
Hookworm	++++	++++	++++	++++	+++++	+++++	+++++		++++
Ascariasis	++++	++++	++++	++++	++++	++++	+++++	+++++	
Trichuriasis	++++	++++	+++	++++	+++	++++	+++		
Tuberculosis	++++	+++	++++	+++	+++	+++	++		+++
Leprosy	++++	+++	++++	+++	±	+++	+		+++
Malaria	++++	++++	++++	++++	++		++		
Filariasis	+		+		±	+	++		
Dengue	+++	+++	+++	+++	+++	+++	++		+++
Venereal diseases	+++	++	++	++	+++	++++	++		++++
Yaws	+++	±	+++		±	+++			
Respiratory diseases	+		+++	++	++				
Rabies	++	±	+++	±	+++	++	++		
Smallpox	–	+	±	±	±	–	0		
Yellow fever	+++		+	++	+	++	++		
Trachoma	++		++		++	+++	++		
Onyongnyong fever							++		
Hepatitis	++	±	±		±	±			
Leishmaniasis	+++		+++	++++	+	++++			
Relapsing fever	+++		+++		±	++++			
Tetanus	+++	++	++	++++	+	++	+++		++
Trypanosomiasis					–	+			++
Meningitis	+++		++++	++++	++++	+++++	++++		
Diphtheria									
Measles							+		
Mumps									
Chicken pox									
Dermatological		+	+	–		+			
Typhus									
Scrub	±				++				
Murine	±	–	++		++	+			
Epidemic	±	++	++			–			

126

TABLE I (*continued*)
Distribution of Important Diseases in the Various Tropical and Subtropical Countries

Disease	Israel	Cyprus	Panama and Canal Zone	Cuba	Haiti—Dom. Rep.	Honduras	El Salvador	Ecuador	British Guiana
Enteric									
Bacillary	±	+	±	+++	++++	++++	+++	++++	++
Cholera	-			-					-
Helminths									
Schistosomiasis	-	-		-	±	-	-	+++	-
Hookworm	±	+++	+++	+++	++++	++++	++++	++++	±
Ascariasis	±	+++		++	++++	++++	++++	++++	±
Trichuriasis	±	+		++	++++	+++	+++	++++	±
Tuberculosis		-	+++	+++	++++	++++	++++	++++	±
Leprosy	-		±	++	+	+	+	+	+
Malaria		+	+	++	++++	++++	+++	+++	±
Filariasis	±		++	++	+	+	+	+++	+
Dengue			+++	+++	++	++	+	+++	++
Venereal disease		+	+	+	+	+	+	+	+
Yaws		-			+	+			+
Respiratory diseases									+
Smallpox	-	-		-	-	-	-	+	-
Yellow fever		±	±	+	-	±	-	±	+
Trachoma		±			-	-		-	-
Onyongnyong fever	++				~				
Hepatitis			±	~	~	±	±	±	±
Leishmaniasis				+	+	±	±	++	+
Relapsing fever					-	-	-		
Tetanus		+	+	++	++	+		+	
Trypanosomiasis								+	
Meningitis	±	++	±	++++	++++	±	+		++++
Diphtheria	±		+	++++	++++	±	++++	+	++++
Measles	±	++	+	++++	++++	±	+++		++++
Mumps	±		+	++	++	±	+		++++
Chicken pox			+	+	+	+	++	+	+
Dermatological									
Typhus									
Scrub	-			±	±	-	±	++	-
Murine	-	-		-	+	-	-	++	-
Epidemic	-	-			-	-	-	+	-
Rift Valley fever									
Chagas' disease							+		

Note: As indicated in the text, vital statistics are inadequate from these countries. The chart presented here was compiled from the best available sources and can be considered only as showing the relative importance rather than specific incidence. + indicates relative frequency of disease, - indicates comparative freedom from disease, ± indicates minimum freedom from disease, a blank indicates no information.

127

tensively if present day problems are to be solved. As shown many years ago in our work in Taiwan,[*] the protein consumption of the rice-eating people was up to approximately 100 gm. a day. This is not to be considered a low protein intake even though 95 per cent of this protein was of vegetable origin. The bulk of the protein came from rice but sufficient soybean was added to the meals daily to supply the missing amino acids, thus the total amino acid mixture was a very adequate one. The serum protein levels of the people we studied were well over 7 gm. per cent indicating the physiologic adequacy of their source of vegetable proteins.

Evidence of what can be done with these vegetable proteins is the development in the Institute for Nutrition for Central America and Panama. This organization has been instrumental in devising a food called Incaparina which is based upon a staple grain of corn to which an oil seed cake is added. The protein quality of this product is essentially equivalent to that of milk and its cost is a fraction of the natural product.

Health problems in each of the various countries of the world reflect in general the level of social, economic and scientific development. By analyzing such demographic indices as morbidity and mortality, growth rate and structure of the population, its urban-rural distribution and the characteristics of its labor force, the nature of the principal health problems can be inferred. By relating these data to data of an economic nature, such as national income, industrial and agricultural production, per capita income, and again to environment, paying special attention to sanitation, nutrition and housing, health problems can be differentiated with great clarity. A brief review of the available data on many of these countries throughout the world (Table I) shows that they are plagued by a series of infectious diseases, undernutrition, poor sanitation, bad housing, poor working conditions, illiteracy and a low per capita income. These conditions lead to a high general mortality, a high infant and child mortality, a high fetal wastage, and the like, and can be related to the poor scholastic performance of the children and the low produc-

tivity of the labor force.

No program related to the nutritional problems of a country can be separated from the total health problem of that country. This includes the previously mentioned social and economic factors as well as the attitudes of the population groups to whom these nutrition programs are to be applied. To date there has been no real effort to develop a technic for measuring the impact of a nutrition program on changes in health, social and economic factors. A format for this type of research would have to be created and would necessitate the association of the technics with sociologic and anthropologic disciplines. In selecting a nutrition program, the effect of which would be studied in this hypothetical situation, it would be preferable to choose one that sets forth results that could be achieved and measured. The goals of these nutrition programs would, of course, depend in large part on the philosophy of those who promoted and operated the programs. It is possible that even the most effective nutrition and public health programs would have to be in force for a long time before their full impact is felt, even though there would be more immediate effects.

The clinical manifestations of nutritional diseases are essentially the same all over the world. However, the social manifestations are determined in a large part by environmental factors which differ from place to place and with time. Thus, it is necessary that each society have at any given point in time its own tailor-made system of nutritional improvement associated with general public health improvements suited to its own resources, needs and particular demands. In other words, the developing countries need not, and indeed perhaps should not, imitate the food patterns of the prosperous areas of the world nor need they imitate the type of public health and medical services. They should be ready to adapt, rather than to adopt, the products of the Western world's health programs.

It is difficult to separate the nutritional problems from the population expansion problems. Gains in life expectancy have been mostly due to the prevention rather than to the cure of disease. Malnutrition and its secondary infections constitute the two most important causes of disease and death in developing countries. The difficulties and failures experienced in controlling the diseases caused by malnutrition and infection do not arise from the lack of scientific

---

[*] POLLACK, H., CONSOLAZIO, C. F., CROWLEY, L. V., ARMSTRONG, F. B., DORSCH, I. F., GUILLORY, R. L., GODBER, J. T., GOLDSTEIN, D. R., SMITH, E. P., LEWIS, O. H., RYER, R. R., III, JEFFERIS, T. C., BROCKETT, J. E., JR., DOSCH, E. L., EBY, T. M., FRICK, L. P., MOON, A. P. and LIN, S. S. Studies on nutrition in the Far East. *Metabolism*, 5: 203, 1956.

knowledge but from economic and social factors that prevent the application of existing knowledge. The most urgent problems to be solved before malnutrition can be diminished in these developing countries cannot be solved by scientific medicine alone, but require in addition attention to the sociologic factors. The objective would be to improve nutrition to the extent that disease and its subsequent disability would be prevented. Coincidentally, environmental factors such as water polution, sewage disposal and housing would have to be improved. A short-term program would focus directly on the therapeutic aspects of supplying the immediate food needs. The results would be visible immediately to the recipient but could not be expected to have the same far-reaching and more permanent effects of well planned, extended agricultural improvement and general nutritional measures. The most effective programs would, of necessity, be a mixture of the two. The immediate therapeutic nutritional program would serve to gain the confidence of the peoples. At the same time, the long-term program, which would cover agricultural developments, nutritional information, housing, recreational facilities, improved working conditions, water supply, sewage disposal and insect vector control, would be promoted.

In addition to the problems of public health are those of transport and communications. Maintenance of nutrition may be dependent upon the introduction of agricultural technics in one area or, in another area, upon the introduction of good transportation in order to bring in food in exchange for local products. What may be needed in other areas is an educational program to alert the people to the proper utilization of local foods. Thus, it becomes clear that a program of this magnitude is more than technology and its application to the problem. It is an intricate complex of social and political attitudes, of values, of judgments and even of religious and other types of faiths. This interdependence upon technologic and social problems must be emphasized because not all technology can be applied intact to a developing nation. The existing technology of the social structure must be modified or a compromise effected in order to achieve the desired objective.

Nutrition programs must serve as a background for the future so that the people can take care of themselves; and any large-scale program should include training in both nutrition and agriculture. However, it must be borne in mind that improving the nutrition and public health status of peoples in underdeveloped countries will create new problems. For example, the resultant population increase might lead to complications that would vitiate the impact of the basic program.

It has been recognized in sophisticated medical circles that attempts to transplant highly sophisticated technologic ideas to developing countries that are not ready for their use may lead to both good and bad results. The success of the Marshall Plan of the United States cannot be correlated with the aid programs to underdeveloped countries. In Western Europe where the Marshall Plan was applied, there were well established social and economic bases which were ready for reconstruction when given aid. These social and economic bases do not exist in the developing countries and it is a question of construction and not reconstruction.

Many questions come to mind. What types of nutrition programs will yield the greatest returns? Are there alternative uses of these scarce resources which would give a greater return to the people? What are the major nutritional problems in the particular areas under study for which a program is required? Are there available modern nutritional and medical health technics for solving these problems? The assumption that a nutrition program will be beneficial in these underdeveloped areas is valid only to the extent that the peoples of these areas are willing and able to utilize it.

It must be recognized that in the more industrially developed nations the increase in life expectancy started long before the introduction of public health measures. This can be attributed to the industrial revolution, the general rise in the standards of living and the improvement in nutrition associated with economic improvement and increased purchasing power.

Most people are fully aware that malnutrition, disease and poverty form a vicious circle. People are sick because they are malnourished. This general relationship between malnutrition, poverty and disease is well illustrated by the vital statistics. Life expectancy at birth in the small part of the world which we characterize as industrially developed is more than double that in the larger part of the world which we characterize as underdeveloped. Infant mortality in countries with high standards of living has been brought down to a fraction of that in the underdeveloped countries. However, let us not forget that even within segments of the so-called developed countries some of these differences still exist.

The current process of social change in the health fields and subsequently in the broader fields of economic, social and educational development differs in many respects from the process which enabled the developed nations to reach their relatively high level. An important difference is that the changes in the underdeveloped countries will evolve in a setting in which knowledge of technics in all fields of nutrition and public health, as well as in agriculture and industry, is available. Thus, the changes can now be accomplished more cheaply, more effectively and certainly much more rapidly.

In order to solve the nutritional problems of a country it is essential to understand the agricultural productivity of the available land. The amount of arable surface available to the individual varies in each country. It is estimated that in Taiwan there is about 0.24 acre for each person; in Viet Nam, 0.5 acre, in Thailand, 6 acres; in Burma, 2 acres; in India, 1.1 acres; in Japan, 0.2 acre; and in Pakistan, 1 acre. These arable areas can be increased by only a small percentage as most of the reclaimable land is in current use. The key to increased production lies chiefly in obtaining better yields per acre. According to FAO figures, Japan has improved its rice production per acre by 22 per cent since 1939. The Philippines have increased their productivity 90 per cent for each acre in the same period of time.

Current programs for improvement of seed and irrigation, fertilization and the like, are all important in this matrix of problems. Since fertilizers cannot always be prepared locally, hard currency is necessary. To obtain hard currency, money crops must be raised and the more money crops produced the less food crops.

Another problem concerned with food is its storage and distribution. Lack of transportation within the country is indeed a vital item. Refrigerated storage for such foods as fish is extremely scarce in the developing parts of the world; therefore, systems such as salting and drying are utilized. The current development of fish flour is an extension of this storage problem.

Food habits and prejudices represent still another problem. It is extremely difficult to change the food habits of people on a large scale because of their cultural backgrounds. Many taboos exist that limit the feeding of children, pregnant women and religious groups. In the areas in which nutritional programs would have to be applied cultures have been established through the centuries, based upon religious beliefs, family relationships, local geography, climate, transportation routes as well as the traditional status of women in the family unit and community, the speed with which the family unit is breaking up or, what is currently occurring in many areas of the world, the pull from rural communities to the large cities.

Many of the nutritional problems might be solved by certain changes in food processing procedures. For example, in Thailand, where there is an abundance of food, a change in rice milling procedures would solve many problems. The common problem of ariboflavinosis is probably the most permanent in all these countries and its solution depends upon the country's local sources.

The basic solution to improved protein nutrition must come from greater use of proteins available locally, that is, from peanuts, soybeans, legumes, as well as animal flesh, fish and the like.

It is evident that the assessment of the nutritional status of these people is dependent upon a factor which has received little attention in the past, that is, the question of the degree and type of intestinal parasitism. Several years ago a direct correlation was shown between the degree of parasitism with the hookworm and the body weights of individuals. It was evident from measurements and calculations that the hookworm burden on the population group in Taiwan consumed approximately 10 per cent of the ingested calories. Although in this particular population group there was no anemia from the hookworm parasitism, it is evident that in other population groups they are part and parcel of the total anemia problem.

To sum up, the problem of nutritional inadequacies and the corrective measures designed to relieve the situation must be considered from the total point of view. Nutrition must compete with all the other aspects of the economy of the country in the allocation of scarce resources. Amelioration of the problems of disease can serve to relieve many nutritional disturbances by lowering the metabolic demands of the patient and increasing the efficiency of utilization of food stuffs and manpower itself.

Ecological Factors in Nutritional Disease

NEVIN S. SCRIMSHAW, PH.D., M.D.*

MEDICINE has always been concerned with the cause of disease. In modern academic medicine, however, the cause of a disease is too often equated with the agent of the disease. From an epidemiologic point of view the agent is merely one of a triad whose two other components are host factors and environmental factors. Neither the presence of a pathogenic agent nor the deficiency of an essential nutrient alone determines whether or not disease will occur.

For example, what is the cause of tuberculosis? If it were merely infection with the tubercle bacillus, nearly all of us would long since have contracted the clinical disease. Yet we know that most of us who have worked extensively with sick people have experienced repeated entries of tubercle bacilli into our lungs without contracting clinical tuberculosis. The same exposure, however, in a malnourished or otherwise susceptible person might have resulted in death from acute febrile tuberculosis.

Infection is obviously not synonymous with disease. Host factors combine with the infectious agent to produce the clinical disease,

From the Department of Nutrition and Food Science, Massachusetts Institute of Technology, Cambridge, Massachusetts. Contribution No. 549.

* Professor of Nutrition, Head, Department of Nutrition and Food Science.

Presented at Colloquium "Man and Environment," Albert Einstein College of Medicine, New York, New York, May 27, 1963.

and environmental factors influence both the agent and the host and may, in turn, determine the nature and outcome of the interaction between agent and host.

Just as identifying the agent of an infectious disease is not sufficient to describe its cause, so the agent of nutritional disease, the deficiency of a specific nutrient, is not sufficient to explain the occurrence of the disease. For example, to what extent is a dietary deficiency of iron the cause of hypochromic, microcytic anemia. The iron intake of a person with such an anemia might be quite adequate were it not for the abnormal iron loss resulting from severe hookworm disease; or from excessive phosphates in the diet interfering with iron absorption; or from abnormal blood loss due to menorrhagia, a duodenal ulcer or a hemolytic disorder, or even from an excessive loss of iron in sweat. Environmental and host factors may make a given intake of the nutrient wholly adequate or grossly deficient. In other words, it is the interaction of host, agent and environment which causes the disease.

Too often the medical student and young house officer is encouraged to identify the agent of disease and then to concentrate on therapeutic action against the agent. Because modern clinical medicine has developed effective counter measures against the agents of most diseases, this approach generally works well in the hospital. However, it may fail miserably in preventing a relapse once the patient returns to the environment from which he

American Journal of Clinical Nutrition, February, 1964, Vol. 14, No. 2, pp. 112-122.

came, and as an approach to prevention of disease in a population, it is irrational and usually ineffective. Preoccupation of public health authorities with the agent as the cause of a disease is likely to result in control measures which are uneconomical or ineffective because they do not attack the disease at a vulnerable link in the chain of multiple causation.

Weanling diarrhea is a good example. As Gordon[1] has pointed out for the first time in a recent review, in most of the technically underdeveloped areas of the world there is a characteristic increase in the frequency of diarrheal disease at the time of weaning which is an epidemiologic rather than an etiologic entity. Microbiological studies of this syndrome give exceedingly varied and equivocal results. Depending upon the population studied, only from 20 to 40 per cent of cases can be accounted for by known pathogens. Shigellas, pathogenic strains of Escherichia coli and salmonellas are found in this decreasing order of frequency. Most viral studies have failed to show that the proportion of enteric viruses is higher in children with weanling diarrhea than in those without.

The characteristic feature of the syndrome is that the diarrhea occurs when the supply of breast milk is no longer adequate for the nutritional needs of the child and when the supplementary or substitute feeding provided is both grossly deficient in protein and other nutrients and contaminated by poor sanitation. In addition the child is more likely to be playing in the dirt and even to be coming in direct contact with feces. At the same time his growth and development have come to a virtual standstill because of nutritional deficiency, and fatality rates from other infectious diseases are also high. The data indicate that although diarrhea can be associated with known pathogens in some cases, in a greater number of cases the diarrhea is due to organisms which normally would not be pathogenic in a well nourished host.

Sabin,[2] in a paper presented in Geneva last February at the United Nations Conference on the Application of Science and Technology for the Benefit of the Less Developed Areas,

came to much the same conclusions. He also emphasized the importance of the high level of normally nonpathogenic organisms in grossly contaminated foods fed to young children in these areas.

The newly recognized syndrome of weanling diarrhea occurs because of the synergism of malnutrition and infection. It is most prominent in the second year of life because various environmental and host factors combine to cause a peak of both malnutrition and massive enteric infection during the weaning and postweaning period. It should be noted that during this time the children are being exposed to many organisms of varying pathogenicity for the first time and possess little acquired immunity.

The vital statistics of a country, which are of course the same ones compiled and used by the international health agencies, do not reveal the true basis for diarrheal disease in preschool children. They indicate only that gastrointestinal disease is the most common cause of death in the one to four year age group. Public health authorities have tended to conclude from these data that they should stress the construction of latrines and sanitary water supplies to prevent infection.

In the rural highland Indian village of Santa Maria Cauqué in Guatemala, the Institute of Nutrition of Central America and Panama (INCAP) has managed experimentally to apply the conventional public health measures for controlling enteric infection far more intensively than could be carried out on a national scale. After three years there still has been no recognizable decrease in diarrheal disease in children under five years of age in the village.

The measures instituted have included safe drinking water, a sanitary privy for every house, the full-time services of a sanitary inspector, and the establishment of a clinic with a nurse and doctor in attendance. These did not reduce morbidity from diarrheal disease when no associated nutritional measures were taken or changes in food preparation and handling made within the home. Spread of the diarrheal disease was shown to be by contact within the family group, not by water or flies.

In a similar village, Santa Catarina, in which no medical or sanitary changes were introduced but in which the children were given a dietary supplement containing 30 gm. of good quality protein per day plus other nutrients, there was a decrease in the duration, severity and frequency of diarrheal disease over the same time period. It is obvious that the search for an infectious agent of diarrhea in the weanling child and identification of a known pathogen in some cases did not really lead to an understanding of the causation of the syndrome; this required recognition of the multiple factors involved.

The occurrence of any disease depends upon all three factors—agent, host and environment. One of the clearest indications of this is the way in which the prevalence and nature of disease varies with time, place and person. The operation of these factors can be illustrated by specific examples drawn from either nutritional or infectious disease.

CHANGES IN DISEASE WITH TIME

In 1900 the death rate from diarrheal disease in children under one year of age in New York City was 4,496 per 100,000. In 1920 it was still 1,796 and in 1961 it was only 45. For children one to four years of age this changed from 470 per 100,000 in 1901 to 120 in 1920 and only 2.4 in 1961. Obviously, many environmental and host factors are involved in this dramatic decline, but the rates in New York City as recently as the early 1900's were worse than in technically underdeveloped areas today.

For somewhat the same reason "mehlnar-schaden" or "starch dystrophy," which was exceedingly common in Europe at the beginning of the century and which came from feeding too much carbohydrate and too little protein to infants, has disappeared. Now mehlnar-schaden is recognized as nothing more than the severe protein malnutrition of kwashiorkor. The best example of the virtual disappearance of a nutritional disease from the United States is pellagra, which in the early 1930's claimed thousands of victims in the South and today is almost unheard of in that region.

Unfortunately, the trend is not always toward disappearance of a disease. Until relatively recently beriberi was not an important problem in rural areas of Thailand and Malaya, but small mechanical mills, which are being introduced extensively, do a more efficient job of polishing the rice than hand-pounding, which had been the standard method for generations. The result has been a tragic increase in beriberi, particularly the infantile form. In the latter case the mother's milk is so deficient in thiamine that many breast-fed infants become suddenly ill and die within a matter of hours.

Kwashiorkor and marasmus are also increasing in many of the burgeoning cities of Latin America and Africa because women are weaning their children earlier, either in imitation of the more well-to-do or in order to work at industrial or domestic jobs. Unfortunately, because of ignorance and poverty, they fail to provide their children with proper food substitutes.

Another aspect of the time distribution of disease is periodic occurrence. For example, we are accustomed to the fact that in the United States type A influenza has a periodicity of about two to three years and type B of not less than four to six years. Epidemics of measles occur about every two years and poliomyelitis generally reaches a peak each year in the late summer. Nutritional diseases also are often periodic. Pellagra appears when the population becomes depleted of niacin as a result of the gradual exhaustion of food supplies during a long winter or dry season. The peak is reached just before the new crops are harvested, at a time when exposure to sunlight as a result of working in the fields, contributes to the exacerbation of the skin lesions.

In some countries kwashiorkor has demonstrated a distinct periodicity usually following, by a few weeks, the peak frequency of diarrheal disease which serves as a precipitating factor. Like other infections, diarrheal disease causes a loss of appetite, and there is a tendency toward ingestion of a more liquid and more deficient diet; the metabolic loss of nitrogen is increased and sometimes the absorption of nitrogen from the gastrointestinal tract is decreased. Purgatives are often administered to get rid of the worms which are believed to be responsible for the condition. With all these factors operating in the same direction, the close relationship between kwashiorkor and diarrheal disease is hardly surprising. For the same reasons, increases in the occurrence of kwashiorkor follow epidemics of measles and other common communicable diseases.

The distribution of hookworm disease and ascariasis is obviously closely related to climate and soil conditions which will support embryonation of eggs. Where the soil is frozen hard or nonexistent, as in the Arctic, or is dry sand, as in the desert, the propagation of these diseases is manifestly impossible. But one must beware of judging the macroclimate and forgetting the microenvironment in which the individual actually lives.

A few years ago surveys in Greenland showed a high frequency of certain intestinal parasites which are considered to be primarily tropical and subtropical in their distribution and not able to survive in the Arctic.[3] The answer was simple. The microclimate within the houses was hot and humid and transmission occurred as if in the tropics. It is pertinent that nineteenth century pictures of East Coast Eskimo households in Greenland show all family members wholly unclothed.

The classic example of place distribution of a nutritional disease is endemic goiter. In the wake of the last Ice Age, vast and diverse areas of the world were left iodine-poor. Mature, iodine-rich soil was swept away and replaced by new soil created by the grinding up of crystalline rock, the iodine content of which was only about one-tenth the average of mature soil. As the great glaciers receded, iodine replenishment of the soil began by iodine liberated from the sea into the air by oxidation and carried by air currents, a process which has now been going on for some 10,000 to 20,000 years. Today areas in which the incidence of endemic goiter is intense can be reciprocally correlated with the length of the postglacial period of iodine replenishment, the prevalence usually being lower in equatorial areas than in those closer to the poles.

The fact that the distribution of endemic goiter is also influenced by goitrogenic substances in the diet, hardness of water and water polution, and that the incidence is currently being reduced by such factors as less monotonous diets, importation of food from nongoitrous areas and prophylactic iodization of salt only strengthens the argument for the importance of all three types of environmental factors—physical, biological and social—in the causation of nutritional disease.

Today most of the classic deficiency diseases are sharply differentiated in place distribution by the degree of social, economic and technical development. In order to understand this distribution, little is contributed from knowing that beriberi is due to a lack of thiamin, pellagra to a niacin-tryptophan deficiency or xerophthalmia to inadequate intakes of vitamin A unless we know the environmental and host factors which account for the actual precipitation of these diseases.

Admittedly, a clinician treating a patient in a hospital may be satisfied to know only that administration of a specific nutrient will result in cure of a given clinical syndrome, but even this is deceptive. Under the conditions in which nutritional deficiencies occur in the population, they are rarely single.

When pellagra was common in the southern United States, treatment with niacin alone sometimes precipitated signs of beriberi. Likewise, treatment of beriberi or ariboflavinosis with thiamin or riboflavin alone frequently resulted in the development of signs of clinical pellagra. Treatment of xerophthalmia with only vitamin A is still likely to limit the resistance and growth of the child suffering from protein deficiency. Conversely, giving a skim milk supplement alone to protein-deficient children whose diets are also low in vitamin A has contributed to widespread precipitation of xerophthalmia.

In 1817 the case fatality from scarlet fever in Richmond, Virginia, ranged from 10 to 12 per cent whereas in 1962 there were essentially no deaths from this disease. In 1960, the last year for which comparable figures were available, the mortality rate from measles in Mexico was 90 times higher and in Guatemala 189 times higher than that in the United States. Measles is a highly communicable disease affecting nearly all children early in life. Death from measles is exceedingly rare among well nourished children, even without the use of sulfonamides and antibiotics, and the virulence of the measles virus does not differ in the three countries. Young children in Guatemala and Mexico are simply more susceptible hosts. The malnutrition which is responsible for their greatly retarded growth and development during the critical period between weaning and school age, also reduces their resistance to infectious diseases.

Earlier in this discussion, reference was made to Santa Catarina, a rural village in Guatemala in which the nutrition of the preschool child has been improved by daily dietary supplements. Although two epidemics of measles have now struck this village, there has not been a single fatality in children receiving the additional food regularly even though no additional medical care has been rendered and the mortality from measles has remained high in surrounding villages. Since the feeding program was introduced, the children in Santa Catarina have also had shorter, less severe and somewhat less frequent episodes of diarrhea than before or than still occur in surrounding villages

HOST FACTORS IN NUTRITIONAL DISEASE

I will now return to the triad of host, agent and environmental factors which are responsible for the variation of disease with time, place and person. Although I wish to emphasize environmental factors in this presentation, we cannot interpret adequately the effects of either environmental or agent factors in nutritional disease without recognizing the host factors with which they interact.

The effects of age and sex are best understood in terms of the physiological changes with which they are associated. In general, the faster the rate of growth and development, the higher the nutritional requirements per unit of body weight. This means that nutrient needs are relatively greatest in the infant and preschool child, as well as during the pubertal growth spurt and during pregnancy and lactation. All the nutrients contained in breast milk must be ingested by the mother in addition to her usual requirements. Even the lack of teeth at a very young and frequently also at old age may be of nutritional significance.

Both environmental and host factors are involved in the highly characteristic age distribution of many nutritional disorders. The age specificity of weaning diarrhea has already been described. Infantile beriberi occurs in breast-fed infants at two to three months of age because this is when the meager stores of thiamin present at birth in a child born of a deficient mother become exhausted if the mother's milk is deficient in thiamin. Iron deficiency anemia in a child not receiving proper supplementary feeding usually begins after six months of age, since innate stores of iron last longer than those of thiamin. Rickets is most frequently seen during the period of most active growth because vitamin D is needed primarily for bone enlargement. Even in marked vitamin D deficiency it is doubtful whether classic rickets can develop when such factors as protein deficiency prevent the growth of the child.

Frequent pregnancies may be a major host factor in malnutrition in women of childbearing age. When the demands of pregnancy and lactation are not met by diet, the mother's own tissues become depleted. If the postpartum diet is not sufficient to allow repletion, the mother becomes progressively more poorly nourished. This also reflects on the early health of successive offspring.

In a study in rural India a direct correlation has been found between the number of previous pregnancies and survival of the infant.[4] In some parts of India there is also an increased incidence of osteomalacia in women who have had repeated pregnancies.[5] A similar relationship to iron deficiency anemia is seen in nearly all lesser developed areas.

PATHOLOGIC STATES

In a person whose food supply is apparently ample, malnutrition can occur as a result of

136

noninfectious pathologic states in the host. Some of these, such as congenital metabolic disorders, are not of immediate environmental origin; others with an environmental component, such as cancer and heart disease, are beyond the scope of this discussion. Infectious diseases, however, are host factors which clearly have their origin in the environment and which have a profound effect on nutritional status. The effect on nutrition is particularly important in technically underdeveloped areas in which a high incidence of infections occurs in populations which are already relatively poorly nourished.

Large increases in the urinary output of nitrogen have been demonstrated in bacterial diseases such as typhoid fever, pneumonia and acute febrile tuberculosis, viral diseases such as measles and chickenpox, and systemic protozoan diseases such as malaria.

For example, in metabolic studies, it has been impossible to maintain nitrogen balance in patients with such acute diseases as typhoid fever and febrile tuberculosis despite greatly increased protein intake.[6-13] In the only such study of a rickettsial disease in man, Harrell and co-workers[14] found that over 4 gm. of protein per kg. of body weight was required to maintain nitrogen balance during the febrile period of Rocky Mountain spotted fever.

Not only do severe infections increase nitrogen losses, but INCAP studies have shown that infections resulting from vaccination against smallpox and administration of the new live-virus measles vaccine also increase the urinary excretion of nitrogen. This is also true for immunization with the 17-D strain of yellow fever vaccine which produces almost no febrile or systemic reaction.[15]

There is no longer any doubt that all infections cause some increased nitrogen loss in the urine, and that some of them decrease protein absorption from the gastrointestinal tract. It would be a mistake, however, to assume that these metabolic effects of infection account for all, or even most, of their influence on nutritional status. As already mentioned, infections are accompanied by a tendency to reduce the intake of solid food and to substitute watery gruels of lower protein content,

to say nothing of the administration of medicines which alter gastrointestinal motility and flora.

It is not surprising, therefore, that an infectious episode is an almost invariable antecedent to kwashiorkor. Kwashiorkor can be thought of as a frequent result of synergism of malnutrition and infection in which the symptoms of malnutrition predominate. In weanling diarrhea there is also a synergism of malnutrition and infection in which the symptoms of the infection predominate. It is doubtful, however, whether either disease would be of public health importance without the presence of both factors.

Avitaminosis A is also closely associated with the stress of infection. In most infections vitamin A blood levels are considerably reduced and in certain pathological states, including pneumonia, obstructive jaundice and chronic nephritis, the vitamin may appear in the urine.[16] Moreover, giardiasis and other intestinal parasites may impair intestinal absorption of vitamin A.[17,18] As early as 1892 Spicer[19] in England reported that xerophthalmia frequently developed in children with meningitis, infantile diarrhea, chronic tuberculosis, measles, whooping cough and severe chickenpox. Measles and other infections are recognized to be a major factor in the occurrence of xerophthalmia and keratomalacia in Indonesia, where large numbers of children become partially or totally blind as a result, and more sporadically in Latin America, Africa and Southeast Asia.

As to thiamin deficiency, the observations of many qualified observers interned in Japanese prisoner of war camps in World War II leave no doubt that dysentery will precipitate acute, clinical beriberi in persons whose diet is chronically deficient in thiamin.[20] Pneumonia, malaria and even bed bugs have been listed as factors capable of precipitating acute beriberi in persons in a borderline state of thiamin deficiency.[21]

The association of infection with decreased blood levels and increased urinary excretion of vitamin C and with clinical scurvy is well established. An interesting paper by Hess[22] in 1917 called attention to the frequency with

137

which florid scurvy developed in children from low income families in New York City after they had contracted a febrile illness such as otitis, pneumonia or nephritis. Even vaccination against smallpox has been reported to precipitate scurvy in malnourished children.[23] and recent INCAP studies have demonstrated an increased excretion of ascorbic acid in the urine at the height of the primary vaccination reaction.

Of the several ways in which infections influence iron metabolism and the occurrence of anemia, blood loss is the most direct. The modern studies carried out by Roche and co-workers[24, 25] in Venezuela using Cr^{51}- and Fe^{59}-tagged hemoglobin have shown that each hookworm causes a daily loss of approximately 0.03 ml. of blood or 2.74 ml. of blood per million eggs excreted. Of persons in a hyperendemic area 10 to 20 per cent will have an egg excretion equivalent to infection with at least 100 worms, and for a single human host to have 500 or more worms is not uncommon. If the diets of persons with severe hookworm infection are low in iron, typical iron deficiency will almost certainly be observed. Another interesting example is the effect of the fish tapeworm, *Diphyllobothrium latum*, which can produce macrocytic anemia in man because of its special avidity for vitamin B_{12}.[26, 27]

Chronic infection may decrease iron-binding capacity, reduce iron retention and shorten the life span of erythrocytes. At the same time, the bone marrow in persons with chronic infections may be unable to increase red cell production sufficiently to compensate for these factors. The result is the so-called anemia of infection.[28]

Burns, fractures, accidental and surgical trauma also result in strongly negative nitrogen balance for prolonged periods of time. These stresses, like that of infection, result in an increased adrenal glucocorticoid secretion which mobilizes nitrogen from muscle and other relatively dispensible tissues for use by the liver and other essential organs. Part of this mobilized nitrogen spills over into the urine. Direct necrosis at the site of the lesions also contributes to the protein loss and in the case of burns may be very large. The negative nitrogen balance of trauma can be minimized and sometimes eliminated experimentally by high protein intakes, but more often protein intake is drastically reduced under these circumstances because of poor appetite and poor dietary therapy.

INFLUENCE OF ENVIRONMENT

Medical schools have great difficulty in conveying to their students an adequate appreciation of the significance of environmental factors in the causation of disease. The specific agent of a disease is usually identified by the physician with the help of the laboratory, and the host is available to him for interview and study, but the environment from which the patient comes may be largely unknown. An oral description of environmental factors may mean little to the physician attending a patient who comes from a socioeconomic group with which he is unfamiliar. Yet frequently the key to the nature and occurrence of the disease lies in the patient's environment. Without personal knowledge of the environment, this key may not be available to the physician. Adequate knowledge of an environment is not usually obtained, however, without firsthand experience.

Environmental factors are particularly significant in the causation of nutritional diseases. Moreover, nutritional diseases are most common in technically underdeveloped areas in which the environmental circumstances are most obscure to western and western-trained physicians. By environment it should be clear that the term includes not only physical and biological factors, but social factors as well. In the case of nutritional disease, the environmental factors may act in at least three different ways: (1) by affecting the availability of nutrients, (2) by affecting nutritional requirements of the host, and (3) by affecting the intake of nutrients.

The environmental factors influencing the availability of nutrients are obviously of major significance, but almost entirely beyond the control of the physician. Included among the environmental factors affecting the availability of nutrients are physical factors such as soil and climate which directly influence agricultural production, biological factors which

138

influence the types of plants and animals which the land can support, and social factors. The latter exert their effect through knowledge of good agricultural practice and its application; availability of agricultural extension services and credit; political and economic stability; freedom from civil disturbance or war; governmental regulations and policies; land distribution and tenure; facilities for food storage and processing; and adequacy of food distribution.

The second category of environmental factors, those influencing the nutrient requirements of the host, are most likely to be understood by the physician. Again, physical, biological and social aspects of the environment are all involved.

At high environmental temperatures there is an increased loss of water and significant quantities of essential nutrients through perspiration. Excessive sodium chloride losses in sweat must be replaced or muscle cramps will develop. The relatively higher incidence of iron deficiency anemia in the tropics may in part be due to excessive iron losses in sweat. Copper, manganese, phosphorus and potassium are also present in at least trace quantities in sweat, and from 5 to 15 mg. of calcium per hour may be lost, depending upon the circumstances. Iodine concentration in sweat appears to vary directly with that in blood plasma; thus it is not likely to be a significant factor in the development of endemic goiter.[29]

The amount of nitrogen lost in sweat is sufficient to influence nitrogen balance experiments and may be one of a number of factors contributing to the high prevalence of protein malnutrition or kwashiorkor in tropical areas. Conditions need not be extreme to produce significant nitrogen loss. At an ambient temperature of 90°F. in New Orleans, an output of 75 mg. of nitrogen per hour in sweat was observed in moderately active young men.[30] Under such conditions from 2.2 to 2.6 gm. of total amino acids would be lost. However this loss decreases with lower dietary protein intakes.

Water-soluble vitamin losses also occur but, in general, they are too small to be of significance in practical nutrition. Nevertheless,

there are reports of studies in rats in which three times as much thiamin per gram of food was required to prevent increased pyruvate excretion in the urine at 35°c. compared with 15°c. Also, it has been reported that avitaminosis A can be induced more rapidly in rats in a hot environment.[29]

The effect of low environmental temperatures is greatly reduced by protective clothing and heated buildings. On the other hand, the necessity of performing work in heavy, clumsy clothing may significantly increase caloric requirements. Thus, persons working out of doors under conditions of extreme cold require more calories and hence more thiamin as well. As environmental temperatures become colder, there is also an increase in the urinary excretion of N-methylnicotinamide.[29] In addition, water requirements may be increased by performance of heavy muscular activity while wearing clothing which is heavier than necessary and which subsequently leads to excessive sweat loss. It is paradoxical that excessive sweating may occur at either high or low environmental temperatures.

Sunshine and humidity also play a role in the adverse effects of high environmental temperatures. On the other hand, beneficial effects are derived from exposure of the skin to sufficient sunshine to prevent the occurrence of vitamin D deficiency. In areas in which there was wintertime shortage of sunlight and protective clothing further reduced exposure of the skin to sunlight, rickets was common until the advent of vitamin D concentrates.

As to the biological factors influencing nutrient requirements of the host, the occurrence of pathogens in the environment, which through infection of the host increase nutrient requirements, is particularly important and has already been discussed.

Examples of social or cultural factors influencing host requirements can also be cited. Persons who acquire nutritional macrocytic anemia because of infection with fish tapeworm would not be in this predicament if it were not for their custom of consuming raw fish. Iron deficiency anemia would not be as common if everyone wore. shoes in areas in which hookworm is endemic.

Dietary habits which result in the consumption of foods containing significant quantities of goitrogens increase iodine requirements. Another example which falls into this category is the occurrence of rickets in children whose parents protect them from the sun to keep their skin from turning darker. This is not uncommon among West Indian Negroes in Panama and the Canal Zone and has recently been described also in the Dominican Republic.

The physical, biological and cultural factors affecting the consumption of food by the host can also be readily identified. Food patterns in either hot tropical or cold arctic climates tend to be different from those in temperate zones. Altitude *per se* has little direct effect but does influence the type of food immediately available. As to biological influences, it has already been emphasized that the effect of infectious diseases in decreasing appetite and influencing the character of the diet is probably more important to nutritional states than to its direct metabolic effects.

By far the most significant group of environmental factors influencing food consumption is socioeconomic. The relatively high cost of the so-called protective foods is a major factor in the appearance of malnutrition in any population; in the United States such costs are particularly conducive to malnutrition in retired persons living on limited incomes. In technically underdeveloped areas there is little hope of improving the nutritional status of the people unless the price of suitable food can somehow be brought within their economic reach. Although free distribution of food may be an effective temporary measure, it is not acceptable as a permanent solution.

Economic factors are closely related to political ones. For example, subsidies and price controls may make it easier for people to buy food; duties and special taxes may raise food costs. Legislation requiring the enrichment of cereals and other staple foods can insure essential nutrients even when changes in food habits are difficult to achieve. Systems of food rationing or food disposal plans imposed by governments represent a direct attempt to influence an individual's food consumption. Depending upon their wisdom and objectives, government policies may be powerful factors in either increasing or reducing the prevalence of malnutrition.

Improved availability of food is significant only to the extent that it leads to increased food consumption. The cultural factors which influence food consumption are often the decisive ones. Malnutrition very often results from dietary habits based on ignorance and food prejudice. From a nutritional point of view many beliefs regarding food are irrational even when there is a rationalization for them in the culture. Nutrition education is so difficult because it involves not only supplying knowledge where there is none, but also displacing deepseated beliefs.

Sometimes food prejudices have a rational basis. For example, in some technically underdeveloped areas cow's milk is considered a potential cause of diarrhea in young children. This belief arises from the poor quality of milk available in many technically underdeveloped areas due to adulteration, contamination and lack of refrigeration. Under such circumstances reluctance to accept even reconstituted dried milk becomes understandable especially when its use is likely to coincide with episodes of infectious diarrhea of other origin. The original basis for avoiding pork is not hard to understand. We know now that pork which is insufficiently cooked is a potential source of sometimes fatal trichinosis and of the pork tapeworm, *Tinea solim*, which, unlike that of beef, can give rise to hydatid disease through autoinfection with fertile ova.

In the United States, food faddism is a common cause of malnutrition. At best the so-called "health" foods are needlessly expensive sources of nutrients and at worst nutritionally imbalanced and irrational. Excessive consumption of some of them to the exclusion of a balanced diet may be dangerous. Although the diets consumed by the lacto-ovo vegetarians are usually excellent, eventually the strict vegetarians are likely to have a megaloblastic anemia due to vitamin B_{12} deficiency. Diet fads, especially some of the reducing diets, are likely to lead to serious nutritional deficiency. Unfortunately, even physicians are guilty of recommending or approving reducing diets which are nutritionally unsound.

Outright food quackery is particularly likely to victimize elderly persons living on fixed incomes. Although nutritional deficiencies are the usual result, quackery, food faddism or ignorance occasionally result in excessive intakes of a nutrient. A number of cases of toxicity from excessively large doses of vitamin A and vitamin D have been reported in the United States. As in other aspects of therapeutics (and of human society), the dangerous misconception that "the more of a good thing the better" is hard to eliminate. Cases of carotenemia have been reported from excessive consumption of carrots, and in Costa Rica carotenemia has been seen in a child who received excessive quantities of African palm oil.

In technically underdeveloped areas the tendency of mothers to withhold solid food from the children at the onset of diarrhea and to substitute watery gruels and starchy solutions is, as already noted, a major factor contributing to the high incidence of kwashiorkor. Unfortunately, this practice is often encouraged and followed by otherwise well trained physicians and, for this reason, is doubly hard to combat. Of course, it is not the physician's intent that the child be maintained on a watery inadequate diet for many weeks, but this is a common result, since protein malnutrition can perpetuate the diarrhea after the infection has passed. Physicians in this country who recommend withholding solid food during diarrheal episodes are fortunate in that their patients are well nourished at the start and that the episodes are short. It has been known for fifty years that the absorption of nitrogen and fat increases quantitatively with intake even though it is less efficient in diarrheal disease. Clinically a patient's recovery is better with adequate feeding even though the volume of his stools is increased.

A discussion of the social factors influencing food consumption would not be complete without mentioning the problem of alcohol. Many countries have a problem with alcoholics in whom serious multiple vitamin deficiencies and cirrhosis of the liver develop because of inadequate food consumption. Among the lower socioeconomic groups in technically underdeveloped countries the expenditure of part of the family income by the father on cheap liquor leaves insufficient money to feed his family. Alcoholic beverages also displace more nourishing foods in his own diet.

It should be clear that the social factors influencing food habits and food consumption are equalled in significance only by the primary availability of food. In the developed and underdeveloped countries alike, educational, anthropological, religious, economic, administrative and political factors all influence the adequacy of the nutrient intake of the individual subject.

CONCLUSION

The causes of the diseases of man can be understood only in terms of his relationship to his environment. The agent of nutritional disease is the relative lack of an essential nutrient, but the etiology of the disease includes host factors which determine whether or not a given nutrient intake will be adequate, and environmental factors which affect both agent and host.

The environment includes biological and social as well as physical factors. All three influence the availability of nutrients, the requirements of the host for specific nutrients, and the consumption of nutrients. Determining the cause of a nutritional disease is a study in human ecology—of the interaction of host, agent and environment.

ACKNOWLEDGMENT

This paper is the outcome of innumerable discussions with Dr. John E. Gordon of Harvard University and represents the application of much of his philosophy and experience with the epidemiology of infectious disease to the understanding of nutritional disease.

REFERENCES

1. GORDON, J. E., CHITKARA, I. D. and WYON, J. B. Weanling diarrhea. *Am. J. M. Sc.*, 245: 345, 1963.
2. SABIN, A. B. Cause and control of fatal, infantile diarrheal diseases. In: Health and Nutrition, vol. 6, p. 54. United States Papers prepared for the United Nations Conference on the Application of Science and Technology for the Benefit of the Less Developed Areas. Washington, D. C., 1963. U. S. Government Printing Office.

3. Babbott, F. L., Jr., Frye, W. W. and Gordon, J. E. Intestinal parasites of man in Arctic Greenland. *Am. J. Trop. Med. & Hyg.*, 10: 185, 1961.
4. India-Harvard-Ludhiana Population Study. Unpublished data.
5. Snapper, I. and Nathan, D. J. Rickets and osteomalacia. *Am. J. Med.*, 22: 939, 1957.
6. Coleman, W. and Gephart, F. C. Clinical calorimetry. vi. Notes on the absorption of fat and protein in typhoid fever. *Arch. Int. Med.*, 15: 882, 1915.
7. Coleman, W. and DuBois, E. F. Clinical calorimetry. vii. Calorimetric observation on the metabolism of typhoid patients with and without food. *Arch. Int. Med.*, 15: 887, 1915.
8. Shaffer, P. A. and Coleman, W. Protein metabolism in typhoid fever. *Arch. Int. Med.*, 4: 538, 1909.
9. Krauss, E. Untersuchungen über den minimalen Eiweissverbrauch des Menschen unter gesunden und krankhaften Bedingungen. *Deutsches Arch. Klin. Med.*, 150: 13, 1926.
10. McCann, W. S. The protein requirement in tuberculosis. *Arch. Int. Med.*, 29: 33, 1922.
11. Narasinga Rao, B. S. and Gopalan, C. Nutrition and tuberculosis. ii. Studies on nitrogen, calcium and phosphorus metabolism in tuberculosis. *Indian J. M. Res.*, 46: 93, 1958.
12. Johnston, J. A. Nutritional Studies in Adolescent Girls and Their Relation to Tuberculosis. Springfield, Ill., 1953. Charles C Thomas.
13. Co Tui, Kuo, N. H. and Schmidt, L. The protein status in pulmonary tuberculosis. *Am. J. Clin. Nutrition*, 2: 252, 1954.
14. Harrell, G. T., Wolff, W. A., Venning, W. L. and Reinhart, J. B. Prevention and control of disturbances of protein metabolism in Rocky Mountain spotted fever; value of forced feedings of high-protein diet and of administration of specific antiserum. *South. M. J.*, 39: 551, 1946.
15. Gandra, Y. R. and Scrimshaw, N. S. Infection and nutritional status. ii. Effect of mild virus infection induced by 17-D yellow fever vaccine on nitrogen metabolism in children. *Am. J. Clin. Nutrition*, 9: 159, 1961.
16. Goldsmith, G. A. Nutritional Diagnosis. Springfield, Ill., 1963. Charles C Thomas.
17. Chesney, J. and McCord, A. B. Vitamin A of serum following administration of haliver oil in normal children and in chronic steatorrhea. *Proc. Soc. Exper. Biol. & Med.*, 13: 887, 1934.
18. Katsampes, C. P., McCord, A. B. and Phillips, W. A. Vitamin A absorption test in cases of giardiasis. *Am. J. Dis. Child.*, 67: 189, 1944.
19. Spicer, H. Keratomalacia in young children. *Lancet*, 2: 1387, 1892.
20. Smith, D. A. and Woodruff, M. F. A. Deficiency Diseases in Japanese Prison Camps. Medical Research Council (London) Special Report Series No. 274. London, 1951. His Majesty's Stationery Office.
21. Platt, B. S. Protein malnutrition and infection. *Am. J. Trop. Med.*, 6: 773, 1957.
22. Hess, A. F. Infantile scurvy. v. A study of its pathogenesis. *Am. J. Dis. Child.*, 14: 337–353, 1917.
23. Stern, R. Uber den Zusammen Nang von Skorbut und Infektion. *Ztschr. Kinderhk.*, 36: 32, 1923.
24. Roche, M. and Perez-Gimenez, M. E. Intestinal loss and reabsorption of iron in hookworm infection. *J. Lab. & Clin. Med.*, 54: 49, 1959.
25. Roche, M., Perez-Gimenez, M. E., Layrisse, M. and DiPrisco, E. Study of urinary and fecal excretion of radioactive chromium Cr^{51} in man. Its use in the measurement of intestinal blood loss associated with hookworm infection. *J. Clin. Invest.*, 36: 1183, 1957.
26. Von Bonsdorff, B. Pernicious anemia caused by *Diphyllobothrium latum* in the light of recent investigations. *Blood*, 3: 91, 1948.
27. Von Bonsdorff, B. *Diphyllobothrium latum* as a cause of pernicious anemia. *Exper. Parasitol.*, 5: 207, 1956.
28. Cartwright, G. E. and Wintrobe, M. M. The anemia of infection xvii. A review. In: Recent Advances in Internal Medicine, vol. 5, p. 165. Edited by Dock, W., and Snapper, I. Chicago, 1952. Year Book Publishers, Inc.
29. Mitchell, H. H. and Edman, M. Nutrition and Climatic Stress. Springfield, Ill. 1951. Charles C Thomas.
30. Bost, R. W. and Borgstrom, P. Cutaneous excretion of nitrogenous material in New Orleans. *Am. J. Physiol.*, 79: 242, 1927.

142

Malnutrition, Learning and Behavior[1,2]

NEVIN S. SCRIMSHAW, PH.D., M.D.[3]

FOR THE GREAT MAJORITY of children in the technically underdeveloped countries of the world, retardation in physical growth and development due to malnutrition and its interaction with infection is a fact of existence. This is visible in the almost universally smaller body size of underprivileged populations, regardless of their genetic background. Early malnutrition which stunts growth has also clearly and repeatedly been shown in experimental animals to reduce subsequent learning ability, memory, and behavior. To the extent that this is true for young children as well, the generations on whom social and economic progress will depend in the remainder of this century are being maimed now in body frame, in nervous system, and in mind.

Evidence is already available to suggest that malnutrition during the first few years of life does have an adverse effect on subsequent learning and behavior. The mechanisms involved are not yet well established, and the precise timing, nature,

and severity of the malnutrition responsible need clarification. Nevertheless, it will be evident that the effects of early malnutrition are so far-reaching that the nutrition and health of young children cannot be neglected if development schemes and aid programs are to achieve their full objectives in developing countries.

EVIDENCE FROM EXPERIMENTAL ANIMALS

In the rat, 80% of the brain growth occurs by 4 weeks of age and in the pig by 8–10 weeks compared with less than 20% of the final body weight at these ages. As early as 1920, Jackson and Stewart (1) showed that rats underfed in the first few weeks after weaning and then placed on an adequate diet had smaller brains at maturity than control animals. Dobbing, McCance, Widdowson and co-workers at the Cambridge University Medical School, Cambridge, England, have confirmed this with both rats (2, 3) and swine (4, 5). Since the brain is growing so much faster than the rest of the body during these early weeks, the result is a brain which is abnormally large for the body weight but small for the age of the animal. The most marked postnatal retardation in brain growth in the rats was produced by having a single mother suckle 15–20 young (6). In this way, undernutrition was made to coincide with the time when the brain was

[1] From Department of Nutrition and Food Science, Massachusetts Institute of Technology, Cambridge, Massachusetts.

[2] Presented at the Twenty-Fifth Anniversary Symposium of the Nutrition Foundation, Inc., November 17, 1966.

[3] Head, Department of Nutrition and Food Science, Massachusetts Institute of Technology, Cambridge, Massachusetts.

American Journal of Clinical Nutrition, May, 1967, Vol.20, No.5, pp. 493-502.

growing most rapidly, relative to the body as a whole. Beyond about 3 weeks of age for the rat and 5 weeks for the pig, the effect of short periods of inanition on brain size becomes increasingly less pronounced.

Experiments of this type simulate nutritional marasmus in the young child. It should be noted, moreover, that marasmus in children is particularly common below 1 year of age (7, 8), when the rate of brain growth is at its peak. After 1 year of age the more common form of protein–calorie malnutrition in children is the severe protein deficiency of kwashiorkor (9). With this type of malnutrition, even more central nervous system damage is observed in the experimental animal.

When Platt and co-workers of the British Medical Research Laboratories in London placed weanling rats and piglets (10) and puppies (11) born of well-nourished mothers on diets severely deficient in protein but adequate in calories, the animals showed functional and histological signs of central nervous system damage. The rats developed spasmodic trembling of head and forepaws after 4 days; the pigs soon walked on tiptoe with a "hobble skirt" gait and some incoordination of the hind legs; and the puppies became hyperirritable. Electroencephalograms showed diminution of rhythmic activity, and histological changes appeared in the nerve cells and neuroglial cells in the spinal cord and medulla. When similarly depleted animals were subsequently fed a high protein diet for 1–3 months, the histological changes were not reversed, although the clinical condition improved promptly. The severity of the changes was increased by lowering the age at which the deficiency was established, by reducing the protein value of the diet, or by increasing the duration of the deficient diet.

Workers at Cornell University have reported comparable findings in similarly treated baby pigs (12). They also described alterations in the brain itself, including swelling of the neurons and a reduction in their numbers in the grey matter. The same group has also shown that food deprivation in male rats during the first 3 weeks of life interferes with subsequent visual discrimination performance in a maze (13).

Nováková et al. (14) of the Czechoslovakian Academy of Science compared rats weaned at 21 days with those weaned at 30 days. They found that learning and behavioral responses to an electric bell sound were inhibited by the earlier weaning. However, if the animals weaned early were fed a high fat–low carbohydrate diet simulating rat milk, the differences were abolished.

Widdowson et al. (5) have recently extended their studies of rats and pigs from ones of simple undernutrition in the early weeks to deficiencies primarily of protein. The undernourished rats and pigs became nervous and ravenously hungry. The protein-deficient animals were more docile and less easily disturbed. Furthermore, they lost their appetites and it was difficult to induce them to eat. In these characteristics, they resembled children with kwashiorkor.

In those studies in which the diets of the mothers during pregnancy were deficient in protein and whose offspring were also fed deficient diets after weaning, the effects were similar but even more pronounced (10).

In addition to the organic damage from early malnutrition which can be detected by anatomical and histological studies, it has been suggested that there may be irreversible biochemical changes as well. Certainly, with early retardation in physical growth and development, there is concurrent retardation in biochemical maturation (15). The water, lipid, cholesterol, and enzyme content of tissues of malnourished infants correspond more to those of normal infants of the same length or height rather than of the same chronological age.

There is only fragmentary and doubtful evidence, however, as to the permanence of these biochemical effects. If there is such an effect of early environment on subsequent brain chemistry, it would be an interesting kind of "biochemical Freudianism." [4]

COMPARABLE OBSERVATIONS IN CHILDREN

In the child, the brain achieves 80% of its adult weight in the first 3 years compared with just over 20% of total body weight. Thus, the first 3 years of development of the young child are comparable to the first 4 weeks in the life of a rat.

The human brain at the time of birth is gaining weight at a rate of 1-2 mg/min. It might be expected, therefore, that protein deficiency serious enough to limit gain in height and weight would also limit brain growth during the first 2-3 years of life when it is undergoing most of its increase in size. Head circumference is a useful, if not absolute indicator of brain size, although not any indicator of normal variations in intellectual capacity. When children are undernourished at an early age, their brain growth, as indicated by head circumference, is significantly poorer in contrast to matched controls.

Stoch and Smythe (16) have demonstrated this in their study of 42 South African children who ranged from 10 months to 3 years of age. One group attended an all-day school where they were well fed. The other group ate in their own homes and were found to be malnourished. It has become apparent in this study that the head circumference of the malnourished group is distinctly smaller than that of the controls. These differences have persisted for a follow-up period which now extends to 10 years, and are presumably permanent.

Similar differences in head circumference of individuals from groups of com-

⁴ See McDermott, W., J. Med. Educ. Part II. Sept. 1966, p. 145.

parable genetic but different nutritional backgrounds have been reported from Uganda by Dean and Brown (17, 18), from Peru by Graham (19), and from Mexico by Ambrosius (20). To the extent that brain growth is impaired concurrently with early retardation in linear growth, the population at risk includes more than half of the world's children.

Hundreds of studies have been reported of the slow growth in height and weight of preschool children in the lower socioeconomic groups which make up the great bulk of the populations of developing countries (21, 22). During the first few months when most of the children are adequately breast fed, their growth parallels that of well-nourished children anywhere. The pattern which these children show thereafter is consistent and tragic.

Beginning no later than 6 months of age, when breast milk is no longer a sufficient source of protein and when the prevalence of diarrheal and other infections is increasing steadily, growth is progressively retarded. Moreover, the mortality rate of these children is from 20 to 30 times higher than for children of comparable age in the industrialized countries. In country after country, the height and weight of children in these circumstances average below the 16th percentile of well-nourished children in the United States and Western Europe.

Whenever comparative studies have been done, however, the growth of children in the middle and upper socioeconomic groups of developing countries has been found similar to that of children of comparable age in the United States and Europe. Sometimes the racial composition of the more privileged groups within a country is somewhat different; sometimes it is identical. It seems to make no significant difference in the findings.

In El Salvador and Guatemala, the predominantly Mayan Indian children are malnourished in the preschool years. They are also greatly stunted in early growth and are much smaller in stature as adults (23). By contrast, the children of families in the middle and upper socioeconomic groups in these two countries show growth rates which do not differ significantly from those of North American children. Although they have a much higher proportion of European genetic background, it is unlikely that this is a major factor. In Costa Rica, among populations which are uniformly of predominantly European origin, children of the poor urban and rural families are as retarded in growth as the Guatemalan Indian children (24). In Costa Rica, also, children attending private schools match United States height standards.

When bone maturation has been appraised by evaluating the number and shape of the small bones revealed by radiograph of the wrist, the results have been similar (25). In several Guatemalan villages in which the Institute of Nutrition of Central America and Panama (INCAP) has conducted studies, preschool children showed a 2- to 3-year delay in bone maturation (26).

A list of the countries reporting severe retardation in growth and maturation among preschool children and, subsequently, adults of small stature, would include nearly all of those considered to be technically underdeveloped.

FACTORS RESPONSIBLE FOR RETARDED
GROWTH AND DEVELOPMENT OF
PRESCHOOL CHILDREN OF
DEVELOPING COUNTRIES

While malnutrition is the primary factor in bringing about these circumstances, they cannot necessarily be corrected by improved diet alone. This is because the malnutrition common among preschool children of developing areas is synergistic with infections (27).

Not only do such children receive a diet grossly inadequate in protein for normal growth and development once breast milk is no longer sufficient, but also the frequent infections worsen their nutritional status in a number of ways. Appetite is reduced and, as a therapeutic measure, solid food tends to be withdrawn and replaced by thin, watery gruels. Moreover, all infections, even those as mild as immunization with live virus vaccines, cause a stress reaction which results in increased loss in the urine of nitrogen and several of the vitamins. To make matters worse, strong purgatives often are administered repeatedly to the sick child, adding to the diarrhea and interfering with absorption of nutrients.

Unfortunately, infections are more frequent and severe in these children because their malnutrition lowers resistance and because they are almost constantly exposed to infection due to poor environmental sanitation and lack of personal hygiene.

Since they are almost universally found in malnourished children, the role of intestinal parasites has been recognized for a long time and is probably exaggerated. Far more important are the frequent bouts of diarrheal disease, of severe upper respiratory infections and their complications, and the common communicable diseases of childhood which are more serious in malnourished children.

Unpublished World Health Organization data from surveys conducted for a 1-month period of children under 10 years of age in communities without water supplies revealed the high diarrheal prevalence rates which can occur. For example, in the United Arab Republic 38% of 317 children examined in nonwater-supplied regions developed diarrhea, as opposed to a 10% incidence among 174 children living in water-supplied areas. In Iran, 36% of 453 children living with water supplies had diarrhea during this period while nearly 49% of 425 children in nonwater-supplied regions had diarrhea during the month when the survey was made.

The data of Gordon and co-workers (28, 29) from Northern India and INCAP in rural Guatemala are based on biweekly visits throughout the year. They indicate that diarrheal rates are highest in the 2nd year of life. For example, in three Guatemalan highland villages the rates averaged 224 diarrheal episodes per 100 children for the first 2 years, with a peak rate of 298 at 15–17 months of age (30). In the Guatemalan village studied most intensively, Santa Maria Cauqué, nearly one-fifth of the children had eight or more episodes of diarrhea in their first 2 years of life (31). Dr. Leonardo J. Mata of INCAP has now followed a number of children in this town from birth to 2 years of age by repeated bacteriological, parasitological, and viral studies as well as by maintaining a detailed record of morbidity (32).

The burden of infection can be illustrated by a case which is not at all unusual. The febrile illnesses in the first 2 years of life of one child totaled 151 days and included, sometimes concurrently, eight episodes of diarrhea, five of severe upper respiratory infections, four bouts of tonsillitis, two of impetigo, and one each of bronchopneumonia, unknown viral infection with rash, cellulitis, conjunctivitis, stomatitis, bronchitis, and chicken pox. In addition, there was laboratory evidence of at least 60 days of enterovirus excretion, 56 days of three different bacterial species responsible for dysentery, 108 days of various intestinal protozoan infections, plus seven episodes in which staphylococci or streptococci were identified. During all of this the child was also harboring several species of intestinal worms.

It is scarcely surprising that this child and millions like her in developing countries around the world fail to grow during this period, and that many of them die of either malnutrition or infection in the 2nd year of life. The psychomotor development of children such as the one described has been found retarded by more than 6 months at 1 year of age.

It should be apparent from this brief account that any association between early retardation in physical growth and impairment of mental development affects very large numbers of the world's children. Permanent physical impairment resulting from malnutrition is certain and mental retardation is probable.

FIELD STUDIES IN HUMAN POPULATIONS

In the study of Stoch and Smythe (16) on African children, a series of intelligence tests was administered to both groups. The malnourished group with the smaller head circumferences and grossly underweight bodies gave significantly lower scores. Moreover, there has been no improvement in relative scores during the 10-year follow-up.

The interpretation of this part of the study of Stoch and Smythe is extremely doubtful, since the malnourished children lived in wretched housing with no sanitary facilities, were from broken, poverty-stricken homes, and suffered gross neglect. By contrast, the families of the control group lived in neat brick houses with running water and sanitary facilities and all of the fathers and mothers were employed. All of the children in this group were legitimate compared with only 38% in the malnourished group. There is no way to separate the nutritional from other environmental influences in this study. Unfortunately, this is also true of the study of Cabak and Najdanvic (33) in which Serbian children who were malnourished in infancy had significantly lower IQ scores.

In 1944, Kugelmass, Poull and Samuel (34) analyzed the effects of nutritional improvement on mental performance of malnourished children in New York City. Fifty malnourished children 2–9 years of age were matched for chronological age and intelligence quotient with the same number who were considered well nourished. After the nutritional status of the malnourished had been improved for periods ranging from 1 to 3.5 years, there was an average rise of 18 points in IQ compared with essentially no change in the well-nourished group. This study suffers from the fatal flaw that improvement in IQ scores is known to occur from increased attention to rejected or neglected children even when no malnutrition is present. The relative influence of this and other psychological factors on the results obtained cannot be evaluated.

The data gathered in the town of Tlaltizapán, Mexico, through the pioneering studies of Cravioto, Ramos-Galván and others from the Children's Hospital in Mexico City (35–39) have played a major role in attracting attention to the relationship between nutritional retardation of growth and development for chronological age and performance on psychological tests. The economic and social status of families in Tlaltizapán was very uniform. Retardation in growth and development depended upon family dietary practices and on the occurrence of infections and was found not to be related to differences in personal hygiene, housing facilities, proportion of total income spent on food, or other indicators of social and economic status of the families. These investigators found performance of preschool and school children on the Terman-Merrill, Gesell, and Goodenough Draw-A-Man tests to be positively correlated with body heights and weights.

In order to extend these studies to another population group, and also to make more prolonged observations, Cravioto and several members of his team joined forces with INCAP. Some of the results have recently been described (40–42). They show clearly that in the rural Guatemalan children, 6 to 11 years old, included in the study, retardation in height for age was accompanied by poorer performance on the psychological tests employed. These included replacing eight differently shaped wooden blocks in their corresponding holes; indicating whether the motion of the subject's hand behind a screen traced a shape which was the same or different from the block placed in front of him; and finally, whether a block placed in his hand behind a screen was the same or different from the one placed in front of him. These three tests were considered measures of visual, haptic, and kinesthetic sensory integration, respectively.

The children in the upper quartiles for either weight or height for age made consistently fewer errors in each age group from 6 to 11 years than those in the lower quartile. When a group of children from upper income families in Guatemala City was studied in a similar way, no relationship between height or weight for age and test scores was encountered. This was, of course, expected. In a population group where malnutrition is no longer a major factor influencing growth, the variation in height should be primarily genetic and show no direct correlation with inherited and other variations in intellectual performance.

COMPLICATING SOCIAL FACTORS

One of the most difficult aspects of conducting and interpreting field studies of the effect of malnutrition on intellectual performance is the multiplicity of factors other than nutrition known to influence performance on intelligence tests. These include such cultural factors as psychological and social deprivation, education of the parents, motivation, and external stimuli. For underprivileged children in the United States and other industrialized countries, these factors are likely to override any effects of nutritional status and make such effects difficult or impossible to detect.

In the industrialized countries, a child's inadequate intellectual or social performance is the result of a complex interaction over a period of time of genetic variables and primarily nonnutritional factors in the social or cultural environment. In the rural villages of many developing areas, however, variations from family to family in educational and economic status and in beliefs and customs may be relatively small, and together with genetic differences, may be insignificant as determinants of intellectual performance because the children are so affected by the synergism of malnutrition and infection in such areas.

NATURE AND TIMING OF THE MALNUTRITION

The greatly impaired response to any performance test in children with acute kwashiorkor is largely irrelevant to the discussion, since one of the symptoms of kwashiorkor is profound apathy. Moreover, kwashiorkor in a child is an acute process developing in a very few weeks, usually after months or years of protein–calorie malnutrition (9). In Central America, children with kwashiorkor are found no more retarded in height, weight and bone maturation than the children remaining in the villages or urban slums from which those with the syndrome come (42, 43).

Certainly, the phenomenon of retarded growth and development is a general one in the child populations of developing countries and is not dependent on the occurrence of kwashiorkor. It is probable that most children who recover from kwashiorkor do so completely, although this is not certain. A possible exception would be those few kwashiorkor cases occurring among children under 1 year of age.

By analogy with animal experiments, the earlier the malnutrition, the more likely that some permanent damage might occur. In developing countries, in those exceptional cases when the mother is unable to breast-feed her child at all, the most serious consequences would be anticipated.

The sensitivity of the child's brain to abnormalities in amino acid proportions in the first weeks of life is illustrated dramatically by the association of mental retardation with uncorrected inborn errors of metabolism, such as phenylketonuria, maple syrup urine disease, and galactosemia, as described by Stanbury et al. (44).

Malnutrition beyond about 3 years of age probably has no direct permanent effect on mental development. For adults, at least, the starvation studies of Keys (45), and the prison and concentration camp experiences of World War II indicate that the depression and loss of ambition accompanying starvation can be wholly reversed by refeeding.

Of course, any disease, including kwashiorkor, may affect learning and behavior by other than organic means. Interference with learning during critical periods of development would be expected to produce some long-term developmental lag. Furthermore, motivation and responsiveness have much to do with performance, and these may be impaired by the experiences surrounding disease. Apathy, whether of parent or child, can provoke more apathy and contribute to a cumulative pattern of reduced adult-child interaction with adverse consequences for learning and behavior. Certainly, chronically malnourished children are almost inevitably underprivileged in a number of other ways as well. This is why the epidemiological approach is essential.

REQUIRED RESEARCH

The subject is of such overwhelming importance to the future of the world that definitive research is imperative in order to determine the circumstances and manner in which malnutrition influences both intellectual and physical development. It must be research that distinguishes, in the preschool child, between the temporary effects of an acute disease process on test performance and behavior and the long-term consequences of chronic malnutrition.

Such research must take fully into account the influence of variations in the social or cultural environment, including the education, intelligence, and behavior patterns of the parents and others with whom the child interacts. It must consider differences in the physical environment of housing, sanitation, and water supply, and the influence of the biological environment through exposure to the causative agents of parasitic and infectious diseases. It must also distinguish between genetic factors and environmental ones.

Such research is multidisciplinary, demands the highest professional competence and dedication, is costly, and is exceedingly difficult; but it must be done. Unfortunately, it is so demanding of funds and talent that it can only be done in a very few localities a very few times. Superficial and poorly controlled or single-factor studies will serve only to confuse the issue further.

Experimental studies in animals have much to contribute to resolving the problems described, but they are no substitute for a few excellent field studies in human populations, continued over an extended period of time.

The future of the developing countries depends upon improving the knowledge and technological competence of their peoples. Investments in other aspects of development, including schools and teachers, will be reduced in value if the generations of the future are being damaged now in mind and body. The data already at hand suggest that this is occurring.

CONCLUSIONS

In conclusion, the reduced physical growth and development and costly morbidity and mortality of preschool children in essentially all developing areas is already reason enough for giving high priority to programs for improving the nutritional status of the preschool child in these regions. The probability that early malnutrition can cause significant retardation of mental development is an important added reason for emphasizing the universal prevention of malnutrition in the preschool child.

To reinforce the motivation of economic planners and the governments they serve to increase the investment in programs for reducing the synergistic impact of malnutrition and infection on the preschool children of developing countries, convincing supplementary data from soundly conceived and executed, multidisciplinary field studies are urgently needed.

REFERENCES

1. JACKSON, C. M., AND C. A. STEWART. The effects of inanition in the young upon the ultimate size of the body and of the various organs in the albino rat. *J. Exptl. Zool.* 30: 97, 1920.
2. DOBBING, J. The influence of early nutrition on the development and myelination of the brain. *Proc. Roy. Soc., London, Ser. B* 159: 503, 1964.
3. DOBBING, J., AND E. M. WIDDOWSON. The effect of undernutrition and subsequent rehabilitation on myelination of rat brain as measured by its composition. *Brain* 88: 357, 1965.
4. WIDDOWSON, E. M., J. W. DICKERSON AND R. A. MCCANCE. Severe undernutrition in growing and adult animals. 4. The impact of severe undernutrition on the chemical composition of the soft tissues of the pig. *Brit. J. Nutr.* 14: 457, 1960.
5. WIDDOWSON, E. M. Nutritional deprivation in psychobiological development: studies in animals. Pan American Health Organization, WHO. *Proc. Special Session Held during the Fourth Meeting of the PAHO Advisory Committee on Medical Research*, June 16, 1965. Published May, 1966, as Scientific Publ. No. 134, p. 27–38.
6. WIDDOWSON, E. M., AND R. A. MCCANCE. Some effects of accelerating growth. I. General somatic development. *Proc. Roy. Soc., London, Ser. B* 152: 188, 1960.
7. JELLIFFE, D. B. Infant nutrition in the subtropics and tropics. *World Health Organ. Monograph Ser. No. 29.* World Health Organization, Geneva, 1955.
8. MCLAREN, D. S., C. AMMOUN AND G. HOURI. The socio-economic background of marasmus in Lebanon. *Lebanese Med. J.* 17: 85, 1964.
9. SCRIMSHAW, N. S., AND M. BÉHAR. Protein malnutrition in young children. *Science* 133: 2039, 1961.
10. PLATT, B. S., C. R. C. HEARD AND R. J. C. STEWART. Experimental protein–calorie deficiency. In: *Mammalian Protein Metabolism*, edited by H. N. Munro and J. B. Allison. New York, London: Academic, 1964, vol. II, Chapt. 21.

11. PLATT, B. S. Proteins in nutrition. *Proc. Roy. Soc., London, Ser. B* 156: 337, 1962.

12. LOWRY, R. S., W. G. POND, R. H. BARNES, L. KROOK AND J. K. LOOSLI. Influence of caloric level and protein quality on the manifestations of protein deficiency in the young pig. *J. Nutr.* 78: 245, 1962.

13. BARNES, R. H., S. R. CUNNOLD, R. R. ZIMMERMANN, H. SIMMONS, R. B. MACLEOD AND L. KROOK. Influence of nutritional deprivations in early life on learning behavior of rats, as measured by performance in a water maze. *J. Nutr.* 89: 399, 1966.

14. NOVÁKOVÁ, V., J. FALTIN, V. FLANDERA, P. HAHN AND O. KOLDOVSKÝ. Effect of early and late weaning on learning in adult rats. *Nature* 193: 280, 1962.

15. ARROYAVE, G., AND D. WILSON. Urinary excretion of creatinine of children under different nutritional conditions. *Am. J. Clin. Nutr.* 9: 170, 1961.

16. STOCH, M. B., AND P. M. SMYTHE. Does undernutrition during infancy inhibit brain growth and subsequent intellectual development? *Arch. Disease Childhood* 38: 546, 1963.

17. DEAN, R. F. A. The effects of malnutrition on the growth of young children. *Bibliotheca Paediatrica* (Supplementa ad Annales Paediatrici), Revue Internationale de Pediatrie, 72. Basel: Karger, 1960, p. 111–122.

18. BROWN, R. E. Decreased brain weight in malnutrition and its implications. *E. African Med. J.* 12: 584, 1965.

19. GRAHAM, G. In: *Diet and Body Constitution. Ciba Found. Study Group 17,* edited by G. E. W. Wolstenholme and Maeve O'Connor. Boston: Little, Brown, 1964, p. 11–13.

20. AMBROSIUS, K. D. El comportamiento del peso de algunos organos en niños con desnutricion de tercer grado. *Bol. Med. Hosp. Infantil* (Mex.) 18: 47, 1961.

21. JACKSON, R. L. Effect of malnutrition on growth of the preschool child. In: *Pre-School Child Malnutrition: Primary Deterrent to Human Progress.* Washington, D.C.: Nat. Acad. Sci.—Nat. Res. Council, publ. 1282, 1966, Chap. 2.

22. WOODRUFF, C. W. An analysis of the ICNND data on physical growth of the pre-school child. In: *Pre-School Child Malnutrition: Primary Deterrent to Human Progress.* Washington, D.C.: Nat. Acad. Sci.—Nat. Res. Council, publ. 1282, 1966, chapt. 3.

23. SCRIMSHAW, N. S., M. BÉHAR, C. PÉREZ AND F. VITERI. Review article—nutritional problems of children in Central America and Panama. *Pediatrics* 16: 378, 1955.

24. SCRIMSHAW, N. S., J. O. MORALES, A. SALAZAR AND C. LOOMIS. Health aspects of the community development project, rural area, Turrialba, Costa Rica, 1948–51. *Am. J. Trop. Med. Hyg.* 2: 583, 1953.

25. GARN, S. M. Malnutrition and skeletal development in the pre-school child. In: *Pre-School Child Malnutrition: Primary Deterrent to Human Progress.* Washington, D.C.: Nat. Acad. Sci.—Nat. Res. Council, publ. 1282, 1966, Chapt. 5.

26. ROHMANN, C. G., S. M. GARN, M. A. GUZMÁN, M. FLORES, M. BÉHAR AND E. PAO. Osseous development of Guatemalan children on low-protein diets. *Federation Proc.* 23: 338, 1964.

27. SCRIMSHAW, N. S., C. E. TAYLOR AND J. E. GORDON. Interactions of Nutrition and Infection. *World Health Organ. Monograph,* Geneva. In press, 1967.

28. GORDON, J. E., I. D. CHITKARA AND J. B. WYON. Weanling diarrhea. *Am. J. Med. Sci.* 245: 345, 1963.

29. GORDON, J. E. Weanling diarrhea—a synergism of infection and nutrition. Chapter 6 in: Interactions of Nutrition and Infection edited by N. S. Scrimshaw, C. E. Taylor and J. E. Gordon. *World Health Organ. Monograph,* Geneva. In press, 1967.

30. GORDON, J. E., M. A. GUZMÁN, W. ASCOLI AND N. S. SCRIMSHAW. Acute diarrhoeal disease in less developed countries. 2. Patterns of epidemiological behaviour in rural Guatemalan villages. *Bull. World Health Organ.* 31: 9, 1964.

31. GORDON, J. E., W. ASCOLI, V. PIERCE, M. A. GUZMÁN AND L. J. MATA. Studies of diarrheal disease in Central America. VI. An epidemic of diarrhea in a Guatemalan highland village, with a component due to *Shigella dysenteriae,* type I. *Am. J. Trop. Med. Hyg.* 14: 404, 1965.

32. MATA, L. J., AND C. E. BETETA. Colonizacion del intestino de niños lactantes por virus, bacterias y levaduras. *Rev. Col. Med. Guatemala* 16: 127, 1965.

33. CABAK, V., AND R. NAJDANVIC. Effect of undernutrition in early life on physical and mental development. *Arch. Disease Childhood* 40: 532, 1965.

34. KUGELMASS, I. N., L. E. POULL AND E. L. SAMUEL. Nutritional improvement of child mentality. *Am. J. Med. Sci.* 208: 631, 1944.

35. GÓMEZ, F., J. VELAZCO-ALZAGA, R. RAMOS-GALVÁN, J. CRAVIOTO AND S. FRENK. Estudios sobre el niño desnutrido. XVII. Manifestaciones psicologicas (communicacion preliminar). *Bol. Med. Hosp. Infantil Mex.* 11: 631, 1954.

36. RAMOS-GALVÁN, R. Aplicación de la prueba de Goodenough a escolares Mexicanos de distintos grupos socioculturales y diverso estado de nutricion, a) Introduction. b) Estudio en niños asistentes a una escuela privada de la ciudad

de México. *Bol. Med. Hosp. Infantil, Mex.* 21: 137, 149, 1964.

37. RAMOS-GALVÁN, R., L. VEGA AND J. CRAVIOTO. Aplicación de la prueba de Goodenough a escolares Mexicanos de distintos grupos socioculturales y diverso estado de nutrición, c) "Operación Zacatepec" VII. Informe preliminar sobre el estudio de 852 dibujos realizados por escolares del poblado de Tlaltizapán, Morelos. *Bol. Med. Hosp. Infantil, Mex.* 21: 157, 1964.

38. RAMOS-GALVÁN, R., AND V. J. VAZQUEZ. Aplicación de la prueba de Goodenough a escolares Mexicanos de distintos grupos socioculturales y diverso estado de nutrición, d) Estudio en 1197 niños asistentes a escuelas—publicas de la ciudad de Mexico. *Bol. Med. Hosp. Infantil, Mex.* 21: 165, 1964.

39. ESPINOSA-GAONA, C., B. PÉREZ ORTIZ AND R. RAMOS-GALVÁN. Aplicación de la prueba de Goodenough a escolares Mexicanos de distintos grupos socioculturales y diverso estado de nutrición, e) Nuevos estudios en Tlaltizapán, Mor. *Bol. Med. Hosp. Infantil, Mex.* 21: 173, 1964.

40. CRAVIOTO, J., AND B. ROBLES. Evolution of adaptive and motor behavior during rehabilitation from kwashiorkor. *Am. J. Orthopsychiat.* 35: 449, 1965.

41. WUG DE LEON, E., E. DE LICARDIE AND J. CRAVIOTO. "Operacion Nimiquipalg" VI. Desarrollo psicomotor del niño en una poblacion rural de Guatemala, perteneciente al grupo Cakchiquel. *Guatemala Pediat.* 4: 92, 1964.

42. CRAVIOTO, J., E. DE LICARDIE AND H. G. BIRCH. Nutrition, growth and neurointegrative development: an experimental and ecologic study. *Pediatrics* 38 (2): Suppl. part II, 319, 1966.

43. BÉHAR, M., C. ROHMANN, D. WILSON, F. VITERI AND S. M. GARN. Osseous development in children with kwashiorkor. *Federation Proc.* 23: 338, 1964.

44. STANBURY, J. B., J. B. WYNGAARDEN AND D. S. FREDERICKSON. *Metabolic Basis of Inherited Disease* (2nd ed.). New York: McGraw-Hill, 1966.

45. KEYS, A., J. BROZEK, A. HENSCHEL, O. MICKELSEN AND H. L. TAYLOR. *The Biology of Human Starvation.* Minneapolis: Univ. Minnesota Press, 1950, vol. II.

Man, the Destroying Biotype

Man's persistent disruption of natural equilibria poses a constant threat to his means of subsistence.

Raymond Bouillenne

Freedom cannot thrive in lands oppressed by hunger and want.

The great technical achievements of our age, which are so wonderfully expressed in the United States, must not make us forget this fundamental truth: Man remains bound to the environment in which he lives.

In this article I want to present some facts and impressions gathered during my travels, especially in certain tropical regions. I want to develop the following points: (i) The place of man within the biosphere; (ii) the ecological significance of the exploitation of natural resources for purposes of human nutrition and industry; (iii) natural equilibra and the regression of soils; and (iv) the protection of the human habitat.

Man can live and find suitable food only under certain geographical conditions. The earth has a surface of about 500 million square kilometers; more than two-thirds of this is covered by the seas. Of the remaining 127 million square kilometers, glacial areas, high mountain peaks, and deserts are un-

The author is professor of botany and director of the Botanical Institute and Garden, University of Liège, Belgium. This article is adapted from one of a series delivered in the United States during 1960 for the Academic Year Institute, organized by the National Science Foundation.

favorable for human habitation. Man is thus confined to less than one-eighth of the total surface of the globe. He is further limited by an extremely thin layer of breathable air and a thin layer of arable land in which plants can grow and on which animals and men can live. The elements of nature—light, air, water, soil, plants, animals, and men—are closely linked to one another; any perturbation of one releases a cascade of repercussions upon the others. In the course of thousands of years certain balances have been established. Sometimes they have been upset.

Man seems reluctant to accept his place in nature. He declares that the power of his genius, the vastness of his technical achievements, and the abundance of his populations places him beyond the limits of nature. He forgets that he is the outcome of a long series of evolutionary adjustments and that his ascendency over nature is recent indeed.

His first appearance dates back about a million years, it is true, but for ninety-nine hundredths of that million-year period he lived in small dispersed groups as a minute part of the jungle, striving against the elements, threatened both by the brutality of wild life and

Science, March, 1962, Vol.135, No.3505, pp. 706-712.

by the ravages of disease. It is only in the last hundredth of his time on earth that he has discovered the means of defending himself and has become able to increase his numbers and acquire greater knowledge. The oldest civilizations, whether Chinese, Indian, or Egyptian, go back less than 30,000 years and did not become of real importance before 7000 to 10,000 years ago. During that 10,000 years, through science and its techniques, man has improved his lot to a fairly marked degree.

His numbers are now extraordinary. The population of the globe, assessed at about 20 millions 5000 years before our era, had increased to 500 millions by the 17th century. The beginning of the industrial era at the end of the 18th century, with the introduction of steam and electricity, the mechanization of agriculture, and the discovery of fertilizers, brought about a staggering advance in production and also a staggering increase in the birth rate. By 1900 the world population had risen to 1.5 billions, and by 1952, to 2.6 billions. The population of the globe has increased fivefold in 300 years. Recent forecasts indicate that 40 years hence, in the year 2000, there will be 6 billion human mouths to feed. Russia today has a population of about 200 millions. In 1990 there will be 400 million Russians. England's demographic expansion came somewhat earlier; at the end of the 18th century there were just over 10 million inhabitants in Britain (Scotland included); today there are some 50 millions. In China each year brings an additional number equivalent to the population of England.

Man has very rapidly conquered and exploited the available natural resources for the needs of his economy. Nothing stops him in his ever more audacious achievements; he pierces mountains, builds dams, casts bridges across arms of the sea, turns rivers from their courses, gains mastery of the air; he hews down forests and vastly extends the areas of cultivation; he releases almost unthinkable nuclear forces. *Homo sapiens* has become *Homo economicus*.

Yet will he ever be able to escape from his nature as a living being, subject like other living beings to biological feeding requirements? Will he be able to escape the conditions of the environment in which vegetation is the only basic producer of the essential organic materials? We must remember that it is strictly from the plant and animal kingdoms that we get our sustenance. All flesh *is* grass; it is the organic matter synthesized by plants which constitutes the basis of our foodstuffs. We are dependent on the wonderful, complex little factory that each green leaf represents. Green plants alone have the power to synthesize from the carbon dioxide of the air and from water, at low temperature and by means of light, chlorophyll, the protoplasm of plant cells, and the sugars that mark the transition from inorganic to organic matter. If land and sea plants ceased to fulfill this function there would be no more sugar nor meat nor oil nor cotton nor flax nor rubber nor paper. All life would come to an end on the surface of the earth. The delay would be one of but a few months, despite the large stocks of certain foodstuffs that are accumulated in some places.

The biological limits of plant synthesis as well as the ecological balance in the medium thus determine the world potential of life. These two factors place limits on man's food supply and on the reserves of energy needed by his industries. Whether he likes it or not, the problem of resources of energy (petroleum, coal, wood) from fossil deposits and the problem of feeding humanity are closely linked to the problem of balance between various elements of the biosphere of which man is inevitably a part. Nuclear energy has opened up new horizons in the sphere of industry, but *not* in the realm of foodstuffs. Before man tries to explore the moon he must continue to eat on earth.

In regions of temporary abundance, such as America and some parts of

Europe, the question of food does not force itself on public attention. We think of it only when we must draw up a medical diet or analyze a cooking recipe or solve pressing problems of markets, of transportation, or of purchasing power. When we look beyond the bounds of these regions of abundance, however, one fact cannot be escaped: there is not enough food for the present number of living beings. One-third of the world's population has enough to eat. This third alone eats three-quarters of the crops harvested over the entire earth. The other two-thirds of the human race have not enough to eat, and this situation is getting worse each day, as 120,000 new beings a day are born. The globe is at present able to feed only 4 billion inhabitants on a ration of 2800 calories per person per day (in America the daily individual consumption is about 4000 calories; in Sweden, 5000). In the year 2000 there will be 6 billion mouths to fed, on a planet where there is less and less useful land.

The surface of cultivated lands cannot be extended indefinitely. To solve the problem some advocate the opening and development of new lands, others urge the application of the results of laboratory research through which such progress has already been made in the fields of plant physiology, selection, agronomy, and phytopharmacy. It is possible and indeed probable that some gains may be made through the use of fertilizers, the judicious application of the laws of plant growth, knowledge of soil conditions and suitable climates, and application of new cultivation techniques. But—though this solution may seem the most obvious and rapid—we must beware of the strictly temporary gains that would come from clearing forest regions which have kept their primitive character. Reliance on such solutions could be disastrous.

The expansion of human populations and the extraordinary increase in the technical means at their command are creating a serious state of disequilib-rium. The speed with which detrimental changes have occurred in recent centuries is fantastic. Cultivation has already so extensively replaced natural conditions, over numerous and vast territories, that very little of virgin nature remains. And reduction of forest areas below a certain limit has been proved to have serious consequences. It disturbs a whole series of natural balances, causing floods, drought, erosion, lowering of the water table, depletion of soils, dust storms, changes of climate, and so on.

In most parts of the world the progressive clearing of forests to acquire virgin humus has been practically unbridled. Only in Europe, where agriculture has been established for a long time and where the consequences of certain states of imbalance have been gradually recognized, is this not true. Elsewhere, cultivation is abandoned when the soil becomes unproductive. Then herbaceous plants appear and are generally used as pasture. Because of the need for pastureland, grassland has been burnt off so that it will not become wooded. Where this is done, a great number of useful plants disappear, to be replaced by a small number of pyrophilous varieties that are often not suitable even for pasture. The vegetative cover disintegrates, especially when, as often happens, there is overgrazing. The soil, laid bare, undergoes extensive changes in structure and composition. It loses its colloids, becomes dust, hardens into laterite, or is carried away by erosion.

Thus we witness, in what was formerly a slow but is nowadays a rapid regressive chain, the degradation of plant groups, on disorganized soils made barren, in areas veering toward aridity. The influence of these climates has an untoward effect on the adjacent forests and zones of cultivation.

The delicacy of the balances in the great tropical forests, the luxuriance and wealth of which seem to suggest great stability, is particularly evident to me, as biogeographer and ecologist.

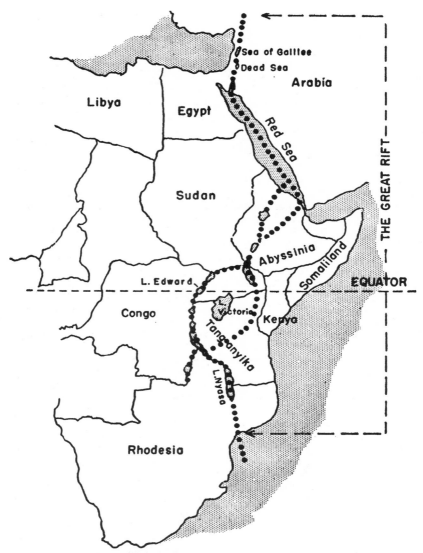

East Africa, showing the location of the "Great Rift" and the general mountain massif. The Albert National Park lies at the point where the Great Rift is intersected by the equator.

This stability does not exist. The great forests of the hot regions are *less* resistant than are the forests of our temperate climate. The equatorial soil is generally poor; the forests can live and subsist in these regions only because they are part of a closed and hence balanced cycle. The organic matter that falls from the trees constitutes the humus; all that the forest produces returns to the forest. If the forest is interfered with, if the soil is laid bare, the humus decomposes very rapidly, and in hot, damp regions it is not renewed. It is reduced to soluble mineral salts, which the rains easily and swiftly wash away.

156

The losses of nitrates and ammonium salts are highly subject to variations in temperature; the rise of a single degree in the atmospheric temperature, between 25° and 26°C, for example, may increase the nitrogen loss by 15 to 20 pounds per acre per year. And the destruction of the forest exposes the soil to conditions that produce a considerable rise in temperature.

The beautiful forest region of the Lubilash, in the Congo, is established on sand covered with a thin layer of humus. Clearing such a forest for agricultural purposes brings about a rapid exposure of the sterile subsoil. The soil becomes unproductive after 3 or 4 years and has to be abandoned. Furthermore, industrial crops such as cotton and *Pyrethrum* do not completely cover the cleared soil, which thus suffers severe depletion the year round as a result of exposure to the hot sun, desiccation, washing away by rain, and erosion. And finally, before undertaking cultivation, it has been necessary to clear away the trees cut down, by burning them. Fire destroys not only the superficial organic bed that has accumulated but also all the microflora of the soil, a large part of which consists of mycorrhizal fungi in symbiosis with the roots of the trees themselves. The microflora of a healthy soil 30 centimeters thick may represent a mass of 5 tons per acre. After the fire the micorrhizal organisms are replaced by a commonplace microflora unsuitable for reconstructing the forest after the cultivated fields have been abandoned. Here, certainly, we may say that between mankind and starvation there are but 20 to 30 centimeters of soil. This precious part of the earth is a mixture of the products of superficial disintegration of the rocks and of humus resulting from the decomposition of living things, particularly of plants which have lived on the surface over past ages. It is my judgment that, under natural conditions in this area, 2 to 3 centimeters of such a humus takes 1000 years to form.

One may, from an aeroplane during long transcontinental flights, observe with dramatic force this decadence of the plant kingdom over the surface of the globe. An experienced observer is amazed to see so many areas without forests, so many desert steppes and brushwood areas at every stage of denudation. This situation is generally the outcome of land clearance, cultivation, conversion to pasture, and fire, by the hand of man. The conditions required for cultivation of plants are completely wiped out. Man's means of feeding himself have become progressively more and more precarious. It is therefore not surprising that archeologists are discovering, precisely in those zones where semiarid or desert conditions prevail today, the remains of dense and prosperous ancient populations. The present-day causes, which we can see quite clearly, must have acted in the past as well, though perhaps more slowly. We do not need to ask ourselves why these civilizations disappeared, why the fields these peoples used to cultivate were abandoned.

Egypt, which now occupies only the Nile Valley, like China, which clings to the valleys of the Blue River and the Yellow River, formerly covered the now desert spaces with its fields. Cyrenaica, at the time of imperial Rome, possessed the famous Gardens of Berenice. The Libyan Desert hides the ruins of great towns such as Thysdrus (El Djem), whose stadium was built to hold 60,000. The French explorer August Chevalier discovered in the Sahara, beneath thick layers of sand, traces of dense forests which, less than 2000 years ago, made a rich colony of what is now synonymous with barrenness and aridity. And the list does not end here; Arabia, Babylon, and Tibet can be added. In Morocco, since the Roman period, 12½ million acres of forests have disappeared as a result of fire and overgrazing by sheep and goats.

In the great forest massif of Central Africa, where the rate of regression is rapid, the present state of affairs is becoming disastrous, owing to the activity of the natives, who still start fires to clear the land for hunting and cultivation. This forest area, which is bounded on the north by the Sahara and on the south by the semiarid regions of the Kalahari, is receding with alarming speed. On all sides the deserts are advancing. It is estimated that in French Equatorial Africa alone the loss of fertilizing matter during the present generation has amounted to half a billion tons, and in a single cotton district in the Congo agronomists have shown that in 6 years 30,000 square kilometers of soil have been ruined. In Madagascar the drama has been played out over a period of 60 years. This island was once covered with splendid forests; today 70 percent of its area is occupied by an ocean of tough grasses, ravaged by fire and unsuitable even for the feeding of herds. In short, we are in the throes of an apparently irreversible progressive *reduction* of the surface of cultivable lands. It is estimated that the area of such lands on the earth has decreased by 20 percent in the last hundred years. Of the 40 billion acres remaining today, at least 20 million disappear irretrievably each year.

The lesson of the past is clear: We *cannot* continue to exploit nature with impunity. We cannot clear away the forests and enlarge the areas of cultivation without bringing about disturbances in the equilibrium which, throughout the globe, result in disappearance of areas of vegetation, impoverishment of the fauna, erosion, disappearance of the water table, depletion of nutritive elements (particularly of nitrogen carried off by the crops and not restored), degeneration of lands to desert wastes, famine, decline of civilizations, migration of populations, revolutions, and wars of extermination.

Today, therefore, we can measure the extent of the threat which hangs over our descendants and the urgency of the problem which it is absolutely necessary that we solve. We must end the degradation of vegetation and the erosion of the earth, everywhere on the surface of the globe. This problem cannot be left to any nation of indifferent or inactive individuals. In some countries, departments with extensive powers are studying and applying the means advocated for preventing complete sterilization of the land. The International Union for the Protection of Nature has undertaken a propaganda campaign. We wish it every success.

Protecting Man's Habitat

The idea that nature must be protected is quite a recent one. Plato, it is true, 2400 years ago, described the erosion of the mountains of Attica and the ruin of villages and farms. He believed that the deforestation carried out by man was the cause of this erosion. But it is only during the last 100 years that many people have become aware of the degradation occurring everywhere and the need to counteract it. A movement has developed recently to check the disturbance of natural equilibria.

It is curious that the first attempts to protect nature were made from esthetic motives, and in the United States. In 1872 the American pioneers, captivated by the charm of the new landscape they had discovered in the Far West, wished to perpetuate the spectacle for their descendants. At the same time artists, tourists, and the general public were reacting against the standardization of the places in which they lived and were seeking relaxation in invigorating nature. From these desires grew the great national parks, of which the first was Yellowstone. Later, naturalists grew alarmed at the progressive transformation wrought in setting up human establishments, either agricultural, industrial, or residential. Today it is the biologists who, studying the problems arising from the disturbance of natural equilibria, have concluded that nature governs the stability of the entire human habitat, controlling not only the production of indispensable foodstuffs but economic and industrial enterprises as well.

Even among our contemporaries,

however, there are many who remain ignorant of the problem. They do not realize that this is a fundamental question for our age, and that the future of our civilization depends upon its solution. They do not see that man is now disrupting the operation of natural laws and leaving to his descendants, through the destruction of plants and soil, the prospect of insufficient food and perhaps of widespread famine. Scientists are therefore insisting that everyone be informed and that defensive measures be taken without delay. But they also insist that any intervention be thoroughly studied *before* steps are taken to stabilize or reestablish equilibria. It is all too likely that improvised decisions may be the starting points for further and unexpected catastrophies.

If we are to protect man's habitat we must first know and understand what it is we are trying to protect. That knowledge is still incomplete. This is particularly true of certain regions situated in the tropics. And the possibility of acquiring much of this knowledge is rapidly slipping through our fingers. We know that 110 species of mammals alone have ceased to exist in the last 2000 years. In 200 years 600 species of animals have declined to the point of extinction. And what about the plants that are subjected, every year, to the assault of land clearance and destructive fires? The plant world is suffering an alarming decimation. In the temperate countries wild plants can live only along the borders of roads and fields; in the hot countries the sunloving species are propagated over degraded areas, which have been tremendously enlarged, at the expense of other, shade-loving species that are now rare.

For half a century the demands of an explosive world economy, careless of consequences, have posed a growing threat to the stability of the habitat of many living species, which are thus condemned to perish. We shall bitterly regret this when we become fully aware of it. Would it not have been a pity,

for example, if the coffee plant had disappeared before we were able to exploit it? Are we sure that there are not other wild species capable of meeting man's ever-growing needs for plant and animal food? Do we not know that research to discover and develop species for such uses requires time? Such research must be carried out by generations of naturalists and biologists having at their disposal the data accumulated through the patient work of a long line of predecessors. Compare this with the speed with which the forces of destruction accomplish their work.

In phytosociological groups there exist species capable of surviving even marked disturbances in their natural medium; there are others, however, which live in narrowly defined habitats and disappear the moment those habitats are disturbed.

All of these questions must be examined in detail, and solved, and the answers must be generalized and applied the world over. Perhaps nowhere in the world can some of them be better studied than in the great region of the Congo watershed, and in no other part of the world can failure to find satisfactory answers have more far-reaching effects. I shall take as an example a region with which I am particularly familiar, since I was a member of the directing council of the National Park Institute of the Belgian Congo for more than 20 years. Let us consider the Albert National Park in Central Africa.

The Albert National Park lies in the high part of Africa, extending over a vast plateau at an altitude of 3000 feet. It is part of the vast chain of mountains which begins with Mount Sinai in Asia Minor, runs along the west bank of the Red Sea, and continues from Abyssinia through the district of the great lakes to Rhodesia and South Africa. The Nile flows at the foot of the western edge of this chain of mountains; its source is in them, and its valley follows what is called the Great Rift Valley. The Albert National Park occupies a section of this rift, between Lake Kivu in the south and latitude 1°N. It is wedged in the bottom of this valley for a distance of nearly 200 miles. To the east and west it is literally walled in by the two escarpments of the Rift; the greatly varying gradients of these walls present a practically insurmountable obstacle to the migration of plants and animals. In the south the horizon is closed by the chain of the Virunga volcanoes (10,000 to 12,000 ft), and to the north by the mighty Ruwenzori massif (15,000 ft). The park is thus roughly divided into four sectors, that of the volcanoes, that of the plain of Lake Edward, that of the Semliki River, and that of the Ruwenzori massif.

Two of the volcanoes, Nyiragongo and especially Nyamuragira, are active. Nyamuragira illuminates the night sky with fearful red glows. The last outflow of lava was in 1948, and the cooling flows are in the process of being colonized by plants and animals. The oldest deposits are already overgrown with forest. At the level of the base of the volcanoes there is a mountain forest, at 4000 feet, which is dense and shadowy. At about 8000 feet there is a curious band of bamboo forest. At 9000 feet the *Hagenia* forest appears, with a typical undergrowth inhabited by a species of endemic gorilla, of very great stature and covered with thick hair. Higher still come the bands of subalpine vegetation, including *Lobelia* and *Alchemilla*, forming an amazing landscape of prehistoric appearance up to an altitude of about 12,000 feet, above which only lichens and mosses are able to grow.

The Lake Edward plain is of recent origin; it is in the stage of herbaceous colonization, with herbaceous vegetation gradually giving place to thornbush and *Euphorbia*. This vegetation is established on the alluvial deposits of Lake Edward. The grassy terrain has favored a tremendous multiplication of antelopes, but as the habitat has changed, the numbers have decreased; elephant and buffalo, which prefer more wooded surroundings, are now increasing. Carnivorous beasts such as lions, leopards, and lycaons (the Cape hunting dog) fulfill their role of natural selection, and sick or unfit animals are weeded out. Hippopotami inhabit the rivers. All these animals, protected as they have been for 30 years, live in absolute peace, untroubled by the presence of human beings, whom they no longer fear.

On the marshy banks of Lake Edward itself live countless flocks of birds, feeding on the great numbers of fish which inhabit the immense expanses of shallow water. The River Semliki sector, which links Lake Edward with Lake Albert in the north, consists of several parts. One of these is the Upper Semliki, consisting of vast expanses of grassy savannas. It was formerly inhabited by a rich fauna, since ravaged by hunting expeditions. Further north a forest section is still inhabited by several families of gorillas. As for the Ruwenzori, its summit reaches glacial levels at an altitude of 15,000 feet. It can be climbed, and here one may see the same bands of vegetation that one sees on the volcanoes, but in a still more impressive setting.

The great importance of the Albert National Park lies in the fact that it spans the very heart of Central Africa, in the region where the flora and fauna of West and of East Africa meet. We thus find here plants and animals of the two great African domains, the Congo and the Nile, at the limit of their range of extension, as well as numerous elements typical of neither of these domains but of Central Africa.

How did it happen that this vast territory was set apart as a reserve? During the latter part of the last century a few men of foresight began to realize the seriousness of the ever-present threats to man's habitat and to take steps to counter them. In 1891 Theodore Roosevelt set aside for public use 150 million acres of forest lands, the "forest reserves." Today they represent about all that remains of nonprivate forest in the United States. Two years later, in 1893, King Leopold II of

160

Belgium, realizing that bush fires in the Congo were so intense as to be fatal to the natural vegetation, issued an edict forbidding them. This edict ended with the sentence: "If we consider the influence of forests on the climate and soil of a region, we must realize how important it is to foster the forest cover." (Leopold, like Roosevelt in the United States, was bitterly criticized by all those who considered the forests a hindrance that delayed exploitation of the earth and reduced the profits to be obtained thereby.) In 1889 this edict was extended by the establishment of big game preserves in Central Africa, the specific purpose being to prevent the destruction of the elephants. After a series of international conferences on the need for protecting African wild life, further decrees for the more general regulation of hunting were issued. Leopold wanted to establish in Africa a series of natural reserves similar to those in the United States, but public opinion was not ready for that step within his lifetime. In 1919 his successor, King Albert, during a trip to the United States, told the Belgian ambassador in Washington, Baron Cartier de Marchienne, of his wish to see a series of national parks created in the Congo, similar to those he had seen in America. Baron de Marchienne, himself an ardent advocate of conservation, gained the support of a number of American conservationists, among them John C. Merriam, then president of the Carnegie Institution in Washington, and the late Henry Fairfield Osborn, president of the American Museum of Natural History in New York.

In 1920 the American Museum of Natural History sent Carl Akeley to the volcanoes of Kivu to study the gorillas which had been reported there. Akeley succeeded in observing these extremely rare and interesting animals at close range and urged that they be effectively protected. Through his efforts and those of the U.S. ambassador in Brussels, William Phillips, and of certain Belgian officials, approval was obtained in 1925, for the creation by the Colonial Council of Belgium, of a national park at Kivu. Akeley met his death in Kivu a year later and was buried on the side of Mikeno volcano at an altitude of about 8000 feet, in the midst of the reserve which he had helped to create.

In 1929 a new decree extended the original reserve to include the entire region of the Virunga volcanoes and the plain of Lake Edward, giving the Albert National Park a total area of about 1 million acres. Later the Park was again enlarged and five other parks were created. The lands were state lands and could not be transferred. The inhabitants, where any existed, were evacuated after amicable agreement and just compensation. Only the Pygmies, the "Batwa," were allowed to live in the national parks, since they, in fact, contributed to the protection of the forests in which they lived.

Today the Congo is in the throes of establishing itself as an independent commonwealth. We can only hope that the new leaders of the region will not allow the destruction of all that which has been preserved with so much difficulty in these areas.

Galloping Technology, A New Social Disease*

Jerome D. Frank

The outstanding characteristic of our time is the headlong rush of technology and science. Scientists and engineers are prying new secrets out of nature and remaking our lives at a breathtaking and ever accelerating rate. The adverse effects on society of their efforts could be referred to as social diseases, although we have preferred the term social issues. Our galloping technology has created or aggravated problems of unemployment, urbanization, racial and international tensions, war, overpopulation, and many others that have been the constant concern of members of SPSSI.

But "social disease" in my title refers to the other, old-fashioned medical meaning of the term—namely, illness caused by the conditions of social living. My particular training has made me sensitive to the direct effects on life and health of man's reckless conquest of the environment, a topic that has been largely neglected by social scientists. The most obvious reason for this neglect is that the problems present themselves as medical or technological. My thesis is that, although the new menaces to life and health may be caused by new machines and poisons, the remedies lie mainly in the realm of human behavior.

* Presidential address for the Society for the Psychological Study of Social Issues (Division 9 of the American Psychological Association) presented at the meetings of the APA in New York City on September 3, 1966.

Journal of Social Issues, 1966, Vol.22, No.4, pp. 1-14.

In its medical meaning, the term "social disease" referred to illnesses contracted, directly or indirectly, by misbehavior, and therefore blameworthy. Most commonly, of course, it was a euphemism for venereal disease, but it was also used for illnesses like tuberculosis, presumably contracted by living under unhygienic conditions. These diseases were reprehensible because our forefathers blamed the slum dwellers for the circumstances under which they were forced to live.

Of the social diseases caused by galloping technology, those caused by air pollution might be thought of as analogous to tuberculosis, whereas injuries and deaths caused by reckless driving—a voluntary, pleasurable, but disapproved activity—would be analogues of venereal diseases.

Like their medical counterparts, technological social diseases can be acute or chronic. The most virulent and acute form, which fortunately has not yet broken out, would be modern war. The threat to survival posed by modern weapons is receiving so much agonized attention from most of us that there is no need to dwell on it. It may be worthwhile to point out, however, that modern weapons symbolize the reversal of man's relation to his environment, a matter to which I shall return again. For the first time in human history, the chief danger to human survival comes from man himself instead of the forces of nature.

Historians have sufficiently described the horrors of war throughout the ages, but actually weapons were a trivial source of death compared to natural causes until very recently. Even when men tried deliberately to kill each other in war, they succeeded only sporadically and in localized areas. The influenza epidemic in 1918, for example, killed ten million people throughout the world in six months. Endemic diseases like malaria and tuberculosis took their tolls in millions every year, as did famine.

World War II claimed about 65 million lives in eight years, if one starts with the Japanese invasion of Manchuria, but in that war, as in all others, the great majority of deaths were caused by disease and starvation resulting from the dislocations of society caused by the fighting. World War II was the first in which, even among the fighting men, more died of wounds than disease. As a great bacteriologist has observed: ". . . soldiers have rarely won wars. They more often mop up after the barrage of epidemics. Typhus . . . plague, typhoid, cholera and dysentery (have) decided more campaigns than Caesar, Hannibal, Napoleon and all the inspector generals of history" (9).

Now, just as we have learned to master the major epidemic illnesses and to produce food in abundance for everyone, we have suddenly created a new, more powerful form of death-dealing that can destroy tens of millions of people in minutes and, indeed, could put an end to mankind. If one were mystically inclined, one might suspect that there is some law of nature which states that the danger to human life remains constant, so that as one source diminishes another must take its place.

I shall assume, without any really valid grounds, that humans will shackle the self-created monster of modern weapons before it is too late. Otherwise there would be no point in continuing with this address, which deals with the causes and cure of chronic forms of technological social disease. These are the subtle, insidious dangers that are the unwanted and incidental by-products of fabulous achievements in raising the level of human welfare. These dangers are at present more apparent in the United States because our society is the most technologically advanced, but in due course they are certain to plague all nations.

The dangers can be grouped into three categories: pollution of the living environment, the biosphere; accidents; and drugs. Let me start with the only brand new danger, of small consequence at present but potentially one of the greatest—the pollution of the biosphere by radioactive products of nuclear power plants.

At this time, twenty-seven nuclear power plants are in operation or under construction, and their number will grow very rapidly. In 1962 nuclear power accounted for only one-half of one percent of the total power generated in this country, but it could be as high as fifty percent by the year 2000. And the growth rate is exponential. In absolute figures nuclear power plants produced one-half million kilowatts in 1960, one and one-half million this year, an estimated five million by 1970, and 68 million kilowatts by 1980.

Nuclear power plants present three types of danger. The first is a break in the protective casing that encloses the radioactive elements. Such an accident to the reactor in Windscale in England in 1957 is said to have released more radioactivity into the atmosphere than the explosion of an atomic bomb of the Hiroshima type. Another serious potential hazard lies in the possibility of a leak in the transportation and storage of high level radioactive wastes that cannot be safely released. Already some sixty million gallons are stored in underground tanks and, of course, the storage problem will become increasingly serious with each passing year.

The third source of potential danger lies in low level radioactive isotopes. These are now released into the environment under carefully monitored conditions, to insure that the dilution is sufficient to prevent any predictable human exposure above levels believed to be harmful. The trouble is that very little is known about these isotopes, since they have only existed for a few years. So far, none has approached the presumed maximal permissible concentration in humans. However, they raise uncomfortable questions. Even though traces of radioactive isotopes in our tissues may be harmless in the short run, we do

164

not yet know enough about what long exposure to slight doses of ionizing radiation does to living systems to be sure that we are not suffering slow damage. In this connection, deaths from cancer in survivors of the Japanese atomic bombings have only now, after about twenty years, started to show a sharp rise.

A more serious problem is that some living creatures accumulate certain isotopes which become increasingly concentrated as they move up the food chain. For example, algae concentrate radioactive zinc to about 6,000 times that of the surrounding water. The algae are eaten by bluegill fish, in whose bones the concentration is about 8,700 times that of the water. Fortunately, humans do not eat bluegill bones, but who knows what edible tissues will be found to store other radioactive substances in the same way?

Dangers of the same type are created by pesticides. In terms of the amount of chemical per unit of body weight, most pesticides are equally toxic to all living creatures, though immunity for some can be built up in time. They kill insects and not men simply because the former receive enormously greater doses in proportion to their weight. The amount found in human tissues to date is far below the concentration that would cause immediate damage. But certain creatures we eat concentrate pesticides to a fantastic degree. The oyster, for example, accumulates DDT to a level some 70,000 times above that of the surrounding water. This happens because water-living creatures lack the enzymes present in adult humans, that metabolize most of these substances into harmless wastes. It turns out—an example of an unanticipated danger—that babies also lack these enzymes, so that they would be damaged by much smaller amounts of pesticide than adults.

Furthermore, some pesticides, like radioactive isotopes, cause cancer in animals on repeated exposure, and some are suspected of damaging the germ plasm, so that their deleterious effects, though long delayed, may eventually be very serious.

A more serious, immediate menace to health is atmospheric pollution from factories and automobiles. It is estimated that 133,000,000 tons of aerial garbage are dumped into the atmosphere of the United States each year—more than the weight of our annual steel production. As to its effects on health, a cautious statement is: "A large fraction of our population is now being exposed to significant concentrations of a variety of toxic chemicals. These levels are often a substantial fraction of those which produce acute effects. There is a possibility that our people may be sustaining cumulative insidious damage. If genetic injury were involved, the results could be especially serious" (1, p. 1527). It is estimated that the chances of a man dying between the ages of 50 and 70 from respiratory disease are twice as great if he lives in an air-polluted area than in a clean-air area.

A particularly subtle form of air pollution, which may have the most inexorable effects, is the slow increase in carbon dioxide in the atmosphere produced by industrial use of fossil fuels. This blocks the radiation of heat energy back to outer space, so that the temperature of the earth is gradually rising. The average temperature today is 8% higher than it was in 1890. This, of course, could be due to other causes. In any case, if it keeps up, among other unpleasant consequences, it will melt the polar ice caps, flooding the world's seaboards.

The social diseases considered so far have been analogous to tuberculosis—the individual cannot do anything about the noxious agents to which he is exposed. Now let us turn to those that are more analogous to syphilis—that is, they result from a person's own actions, whether deliberate or heedless. This category includes disability and deaths caused by accidents or by drugs. Accidents have become the leading cause of death from ages 1 to 37 and the fourth cause of death at all ages, being exceeded only by heart disease, cancer and stroke. Their prominence obviously results, in part, from the sharp reduction in natural causes of death, especially in the younger age group, but in absolute figures they claim an impressive toll. In 1964, the last year for which figures are available, they killed 105,000 people and injured 10,200,000. The worst offender, of course, is the automobile—or rather the automobile driver. On United States highways a death or injury occurs every 18 seconds. In 1965, 49,000 people were killed—or almost half of those who were killed in all accidents—and 3,500,000 maimed. I shall return to the question of the causes of this carnage presently, but for the moment wish to pass on to a brief look at the last category of new environmental hazards to be considered. Ironically, these are created by the medical profession or, more broadly, the life sciences.

The worst, fortunately, is only hypothetical so far. Now that biologists have been able to rearrange living molecules, they can create self-reproducing viruses that never before existed. Probably some are doing this in the service of biological warfare, but many are working on such projects purely out of that powerful human urge, scientific curiosity. A Nobel prize winning biologist views such research with profound alarm. He speaks of the good possibility that these tinkerers will create a new poliomyelitis virus, for example, against which humans have built up no immunity. "Any escape into circulation . . . could grow into the almost unimaginable catastrophe of a 'virgin soil' epidemic involving all the populous regions of the world" (4, p. 38). He concludes: "there are dangers in knowing what should not be known," (4, p. 39) a feeling shared by many atomic scientists. Apparently, splitting the molecule may have consequences as disastrous as splitting the atom.

To return to more mundane but more immediate hazards arising directly from efforts to prolong life and health, floods of new medications are being put on the market. Despite increasingly stringent laws, some that cause serious damage to health or even death get past the guards. Examples were the contaminated strain of polio vaccine, and, more recently, the malformed babies caused by an apparently harmless sleeping medicine, thalidomide.

Finally, there is the growing menace of drugs that alter states of consciousness, including sedatives, stimulants, mood-lifters and so-called psychotropic drugs such as LSD. Most of these drugs were thought to be harmless when first introduced. Cocaine, barbiturates, dexedrine, and now LSD, to name a handful, were first viewed as great boons to man.

We should have learned by now that no drug powerful enough to cause a change in psychic state is harmless if taken over a long enough period of time or in large enough doses. Barbiturates proved to be superb suicidal agents, dexedrine produces serious psychoses (in one series 83% of those who used this supposedly harmless pep pill for one to five years showed psychotic symptoms), and increasing numbers of sufferers from the acute and chronic ill effects of LSD are appearing in psychiatric emergency rooms.

Hundreds of common drugs, moreover, impair driving ability. One physician found that a group of patients receiving a tranquilizer for 90 days had 10 times more traffic accidents than the population at large. He concludes, glumly, "No matter how strenuously doctors warn patients about drugs and driving, the advice probably wears off faster than the drug" (5).

This reminder that our topic is people, not technology, may serve to conclude this very spotty survey of the new hazards to life and health created by man. I have not even mentioned, for example, water pollution by industrial wastes, the more than 150 poisons that can be found in any household, or the host of new industrial hazards.

The psychological questions I should like to raise concerning this new group of social diseases are, first, why do we not pay more attention to them and, second, why are our countermeasures so ineffective.

The obstacles are both perceptual and motivational. Perceptually, most of the dangers are remarkably unobtrusive. In fact, they are undetectable by the senses. Radioactive isotopes and pesticides in our tissues, and the slowly rising carbon dioxide content of the air cannot be seen, heard, tasted, smelled or felt, so it is easy to forget about them. When they do intrude on consciousness, in the form of eye-burning smog or brown water, in the language of perceptual psychology, they are ground rather than figure. As an authority on air pollution says: ". . . the private citizen is unaware of the fact that the substance he is inhaling may eventually cause cancer of the lungs. He does not associate a bad cough with atmospheric conditions. It may be only on days of particular wind direction that a housewife will be bothered by fly ash on her clothesline; immediately thereafter, she'll forget it. . . . The offensive odors of some industries, the dust on windowsills, the haze that obscures an otherwise beautiful day—all are taken as features of urban living about which nothing can be done. And when the air is clear, the facts of the matter might as well not exist" (6, p. 262). One is reminded of the old man in Arkansas whose roof didn't leak when it didn't rain.

Occasionally the dangers do spring into focus, as when at least 4000 people died during a four-day London fog in 1952, or when traffic deaths hit the headlines on a holiday weekend, but these occasions are too brief and infrequent to sustain attention.

A further difficulty in identifying the damage to health caused by noxious environmental agents is that illnesses have multiple causes, so in any given case it is hard to single out what really is to blame. If an elderly man with chronic lung disease dies during a heavy smog, who can say for certain that the smog was the cause of death? In other terms, statistical variations in various environmental and internal factors are so great that the true noxious agent may be hidden by them. The problem is analogous to that of detecting evoked potentials on the electroencephalogram. These are spike waves occurring a fraction of a second after the stimulus. They can only be detected by superimposing hundreds of tracings so the random variations cancel each other out.

Finally, although the damage done by environmental poisons is constantly increasing, the increments are very small compared to the base level. So, in accord with a well known psychophysiological law, they do not rise above the threshold of awareness. Humans may be in the same plight as a frog placed in a pan of cold water, which is very slowly heated. If the rise in temperature is gradual enough, he will be boiled without ever knowing what happened to him.

These perceptual obstacles to appreciating the dangers created by technological advances play into strong motives for not doing much about them. The major source of complacency, I believe, is that the new dangers to life and health are tiny compared to the benefits. For example, American industry, the chief source of pollution of the biosphere, produces half the world's goods in addition to a fabulous arsenal of weapons—a technological triumph that could, in a flash, nullify the gains produced by all the others. And our society could not function at all without that space-annihilator, the automobile. Pesticides are mainly responsible for enabling less than 10% of the American population not only to feed the rest too well, but to produce millions of tons of surplus food.

Medical science has prolonged the average length of life in the United States by about 50% in the last half century and has virtually conquered the major epidemic diseases, although this battle is never permanently won. (Recently new strains of resistant malaria have been reported from Vietnam.) And the lives of millions have been made more tolerable by relatively harmless sedatives and anti-depressants.

Surely, it will be said, these huge gains in human welfare (and I have named only a few) far outweigh the relatively minute increases in illnesses and deaths that accompany them.

True, but in absolute numbers over 100,000 accidental deaths a year and the rising death rates from cancer and lung disease are far from insignificant. And even though the immediate danger to health and life may be small, some types of damage are cumulative and some may be irreversible. For example, no one knows how to restore to the water of Lake Erie the oxygen it has lost through a complex chain of biological and chemical reactions set off by industrial wastes, resulting in destruction of its edible fish.

In any case, the rewards yielded by our galloping technology are large, tangible and immediate, and the penalties are remote and contingent. It does not take a learning theorist to know which will determine behavior. The pleasure of a puff on a cigarette far outweighs the probability that it will shorten the smoker's life by a few years in the distant future. The increased risk of getting killed influences the automobile driver much less than the joy of speeding, especially after a few drinks. And, at the social level, the prospects of increased revenues to a community from a new industry dwarf the hazard to health it might create.

So, everyone is motivated to minimize the dangers, especially when taking them seriously might jeopardize some of the gains. Perhaps this universal underestimation also partly reflects the proverbial American optimism. Even scientists, whose sole task should be to establish the facts, seem to be affected. One is constantly running across news items like: "New tests developed at Pennsylvania State University reveal that pesticide residue in plants is fifty per-cent to a hundred per-cent greater than present tests indicate" (7). Or: "Radioactive caribou and reindeer may pose a health threat to nearly all the residents of Alaska. Scientists previously had believed that only Eskimos living near the Arctic Circle were endangered" (2).

When profits, not merely truth, are at stake, optimism becomes literally blind. One example may suffice. Fluorides discharged into the air by phosphate plants in two Florida counties have damaged citrus crops over a radius of about 50 miles, cut production in some groves by as much as 75%, and have resulted in a 20 million dollar reduction in property values. In the face of these facts a spokesman for the Florida Phosphate Council told local citrus growers: "Gentlemen, there's no problem of air pollution in this area that is affecting citrus groves. All you boys have to do is take better care of your groves and you will have no complaints about air pollution" (6, p. 261).

Since local chambers of commerce wish to attract people to their localities, they join the creators of pollution in minimizing it, so whatever tendency the average citizen has to overlook his slow poisoning is aided by the absence of corrective information. A recent poll of the inhabitants of Nashville, where substantial numbers die every year from heart and respiratory diseases aggravated by heavy air pollution, found that 85% believed it to be a healthy place to live, and less than 3% suggested that measures be taken to reduce air pollution.

Despite these impediments, Americans have at last officially recognized the existence of the problems and taken action to solve them. Congress has appropriated funds for fighting air pollution, water pollution and highway accidents. So, you may ask, what is there to worry about? Unfortunately, in comparison with the size of the dangers, the efforts to combat them are so small as to be pitiable, or laughable, depending on one's point of view. For example, only 130 air pollution control programs are in effect in the nation's 7,000 communities, and most of these are considered inadequate.

The two main sources of air pollution are industry and the automobile. By 1970 there will be 60% more industries pouring pollutants into the air than in 1960, many of them new, so no one knows how toxic they will be. In 1960 74 million automobiles travelled 728 billion passenger miles. In 1980 these figures will be about doubled.

Thus, emission of poisons into the atmosphere would have to be reduced at least fifty percent merely to keep pace with their increased production. To do this would cost an estimated three billion dollars a year. Even this would only be about one-half of one percent of our gross national product. Actually industry and the government today are spending only about 35 million—that is, slightly over one-tenth as much as would be needed to do a minimal job. To quote an expert: "America of the near future will be filthy and foul, and our air will be unfit to breathe. Indeed, this dark, dangerous era ahead of us is inevitable" (6, p. 271).

In short, so far, efforts to halt the diseases created by our galloping technology have been too little and too late. That this state of affairs is a pressing social issue seems self-evident, so it is appropriate to ask why it has aroused so little interest among social psychologists. The basic trouble may be that, in contrast to our other concerns such as war, poverty and racial discrimination, this one has no focus and no villians. Ironically, the ills caused by technology are by-products of benevolent efforts to promote the general welfare. It is hard to get indignant over this, and indignation seems to be the initial goad to becoming concerned about a social issue.

Moreover, if one looks about for a focus, one can find only familiar and universal aspects of human nature—such as failure to appreciate the seriousness of dangers that are not in awareness, unwillingness to forego immediate rewards in order to forestall future disasters, and the general inertia of social organizations. We may be dealing with a new manifestation of the illness that, according to the Spanish philosopher, Ortega Y Gasset, afflicts all civilized societies and eventually kills them—the desire of the citizens to enjoy the fruits of civilization without putting forth the effort or accepting the discipline necessary to maintain it. Perhaps the last word was really said by Descartes over three centuries ago: "Defects are always more tolerable than the change necessary for their removal" (6, p. 221).

Lest we throw up our hands prematurely, however, let me suggest some aspects of the problem to which social psychologists might be able to contribute.

One is the American faith in the quick fix. Our history of incredible inventiveness has fostered the belief that some new technological invention can always be devised to correct the evils created by the last one, without causing anyone too much cost or inconvenience. No doubt, new inventions will be required to help combat new dangers, and all of the diseases created by technology have partial technological antidotes. But right now we have the techniques to sharply reduce such evils as air and water pollution, if only we would apply them, and the most efficient way to relieve many other dangers would be through modifying the behavior of people, not machines.

Traffic fatalities are a case in point. When the disgraceful carnage on our highways finally passed the threshold of awareness, a great cry went up for safer cars, whereas what we need more are safer drivers. Certainly cars could and should be made much safer than they are today, but just consider a few facts. Twenty percent of drivers are involved in 80% of accidents. If they were all kept off the roads, accidents would be sharply reduced at one blow. Many studies have found that in about 50% of fatal accidents one or both of the persons involved had been drinking. And I have mentioned the tenfold increase in accidents found among one group of patients on tranquilizers.

Finally, speeding is involved in nearly 2 out of 5 driving deaths. No amount of tinkering with automobiles will change the fact that the human reaction time is about three-fourths of a second, which means that at 70 miles an hour a car will cover 77 feet or about three car lengths before the driver can even press the brake. So if a driver is tailgating at that speed and the car in front stops suddenly, no safety devices on earth can keep him from crashing, although they could, to be sure, reduce his resulting injuries.

Nor are these considerations merely theoretical. Three New

England states have reduced their accident rate to about half the national average simply by enforcing laws against speeding and drunken driving. If to these were added universal driver education courses, and effective measures to keep accident-prone drivers permanently off the roads, traffic fatalities would drop to a negligible level without changing the design of a single car.

Insofar as improved safety features on cars are involved, the human problem has only been pushed one step back to the auto makers. It is much easier to invent safety devices than to get auto manufacturers to install them. No manufacturer can afford the additional cost of making his cars safer unless all his competitors do likewise.

This consideration calls attention to a broad social issue that creates serious impediments to combatting technological sources of damage to health—the competitive orientation of our society. The American social philosophy assumes that competition is the mainspring of social and economic advance. The general welfare is believed to emerge from the interaction of conflicting economic interests. Every American inevitably belongs to several overlapping interest groups, but, by and large, he assigns the highest priority to the one centering on his means of livelihood, whether it be producing or selling goods, working for wages, or selling services. Groups are formed to protect other interests than making money, to be sure, but they do not exert as powerful or pervasive an influence. If an interest does not affect income and offers no dramatic focus for attention, no group will form to protect it, regardless of how vital it may be. It is safe to predict that there will never be a National Association of Air Breathers or an Amalgamated Water Drinkers Union. As a result, efforts to combat the poisoning of the biosphere are bound to receive a low priority. Everybody's business is nobody's business.

Another social issue implicit in technologically-caused ills arises from the fact that they cannot be effectively combatted by local action. The dangers are seldom confined to political units. When they are, as when fumes from a factory pollute the air of a town, the industry involved is seldom locally owned, and so is relatively immune to local pressures. The characteristics of local administrative agencies also impede effective action. If the job of policing water pollution, for example, is assigned to an established agency like the Health Department, it must take its place at the end of the line behind the department's established duties, and must compete for funds and personnel that are usually already inadequate. If a new department is formed, it must battle established agencies, resistant to encroachments on their terrains.

Nor can local communities meet the financial burdens involved in adequate safety measures. A major reason for the success of the federal highway program seems to be that the federal government footed 90% of the bill. It will probably have to assume a similar share of the cost of combatting environmental ills, instead of the meagre 40% it now offers.

And so we find ourselves once again facing in a new guise the perennial problem of the place of government regulation and control in a free society—a manifestation of the inevitable and universal tension between freedom of the individual and the welfare of the group.

In other words, it appears that technologically-caused ills of individuals can be successfully combatted only by correcting the ills of society with which they are intertwined. At this point certain new tools that psychologists have helped to develop may come to our aid.

One is computerized systems analysis. The biosphere is a single system, of which human beings are an integral part. So attempts to modify any aspect of it may have repercussions on the rest, sometimes unforeseen. For example, the introduction of methods to control air pollution might affect patterns of mass transportation and employment, which in turn may influence rates of crime, alcoholism and drug addiction. Computerized techniques of systems analysis, that enable rapid gathering of many types of data and analysis of their interactions, for the first time permit solution of such problems. They analyze the relationships of the different aspects, make it possible to anticipate the effects of various remedies before actually implementing them and provide continuous feedback on the success of the measures finally undertaken. California has pioneered in a pilot application of systems analysis to problems of air and water pollution, mass transportation, and crime, with encouraging results.

To combat the ills caused by technology also requires bringing about major changes in the attitudes of the American people. We would have to learn to view our problems in a broader context—to realize that the quick fix will not work and that adequate solutions require consideration of the social and ethical implications of remedial measures. In addition, we shall have to learn how to cope with a constantly changing environment.

The achievement of both these aims would require drastic and large-scale changes in our philosophy and methods of education. There would have to be more emphasis on general principles, and on learning how to solve problems, and less on sheer information and development of technical skills. It would be necessary to introduce these orientations into the school curriculum from the earliest grades. Their implementation would require full use of new methods of teaching that eliminate the enormous waste motion of traditional methods.

A massive program of adult education along similar lines would also be necessary. Electronic communications media could be used very much more effectively for such a purpose than they are today.

Many industrially backward nations are using radio and television to speed the education of their people, as well as for other less worthy aims. Today, educators, political leaders and other molders of the public mind can drop in for a chat, via television, in over 93% of American homes. Attempts to use the educational potentialities of television more fully would run into the same obstacles as any other social innovation. The mere existence of television, however, gives grounds for hope that it will be used to speed the changes in public attitudes required by the changes in the environment.

Lurking behind all the problems I have discussed is a brand new psychological issue, to which I should like to call your attention. It probably concerns philosophers, theologians and poets primarily, but, as psychologists, we cannot be indifferent to it. Let me introduce the topic by taking as a text a comment of a State Conservation Commissioner defending a public utility, one of whose atomic power plants had caused an enormous fish kill by its effluent. He described this mishap as "almost in the vein of an act of God" (8). I do not think he really meant to imply that God is dead and has been replaced by Consolidated Edison. But such a proposition might contain a germ of truth. Our generation is living through the culmination of a struggle between man and nature that began when someone first resolved to sail into the wind, rather than letting currents and breezes carry him where they would. After he learned how to do it, he became able to choose his destination, so he had to develop navigational instruments to tell him where he was and how to reach his goal. From then on, step by step, man has gradually bent the forces of nature to his will, until today, barring only his inability to conquer death, he seems to be nature's master. But let us not become too self-confident. At first the benefits of our assault on the natural environment far exceeded the costs, but now the latter are rapidly mounting. Nature may simply have been biding its time.

The interesting psychological point is that our increasing power over nature has been accompanied by growing despair about ourselves. Playwrights, novelists, poets, philosophers keep hammering away on the related themes that life is meaningless, absurd, a kind of bad joke, and that man is capable only of making himself and his fellows miserable. And these statements find a wide response. Could they spring, in part, from a feeling of terror at our inability to live up to the appalling responsibilities of our new power?

In the past, men could shrug their shoulders in the face of most of the evils of life because they were powerless to prevent them. A misfortune like a fish kill could be blamed on God or Fate. Now there is no one to blame but ourselves. Nothing is any longer inevitable. Since everything can be accomplished, everything must be deliberately chosen. It is in human power, for the first time, to achieve a level of welfare exceeding our wildest imaginings or to commit race suicide, slowly or rapidly. The choice rests only with us.

Perhaps we are realizing that no degree of control over nature can solve basic problems of social living. Our dazzling material triumphs are, rather, a warning that in the end, all depends on improving the quality of our relationships with each other. Without this, all our scientific and technological triumphs may only hasten our destruction.

Man has been characterized as the only creature with an infinite capacity for making trouble for himself, and we seem to be exercising that capacity fully today. It may be some comfort to recollect, with a student of man's origins, that "man is a bad weather animal, designed for storm and change" (3).

Today man is making his own stormy weather. Perhaps it is not too much to hope that the same qualities which enabled him to triumph over the destructive forces of nature will enable him to master those he himself has created.

REFERENCES

1. ABELSON, P. H. Air pollution. *Science,* March 26, 1965, 147, 1527.
2. *AMA News,* January 10, 1966.
3. ARDREY, R. *African Genesis.* New York: Atheneum, 1961.
4. BURNET, F. M. Men or molecules? A tilt at molecular biology. *The Lancet,* January 1, 1966, 7427.
5. HOLLISTER, L. E. *Baltimore Sun,* March 20, 1966.
6. LEWIS, H. R. *With Every Breath You Take.* New York: Crown Publishers, 1965.
7. *Medical World News,* October 8, 1965.
8. WILM, H. G. *New York Times,* May 20, 1965, p. 45, Col. I.
9. ZINSSER, HANS, *Rats, Lice and History.* Boston: Little Brown, 1935.

Water Pollution

Robert D. Hennigan

Introduction

Water pollution is one of the major environmental problems of our times. As with most other forms of environmental pollution, it has come about because of the industrial-urban growth and development over the past 60 to 70 years, particularly the past 20 years.

Water pollution results when any input into the water cycle alters water quality to the extent that a legitimate use is impaired or lost. Water pollution abatement—or rather water quality management—has social, economic, political, and technical aspects. Consequently, it must be approached as a complex social and technical system requiring an interdisciplinary input if problems are to be accurately defined and effective remedial action taken.

Understanding of the water pollution problem requires a knowledge of:

1) Water quantity and quality relationships

2) The source, type, and volume of pollutants

3) The effect of pollutants on water use

4) The objectives of water quality management

5) The historical background of regulatory efforts

6) Social and economic development and its impact on water quality

From such basic knowledge and background, the contribution of the educational community can be determined in terms of manpower to be trained, problems to be studied and researched, and community education to be undertaken.

The author is P. E. Director of SUNY Water Resources Center, College of Forestry, Syracuse University, Syracuse, New York. This is the fourth paper from the Pollution Conference, held at State University, Oneonta, N.Y.

Water Resources

The water resource includes water in all its forms, uses, movements, effects, and locations. Rain, hail, snow, ice, fog, atmospheric vapors, soil moisture, surface water, and ground water are all part of the water resource as are streams, rivers, estuaries, ponds, lakes, oceans, wells, and springs.

Water is a renewable natural resource. It is delivered from the atmosphere in the form of rain, snow, hail, fog, and condensation and returns to the atmosphere by evaporation and transpiration. While on the earth, it runs over the ground to lakes, rivers, streams, and oceans and seeps into the ground to be taken up by growing plants to become a part of the ground-water reservoir, eventually discharging also to streams, lakes, or the ocean. There is a continual cycling of water through this system, propelled largely by solar radiation. Precipitation, transpiration, evaporation, ground-water infiltration and discharge, and surface runoff and streamflow vary from place to place and time to time. Furthermore, at any specific location and time, variation is the characteristic pattern to be expected.

Water is one of the essential elements of life. Because of its need and use, water availability is a shaper of civilization and cultures. The rise of cities and burgeoning modern urbanization, such as the Niagara Frontier Region, the city of New York metropolitan complex, and the urban-industrial concentration along the shores of the Great Lakes, is directly related to water availability and development.

In days past, activities and cultures developed where the water could be conveniently put to use. Water location

Bioscience, November, 1969, Vol.19, No.11, pp. 976-978.

is no longer the constraint it once was; techniques for water development, use, and transpiration have expanded man's control over water immensely.

Man's concern over water includes water quantity; its availability and volume, in time and place; and water quality, its physical, chemical, radiological, and biological condition, which directly affect its availability for use.

Water Quality

Water quality is determined by natural conditions, by man's activities, by land use development and treatment, and most drastically by waste water disposal.

Water found in nature is acid and alkaline, hard and soft, colored and uncolored, highly mineralized and low in minerals, turbid and clear, mildly and significantly radioactive, saline and fresh, saturated and devoid of oxygen, cold and hot, with and without a variety of elements in trace concentration, highly productive and unproductive of biological life.

Influencing factors are surface and subsurface geology; geographic and hydrologic conditions; storage availability; the size and nature of waters under consideration, urban and industrial development; other land use; climate, both seasonal and long term; and the physical, chemical, and biological interaction of all these things.

Natural conditions have been and are drastically affected by man's activities. These include development projects which alter stream and lake regimens as noted further on, and waste water inputs, both from point and diffuse sources.

Point sources include municipal sewage treatment plants; sanitary and storm sewer systems; waste outlets from steel mills, petroleum refineries, chemical plants, dairies, food processing plants, paper mills, metal processing and plating works, tanneries, thermal electric power plants, and coke plants; commercial and pleasure boats; irrigation return water, cattle feeding pens and areas; and radioactive processing and use facilities.

The diffused or nonpoint sources are overland runoff from urban, rural, agricultural, forest, and swamp land; fallout from the atmosphere; ground-water discharge to lakes and streams; and sometimes solid waste from dredging, individuals, municipalities, and industries.

The waste water inputs from runoff generally contribute silt, salts, oil, and other deleterious matter from city streets; radioactive material from fallout; sediment from highway construction and urban and farm land erosion; and pesticides, nutrients, and herbicides from land and area application. Point sources sometimes include these elements but, in addition, contribute sewage, phenols, oil, acids, alkalies, heat, solid waste, radioactive material, heavy metals, bacteria and viruses, detergents, salts, floating and settled solids, organic and inorganic material, dissolved solids, biochemical and chemical oxygen-demanding wastes, and toxic and inert material.

The effect of waste loading is dramatic. Water supply quality deteriorates; beaches are closed; the ecological balance is upset; fish and wildlife are killed; areas of lakes and rivers become cesspools; aesthetic sensibilities are offended by floating solids, colors, oil, and odors; recreational use is severely curtailed; nuisances are created; the commercial fishery declines; algae and weeds proliferate; and the mineral content of waters rises.

Interaction

Water quantity and quality considerations cannot be considered unilaterally. They are intimately related. The water supply becomes the used water to be returned as waste water. The impoundment changes the environment and the ecology of the stream or lake. Changing land use from rural to urban changes the stream regimen, frequently resulting in local flood problems and stream pollution because of loss of base flow and increased waste loadings caused by urban runoff. Inter-basin transfer of water alters downstream conditions because of the loss of

177

water. Impoundments may release cold, deoxygenated water high in manganese to the debasement of downstream uses. Peak power releases from hydro projects create surges and rapid changes in stage with consequent shock to downstream areas. Waste water inputs greatly exceed available capacity of unregulated streams in many places, even with the use of advanced treatment methods, particularly in urban areas.

Ideally, quantity and quality considerations are part of a whole or single system and should be considered accordingly.

System Elements

Water resource and quality management involves the physical resource, the people, and the governmental or institutional arrangement.

It is a multi-layered system: the first layer is the geography and hydrology of the locale; the second is the population distribution; the third is the international, state, and local boundary lines setting forth jurisdictional-geographic areas.

The needs and demands of the people will dictate program goals; the physical resource will be the determinant of technological input and facilities or programs needed; and the institutional pattern will identify the agency or instrumentality charged with the responsibility for implementation.

In addition, there are a myriad of other elements such as the legal foundation, economic concerns, and the relationship between adjacent or related areas within levels of government and between the various disciplines concerned with some band of the water resource spectrum. Consequently, the water resource system is not only multi-layered, but it is also marbled, including diverse and, at times, competing and conflicting interests. This is illustrated by the varied objectives of water pollution control.

Major water quality management objectives include:

1) Domestic water supply for public water systems and for facilities and individuals not served by such systems

2) Industrial water supply for manufacturing, food processing, and cooling purposes

3) Agricultural water supply for livestock and for irrigation

4) Water-borne transpiration and navigation

5) Optimal water conditions for fish and wildlife propagation and survival

6) Recreational use of water for boating, swimming, fishing, water skiing, and aesthetic enjoyment

7) Hydroelectric power development and cooling water for steam electric power generation, and

8) Responsible waste water disposal from point and diffuse sources into the environment.

All of these objectives are not totally compatible. One use may conflict with another: limiting recreational use of a watershed to protect public water supply quality; maintaining impoundment or lake levels for recreational purposes, thereby losing storage for stream flow regulation; use of water for irrigation or transfer of water out of a watershed, thereby decreasing downstream flow; increasing the rate of eutrophication by warming up water because of use for cooling purposes, or by addition of nutrients; and loss of fishery and recreational use because of waste water disposal.

The complex interdisciplinary and systematic elements of water pollution are demonstrated by this conference. All of the individual topics, including radiation, pesticides, population, solid waste, heat, and air, are part and parcel of the water pollution package.

Based on the foregoing general understanding, let us address ourselves to the questions of "Where are we?," "How did we get here?," and "What must be done to reclaim and protect the water resource?"

Where Are We?

It is no longer necessary to convince people that serious water pollution problems exist; this is a generally acknowledged fact. Both the popular and scientific press are loaded with articles and stories on the dismal position we find ourselves in. A prime current example is the oil well debacle at Santa Barbara as well as the continuing issues of eutrophication, pesticides, nutrients, and heat.

The waters of the nation and the state have been degraded. There is hardly a lake or a stream that is untouched. Some of the most obvious examples include the Great Lakes, particularly Lake Erie, where accelerated eutrophication brought on by massive waste water inputs has resulted in impairment and loss of many water uses such as fishery and recreational and aesthetic values; the Hudson River; the marine and harbor waters of New York; the ground waters of Long Island; and the local area waters around all metropolitan centers such as the Buffalo River which is a veritable cesspool of sewage and industrial waste. The number of situations that could be listed is truly endless. Naturally, most are familiar with the stories on the pollution of the Mississippi River, the Potomac River, and Puget Sound to name a few. Even the pollution by paper mills of Lake Baikal in the Soviet Union has been documented in the press.

Analysis of the present water pollution situation results in two major conclusions:

1) The water pollution problem is an urban-industrial phenomena, and

2) The great bulk of pollution input is from sewage and industrial waste water.

How Did We Get Here?

The critical water pollution situation developed because of the great urban-industrial growth coupled with a weak regulatory effort. The foundation of water pollution regulation was the prevention of epidemic, water-borne diseases. Water-borne disease was eliminated for all practical purposes by the mid-thirties by water treatment, disinfection, and abandonment of polluted sources. The emphasis was on municipal water supplies, with little attention paid to waste disposal. A resurgence of interest and concern developed after World War II and has intensified since that time.

The unexpected postwar boom brought with it industrial expansion, new industrial processes, detergents, development, and manyfold increases in use of pesticides, fertilizers, and herbicides, increasing urbanization, an exploding population, prosperity, and increased leisure time. Domestic and industrial demands for water started to spiral out of sight as did the demands for water-based recreation, coupled with a parallel increase in the production of waste water. Rising community standards and a greater concern for the quality of life and aesthetic concerns as well as increasing water usage resulted in a public demand that government undertake programs to properly protect, develop, enhance, and reclaim the water resources, particularly as water shortages occurred and pollutional situations worsened.

Urban Growth

The urban nature of much of the water pollution problem has become increasingly apparent.

The great growth of metropolitan areas is well recognized and well documented. The change in the past 50 years has been truly fantastic. In 1900, one out of 20 Americans lived in an urban areas; and in 1968, 14 out of 20 Americans live in an urban area. During this same period of time, the population has doubled, meaning that while the rural population has dropped about 30%, the urban population has increased 2800%. It is estimated that the existing population will double within the next 30 years and some 80% of this will be in urban areas.

Additionally, the per capita use of water has increased four-fivefold over the past 5 decades from 30 to 150 gallons per capita per day. Similar increases have taken place for other water uses—industrial, recreational, etc.

It is in metropolitan areas where over 80% of the people live, provide the support for industrial development, generate the increasing demand for water, and produce most of the pollutant input into the water system.

Another offshoot of this growth is the increased recreational use of the waters. Boat registrations, for example, have increased from about 100,000 in 1960 to 400,000 in 1966.

Cost analyses for water pollution abatement show that over 90% of the needed expenditures of $26 to $29 billion for the next few years are for industrial and municipal waste collection and treatment facilities, again located in urban areas.

It is estimated that the power needed to serve this increasing population and industrialization will increase from 18,000 megawatts to 48,000 megawatts in the next 24 years. This increase in power demand represents 270% of present capability. Practically all of it will be supplied by nuclear steam electric plants since the state's hydropower capability is almost fully developed with the possible exception of some river basin development or off-stream storage for peak power usage.

The increasing usage of water for domestic, industrial, and cooling purposes will produce like amounts of waste water to be treated and disposed of, and the accelerating land urbanization will likewise intensify waste quality and quantity problems, both locally around metropolitan centers and generally throughout the whole water system.

Out of all these changes and demands has come a new frame of reference. This new frame of reference is one which recognizes the limited water resource base, the ever-expanding need and demands, rising standards, and the public insistence that effective action be taken to bring a halt to exploitation and degradation of the water resource. Simply expressed, it constitutes a change of emphasis from, "How much waste can be put into the waters?" to, "How much waste can be kept out of the waters?" and recognition that any approach made be socially, economically, and technically viable.

Action

Barriers to effective action are a sometimes ill-informed public, lack of manpower, limited capability (particularly in metropolitan areas with multiple governments), fiscal resources, ineffective state and federal programs, limited technical knowledge or inability to bring current knowledge to bear on problems, and conflict between various interests.

An effective water quality management program is possible through: (1) system and process changes, both in municipal and industrial water management use, to reduce the volume of water used and subsequent waste water and to reduce the type or amount of polluting substances or materials. Cases in point would be metering of all water services to reduce water consumption, manufacture of paper by a dry process or with a closed system, and the recent change in detergent manufacture to produce a biodegradable product instead of the former stable, persistent material; (2) design, construction, and operation of necessary drainage and sewage collection and treatment facilities and industrial waste treatment facilities; (3) effective control measures to eliminate or reduce input of heat, oil, sediment, pesticides, nutrients, dissolved salts, boat discharges, and solid waste; and (4) impoundments for stream flow regulation to eliminate nuisance conditions to equalize waste dilution and to maintain acceptable environmental conditions.

The problems and needs in water pollution control are world-wide as well as national, state, and local concerns. The nature and seriousness of the problems depend on the particular situation faced and its technical, legal, economic, and social ramifications. However, the common element is the need for: (1) research programs in physical, social, and biological sciences; (2) education and training at the graduate, undergraduate, and technician level to provide needed manpower; (3) a comprehensive, continuously-operating surveillance program to show long-term trends, to pinpoint problems, to evaluate activity, and to help plan future action; and (4) a public education program to develop support for effective action and to counter misinformation about the water resource and water quality management.

Conclusion

At the present time where changing rules, policies, and standards are the order of the day, some bitter battles will be fought between antagonists over water pollution. I think that the following quote from Schlesinger puts this into proper perspective: "Reason without passion is sterile, but passion without reason is hysterical. I have always supposed that reason and passion must be united in any effective form of public action." At the same time, the changing needs and demands must be recognized, accepted, and accommodated.

The Effects of Pesticides

William A. Niering

The dramatic appearance of Rachel Carson's *Silent Spring* (1962) awakened a nation to the deleterious effects of pesticides. Our technology had surged ahead of us. We had lost our perspective on just how ruthlessly man can treat his environment and still survive. He was killing pesty insects by the trillions, but he was also poisoning natural ecosystems all around him. It was Miss Carson's mission to arrest this detrimental use of our technological achievements. As one might have expected, she was criticized by special vested industrial interests and, to some degree, by certain agricultural specialists concerned with only one aspect of our total environment. However, there was no criticism, only praise, from the nation's ecosystematically oriented biologists. For those who found *Silent Spring* too dramatic an approach to the problem, the gap was filled two years later by *Pesticides and the Living Landscape* (1964) in which Rudd further documented Miss Carson's thesis but in more academic style.

The aim of this chapter is to summarize some of the effects of two pesticides — insecticides and herbicides — on our total environment, and to point up research and other educational opportunities for students of environmental science. The insecticide review will be based on representative studies from the literature, whereas the herbicide review will represent primarily the results of the author's research and experience in the Connecticut Arboretum at Connecticut College. Although some consider this subject controversial, there is really no controversy in the mind of the author—the issue merely involves the

sound ecological use of pesticides only where necessary and without drastically contaminating or upsetting the dynamic equilibrium of our natural ecosystems. I shall not consider the specific physiological effects of pesticides, but rather their effects on the total environment — plants, animals, soil, climate, man — the biotic and abiotic aspects.

Environmental science or ecosystematic thinking should attempt to coordinate and integrate all aspects of the environment. Although ecosystems may be managed, they must also remain in a relative balance or dynamic equilibrium, analogous to a spider's web, where each strand is intimately interrelated and interdependent upon every other strand.

The Impact of Insecticides

Ecologists have long been aware that simplifying the environment to only a few species can precipitate a catastrophe. Our highly mechanized agricultural operations, dominated by extensive acreages of one crop, encourage large numbers of insect pests. As insurance against insect damage, vast quantities of insecticides are applied with little regard for what happens to the chemical once it is on the land. Prior to World War II, most of our insecticides were nonpersistent organics found in the natural environment. For example, the pyrethrins were derived from dried chysanthemum flowers, nicotine sulphate from tobacco, and rotenone from the tropical derris plants. However, research during World War II and thereafter resulted in a number of potent persistent chlorinated hydrocarbons (DDT, dieldrin, endrin, lindane, chlordane, heptachor and others) to fight the ever-increasing hordes of insects, now some 3000 species plaguing man in North America.

In 1964, industries in the United States produced 783 million lb. of

This paper will appear in the symposium volume *Environmental Problems* to be published by J. B. Lippincott, Summer, 1968.

The author is Professor of Botany and Director of the Connecticut Arboretum, Connecticut College.

Bioscience, September, 1968, Vol.18, No.9, pp. pp. 869-875.

182

pesticides, half insecticides and the other half herbicides, fungicides, and rodenticides. The application of these chemicals on the nation's landscape[1] has now reached the point where one out of every ten acres is being sprayed with an average of 4 lb. per acre (Anonymous, 1966).

Positive Effects on Target Organisms

That market yields and quality are increased by agricultural spraying appears to have been well documented. Data from the National Agricultural Chemical Association show net increased yields resulting in from $5.00 to $100.00 net gains per acre on such crops as barley, tomatoes, sugar beets, pea seed, and cotton seed. However, Rudd (1964) questions the validity of these figures, since there is no explanation just how they were derived. His personal observations on the rice crop affected by the rice leaf miner outbreak in California are especially pertinent. The insect damage was reported as ruining 10% to 20% of the crop. He found this to be correct for some fields, but most of the fields were not damaged at all. In this situation, the facts were incorrect concerning the pest damage. It appears that not infrequently repeated spraying applications are merely insurance sprays and in many cases actually unnecessary. Unfortunately, the farmer is being forced to this procedure in part by those demanding from agriculture completely insect-free produce. This has now reached ridiculous proportions. Influenced by advertising, the housewife now demands perfect specimens with no thought of or regard for how much environmental contamination has resulted to attain such perfection. If we could relax our standards to a moderate degree, pesticide contamination could be greatly reduced. Although it may be difficult to question that spraying increases yields and quality of the market-

able products, there are few valid data available on how much spraying is actually necessary, how much it is adding to consumer costs, what further pests are aggravated by spraying, and what degree of resistance eventually develops.

Negative Effects on Nontarget Organisms

Although yields may be increased with greater margins of profit, according to available data, one must recognize that these chemicals may adversely affect a whole spectrum of nontarget organisms not only where applied but possibly thousands of miles from the site of application. To the ecologist concerned with the total environment, these persistent pesticides pose some serious threats to our many natural ecosystems. Certain of these are pertinent to review.

1. Killing of nontarget organisms. In practically every spray operation, thousands of nontarget insects are killed, many of which may be predators on the very organisms one is attempting to control. But such losses extend far beyond the beneficial insects. In Florida, an estimated 1,117,000 fishes of at least 30 species (20 to 30 tons), were killed with dieldrin, when sand flies were really the target organism. Crustaceans were virtually exterminated — the fiddler crabs survived only in areas missed by the treatment (Harrington and Bidlingmayer, 1958).

In 1963, there was a "silent spring" in Hanover, New Hampshire. Seventy per cent of the robin population — 350 to 400 robins — was eliminated in spraying for Dutch elm disease with 1.9 lb. per acre DDT (Wurster et al., 1965). Wallace (1960) and Hickey and Hunt (1960) have reported similar instances on the Michigan State University and University of Wisconsin campuses. Last summer, at Wesleyan University, my students observed dead and trembling birds following summer applications of DDT on the elms. At the University of Wisconsin campus (61 acres), the substitution of methoxy-

[1] Dr. George Woodwell estimates that there are 1 billion lbs. of DDT now circulating in the biosphere.

chlor has resulted in a decreased bird mortality. The robin population has jumped from three to twenty-nine pairs following the change from DDT to methoxychlor. Chemical control of this disease is often overemphasized, with too little attention directed against the sources of elm bark beetle. Sanitation is really the most important measure in any sound Dutch elm disease control program (Matthysse, 1959).

One of the classic examples involving the widespread destruction of non-target organisms was the fire ant eradication program in our southern states. In 1957, dieldrin and heptochlor were aerially spread over two and one-half million acres. Wide elimination of vertebrate populations resulted; and recovery of some populations is still uncertain (Rudd, 1964). In the interest of science, the Georgia Academy of Science appointed an ad hoc committee to evaluate this control-eradication program (Bellinger et al., 1965). It found that reported damage to crops, wildlife, fish, and humans had not been verified, and concluded, furthermore, that the ant is not really a significant economic pest but a mere nuisance. Here was an example where the facts did not justify the federal expenditure of $2.4 million in indiscriminate sprays. Fortunately, this approach has been abandoned, and local treatments are now employed with Mirex, a compound with fewer side effects. Had only a small percentage of this spray expenditure been directed toward basic research, we might be far ahead today in control of the fire ant.

2. *Accumulation in the food chain.* The persistent nature of certain of these insecticides permits the chemical to be carried from one organism to another in the food chain. As this occurs, there is a gradual increase in the biocide at each higher trophic level. Many such examples have been reported in the literature. One of the most striking comes from Clear Lake, California, where a 46,000-acre warm lake, north of San Francisco, was sprayed for pesty gnats in 1949, 1954, and 1957, with DDD, a chemical presumably less toxic than DDT. Analyses of the plankton revealed 250 times more of the chemical than originally applied, the frogs 2000 times more, sunfish 12,000, and the grebes up to an 80,000-fold increase (Cottam, 1965; Rudd, 1964). In 1954 death among the grebes was widespread. Prior to the spraying, a thousand of these birds nested on the lake. Then for 10 years no grebes hatched. Finally, in 1962, one nestling was observed, and the following year three. Clear Lake is popular for sports fishing, and the flesh of edible fish now caught reaches 7 ppm, which is above the maximum tolerance level set by the Food and Drug Administration.

In an estuarine ecosystem, a similar trend has been reported on the Long Island tidal marshes, where mosquito control spraying with DDT has been practiced for some 20 years (Woodwell et al., 1967). Here the food chain accumulation shows plankton 0.04 ppm, shrimp 0.16 ppm, minnows 1 to 2 ppm, and ring-billed gull 75.5 ppm. In general, the DDT concentrations in carnivorous birds were 10 to 100 times those in the fish they fed upon. Birds near the top of the food chain have DDT residues about a million times greater than concentration in the water. Pesticide levels are now so high that certain populations are being subtly eliminated by food chain accumulations reaching toxic levels.

3. *Lowered reproductive potential.* Considerable evidence is available to suggest a lowered reproductive potential, especially among birds, where the pesticide occurs in the eggs in sufficient quantities either to prevent hatching or to decrease vigor among the young birds hatched. Birds of prey, such as the bald eagle, osprey, hawks, and others, are in serious danger. Along the northeast Atlantic coast, ospreys normally average about 2.5 young per year. However, in Maryland and Connecticut,

reproduction is far below this level. In Maryland, ospreys produce 1.1 young per year and their eggs contain 3 ppm DDT, while in Connecticut, 0.5 young ospreys hatch and their eggs contain up to 5.1 ppm DDT. These data indicate a direct correlation between the amount of DDT and the hatchability of eggs — the more DDT present in the eggs, the fewer young hatched (Ames, 1966). In Wisconsin, Keith (1964) reports 38% hatching failure in herring gulls. Early in the incubation period, gull eggs collected contained over 200 ppm DDT and its cogeners. Pheasant eggs from DDT-treated rice fields compared to those from unsprayed lands result in fewer healthy month-old chicks from eggs taken near sprayed fields. Although more conclusive data may still be needed to prove that pesticides such as DDT are the key factor, use of such compounds should be curtailed until it is proved that they are not the causal agents responsible for lowering reproductive potential.

4. Resistance to sprays. Insects have a remarkable ability to develop a resistance to insecticides. The third spray at Clear Lake was the least effective on the gnats, and here increased resistance was believed to be a factor involved. As early as 1951, resistance among agricultural insects appeared. Some of these include the codling moth on apples, and certain cotton, cabbage, and potato insects. Over 100 important insect pests now show a definite resistance to chemicals (Carson, 1962).

5. Synergistic effects. The interaction of two compounds may result in a third much more toxic than either one alone. For example, Malathion is relatively "safe" because detoxifying enzymes in the liver greatly reduce its toxic properties. However, if some compound destroys or interrupts this enzyme system, as certain organic phosphates may do, the toxicity of the new combination may be increased greatly. Pesticides represent one of many pollutants we are presently adding to our environment. These subtle synergistic effects have opened a whole new field of investigation. Here students of environmental science will find many challenging problems for future research.

6. Chemical migration. After two decades of intensive use, pesticides are now found throughout the world, even in places far from any actual spraying. Penguins and crab-eating seals in the Antarctic are contaminated, and fish far off the coasts of four continents now contain insecticides ranging from 1 to 300 ppm in their fatty tissues (Anonymous, 1966).

The major rivers of our nation are contaminated by DDT, endrin, and dieldrin, mostly in the parts per trillion range. Surveys since 1957 reveal that dieldrin has been the main pesticide present since 1958. Endrin reached its maximum, especially in the lower Mississippi River, in the fall of 1963 when an extensive fish kill occurred and has since that time decreased. DDT and its cogeners, consistently present since 1958, have been increasing slightly (Breidenbach et al., 1967).

7. Accumulation in the ecosystem. Since chlorinated hydrocarbons like DDT are not readily broken down by biological agents such as bacteria, they may not only be present but also accumulate within a given ecosystem. On Long Island, up to 32 lb. of DDT have been reported in the marsh mud, with an average of 13 lb. presumed to be correlated with the 20 years of mosquito control spraying (Woodwell et al., 1967). Present in these quantities, burrowing marine organisms and the detritis feeders can keep the residues in continuous circulation in the ecosystem. Many marine forms are extremely sensitive to minute amounts of insecticides. Fifty per cent of a shrimp population was killed with endrin 0.6 parts per billion (ppb). Even 1 ppb will kill blue crabs within a week. Oysters, typical filter feeders, have been reported to accumulate up to 70,000 ppm. (Loosanoff, 1965). In Green Bay along Lake Michigan, Hickey and Keith (1964) report up to 0.005 ppm wet weight of DDT, DDE, and DDD in the lake sediments. Here the accumulation has presumably been from leaching or run-off from surrounding agricultural lands in Door County, where it is reported that 70,000 pounds of DDT are used annually. Biological concentration in Green Bay is also occurring in food chain organisms, as reported at Clear Lake, California. Accumulation of biocides, especially in the food chain, and their availability for recycling pose a most serious ecological problem.

8. *Delayed response.* Because of the persistent nature and tendency of certain insecticides to accumulate at toxic levels in the food chain, there is often a delayed response in certain ecosystems subjected either directly or indirectly to pesticide treatment. This was the case at Clear Lake, where the mortality of nontarget organisms occurred several years after the last application. This is a particularly disturbing aspect, since man is often the consumer of those food chain organisms accumulating pesticide residues. In the general population, human tissues contain about 12 ppm DDT-derived materials. Those with meatless diets, and the Eskimos, store less; however, agricultural applicators and formulators of pesticides may store up to 600 ppm DDT or 1000 ppm DDT-derived components. Recent studies indicate that dieldrin and lindane are also stored in humans without occupational exposure (Durham, 1965). The possibility of synergistic effects involving DDT, dieldrin, lindane, and other pollutants to which man is being exposed may result in unpredictable hazards. In fact, it is now believed that pesticides may pose a genetic hazard. At the recent conference of the New York Academy of Science, Dr. Onsy G. Fahmy warned that certain chlorinated hydrocarbons, organophosphates and carbamates were capable of disrupting

the DNA molecule. It was further noted that such mutations may not appear until as many as 40 generations later. Another scientist, Dr. M. Jacqueline Verrett, pointed out that certain fungicides (folpet and captan) thought to be nontoxic have chemical structures similar to thalidomide.

We are obviously dealing with many biological unknowns in our widespread use of presumably "safe" insecticides. We have no assurance that 12 ppm DDT in our human tissue, now above the permissible in marketable products for consumption, may not be resulting in deleterious effects in future generations. As Rudd warns (1964): ". . . it would be somewhat more than embarrassing for our 'experts' to learn that significant effects do occur in the long term. One hundred and eight million human guinea pigs would have paid a high price for their trust."

Of unpredicted delayed responses, we have an example in radiation contamination. In the Bravo tests on Bikini in 1954, the natives on Rongelap Atoll were exposed to radiation assumed to be safe. Now more than a decade later, tumors of the thyroid gland have been discovered in the children exposed to these presumably safe doses (Woodwell et al., 1966). Pesticides per se or synergisms resulting from their interaction could well plague man in now unforeseen or unpredictable ways in the future.

The Sound Use of Herbicides

In contrast to insecticides, herbicides are chemical weed-killers used to control or kill unwanted plants. Following World War II, the chlorinated herbicide 2, 4-D began to be used widely on broadleaf weeds. Later, 2, 4, 5-T was added, which proved especially effective on woody species. Today, over 40 weed-killers are available. Although used extensively in agriculture, considerable quantities are used also in aquatic weed control and in forestry, wildlife, and right-of-way vegetation management. Currently, large quantities are being used as defoliators in Vietnam.

Although herbicides in general are much safer than insecticides in regard to killing nontarget organisms and in their residual effects, considerable caution must be exercised in their proper use. One of the greatest dangers in right-of-way vegetation management is their indiscriminate use, which results in habitat destruction. Drift of spray particles and volatility may also cause adverse effects on nontarget organisms, especially following indiscriminate applications. In the Connecticut Arboretum, shade trees have been seriously affected as a result of indiscriminate roadside sprays (Niering, 1959). During the spring of 1957, the town sprayed the marginal trees and shrubs along a roadside running through the Arboretum with 2, 4-D and 2, 4, 5-T (1 part chemical: 100 parts water). White oaks overarching the road up to 2 feet in diameter were most seriously affected. Most of the leaves turned brown. Foliage of scarlet and black oaks of similar size exhibited pronounced leaf curling (Fig. 1). Trees were affected up to 300 feet back from the point of application within the natural area of the Arboretum. White oak twigs near the sprayed belt also developed a striking weeping habit (Fig. 2) as twig elongation occurred — a growth abnormality still conspicuous after 10 years.

The effectiveness of the spray operation in controlling undesirable woody growth indicated a high survival of unwanted tree sprouts. Black birch and certain desirable shrubs were particularly sensitive. Shrubs affected were highly ornamental forms often planted in roadside beautification programs. The resulting ineffectiveness of the spray operation was indicated by the need for cutting undesirable growth along the roadside the following year.

In the agricultural use of herbicides, drift effects have been reported over much greater distances. In California, drift from aerial sprays has been reported up to 30 miles from the point of application (Freed, 1965).

Although toxicity of herbicides to nontarget organisms is not generally a problem, it has been reported in aquatic environments. For example, the dimethylamine salt of 2, 4-D is relatively safe for bluegill at 150 ppm, but the butyl, ethyl, and isopropyl esters are toxic to fish at around 1 ppm (R. E. Johnson, personal communication). Studies of 16 aquatic herbicides on *Daphnia magna,* a microcrustacean, revealed that 2, 4-D (specific derivative not given) seemed completely innocuous but that several others (Dichlone, a quinone; Molinate, a thiolcarbamate; Propanil, an anilide; sodium arsenite and Dichlopenil, a nitrile) could present a real hazard to this lower food chain organism (Crosby and Tucker, 1966).

Effects on rights-of-way. The rights-of-way across our nation comprise an estimated 70,000,000 acres of land, much of which is · now subjected to herbicide treatment (Niering, 1967). During the past few decades, indiscriminate foliar applications have been widespread in the control of undesirable vegetation, erroneously referred to as brush (Goodwin and Niering, 1962). Indiscriminate applications often fail to root-kill undesirable species, therefore necessitating repeated retreatment, which results in the destruction of many desirable forms. Indiscriminate sprays are also used for the control of certain broadleaf weeds along roadsides. In New Jersey, 19 treatments were applied during a period of 6 years in an attempt to control ragweed (Dill, 1963). This, of course, was ecologically unsound, when one considers that ragweed is an annual plant typical of bare soil and that repeated sprayings also eliminate the competing broadleaved perennial species that, under natural successional conditions, could tend to occupy the site and naturally eliminate the ragweed. Broadcast or indiscriminate spraying can also result in destruction of valuable wildlife habitat in addition to the needless destruction of our native flora — wildflowers and shrubs of high landscape value.

Nonselective spraying, especially along roadsides, also tends to produce a monotonous grassy cover free of colorful wildflowers and interesting shrubs. It is economically and aesthetically unsound to remove these valuable species naturally occurring on such sites. Where they do not occur, highway beautification programs plant many of these same shrubs and low-growing trees.

Recognizing this nation-wide problem in the improper use of herbicides, the Connecticut Arboretum established, over a decade ago, several right-of-way demonstration areas to serve as models in the sound use of herbicides (Niering, 1955; 1957; 1961). Along two utility rights-of-way and a roadside crossing the Arboretum, the vegetation has been managed following sound ecological principles, as shown in Figures 3 and 4 (Egler, 1954; Goodwin and Niering, 1959; Niering, 1958). Basic techniques include basal and stump treatments. The former involves soaking the base of the stem (root collar) and continuing up the stem for 12 inches; the stump technique involves soaking the stump immediately after cutting. Effective formulations include 2, 4, 5-T in a fuel oil carrier (1 part chemical: 20 parts oil). Locally, stem-foliage sprays may be necessary, but the previous two techniques form the basic approach in the selective use of weed-killers. They result in good root-kill and simultaneously preserve valuable wildlife. habitat and aesthetically attractive native species, all at a minimum of cost to the agency involved when figured on a long-range basis. In addition to these gains, the presence of good shrub cover tends to impede tree invasion and to reduce future maintenance costs (Pound and Egler, 1953; Niering and Elger, 1955).

Another intriguing use of herbicides is in naturalistic landscaping. Dr. Frank Egler conceived this concept of creating picturesque natural settings in shrubby fields by selectively eliminating the less attractive species and accentuating the ornamental forms (Kenfield, 1966). At the Connecticut Arboretum we have landscaped several such areas (Niering and Goodwin, 1963). The one shown in Figure 5 was designed and created by students. This approach has unlimited application in arresting vegetation development and preserving landscapes that might disappear under normal successional or vegetational development processes.

Future Outlook

Innumerable critical moves have recently occurred that may alter the continued deterioration of our environment. Secretary Udall has banned the use of DDT, chlordane, dieldrin, and endrin on Department of the Interior lands. The use of DDT has been banned on state lands in New Hampshire and lake trout watersheds in New York State; in Connecticut, commercial applications are limited to dormant sprays. On Long Island, a temporary court injunction has been granted against the Suffolk County Mosquito Control Board's use of DDT in spraying tidal marshes. The Forest Service has terminated the use of DDT, and in the spring of 1966 the United States Department of Agriculture banned the use of endrin and dieldrin. Currently, the Forest Service has engaged a top-level research team in the Pacific Southwest to find chemicals highly selective to individual forest insect pests and that will break down quickly into harmless components. The Ribicoff hearing, which has placed Congressional focus on the problem of environmental pollution and Gaylord Nelson's bill to ban the sale of DDT in the United States are all enlightened endeavors at the national level.

The United States Forest Service has a selective program for herbicides in the National Forests. The Wisconsin Natural Resources Committee has instituted a selective roadside right-of-way maintenance program for the State. In Connecticut, a selective approach is in practice in most roadside and utility spraying.

Although we have considerable knowledge of the effects of biocides on the total environment, we must continue the emphasis on the holistic approach in studying the problem and interpreting the data. Continued observations of those occupationally exposed and of residents living near pesticide areas should reveal invaluable toxicological data. The study of migrant workers, of whom hundreds have been reported killed by pesticides, needs exacting investigation.

The development of more biological controls as well as chemical formulations that are specific to the target organism with a minimum of side effects needs continuous financial support by state and federal agencies and industry. Graduate opportunities are unlimited in this field.

As we look to the future, one of our major problems is the communication of sound ecological knowledge already available rather than pseudoscientific knowledge to increase the assets of special interest groups (Egler, 1964; 1965; 1966). The fire ant fiasco may be cited as a case in point. And as Egler (1966) has pointed out in his fourth most recent review of the pesticide problem: ". . . 95% of the problem is not in scientific knowledge of pesticides but in scientific knowledge of human behavior. . . . There are power plays . . . the eminent experts who deal with parts not ecological wholes."

One might ask, is it really good business to reduce the use of pesticides? Will biological control make as much money? Here the problem integrates political science, economics, sociology, and psychology. Anyone seriously interested in promoting the sound use of biocides must be fully cognizant of these counter forces in our society. They need serious study, analysis, and forthright reporting in the public interest.

With all we know about the deleterious effects of biocides on our environment, the problem really challenging man is to get this scientific knowledge translated into action through the sociopolitical pathways available to us in a free society. If we fail to communicate a rational approach, we may find that technology has become an invisible monster as Egler has succinctly stated (1966).

Pesticides are the greatest single tool for simplifying the habitat ever conceived by the simple mind of man, who may yet prove too simple to grasp the fact that he is but a blind strand of an ecosystem web, dependent not upon himself, but upon the total web, which nevertheless he has the power to destroy.

Here environmental science can involve the social scientist in communicating sound science to society and involve the political scientist in seeing that sound scientific knowledge is translated into reality. Our survival on this planet may well depend on how well we can make this translation.

References

Ames, P. L. 1966. DDT residues in the eggs of the osprey in the northeastern United States and their relation to nesting success. *J. Applied Ecol.*, 3 (suppl.): 87-97.

Anonymous. 1966. Fish, wildlife and pesticides. U.S. Dept. of Interior, Supt. of Doc. 12 p.

Bellinger, F., R. E. Dyer, R. King, and R. B. Platt. 1965. A review of the problem of the imported fire ant. *Bull. Georgia Acad. Sci.*, Vol. 23, No. 1.

Breidenbach, A. W., C. G. Gunnerson, F. K. Kawahara, J. J. Lichtenberg, and R. S. Green. 1967. Chlorinated hydrocarbon pesticides in major basins, 1957-1965. *Public Health Rept.* 82: 139-156.

Carson, Rachel. 1962. *Silent Spring.* Houghton Mifflin, Boston, 368 p.

Cottam, C. 1965. The ecologists' role in problems of pesticide pollution. *BioScience*, 15: 457-463.

Crosby, D. G., and R. K. Tucker. 1966. Toxicity of aquatic herbicides to *Daphnia magna. Science*, 154: 289-290.

Dill, N. H. 1962-63. Vegetation management. *New Jersey Nature News,* **17:** 123-130; **18:** 151-157.

Durham, W. F. 1965. Effects of pesticides on man. *In* C. O. Chichester, ed., *Research in Pesticides.* Academic Press, Inc., New York.

Egler, F. E. 1954. Vegetation management for rights-of-way and roadsides. *Smithsonian Inst. Rept. for 1953:* 299-322.

———. 1964a. Pesticides in our ecosystem. *Am. Scientist,* **52:** 110-136.

———. 1964b. Pesticides in our ecosystem: communication II: *BioScience,* **14:** 29-36.

———. 1965. Pesticides in our ecosystem: communication III. *Assoc. Southeastern Biologist Bull.,* **12:** 9-91.

———. 1966. Pointed perspectives. Pesticides in our ecosystem. *Ecology,* **47:** 1077-1084.

Freed, V. H. 1965. Chemicals and the control of plants. *In* C. O. Chichester, ed., *Research in Pesticides.* Academic Press, Inc., New York

Goodwin, R. H., and W. A. Niering. 1959. The management of roadside vegetation by selective herbicide techniques. *Conn. Arboretum Bull.,* **11:** 4-10.

———. 1962. What is happening along Connecticut's roadsides. *Conn. Arboretum Bull.,* **13:** 13-24.

Harrington, R. W., Jr., and W. L. Bidlingmayer. 1958. Effects of dieldrin on fishes and invertebrates of a salt marsh. *J. Wildlife Management,* **22:** 76-82.

Hickey, J. J., and L. Barrie Hunt. 1960. Initial songbird mortality following a Dutch elm disease control program. *J. Wildlife Management,* **24:** 259-265.

Hickey, J. J., and J. A. Keith. 1964. Pesticides in the Lake Michigan ecosystem. *In* The Effects of Pesticides on Fish and Wildlife. U.S. Dept. Interior Fish and Wildlife Service.

Keith, J. A. 1964. Reproductive success in a DDT-contaminated population of herring gulls, p. 11-12. *In* The Effects of Pesticides on Fish and Wildlife. U.S. Dept. Interior Fish and Wildlife Service.

Kenfield, W. G. 1966. *The Wild Gardner in the Wild Landscape.* Hafner, New York. 232 p.

Loosanoff, V. L. 1965. Pesticides in sea water. *In* C. O. Chichester, ed., *Research in Pesticides.* Academic Press, Inc., New York.

Matthysse, J. G. 1959. An evaluation of mist blowing and sanitation in Dutch elm disease control programs. N.Y.

State Coll. of Agric. Cornell Misc. Bull. 30, 16 p.

Niering, W. A. 1955. Herbicide research at the Connecticut Arboretum. *Proc. Northeastern Weed Control Conf.,* **9:** 459-462.

———. 1957. Connecticut Arboretum right-of-way demonstration area progress report. *Proc. Northeastern Weed Control Conf.,* **11:** 203-208.

———. 1958. Principles of sound right-of-way vegetation management. *Econ. Bot.,* **12:** 140-144.

———. 1959. A potential danger of broadcast sprays. *Conn. Arboretum Bull.,* **11:** 11-13.

———. 1961. The Connecticut Arboretum right-of-way demonstration area— its role in commercial application. *Proc. Northeastern Weed Control.,* **15:** 424-433.

———. 1967. Connecticut rights-of-way — their conservation values. *Conn. Woodlands,* **32:** 6-9.

Niering, W. A., and F. E. Egler. 1955. A shrub community of *Viburnum lentago,* stable for twenty-five years. *Ecology,* **36:** 356-360.

Niering, W. A., and R. H. Goodwin. 1963. Creating new landscapes with herbicides. *Conn. Arboretum Bull.,* **14:** 30.

Pound, C. E., and F. E. Egler. 1963. Brush control in southeastern New York: fifteen years of stable treeless communities. *Ecology,* **34:** 63-73.

Rudd, R. L. 1964. *Pesticides and the Living Landscape.* University of Wisconsin Press, 320 p.

Wallace, G. J. 1960. Another year of robin losses on a university campus. *Audubon Mag.,* **62:** 66-69.

Woodwell, G. M., W. M. Malcolm, and R. H. Whittaker. 1966. A-bombs, bug bombs & us. Brookhaven National Lab. 9842.

Woodwell, G. M., C. F. Wurster, Jr., & P. A. Isaacson. 1967. DDT residues in an east coast estuary: a case of biological concentration of a persistent insecticide. *Science,* **156:** 821-824.

Wurster, Doris H., C. F. Wurster, Jr., & W. N. Strickland. 1965. Bird mortality following DDT spray for Dutch elm disease. *Ecology,* **46:** 488-499.

Adaptive Strategy for Air Pollution

Frederick Sargent, II
University of Illinois

The recently published hearings of the Daddario Subcommittee (1966, p. 10), focused on the fundamental goal of an adaptive strategy, viz.

> managing the quality of the renewable resources of air, water, and land to yield the greatest net benefit to society . . . Specification of quality objectives, of course, brings contending needs into conflict. The management which is called for must balance risks and benefits of many future actions. Too often the benefits are more easy to evaluate than the risks. It is in this way that technology is most inadequate for pollution abatement. This inadequacy prevents agreement on the many subobjectives of criteria and standards which comprise the overall goal.

Man has long taken for granted his habitat and its apparently limitless bountifulness. Rather abruptly, and only recently, he discovered that not only were the bounties of his habitat limited but also that his imprint on that habitat could be seriously disruptive. Thus he came to realize that environment could not be taken for granted. Now he searches for processes that will ameliorate his environmental imprint. And he hopes it will not be too late. Air pollution is one dimension of that human imprint. My objective is to consider some concepts and actions that might contribute to the formulation of an adaptive strategy for air pollution.

Demitri Shimkin (1966, p. 38) identifies adaptive strategy as a system of "cognition and behavior maximizing the well-being and minimizing the hazards to survival of human populations." The concepts fundamental to this strategy are habitat, biological population, and behavioral codes. Habitat and population are linked in the concept of ecosystem. Behavioral codes translate man's perception of himself in relation to ecosystem into a set of rules for resource management, for the ecosystem is a resource. The atmospheric environment, a part of the ecosystem, is equally a resource. Consequently, for an adaptive strategy for air pollution to be effective, it must treat air pollution ecologically. Although this viewpoint does not simplify the strategic decisions, it does assure, as I will attempt to bring out, that risks are evaluated and hazards minimized.

The adaptive strategy is prospective, but the time for decision is upon us. The projections for continuing growth of the human population and its technological expectations suggest that current management practices will not keep pace, that atmospheric pollution will become more intense and more widespread. The urgency for instituting effective regulations was emphasized by President Johnson in his message to Congress on "Protecting Our National Heritage." In that message he called for an Air Quality Act which would establish regional regulatory commissions, promulgate uniform air quality standards, and expand investigative efforts. This message is an enlightened judgment, for it recognizes the fundamental dichotomy in an adaptive strategy, viz., the regulation of industrial

Presented in Session on "Air Pollution Control" at 27th Annual Meeting of Illinois Public Health Association, Peoria, Illinois, April 7, 1967.

growth (the cost) so that the wastes of technology will not irreparably destroy the fitness of the ecosystem (the risk).

Ecosystem as a Renewable Natural Resource

All living organisms are linked to one another and to their environment by complex flows of energy and matter. This linkage is an open system which is called the ecosystem. Energy continually flows into the system from the sun. The energy is captured by the green plants in the process of photosynthesis. The energy stored in these primary producers is then distributed in a hierarchal manner to the herbivores, carnivores, and, ultimately, the consumers of detritus. Because the energy of the system is finally dissipated as heat, it must be continually replenished from the sun. Materials, such as carbon, nitrogen, and water, flow through this system cyclically moving from environment, through the biomass, and back to environment. These hierarchal flows of energy and matter constitute the metabolism of the ecosystem.

During the course of terrestrial and organic evolution, adaptation was achieved between organism and environment, an adaptation which may be viewed as fitness of the ecosystem (Sargent & Barr, 1965). By virtue of this reciprocal fitness, continuing stability was achieved. This was before man became the dominant of the ecosystem. Eiseley (1962, p. 121) described that universe thus:

> If we examine the living universe around us which was before man and may be after him, we find two ways in which that universe, with its inhabitants, differs from the world of man: first, it is essentially a stable universe; second, its inhabitants are intensely concentrated upon their environment. They respond to it totally, and without it, or rather when they relax from it, they merely sleep. They reflect their environment but they do not alter it.

Man has changed this universe: he has become its dominant. He extracts from the ecosystem energy and raw materials not only to sustain his metabolic requirements and to provide clothing and shelter for himself but also to support his technological establishment. He has learned to manipulate the ecosystem so as to enhance its productivity. In essence, he has created a human ecosystem. Eiseley (1962, pp. 123-4) has this to say about the present universe:

> It is with the coming of man that a vast hole seems to open in nature, a vast black whirlpool spinning faster and faster, consuming flesh, stones, soil, minerals, sucking down the lightning, wrenching power from the atom, until the ancient sounds of nature are drowned in the cacophony of something which is no longer nature, something instead which is loose and knocking at the world's heart, something demonic and no longer planned — escaped it may be — spewed out of nature, contending in a final giant's game against its master.

Man's manipulations of the ecosystem have come to pose a serious threat to the stability of this system. The view has emerged in recent years that, to assure his survival, man must manage, not manipulate, the ecosystem. In the context of this view, the ecosystem becomes a renewable natural resource. Its natural stability bespeaks its capacity for renewal. For example, the metabolic cycles assure a continuing supply of nutrient energy and raw materials, and photosynthesis maintains the concentrations of atmospheric oxygen and carbon dioxide. Management thus becomes the keystone of adaptive strategy. The objective of management must be to augment the productivity to fulfill man's specific needs and requirements. This objective must be pursued ecologically so that the essential but delicate stability of the ecosystem is maintained.

A metabolic corollary of the renewable processes of the ecosystem is its capability of handling detritus. Atmospheric processes such as rainfall and sedimentation cleanse the air. Green plants play a role in regulating the concentration of carbon dioxide. Bacteria and fungi degrade animal and vegetable wastes and dead organisms. The basic ecological problem posed by air pollution is that the detritus of man's technology — heat, particulates, gases, and aerosols — are discharged into the atmosphere at a rate greatly exceeding the natural processes for recycling wastes. Thus, there is a net and continuing accumulation of technological detritus in the air. Some figures collected by Middleton (1966) illustrate the magnitude of the emission from man's industrial establishment. In 1960, 23.3×10^6 tons of sulfur dioxide were released into the air. Most of this waste derives from the combustion of coal. By 1980 the figure for sulfur dioxide may reach 36.0×10^6 tons. In Los Angeles alone, the daily discharge of sulfur dioxide is 455 tons. Nitrogen oxides are emitted at a rate of 835 tons per day. Organic vapor losses each day amount to 2755 tons. Each day some 10,660 tons of carbon monoxide are discharged into the air.

These emissions derive primarily from the combustion of fossil fuels in industry and in automobiles. To capture the energy stored in these fuels, a remarkable volume of air is utilized. Middleton (1966) estimates that each year 3000 cubic miles of air are used to release the energy from the fossil fuels consumed in the United States. Automobiles alone account for 21% · of this volume of air.

The atmospheric accumulation of detritus has initiated a degradation of the ecosystem in two distinctly different ways. First, the mounting discharge of wastes into the atmosphere has led to what has been euphemistically called "inadvertent" modification of weather and climate. Second, some of the wastes have proved toxic for various living organisms. For some time man did not perceive the ecological consequences of the growing bulk of atmospheric detritus. When, finally, some of the consequences were perceived, he labeled them "inadverent." Of course, this was just rationalization for lack of ecological foresight. Now, the problems of air pollution have become so complex that man must make very difficult behavioral decisions, decisions upon which his continued survival may well depend. Now, it is imperative that he understand the ecological implications of air pollution so that he may formulate an effective adaptive strategy.

Threats to the Fitness of Ecosystem

A brief ecological analysis of four problems stemming from air pollution will serve to emphasize the complexity of the situation facing man at this point in time. These problems are: (1) inadvertent modification of weather and climate, (2) atmospheric dispersal of pollutants, (3) the green plant, and (4) human health.

Inadvertent Modification of Weather and Climate

Because of thermal pollution, urban areas are "heat islands." Large quantities of waste heat are dispersed into the atmosphere. It is not unusual to find the air over cities several degrees Celsius above that of the rural surroundings (Comm. Atmos. Sci., 1966). Hickman (1965), for example, calculated that the total heat released into the atmosphere daily amounts to 0.2% of that received from the sun. He emphasized that since this discharge is confined largely to urban areas, its effect can account for an increment of 3-4 Celsius.

Carbon dioxide tends to trap outgoing infrared radiation. During the past three or four decades, there has been an increase of 15-25% in the concentration of carbon dioxide in the atmosphere. It has been suggested that this green-house effect of carbon dioxide has contributed to the rise of the mean global temperature of about 1.6 Celsius since 1900. Extrapolating from these correlations, predictions have been that by 2000 A.D. the mean global temperature may have risen 4 Celsius. These predictions are difficult to accept without reservation, for, since 1940, the mean global temperature has actually declined about 0.3 Celsius (Mitchell, 1961, 1963).

Concurrently, the turbidity of the atmosphere has shown substantial increases (McCormick, 1967). The increments have taken place not only in the air over cities but, more meaningfully, in the air over places far removed from cities. The greater turbidity arises from dusts and aerosols accumulating in atmosphere. Since turbidity reflects incoming solar radiation, it acts to reduce the solar energy reaching the earth's surface. Significant cooling is the consequence. Whether the decline in mean global temperatures since 1940 should be ascribed to rising turbidity is difficult to say. The main reason for making a conservative judgment is that appreciable variations of mean global temperature have been clearly demonstrated far back in geologic time (Brooks, 1926).

Two other processes may be acting to reduce incoming solar radiation through the production of cloudiness. First, meteorologists at the National Center for Atmospheric Sciences have traced the evolution of cirrus clouds from the vapor trails of jet aircraft (Fig. 1). Certainly these jets are carrying water vapor and freezing nuclei high into the troposphere. Second, Dr. V. J. Schaefer (1966) has shown that lead from automobile exhaust serves as a potent freezing nucleus. He speculates that lead in the atmosphere may lead to increased cloudiness. He also reported that in recent decades the number of condensation nuclei in the air has increased by several orders of magnitude.

All these man-made alterations argue for a growing disturbance in the energy budget for the ecosystem. What direc-

tion the disturbance will take is difficult to foresee.[1] It is possible that the water budget may also be altered. Turbidity can act to stabilize the atmosphere. Increased stability means decreased convective activity and decreased rainfall. It may be that megalopolis will eventually produce its own drought.

Atmospheric Dispersal of Pollutants

Meteorological processes, particularly wind and turbulent mixing, tend to disperse emissions for sources of pollutants. There is one important meteorological condition which, however, impedes dispersal; in fact, it traps air pollutants so that they may accumulate to very high levels. This situation is the inversion. The inversion has been the principal meteorological element in most air pollution disasters and alerts. Petterssen (1966) has shown that those geographic regions where conditions favor frequent development of inversions will be just the regions where the human population will congregate in 2000 A.D. (Fig. 2).

The Green Plant

If I were asked to name a weak link in the metabolism of the ecosystem most susceptible to the toxic influences of air pollutants, I would reply, "The primary producers or the green plants." These organisms are most sensitive to a variety of atmospheric contaminants deriving from man-made sources. Plants, in fact, are better sensors of air pollution than most instruments. This sensitivity has serious ecological implications, for the green plants play a number of vital roles in the metabolic flows of the ecosystem: The green plants capture solar energy and store it in forms useful to consumers. The plants participate in regulating atmospheric CO_2 and oxygen; in fact, green plants are primarily responsible for

[1] In a recent article Bryson and Baerris (1967) discuss man's role in the creation of the Rajputant Desert of northwestern India.

maintaining an oxidative environment for all living organisms. In spite of these basic ecological functions, man's onslaught on the green plants has extended beyond the impact of air pollution. In assessing the role of green plants in the fitness of the ecosystem, the impacts of the urban sprawl and the rapid expansion of networks of highways must not be overlooked. These invasions are progressively reducing the land surface covered by green plants. Although there is presently no evidence that the oxygen content of the atmosphere has begun to decline measurably, the AAAS Air Conservation Commission (1965) foresaw such a decline as a distinct possibility in the future. In view of the fact that the vast quantities of air consumed by man's technology also place appreciable demands on the capacity of green plants to maintain the atmospheric oxygen, it would not seem unreasonable to propose that oxygen be one of the gases monitored regularly by networks of air pollution sensors.

A logical reaction to these grim prospects might be to suggest that a search be made for species of useful plants less susceptible than average to air pollutants and introduce them into areas where the potential for air pollution is particularly high. Such an introduction might be an adaptive strategy. Reactions of green plants to fluoride in the environment provide a striking example of the problems and implications of this strategy. Furthermore, when fluoride phytopathology is examined in terms of this concept, a number of questions are raised for which plant physiologists cannot now provide answers.

The reactions of plants to fluoride span the range from fatal damage to adaptation. These effects may be induced by fluoride in the air environment about the leaves or by fluoride in the aqueous environment of the soil surrounding the root system. Many plants accumulate fluoride by these processes. Damage to the plant may accrue from this storage, but there is great variability in resistance of plants to fluoride intoxication. One measure of this resistance is the level to which fluoride must rise before the plant reveals that it has been injured. Gladiolus leaves, for example, often show necrosis at 10-20 ppm, whereas for the camellia 3000 ppm is innocuous.

Some plants appear to have made an adaptation to environmental fluoride via a mechanism which can reasonably be described as detoxification. The adaptation has been achieved by enzyme induction, for in these plants fluoride is present as organo-fluoride. The compound most commonly identified has been monofluoroacetate (Delrich and McEwan, 1962). This adaptation — if that is what it is — has been accomplished by a wide variety of species: *Dichapetalum cymosum* and *D. toxicorum* from Africa, *Acacia georginae* and *Gastrolobium grandiflorum* from Australia, and *Palicourea marcgravii* from South America. The adaptation may not be complete; for *Acacia georginae*, for instance, can be damaged by inorganic fluoride. This detoxification is probably an adaptation to fluoride in the soil water. It has not yet been convincingly demonstrated whether fluoride occurring as an air pollutant is capable of inducing synthesis of organo-fluorides. Because the adaptation is not species specific, a reasonable likelihood exists that such an enzyme induction can be achieved by other plants.

By storage and by incorporation in organic compounds, fluoride enters the food chain. The next organism in the hierarchy of the biomass to deal with this mineral is the herbivore or primary consumer. Both the potential for storage and the formation of organo-fluoride may have serious consequences for these primary consumers.

In areas where there is a fluoride-polluted atmosphere, alfalfa and orchard grass accumulate the element.

The fluoride content of these plants may reach 40 ppm or more. Cattle fed solely on this material often develop fluorosis as a reaction to inorganic fluoride.

When plants rich in organo-fluoride are consumed by domestic animals, most of them die (Oelrich and Mc-Ewan, 1962). Death is caused by inhibition of the enzyme aconitic hydratase by fluorocitrate. The fluoroacetate enters the Kreb's cycle as fluoroacetyl-CoA, condenses with oxaloacetate to form fluorocitrate, blocks aconitic hydratase, and brings about a rapid build-up of fluorocitrate (Fig. 3). This aberrant production of citrate has been termed the "lethal synthesis" by Sir Rudolph Peters (1952, 1957).

There is an important ecological lesson in this story of fluoride. Several species of useful plants have adapted to fluoride. When these plants are eaten by mammals, the consumers die. In the plant there has been enzymatic adaptation. In the mammal, in contrast, enzymatic blocking takes place and the resulting metabolic disturbance leads to death. Thus as one traces fluoride through the food chain of the ecosystem, one finds several plants which have adapted to fluoride in their environment by synthesizing organo-fluoride, while the great majority of plants have not so adapted. Adaptability at one level in the food chain does not assure comparable adaptability at other trophic levels in the biomass. The introduction of fluoride-resistant plants into areas where there is a high potential for air pollution may be advantageous from the viewpoint of the plant but disadvantageous from the viewpoint of the mammal. In a sense this analysis has been speculative. Airborne fluoride has not yet been shown to cause an enzyme induction permitting the detoxification of fluoride. Nevertheless, the analysis illustrates the complexity of decisions that must be taken in developing an effective adaptive strategy.

Human Health

One cannot gainsay that man's health is at risk from air pollution. The risks are acute and chronic, overt and subtle, and direct and indirect. The "air pollution episode" is one epidemiologic expression of the acute, overt, and direct effect and it provides several ecologically useful insights. We learn of the role of meteorological processes, of toxic levels of air pollutants, of predisposing pathological conditions, of differential susceptibility, and of time-course for acute morbid events. Such facts as these are each important elements in adaptive strategy, for they provide inputs into the decision process of weighing costs and benefits. However, I would argue that even though the air pollution episode is a danger flag, it is not a signal on which to focus all attention. The risks to human health most difficult to evaluate are the subtle ones accruing from chronic exposure to low levels of air pollutants and the ones that develop indirectly through deterioration in the fitness of the ecosystem. The rising curves of morbidity and mortality from chronic respiratory disease (e.g., bronchitis, emphysema, and pulmonary cancer) are most likely indices of the subtle actions of air pollutants. We have already seen in weather modification and the action of air pollutants on plants some aspects of the problems arising from a deteriorating biosphere. The subtle, chronic, and indirect processes demand a prospective outlook. Vis-à-vis this viewpoint, Dubos (1963) writes of prospective epidemiology and Goldsmith (1967), of environmental epidemiology.

The critical datum for prospective epidemiology is a baseline against which to judge the effects on man that his alterations of the environment have produced. One baseline is human health; another is the environmental configuration that sustains the healthy state. Health is an elusive quality that is extremely difficult to define primarily because one's concept of it is closely interwoven with cultural traditions and perceptions. (Sargent, 1966).

A concept of health that is most useful for adaptive strategy is one stated by Dubos (1965, p. 10). He views health as "a process of continuous adaptation to the myriad microbes, irritants, pressures and problems which daily challenge man." According to this view, health exhibits ontogeny, i.e., it matures, reaches a maximum, and declines during the life sequence of the individual. Furthermore, this view of health subsumes adaptive plasticity or the capacity of the individual to adjust to changing environmental circumstances. Certainly there is ample evidence to support the ontogenic characteristic of health. The problematic characteristic is adaptive plasticity. This plasticity is largely past-oriented. We know that man can adapt to experiences through which he has come during his evolution. We are uncertain whether he will be able to adapt to the environmental changes that he is producing. Our uncertainty stems primarily from the fact that the rate of environmental change has been so rapidly accelerated. In the long course of time, genetic variability, which is so great in man, may assure survival through the action of selection pressures. But since the environment is being altered so rapidly, the process that most concerns us is the adaptability of men now peopling the earth.

Several ways are open to obtain information on these matters. One approach would be to study populations representing different genetic backgrounds living in contrasting habitats and cultural circumstances. A second approach would be to identify in a population the range of adaptability to diverse environmental circumstances. A third approach would be to investigate populations migrating between contrasting habitat and cultural circumstances. Each approach should be longitudinal, for adaptability can only be judged realistically by continuing observation. Each requires detailed and intensive study of the members of the selected populations. To fulfill the objectives of these studies, detailed measurements of the sort performed by clinical investigators must be carried out on representative populations. In a sense, this is human experimentation. It can be argued that since man is already at risk, but at risk of unknown magnitude, such measurements are justified, indeed imperative.[2] Investigations of the nature here outlined are envisioned for the International Biological Programme of the International Council of Scientific Unions.

The concept of health cannot be separated from a concept of environment. Insofar as environment is concerned, we are interested in environmental configurations which will permit adaptability to function effectively. In the context of this discussion, the particular environmental configuration that is the focus of our attention is "air quality." Here the baseline might simply be atmospheric air polluted no more than might be expected by natural processes—dust storms; sea spray; pollen from grasses, flowers, and trees; and volcanoes. From the viewpoint of human health, how much of a departure from such a natural atmosphere can be accommodated by man's adaptive plasticity? The answer to this question is given in the decision man makes about "air quality standards." If the "air quality standards" are set so that some man-made pollution is permitted, there is a risk that a deterioration of health will accrue. Since very little is known about human adaptability for air pollution, the mag-

[2] I have argued this matter more fully in another context (Sargent, 1967b). In addition, there is an extended discussion of the legal and ethical problems of investigating human responses and adaptability to air pollutants in a symposium published in the *Archives of Environmental Health* (Webster, 1963).

nitude of the risk cannot now be assessed. Indeed, the only information available on this point is the report of Killick (1948) that short-term acclimatization to carbon monoxide could be induced in a small group of male volunteers. Consequently, since enforcement of air quality standards will entail great cost, it is imperative that the risks be established so that the standards can be realistic. In other words, in our strategic thinking we must weigh the risk of man's adapting to a polluted atmosphere against the cost of regulating the atmosphere so that it fulfills man's needs and requirements. Certainly, man's capacity "to adapt to a wide range of circumstances deserves more explicit recognition in our environmental planning as an alternative to a policy of effecting adjustments of the environment aimed toward some assumed set of maximally satisfying conditions" (Kates & Wohlwill, 1966, p. 17).

A further important consideration in evaluating human risk is the question, "Risk to Whom?" Goldsmith (1961) and I (Sargent, 1966, 1967a) have argued that the risk should be evaluated in terms of the most sensitive, the least adaptable segment of the human population. The criteria by which this segment can be identified have not yet been established; and it is for this reason that studies of the range of adaptability to diverse environmental circumstances must be undertaken.[3]

We have now shown that there are at least two potential weak links in the ecosystem: the green plant and the human being. Both show some evidence of adaptability to air pollution, but the adaptability of the plant may disrupt the metabolic flow of the ecosystem. This has serious implications,

---

[3] Although it is a tangential consideration to the thesis of this discussion, the matter of civil action for air pollution is nevertheless a most important application of air quality standards to individuals allegedly suffering from illness or disability caused by air pollution. Rheingold (1966) has examined this legal arena in considerable depth and his paper should be consulted for precedences and their implications.

for the plant is the primary producer of nutrient energy for the hierarchy of dependent consumers including man. Thus from the viewpoint of an adaptive strategy, air quality standards must take into account the impact of air pollution on the weakest link in the metabolic flows of the ecosystem. Whereas human health might be directly affected by air pollution, it might be more profoundly jeopardized by a deterioration of the fitness of the ecosystem.

Behavioral Codes in the Adaptive Strategy

The essence of what I have said up to this point is that man must now make a number of complex decisions for managing the ecosystem. The decisions must be made so that industry can have "a basis for planning and action" (Daddario, 1966), so that the fitness of the ecosystem will be preserved, indeed so that the survival of the human species will be assured. These decisions must become behavioral codes. The success of these codes will depend upon two factors: first, man's perception of himself and, second, the quality of the information transmitted to the politician so that informed decisions can be made.

Nature of Behavioral Codes

Human evolution has depended in large part on the control of behavior through codes, traditions, and institutions. In fact, this control is so unique to man that one cannot separate culture from his biology. Geetz (1965, p. 112-113) remarks, ". . . there is no such thing as a human nature independent of culture. . . . We are, in sum, incomplete or unfinished animals who complete or finish ourselves through culture — and not through culture in general but through highly particular forms of it. . . ." If for no other reason than that he evolved that way, man is an animal "desperately dependent upon cultural programs for ordering his behavior" (Geetz, 1965, p. 107). Geetz views these cultural programs as "a set of control mechanisms — plans, recipes, rules, instructions (what computer engineers call 'programs') — for governing human behavior."

Man's Perception of Himself

One problem for an adaptive strategy is man's perception of himself. Man is now educated and trained to have a very parochial view of himself (Chisholm, 1963). His loyalties are primarily to small groups such as family, club, church, school. They can enlarge to state and nation. But now those loyalties must become international and focus on all mankind. Environmental pollution is a problem that confronts all men and all men must be participants in its solution. The realization of this fact is threatening. It requires concern for people beyond one's immediate kin, indeed for people not even born. It symbolizes legal regulation, loss of individual liberty, and invasion of privacy. As Kates (1966) has emphasized, these are serious matters. They are as important, but inadequately studied, aspects of human adaptability as are the physiological regulations that make for biological adaptation. One urgent aspect of strategic planning thus will be to enlarge man's perspective of his place in, and relation to, the ecosystem in order to assure its continued fitness.

Informed Political Decisions

Another serious problem for adaptive strategy is informed political decisions on complex ecological matters. All too often, political decisions are based on inadequate or incomplete information (Sargent, 1966). It is equally the responsibility of the scientist to speak out on these matters and the responsibility of the politician to seek out appropriate and adequate information (Brain, 1965). I regret to say that ecologists have been negligent

in this important regard, for the Daddario Subcommittee (1966, p. 6) has this to say about them: "Ecology, as an organized profession, is not in good condition to become an umbrella for increased research. As a scientific discipline, it is the logical focal point. As a point of view, it is already effective in coordinating other sciences and this may be the most important function in the long run."

Summary

We have pursued a complex path along which we have glimpsed some vistas where investigations might lead to a sharper definition of an adaptive strategy. We have learned that this strategy will involve full participation by government, industry, science, and the public. We have seen that, as the Daddario Subcommittee (1966, p. 32) noted, "Pollution abatement is affected by so many factors that no one existing institution can have control over all of them." I would agree with the view of this Subcommittee (Daddario, 1966, p. 32) that "A consortium of public and private interests will be necessary to accomplish what — in very real terms — may be a marked change in the American way of life."

Acknowledgment

The author gratefully notes the constructive criticisms and valuable suggestions received from Drs. John E. Goldsmith and Leonard H. Weinstein.

References

Air Conservation Commission. 1965. *Air Conservation*. Publ. No. 80, American Association for the Advancement of Science, Washington, D.C.

Brain, W. R. 1965. Science and anti-science. *Science,* **148**: 192-198.

Brooks, C. E. P. 1926. *Climate Through the Ages*. R. V. Coleman, New York.

Bryson, R. A., and D. A. Baerris. 1967. Possibilities of major climatic modification and their implications: northwest India, a case for study. *Bull. Am. Meteorol. Soc.,* **48**: 136-142.

Chisholm, B. 1963. The future of the mind. In *Man and His Future* (G. Wolstenholme, ed.). Little, Brown & Co., Boston, Mass., pp. 315-321.

Committee on Atmospheric Sciences. 1966. *Weather and Climate Modification. Problems and Prospects.* Publ. No. 1350. National Academy of Sciences–National Research Council, Washington, D.C., pp. 83-108.

Daddario, E. Q. (Chm.). 1966. *Environmental Pollution: A Challenge to Science and Technology.* Report of Subcommittee on Science, Research, and Development to Committee on Science and Astronautics. U.S. House of Representatives. Washington, D.C.

Dubos, R. 1963. Man meets his environment. In *Health and Nutrition.* Vol. VI. *Science, Technology and Development.* U.S. Government Printing Office, Washington, D.C., pp. 1-11.

Dubos, R., M. Pines, and Editors of Life. 1965. *Health and Disease.* Life Science Library, Chicago, Ill.

Eiseley, L. 1962. *The Firmament of Time.* Atheneum, New York.

Geertz, C. 1965. The impact of the concept of culture on the concept of man. In *New Views of the Nature of Man.* (J. R. Platt, ed.). University of Chicago Press, Chicago, Ill., pp. 93-118.

Goldsmith, J. R. 1961. Urban air conservation. *Bull. At. Sci.,* 17: 376-379.

Goldsmith, J. R. 1965. Environmental epidemiology and the metamorphosis of the human habitat. *Am. J. Public Health,* in Press.

Hickman, K. 1966. Oases for the future. *Science.* 154: 612-617.

Kates, R. W. 1966. Stimulus and symbol: The view from the bridge. *J. Social Issues,* 22 (4): 21-28.

Kates, R. W., and J. F. Wohlwill (eds.). 1966. Man's Response to the Physical Environment. *J. Social Issues,* 22 (4): 1-140.

Killick, E. M. 1948. Nature of the acclimatization occurring during repeated exposure of the human subject to atmospheres containing low concentrations of carbon monoxide. *J. Physiol.,* 107: 27-44.

McCormick, R. A., and J. H. Ludwig. 1967. Climate Modifications by Atmospheric Aerosols. *Science,* 156: 1358-59.

Middleton, J. R. 1966. Control of environment — economic and technological. In *Environmental Control.* The Graduate College, USDA, Washington, D.C., pp. 53-71.

Mitchell, J. M., Jr. 1961. Recent secular changes of global temperature. In *Solar Variations, Climatic Change and Related Geophysical Problems* (R. W. Faribridge, ed.). *Ann. N. Y. Acad. Sci.,* 95 (1): 235-250.

Mitchell, J. M., Jr. 1963. On the world-wide pattern of secular temperature change. In *Changes of Climate. Arid Zone Research.* (UNESCO), 20: 161-181.

Oelrichs, P. B., and T. McEwan. 1962. The toxic principle of *Acacia georginae. Queensland J. Agr. Sci.,* 19: 1-17.

Peters, R. A. 1952. Lethal synthesis. *Proc. Roy. Soc. London, Ser. B,* 139: 143-170.

Peters, R. A. 1957. Mechanism of the toxicity of the active constituent of *Dichapetalum cymosum* and related compounds. *Adv. Enzymol.,* 18: 113-159.

Petterssen, S. 1966. Recent demographic trends and future meteorological services. *Bull. Am. Meteorol. Soc.,* 47: 950-963.

Rheingold, P. O. 1966. Civil cause of action for lung damage due to pollution of the urban atmosphere. *Brooklyn Law Rev.* (Fall), pp. 17-33.

Sargent, F., II. 1966. Ecological implications of individuality in the context of the concept of adaptive strategy. *Intern. J. Bioclimatol. Biometeorol.,* 10: 305-322.

Sargent, F., II. 1967a. Air pollution: a problem for human ecology. *Arch. Environ. Health,* 14: 35-40.

Sargent, F., II. 1967b. A dangerous game — taming the weather. *Bull. Am. Meteorol. Soc.,* 48 (No. 7): 452-458. *Science and Citizen,* in press.

Sargent, F., II, and D. M. Barr. 1965. Health and fitness of the ecosystem. In *The Environment and Man.* Travelers Research Center, Inc., Hartford, Conn., pp. 28-46.

Schaefer, V. S. 1966. Ice nuclei from automobile exhaust and iodine vapor. *Science,* 154: 1555-1557.

Shimkin, D. B. 1966. Adaptive strategies: A basic problem in human ecology. In *Three Papers on Human Ecology.* Mills College Assembly Series 1965-66. Oakland, Calif., pp. 37-52.

Webster, R. G. (Chm.). 1963. Legal and ethical problems of human exposures. Fifth Ann. Air Pollution Medical Research Conference, California State Dept. Public Health. *Arch. Environ. Health,* 6: 771-798.

Population Pollution

Francis S. L. Williamson

I do not believe that we would still discuss this problem if we did not look hopefully ahead to the technological achievements that may curb--or at least bring to within "tolerable" limits--the tragic, massive, and still-expanding pollution of the air, soil, and water of the earth. This optimism stems from the long overdue consideration of this problem and the implementation of programs dealing with many of its aspects. Environmental pollution, however, is not a priori inexorably linked to human population growth (Daddario, 1968); and we must assume that although numbers of people will increase, the technology now available can and will provide some of the solutions necessary for our health and survival. Additionally, many of us have similar hopes for our less fortunate cohabitants of the earth--those lacking a technology or a freedom of choice. These solutions include the provision in adequate amounts of clean air to breathe, clean water to drink, and clean food to eat. Even if we make the assumption that, as human population growth continues, strict curbs can be simultaneously placed on environmental abuses, we are still confronted with the unresolved problem of population pollution. This I define as the consequences, mental and physical, of life in a world vastly more populous and technologically more complex than the one in which we currently find ourselves. In such a world the goals of healthy and happy human beings, free from malnutrition, poverty, disease, and war, seem to me convincingly elusive. The expression of man's full range of

The author is Director of the Chesapeake Bay Center for Field Biology (Smithsonian Institution, Office of Ecology), Edgewater, Md.
This is the fifth paper from the Pollution Conference, held at State University College, Oneonta, N.Y.

genetic potential is perhaps impossible.

Human Population Growth

I believe there is general agreement among *knowledgeable* men that current trends in the growth of human populations are not only unacceptable but will result in disaster. The current rate of growth, 2% per year (McElroy, 1969), will result in 150 billion people in 200 years. In terms of the time necessary to double the world's population, it represents only about 35 years. As Ehrlich (1968) points out, this "doubling time" has been reduced successively from one million years to 1000, to 200, to 80, and finally to the present 35 years. If the latter rate continues for 900 years, the earth's population will be 60 million people, or about 100 persons for each square yard of the *total* earth surface. Unfortunately, we have no evidence that indicates any lessening of this doubling rate.

Of immediate concern is the world food crisis, a subject dealt with at the Plenary Session of the 19th Annual AIBS Meeting. At that session it was indicated that no efforts are presently being made that would avert global famines by 1985 (McElroy, 1969). Ehrlich (1968) has stated that such famines will be prevalent in the 1970's. What we are prepared to consider as "widespread global famine" is questionable, but apparently it is not the 3.5 million people or more who will starve this year (Ehrlich, 1968); nor is it the general agreement that one-half of the world's people are presently either malnourished or undernourished. I agree with those who feel that we must increase food production at home and abroad in an intensive effort to avert famine, but obviously the successes of such an effort will be pitifully short-lived unless population control is achieved.

While there appears to be general agreement that the growth of human populations must be controlled, both in the long-term sense of allowing for survival and in the immediate sense of averting or alleviating famines, there is little agreement as to how this control is to be achieved.

On 7 January of this year, the Presidential Committee on Population and Family Planning proposed a $120 million increase in the federal appropriation for family planning services to make such services available to all American women who want them. At that time the President stated that no critical issue now facing the world, with the exception of peace, is more important than that of the soaring population. He further stated that world peace will probably never be possible if this latter problem goes unsolved, and he noted that the federal investment in family planning activities had risen from $6 million in fiscal 1964 to $115 million in fiscal 1969. This funding may indicate progress, but certainly not of a magnitude proportional to the enormity and urgency of this situation. A value judgment has been made as to the priority of this problem with that of landing a man on the moon, at least regarding funding and the attraction of intellectual effort.

In my opinion the focus continues to be on family planning, not on population control, and this does little more than achieve a reduction in birth rate of an inadequate nature. I find that I must agree with Kingsley Davis (1967) that "There is no reason to expect that the millions of decisions about family size made by couples in their own interest will automatically control population for the benefit of society." As Davis points out, the family planning campaigns in such "model" countries as Japan and Taiwan have hastened the downward trends in birth rates but have not provided population control. Results of the present approach can only be measured as the difference between the number of children women have been having and the number they want to have. For

example, the family planning program in Taiwan, assuming that the contraceptives used are completely effective, would be successful if it resulted in the women having the desired 4.5 children each. This represents a sharp drop from the average 6.5 children previously borne to each woman but results in a rate of natural increase for the country of close to 3%. If the social and economic change of Taiwan continues, a further drop in fertility may occur. It may even reach that of the United States, where an average of 3.4 children is currently desired. This would result in Taiwan in a 1.7% per year increase, or a doubling of the population in 41 years, and hardly suggests that our country be used as a model or yardstick for other nations.

The plan of Taylor and Berelson (1968) to provide family planning instructions with maternity care may be a logical step in population control, but I fail to see in what way this plan can alter the basic desire of women in the underdeveloped nations to have more than two children. The natural processes of modernization and education have failed to do this in those nations that are developed. With these facts in mind, it is difficult to imagine the acceptance anywhere that *any* population increase, no matter how trivial, can be tolerated and that the goal must be zero growth.

There is no easy single solution to achieving a zero or near-zero growth rate. Berelson (1969) has recently reviewed the further proposals which have been made to "solve" the population problem. He has appraised them according to scientific, political, administrative, economic, and ethical criteria as well as to their presumed effectiveness. The proposals range from the very nebulous one of augmented research effort to the stringent one of involuntary fertility control. The barriers to acceptance of these criteria, for the truly effective measures, seem insurmountable at the present time. It is my personal view that in the United States a system of tax and welfare benefits and penalties; a liberal, voluntary program of abortion and sterilization (government sponsored and financed, if necessary); attempts at the development in women of substitutes for family interests; and greatly intensified educational campaigns are in order. If the United States is to lead the way, and certainly no other nation appears economically prepared to do so, it seems reasonable that we might begin by abolishing those policies that promote population growth. However, I do not believe we will do these things until economic hardship makes them mandatory. Nonetheless, we are nearing the point of either exercising the free choice of methods of population control still available or facing the compulsory ones that otherwise will be necessary for survival.

In the long interim, however, the emphasis of our efforts can be logically focused on the improvement of the quality of the environment and of the people who are to live here. Here, at least temporarily, we can "do things" with some expectation of success.

The Shift to Urban Life

The rapidly rising number of human beings is not resulting in their general distribution over the landscape but rather in the development of enormous urban centers. In 1800, over 90% of the population of the United States, albeit only some 5-1/2 million people, lived in a rural environment. By 1900, the population of this country was nearly equally divided between cities and rural areas. In 1950, the urban population was 64%; in 1960, 70%; and it is presently about 75%. The projection for 1980 is 78% and for the year 2000 about 85% of the expected 300 million people will be urban dwellers. The number of residents in rural areas has not changed over the last 30 years, and is not expected to vary from its present approximately 53 million persons for the next 10 years. There resides in these data, however, the basic fallacy that what we term "rural" is changing also.

Gigantic urban concentrations are developing within the United States, and these have been termed megalopolises.

The three best known have been recently termed "Boswash," "Chipitts," and, for lack of an equally ominous name, "Sag." "Boswash" reaches from New England to Washington, D.C., "Chipitts," from Chicago to Cleveland and south to Pittsburgh and, "Sag," a seaside city occupying the coast of California from San Francisco to San Diego. Demographers and urban planners predict the development of hosts of such "super cities." The Task Force on Environmental Health and Related Problems reported to Secretary Gardner in 1967 that virtually no effort is being made to explore ways of preventing this startling growth. A research program must be inaugurated, they reported, aimed at determining and perfecting measures to shift the focus of future population growth away from already crowded urban areas to parts of the country that are *not now* (emphasis mine) burdened by too many people. Unless such an effort is successful, the pollution control efforts of today, and those planned for the future, could be reduced literally to zero by the sheer increase of people and their correspondingly increased demand for goods, services, and facilities. Similarly, Mayr (1963) earlier pointed out that long before man has reached the stage of "standing room only" his principal preoccupation will be with enormous social, economic, and engineering problems. The undesirable by-products of the crowded urban areas are so deleterious that there will be little opportunity left for the cultivation of man's most uniquely human attributes. This could be what is in store for "Chipitts," "Boswash," "Sag," and others.

It seems that there is not only an urgent need for population control but for planned communities and the de-emphasis of the enormous urban concentrations that compound our problems of coping with environmental pollution.

Urbanization, Pollution, and Man's Welfare

Thus far the data substantiating my remarks are more than adequate. The growth of the world's population is staggering and is attended by increasing urbanization. I still have neglected consideration of man's welfare under these circumstances. The steadily mounting volume of published and unpublished data regarding environmental pollution has focused primarily on the impact of man's activities on his environment and less on the reverse, i.e., the impact of the resultant changes on man himself. Some of these changes are quantifiable, especially those affecting physical well-being. Unfortunately, others affecting such things as mental health and what we refer to vaguely as the "quality of life" are not quantifiable although certainly they are no less real. Obviously, some of these matters cross a number of areas of interest. Consideration of them will be incorporated in the papers of other participants in this symposium.

I would like to consider first some of the quantifiable effects, prefacing my remarks by reiterating the well-known fact that many environmental hazards are so subtle as to be beyond an individual's perception and control. It is less well known that there are frequently some deleterious effects stemming from the most cleverly contrived technological efforts to improve man's general well-being. If we look briefly at selected data from the United States, there is evidence linking air pollution with major respiratory diseases (Task Force on Environmental Health and Related Problems, 1967). Deaths from bronchiogenic carcinoma range from 15 per 100,000 population in rural areas to 30 or more in urban centers with over one million population. Deaths due to emphysema have risen from 1.5 per 100,000 population in 1950 to about 15 in 1964. The correlation of bigger cities with more air pollution with more related deaths seems well-substantiated. Almost half of the people in the United States, 95 million, drink water that is below present federal standards or of unknown quality. Such diseases as infectious hepatitis appear to be directly related to contaminated drinking water, but very little is known about how the agent of hepatitis gets into the water or how it

can be removed (The Task Force on Environmental Health and Related Problems, 1967). The concentration of lead is increasing in the air, water, and food, and the blood levels are sufficiently high in many cases to be associated with subacute toxic effects (Dubos, 1965). The accumulation and effects of nonbiodegradable biocides present another serious problem. Documentation is growing that a number of other diseases are associated with environmental pollution, frequently those associated with urbanization.

As alluded to earlier, our best efforts to reduce environmental hazards often have proceeded without adequate knowledge. The development of efficient braking systems for motor vehicles has led to increased exposure of the public to asbestos particles produced by the gradual wearing of brake linings. There is a scientific basis for concern that these particles may promote bronchiogenic carcinoma (Task Force on Environmental Health and Related Problems, 1967). Subsequent to the inoculation of millions of people with a vaccine to prevent poliomyelitis was the discovery that some of the stocks of vaccine, perhaps as many as 25-35%, contained Simian Virus 40 (Sweet and Hilleman, 1960), previously unknown to be resident in the rhesus monkey cells used to culture the virus of poliomyelitis and thus to manufacture the vaccine. The high prevalence of the virus in the cell cultures was compounded by pooling cells from several monkeys. Simian Virus 40 was subsequently shown to be tumorogenic when injected into young hamsters (Eddy, 1962), to possess the capacity of transforming human renal cell lines in vitro (Shein and Enders, 1962), and to result in the production of neutralizing antibodies in 5.3% of cancer patients living in the known limits of distribution of the rhesus monkey (Shah, 1969). Its carcinogenicity in man remains unknown. Poliomyelitis itself is a disease whose spread is enhanced by close human association. Numerous facts support the view that the disease is an enteric infection spread primarily by contaminated excreta (Bodian and Horstmann, 1965).

Without belaboring the matter of pollution and physical well-being excessively, I would like to add that the Food and Drug Administration has estimated that the American people are being exposed to some 500,000 different alien substances, many of them over very long periods of time. Fewer than 10% of these have been analyzed in a manner that might provide the basis for determining their effects, and it has been emphasized that we simply cannot assess potential hazards. The Simian Virus 40 example seems to substantiate this opinion. Nonetheless, severe physical manifestations can ultimately result from repeated exposure to small concentrations of environmental pollutants. These pollutants can have cumulative delayed effects such as cancers, emphysema, and reduced life span (Task Force on Environmental Health and Related Problems, 1967). A three-session symposium of the recent meeting of the American Association for the Advancement of Science was devoted to discussions of such unanticipated environmental hazards, including interactions between contaminants and drugs, food and drugs, and among different drugs.

Earlier I stated my view that environmental pollution and population growth are not inexorably linked. Assuming that our technology renders the environmental scene once again "pristine" in the sense of allowing for sufficient ecosystem function, perhaps even to the point of eliminating the potential health hazards just mentioned, what are the consequences to man's mental well-being of continued population growth and social contacts? If, for instance, we eliminate the dangerous substances in automobile exhausts and asbestos brake linings, how will we be affected by the increase in vehicles from the present 90 million to the 244 million expected to be present in 30 years? We have no data which allow us to establish levels of tolerance for congestion, noise, odor (perhaps removable), general stress, and accident threats, including those from traffic. Excessive exposure to high noise levels can impair hearing or cause total deafness, but the effects of daily noise and

disruptions of all kinds, in terms of average human tolerance, is largely unknown (Task Force on Environmental Health and Related Problems, 1967). René Dubos states that: "You can go to any one of the thoughtful architects or urban planners . . . none of them knows what it does to the child to have a certain kind of environment, as against other kinds of environments. The whole process of mental development, as affected by physical development of cities, has never been investigated."

I believe it is germane to this discussion to go back to the pioneer work of Faris and Dunham (1939) on mental disorders in urban areas. A brief summary of the data supplied in that study indicates how the incidence of major psychoses are related to the organization of a city. Mental disorders show a decrease from the center to the periphery of the city—a pattern of distribution shown for other kinds of social and economic phenomena such as poverty, unemployment, juvenile delinquency, crime, suicide, family desertion, infant mortality, and communicable disease. Positive correlations are difficult to draw from these data, but they are certainly suggestive and tempting. Each of the chief types of mental disorders has a characteristic distribution with reference to the differentiated areas found within the large, modern city. There is a high degree of association between different types of psychoses as distributed in different urban areas and certain community conditions. It is pointed out that social conditions, while not primary in causation, may be underlying, predisposing, and precipitating factors. Situations involving stress and strain of adjustment may, in the cases of persons constitutionally predisposed, cause mental conflict and breakdown. If social conditions are actually precipitating factors in causing mental illness, then control of conditions making for stress in society will become a chief objective of a preventive program. The study of Faris and Dunham was the first to indicate a relationship between community organization and mental health and to show that urban areas characterized by high rates of social disorganization are also those with high rates of mental disorganization. Finally, it appears that the effect of movement is important to the social and mental adjustment of the person, and precipitating factors in mental breakdown may be found in the difficulties of adjustment to a new situation. Similarly, Dubos (1968) points out that the amount of physical and mental disease during the first phase of the Industrial Revolution had several different causes, one of the most important being the fact that large numbers of people from nonurban areas migrated within a few decades to urban centers. These persons had to make the necessary physiological and emotional adaptations to the new environment.

Our public concern for health, including mental health, has been mainly with frank, overt disease. Since World War II, there has been an increasing understanding of tensions and social stresses, enabling workers in mental health to increase their viewpoints and to include these largely psychologically determined disturbances within their area of interest. The solution of such problems requires the skills of many professions and governmental action nationally and internationally (Soddy and Ahrenfeldt, 1965).

Selection in a Changing World

The concentration of urban life is evidenced by the fact that approximately 70% of our population is crowding into urban areas which represent 10% of the land in the United States. There are presently about 140 million people living on 35 thousand square miles. The evidence reviewed thus far can be reasonably assumed to form the basis for predicting that there will be little or no change in the trend of increasing urbanization. This sequence imposes on man the necessity of ultimately adapting to an environment almost wholly alien to any present today. While our current cities may be no more densely populated than some urban centers have been for centuries, they are infinitely larger and rapidly threaten the existence of all open space. Voluntary population control seems quite unlikely. As long as space and food exist anywhere, it seems reasonable to assume that urbanization will continue until mankind is spread densely over the face of the earth. The luxury of open space appears already threatened and the concept of "getting away from it all" a vanishing one. By 1980, to keep up with today's·ratios of people to public space, we will need 49 million acres of national parks, monuments, and recreation areas instead of our present 25 million, and we will require 57 million acres of national forests and 28 million acres of state parks (Task Force on Environmental Health and Related Problems, 1967). It is difficult to speculate what such needs will be in the year 2000, or if at that time it will even be legitimate to consider them as needs.

Dubos (1968) has pointed out that the effects of crowding, safe limits so to speak, cannot be estimated simply from the levels of population density. The populations of Hong Kong and Holland, for example, are among the most crowded on earth, and yet the inhabitants enjoy good physical and mental health. Centuries of crowding have resulted in patterns of human relationships minimizing social conflicts.

The cultural evolution of man from the Neolithic to modern times has taken place without visible biological evolution (Stebbins, 1952). Mayr (1963) points out that Cro-Magnon man differed physically from modern man no more than do the present members of various races one from the other. Crow (1966) views human evolutionary changes as being of such long-term nature as to be considerably less urgent than the problems of increasing population and its relation to natural resources and the quality of life.

Nonetheless, natural selection is important for modern man because it will result in populations of those human beings for whom survival is possible in a uniformly and densely populated world. It is difficult to imagine that time will allow for any considerable shift in man's present

206

genetic makeup, but rather that within the confines of that limitation he must demonstrate the adaptability necessary for continued existence. Such adaptability will necessarily need to be sufficiently flexible to allow for the disappearance of what we now consider basic freedoms and for the increasing regimentation that seems a certain concomitant of future life on earth.

Summary

I would like to summarize by saying that I am optimistic that modern technology can exercise some considerable control over environmental pollution, and that the current ecological crisis in the world makes it seem certain that some progress, perhaps a goodly amount, will be made. I believe that there is less possibility that current trends in the growth of human populations can be changed for a long period of time. Alterations in these trends require changes in the social and cultural fabric of man and society that are linear in nature, while the growth of population numbers is exponential. Family planning is a start, but it must be followed promptly by other programs much more decisive in character. The United States should take the immediate initiative by abolishing all policies promoting population growth and should use its vast economic and intellectual resources to aid in suitable programs elsewhere. Following our earlier and continuing largess in supplying food and medical services abroad, such accompanying programs of aid in population control would seem to constitute a moral responsibility of considerable magnitude.

In the United States efforts must be made to de-emphasize the trend toward huge urban concentrations, to strive for better planned communities, and thus to alleviate simultaneously the problems of pollution and create greater environmental diversification. Predictive technology must be radically increased, and the liberation of substances into the environment curtailed to allow for *at least* a preliminary assessment of effects.

We are presently unable to adequately evaluate those factors influencing mental hygiene in populations and thus to know what the effects of crowding will be on future generations. However, I think it highly unlikely that those people will either think or react as most of us do today. The prospects for continued life as we presently know it seem to me rather remote. Haldane remarked that the society which enjoys the greatest amount of liberty is the one in which the greatest number of human genotypes can express their peculiar abilities. I am apprehensive as to what these genotypes might be, and in what kind of society they will appear, because the complex environment in which man evolved as the most complex biological species is rapidly disappearing. We must realistically face up to the fact that our biological inheritance, in its currently recognizable form, is not going to persist. I agree that to live is to experience, and that to live well we must maintain ecological diversity, a full range of environmental options so to speak, to insure that a wide range of possibilities exist among men (Ripley, 1968). Nonetheless, a full range of environmental options is different things to different people, and survival in a world restricted in options, of a sort alien to me, brazenly confronts mankind.

References

Berelson, Bernard. 1969. Beyond family planning. *Science,* 163: 533-543.

Bodian, David, and Dorothy M. Horstmann. 1965. Polioviruses. In: *Viral and Rickettsial Infections of Man,* 4th ed., Frank L. Horsfall, Jr., and Igor Tamm (eds.). J. B. Lippincott Co., Philadelphia.

Crow, James F. 1966. The quality of people: Human evolutionary changes. *BioScience,* 16: 863-867.

Daddario, Emilio Q. 1968. A silver lining in the cloud of pollution. *Med. Opinion and Rev.,* 4: 19-25.

Davis, Kingsley. 1967. Population policy: Will current programs succeed? *Science,* 158: 730-739.

Dubos, René. 1965. *Man Adapting.* Yale University Press, New Haven.

————— 1968. The human environment in technological societies. *Rockefeller Univ. Rev.,* July-August.

Eddy, B. E. 1962. Tumors produced in hamsters by SV40. *Fed. Proc.,* **21:** 930-935.

Ehrlich, Paul R. 1968. *The Population Bomb.* Ballantine Books, Inc., New York.

Faris, Robert E. L., and H. Warren Dunham. 1939. *Mental Disorders in Urban Areas.* University of Chicago Press, Chicago.

Mayr, Ernst. 1963. *Animal Species and Evolution.* Harvard University Press, Cambridge.

McElroy, William D. 1969. Biomedical aspects of population control. *BioScience,* **19:** 19-23.

Ripley, S. D. 1968. Statement in Joint House-Senate Colloquium to Discuss a National Policy for the Environment. Hearing before the Committee on Interior and Insular Affairs, United States Senate and the Committee on Science and Astronautics, U.S. House of Representatives, 90th Congress, 2nd Session, 17 July 1968, No. 8, p. 209-215.

Shah, Keerti V. 1969. Investigation of human malignant tumors in India for Simian Virus 40 etiology. *J. Nat. Cancer Inst.,* **42:** 139-145.

Shein, H. M., and J. F. Enders. 1962. Transformation induced by Simian Virus 40 in human renal cell cultures. I. Morphology and growth characteristics. *Proc. Nat. Acad. Sci.,* **48:** 1164-1172.

Soddy, Kenneth, and Robert H. Ahrenfeldt (eds.). 1965. *Mental Health in a Changing World.* Vol. 1 of a report of an international and interprofessional study group convened by the World Federation for Mental Health. J. B. Lippincott Co., Philadelphia.

Stebbins, George L., Jr. 1952. Organic evolution and social evolution. *Idea Exp.,* **11:** 3-7.

Sweet, B. H., and M. R. Hilleman. 1960. The vacuolating virus, SV40. *Proc. Soc. Exp. Biol. Med.,* **105:** 420-427.

Taylor, Howard C., Jr., and Bernard Berelson. 1968. Maternity care and family planning as a world problem. *Amer. J. Obstet. Gynecol.,* **100:** 885.

The Task Force on Environmental Health and Related Problems. A Report to the Secretary of Health, Education, and Welfare. 1967. U.S. Govt. Printing Office, Wash., D.C.

The Population Crisis
Is Here *Now*

Walter E. Howard

Preface

At the present world rate of population growth of 2% per year, a mere dozen people a thousand years ago could have produced the present world population, and in another thousand years each one of us could have 300 million living descendants. Obviously, that cannot be—something must be done. Either the birth rate must be significantly curtailed or the death rate drastically increased.

The world's overpopulation crisis is of a magnitude beyond human comprehension, yet the government and the public remain seemingly indifferent. Better awareness and a more forthright leadership are obviously needed, from biologists and politicians alike. Will you help? A vastly increased rate of involuntary premature deaths can be prevented only by an informed public, here and abroad, following dynamic leadership. No population can continue to increase indefinitely, no matter how much food there is. If civilization is to be viable, we must end the arrogant assumption that there are unlimited resources and infinite air and water. People must develop much greater voluntary restraint in reproduction—or conception itself will have to come under government control.

This earth does not have the resources necessary to provide even the present world population with the degree of affluence that the middle-class citizen enjoys. Even though the average birth rate

in the United States has declined during the past decade from about seven children per family to fewer than three, the population density has been growing much more rapidly than before. The reason is the high population base level; there are now so many more women that their "small" families add a greater number of new people to the population each year than did their grandmothers, even with much larger families.

No population can continue to grow beyond certain limits; eventually, involuntary self-limitation—in the form of premature deaths from starvation, pestilence, and wars—will prevent any further increase in density. Since all finite space is limited, it is an indisputable fact that birth rates and death rates must someday be balanced. Already the rich are devouring the poor—the survival of the fittest.

Introduction

The intent of this article is not to alarm the reader unnecessarily. But how is that possible? Alarm is called for; man should be alarmed. Man must be aware of his dilemma, for if he attempts to feed the world without effective control of the birth rate, he actually is only deferring the starvation of an even greater number of people to a later date.

The world is facing this acute overpopulation situation specifically because of advances in agriculture and health, through science and technology, and a lack of similar progress in the field of sensible birth control. Families are not having more babies, it is just that more

The author is a professor of wildlife biology in the Department of Animal Physiology and a vertebrate ecologist in the Experiment- Station, University of California, Davis.

Bioscience, September, 1969, Vol.19, No.9, pp. 779- 784.

now survive.

Passion between the sexes must, of course, remain a basic human right, but it cannot include the having of children at will. While intercourse remains an individual and private matter, procreation must become of public concern. Conception should not be a euphemism for sexual relations. The obvious goal for all societies wishing an abundant life and freedom from want should be a low-birth-rate, low-death-rate culture. Man's responsibility to the next generation includes a primary duty of limiting the size of that generation.

Our problem is uncontrolled human fertility—not underproduction and mal-distribution—and corrective action is being dangerously delayed by wishful thinking that some miracle will solve the problem. There is a prodigious need for immediate public awareness of the current critical situation, since overpopulation is intimately involved with political, economic, and sociological problems—in fact, with everyone's peace, security, and general well-being. All of the world's desperate needs—ample food, permanent peace, good health, and high-quality living—are unattainable for all human beings both now and in the foreseeable future for one obvious reason: there are too many people. A soaring population means a shrinking of man's space on this earth.

Not only is population growth the most basic conservation problem of today, but its dominating influence will affect the ultimate survival of mankind. Man can no longer be indifferent to this basic population problem. Its severity behooves all to act now. Hunger and overpopulation will not go away if we do not discuss them, and the bringing of too many babies into this world is not just someone else's problem; it is everyone's concern. The destiny of overpopulation is erosion of civilized life.

The World's Population

To appreciate the recent rapidity with which the world's population has grown—it took from the beginning of man until 1850 to reach a population of one billion people, only 80 years more (1930) to reach two billion, then only 30 years (1960) to reach the three billion mark, and in less than 15 years after 1960 we expect four billion. In the next 25 years after that, the population is expected to increase by another three and one-half billion people. If there have been about 77 billion births since the Stone Age, then about 1 out of every 22 persons born since then is alive today; but in only 30 or 40 years from now, if current rates of increase continue, 1 out of every 10 people ever born will be living at that time. The youth of today might see the United States with a population equal to what India has now.

Only a small proportion of the world's population has made the demographic transition of attaining both a lower fertility and a lower mortality; most have decreased only the premature death rate. The population has continued to increase rapidly because reductions in fertility have not been sufficient to offset the effects of current reductions in mortality produced by technological sanitation, disease control, and pesticide use.

The reproductive potential of the world is grim, for 40 to 45% of the people alive today are under 15 years old. How can this tremendous number of babies soon be fed solid foods? And look how soon those who survive will be breeding.

Even though technology exists that could manufacture enough intrauterine devices for every woman, the problems of distribution and the shortage of doctors make it impossible for the devices to be inserted fast enough to control the world's population growth. Within a few years the number of people dying each year from causes related to poor nutrition will equal what is now the entire population of the United States.

In the United States if the fertility and mortality trends of 1950-60 should be reestablished, replacing the 1968 low birth rate, in only 150 years our country alone could exceed the current world population of over 3.3 billion, and in 650 years there would be about one person per square foot. This will not happen, of course, because either the birth rate will decline, or more likely, the death rate will increase.

Rate of Population Increase

The basic factor is the difference between birth and death rates, not what the levels of births and deaths happen to be. Continued doubling of a population soon leads to astronomical numbers. If the world population increase continued at the low rate of only 2%, the weight of human bodies would equal the weight of the earth in about 1500 years.

The world population is reported to be currently growing by 180,000 a day, more than a million a week, or about 65 million a year, and each year it increases in greater amounts. If current trends continue, the population will reach about 25 billion in only 100 years.

Prior to Christ, it took about 40,000 years to double the population, but the current growth rate of about 2% would require only 35 years to double the present population. Populations that grow by 3% per year double within a generation and increase eighteen-fold in 100 years.

Population Dynamics

If 90% of a population survives long enough to reproduce, an average of 2.3 children per family will keep the population stable. Only a very slight increase to 2.5 children would produce an increase of 10% per generation, and 3.0 children per family would cause an increase of 31% per generation. If child-bearing families averaged 3.0 children, about one woman in four would need to be childless for the population to remain stable.

A sustained geometric increase in human beings is, of course, impossible; once the population's base level of density is high, as it now is, birth rates cannot continue much above the death rates for long without a truly impossible density being produced. As the base population density rises, even a lower birth rate can still mean that there will be a greater absolute increase in total numbers than was occurring before, when population was less and birth rates were higher.

Obviously, if input (natality) continues to exceed outgo (mortality), any finite space must eventually fill up and overflow. Populations increase geometrically, whereas food and subsistence increase arithmetically. The geometric ratio of population growth is also known as the ever-accelerating growth rate, the logistic curve, the well-known S-shaped or sigmoid growth curve, and compound interest.

When populations of people are exposed to stressing pressures, including those due to overpopulation, they may respond in a strange way of breeding earlier and more prolifically, further aggravating the situation. The principal way in which man differs from other animals is in his intellect, his ability to read and communicate, to learn, to use tools, and his society; and he also differs from other species in that he attempts to protect the unfit and all "surplus" births.

Predisposition to Overpopulate

Nature has seen to it that all organisms are obsessed with a breeding urge and provided with the biological capacity to overproduce, thereby ensuring survival of the species. Since man now exercises considerable control over so many of the natural factors which once controlled his population, he must also learn to control his innate trait to reproduce excessively.

It is not a question of whether this earth has the resources for feeding a much greater population than is now present—of course, it has. The point is that the human population is now growing too fast for food production ever to catch up without stringent birth control.

Carrying Capacity and Self-Limitation

No matter how far science and technology raise the carrying capacity of the earth for people, involuntary self-limiting forces will continue to determine man's upper population density. Surplus populations do not just quietly fade away—quite the contrary. Before surplus individuals die, they consume resources and contribute in general to other population stresses, all of which make the environment less suitable, thus lowering its carrying capacity. Man needs space to live as much as do plants and animals.

The balance of nature is governed primarily by the suitability of the habitat and species-specific self-limitation, where members of each species involuntarily prevent any further increase in their kind. This self-limitation consists of undesirable stresses which cause individual births in a family to be unwanted or cause a compensating increase in death rates. Members of the population become their own worst enemy in the sense that they are responsible for the increased rates of mortality and, perhaps, also some reduction in natality.

Nearly all organisms that are well-adapted to their environment have built-in mechanisms for checking population growth before the necessary food and cover are permanently destroyed. But nature's population control processes are unemotional, impartial, and truly ruthless, a set of conditions that educated men will surely wish to avoid.

Instead of man learning how to conquer nature, he may annihilate it, destroying himself in the process. In current times at least, there is no hope that man as a species will voluntarily limit his birth rate to the low level (zero or even minus replacement) that the overall population must have. Also, unfortunately, when a population level is below carrying capacity the innate desire to have larger families then becomes very strong, making human husbandry difficult to practice.

Nature does not practice good husbandry—all its components are predisposed to overpopulate and, in fact, attempt to do so, thus causing a high rate of premature deaths. If food supply alone were the principal factor limiting the number of people, man would long ago have increased to a density where all of the food would have been consumed and he would have become an extinct species.

When other organisms follow a population growth curve similar to what man is currently experiencing—and they do this only in disturbed (usually man-modified) environments—they can then become so destructive to their habitat that the subsequent carrying capacity may be dramatically reduced if not completely destroyed, thus causing not only mass individual suffering and a high rate of premature deaths but also a permanent destruction of the ecosystem.

Whenever man's population density has been markedly reduced through some catastrophe, or his technology has appreciably increased the carrying capacity of his habitat (environment), the growth rate of his population increases. The population then tends to overcompensate, temporarily growing beyond the upper limits of the carrying capacity of the environment. The excess growth is eventually checked, however, by the interaction of a number of different kinds of self-limiting population stress factors. These include such forces as inadequate food and shelter, social stress factors, competition for space, wars, an increase in pestilence, or any of many other subtle vicissitudes of life that either increase the death rate, reduce successful births, or cause individuals to move elsewhere. Unfortunately, in the developed countries, science and technology are developing at an exponential rate, so the population growth may not again be sufficiently halted by self-limitation until the earth's resources are largely exploited or a world famine or other drastic mortality factor appears.

Although nature practices survival of the fittest, man believes that all who are born should be given every opportunity to live to an old age. If this is to be our objective, and I am sure it will, then we have only one other alternative, i.e., to restrict the number of births. And to accomplish this, it seems better to reduce conception rather than to rely on abortions. Abortions are a solution, however, when other means of preventing conceptions have broken down. Surprising to most people, abortions induced by a doctor are safer than childbearing.

There is a need too for man to establish a stable relationship with the environment. Man must recognize that he also responds to many, in fact, most of the laws of nature. And his population checks are largely famine, pestilence, and war. Man has transferred himself from being just a member of the ecosystem to a dominant position, where he now mistakenly assumes that the ecosystem is his to control at will. He forgets that he is part of nature. To see his true place in the world he must not attempt to transcend too much over nature, but to discover and assimilate all he can about the truth of nature and his own role in nature.

Only self-limitation can stem the population tide, and the only voice man has in the matter is whether it will be done involuntarily by nature's undesirable stresses, as witnessed by the history of civilization, or will be done consciously by not allowing his kind to exceed an optimum carrying capacity.

Socio-Economic Situations

It is incongruous that student unrest is so great and race problems so much in the front, yet almost everyone seems unaware that the basic cause of most of these socio-economic stresses is overpopulation, about which almost nothing is said by all of these energetic and sometimes vociferous groups. The daily economic pressures of individuals attempting to provide a decent civilization, especially for themselves, may lead to the ultimate destruction of all ecosystems. Surplus individuals do not quietly fade away.

In spite of man's power of conscious thought, the only species so endowed, he seldom thinks beyond his lifetime or his own family's particular needs. The great desire of most people to provide their children and themselves with all of today's advantages is an important factor

in reducing family size. That is not enough, however, for these families are still raising the population level.

At the same time that the world's population is increasing, both the number and the percentage of the "have-nots" increase and, in addition, the gap widens between the "haves" and "have-nots." As tragic as it may sound, when an underdeveloped country's population density is growing rapidly, both health and agricultural aid from the United States may not only be wasted but may severely aggravate the already deplorable social and economic situation in that country.

In industrially developed countries, middle-class couples often have fewer children than they would like (if they only had more money, domestic help, etc.), whereas in underdeveloped countries and ghettos the reverse is too frequently true. High birth rates tend to nullify national efforts to raise average per capita income since there is less money for savings and developmental investments. Neither families nor a nation can escape when life is held close to the margin of subsistence.

Overpopulation inevitably commits too many people to poverty and despair. With perpetual pregnancies the bonds of welfare become inescapable, for unskilled parents cannot feed a large family from the wages they can earn. No matter how you look at it, families of more than two or three children intensify the problem of national development, and this happens whether the parents are poor, middle class, or wealthy.

A complete reorientation of social values and attitudes regarding births is urgently needed now. We need new baby ethics, an awareness of the tragedies associated with too many babies. Bringing births and deaths into balance will demand great social, economic, and political changes.

With reference to our affluence, we cannot turn back—if for no other reason than the fact that there are now too many people to permit going back—to a less materialistic existence without cars, pesticides, diesel exhaust, sewage and garbage disposal, etc. The stork has passed the plow. Food prices in developing nations are rising faster than the purchasing power.

Economic Interests

Man seems to be governed by economic self-interest. Societies become conditioned to the tenets of the economists—that money can buy anything. Without the basic resources there can be no wealth and affluence; but, unfortunately, the exploitation of resources seems to be considered the very foundation of all "progress."

"Progress" is the magic word. It means to increase property values and returns on one's investment; it is the deity of modern civilization. Yet, do any of us really know what we are progressing toward? Too often, the chamber-of-commerce form of "progress" is the next man's destruction.

Man seems to be more concerned with the quality of his goals than with the quantity of his goods. The more slowly a population increases the more rapid is the growth of both its gross and per capita income.

The harmful consequences of overpopulation are blindly overlooked by those who favor an expanding population for reasons of military strength, economic progress, scientific and agricultural development, and eugenics.

Man's economic dreams, his selfishness, and his materialism interfere with his awareness of the fate of the unborn. He is too busy in the United States in covering two acres per minute with houses, factories, and stores. His highways are now equivalent to paving the entire state of Indiana. Every day, California loses 300 acres of agricultural land.

Unfortunately, little planning has been done on how the socio-economic problems can be handled once the population growth is stopped. If the rush of today's living and industrial development or defense spending just slows down, a painful recession is upon us. We have no government study on how the nation could exist without a growing population.

Resource Management

Insidious economic pressures seem to prevent any effective management of resources in a manner that would provide for their utilization in perpetuity. Concrete and pavement surely are not the epitome of the human species' fulfillment. An ecological appreciation of resource management is needed, and ecological ethics must replace ecological atrocities.

Man is rapidly depleting the nonreplenishable resources. Half of the energy used by man during the past 2000 years was used in the last century. Man is reported to have mined more in the past 100 years than during all previous time. But, every barrel has a bottom; unbridled technology promises to speed us faster toward that bottom. Our planet's resources diminish faster as society's affluence is increased. Our qualitative sense of appreciation of our environment seems to be replaced by mere quantitative values. Why cannot civilization fulfill its obligation of being a competent steward of all resources?

It is inevitable that the limited legacy of natural resources must steadily yield in the face of the current explosion in the world population. As the population swells, open spaces are inundated by a flood of housing, and resources shrink faster. The United States and other developed nations are consuming a disproportionately large share of the world's nonrenewable and other resources at an ever-accelerating rate, perhaps 20 to 30 times as much on a per capita basis as are individuals in undeveloped countries. In 1954, the United States was reported to be using about 50% of the raw-material resources consumed in the world each year, and by 1980 it might be 80%. But we do not have an endless earth of boundless bounty. Any finite resource is subject to eventual exhaustion.

Effect of Science and Technology

The world may have sufficient resources, but it has never provided enough food and other necessities of life for all people at any one time. As technology improved, enabling better utilization of resources, the population similarly increased, so that there have always been many who died prematurely, as Malthus predicted.

No one anticipated the scope and rapidity of the technological changes that have occurred in Western society. About one-third of the people now consume about two-thirds of the world's food production, while the other two-thirds go undernourished. But, unfortunately, these starving people reproduce at a high rate. As individual aspirations rise and per capita resources fall, the widening gap between the haves and the have-nots could well generate some serious social and political pressures.

In recent times spectacular gains have been made in controlling mass killers such as typhus, malaria, yellow fever, small pox, cholera, plague, and influenza; but no corresponding checks have been made on birth rates. It is ironic that the root of our overpopulation problem is technical advances brought about by our increasing intellect (the knowledge explosion of the last hundred years).

Technology can produce almost anything, but only at the usually recognized high price of resource consumption and waste accumulation. As our technology advances, the amount of resources utilized per person also increases, and the supply is not endless.

Technology and science can and do progress at an ever-increasing rate, but can social, political, and religious views change rapidly enough to cope with this "progress"? The fruits of all our scientific and technological advances will be ephemeral if the world's population continues to explode. Our intelligence is so powerful that it may destroy us because we lack the wisdom and insight to recognize and correct what we are doing to ourselves and, especially, to future generations. We are passing on an enormous population problem to the next generation.

Pollution and Waste Disposal

Affluent societies have also been labeled "effluent" societies. That man is a highly adaptable species that can live in polluted environments, in extremely crowded conditions, in situations of acute malnutrition, and in some of the most depressing of environments is well exemplified today. But why should he? And how much lower can he sink and still survive as a "successful" species?

Mushrooming with the population are pollution and litter. We produce 70% of the world's solid wastes but have only 10% of the world's population. There is a need to make the reuse and disposal of rubbish more economical.

Popular Solutions and Misconceptions

Hopeful but inadequate panaceas include synthetic foods (proteins and vitamins), hydroponics, desalinization of seawater, food from the ocean, more agricultural research, fertilizers, irrigation, the vast unused lands, land reforms, government regulation, price support, migrations, redistribution of food and wealth, and private enterprise.

Science and technology may find a way to produce more food and to accommodate more people, but in the end this, of course, will only make matters that much worse if birth control is not effective. It should be obvious that the only solution is a drastically reduced birth rate or a greatly increased death rate. The one inescapable fact about a country's population—about the world's population—is that the death rate must someday equal the birth rate, regardless of how plentiful food may be.

Unfortunately, a basic American philosophy is the belief that our free-enterprise system can produce anything that is necessary, a false cornucopian faith that our population growth is not a real threat. Our overpopulation-underdevelopment dilemma is not a matter of increasing production to meet the demand for more food; rather, the only solution is to limit demand for food so that production may someday catch up to the population's needs.

Role of Family Planning

There is no question that family planning has made great progress. But today's society and religious groups must recognize the urgency for adopting the pill, IUD, other chemical and mechanical devices (both undependable), sterilization, abortion—in fact, any means of limiting childbirth. The promotion of some form of effective means of artificial birth control is the only moral, human, and political approach available to prevent the misery and suffering which will result if people are permitted to have as many "planned" children as they want.

Despite the great benefits of family planning programs, especially the benefits to the families concerned, family planning is not a euphemism for birth control. We need to develop a social and cultural philosophy that even a family of three children is too large and to overcome the fear of some ethic and religious sects that other groups may multiply faster, becoming more dominant. Family planning per se has little relevance to the underdeveloped countries of the world or to poverty groups in the more advanced countries. Therefore anything other than government control of conception may be self-defeating.

Sexual Desire and Love of Children

The basic conflict with the overpopulation problem is that of desires—actually drives—and the fact that most young women are fecund; without either the strong drives or the ability of women to conceive, there would be no problem. As with all organisms, man's potential fecundity and predisposition to overproduce are the basic causes for his excess fertility over deaths. Most babies are the consequence of passion, not love. But children are loved.

Motherhood must become a less significant role for women. We must forego some of our love for children and learn to be content with fewer numbers. What is needed in the way of governmental control of births is not control of an individual's behavior but control of the consequence of such behavior, the prevention of intemperate breeding.

There is no question that children make family ties more intimate, but man has already done too well toward "fathering" the country. Compassionate relations between spouses, not the having of children, must become the primary goal of marriages in the future. There is no need to find drugs that destroy sexual desire; the objective is to control the conception rate, not frequency of intercourse.

Is Having Children a Basic Right?

One price that society must be willing to pay for sustained world peace is a stringent universal birth-control program, which will require revolutionary revisions of modes of thought about our basic human rights with regard to family planning.

The increasing disparity between population density and food supply, by itself, justifies effective birth control regardless of the "morality" associated with depriving parents of the right to have as many planned children as they choose.

Having too many children can no longer be dismissed as an act of God, for it is now truly. the consequence of a complacent society that is unwilling to take any of many steps available for preventing surplus births. Our primitive reproductive instincts cannot be condoned in the face of modern survival rates. The two are no longer in balance.

To say that the opportunity to decide the number and spacing of children is a basic human right is to say that man may do whatever he wants with nature without thought of its inevitable consequence to future generations. Our legal and ethical right should be to have only enough children to replace ourselves.

No longer can we consider procreation an individual and private matter. Intercourse, yes, but not unregulated numbers of conceptions since they affect the welfare of all other individuals living at that time plus those to be born in the future.

Religious Complications

It needs to be said over and over again that the bringing of surplus children into this world, whether from personal desire or from religious edicts, destines not only some of these children but many others to a premature death. Overproduction actually lowers the maximum density that can be sustained for normal life spans, thereby increasing the number of souls in need of salvation.

The "morality" of birth control in today's burgeoning human population has taken on an entirely new aspect. God clearly never meant for man to overpopulate this earth to the point where he would destroy many other forms of life and perhaps even himself. The religious doctrines we lean on today were established before science and technology had dramatically raised the carrying capacity for man.

The question of complete abstinence as the only acceptable means of family regulation is as ludicrous as compulsory euthanasia. The mortal sin, if there is one, in God's eyes surely would be associated with those who do *not* practice birth control, for to let babies come "as they naturally do" will prove to be a form of murder—through starvation, pestilence, and wars resulting from excess babies. It must be recognized that the number of children can no longer be left to "the will of God" or to our own desires and family plans, and if population controls are to be successful, they may have to be determined by government regulations.

Religious views that do not condone rigorous birth control must realize that every surplus birth their philosophy promotes will guarantee, on the average, a horrible death some day to more than one individual.

Although the Christian attitude implies that everything on this earth was created for man's use, in reality man is inescapably also part of nature.

Some form of compulsory control of birth rates is essential, although I see no reason why various religious groups cannot be permitted to achieve birth limitations in whatever manner they choose. If a woman or a couple exceeds the limit set by society, however, then they must be dealt with by law compelling them to be sterilized, to have an abortion, or by some other repayment to society.

Birth control is not murder, as some claim, but lack of it in today's overpopulated world most surely will be. For those who strongly oppose the setting of any limit on the number of children a family can have, I ask them to tell the rest of us just how they think the premature death rate should be increased to offset their extra births.

Wealth vs. Number of Children

Civilization can no longer endure a way of life in which people believe they have the right to have as many children as they can afford. This is hypocritical, for those who can "afford" luxurious living are already utilizing many times their share of the limited food and other resources, and also they are contributing much more pollution to the environment than are the have-nots. The affluent population needs to be made aware of the overpopulation problems, for they often desire to have more children per family than those who are in poverty.

Too much of today's religious climate makes birth control a politically sensitive area, thus constraining public officials. But, as citizens, are we not justified in asking why our governmental officials have not done more to make us aware of the urgency of population control—political sensitivities notwithstanding?

Governments should be guiding the development of a better life and world to live in, but if it does not recognize the need for human husbandry, then it will be fostering the ultimate destruction of the earth rather than the goals it seeks.

Man, in spite of his intellect, is so concerned with the present that he too often turns a deaf ear to alarming sounds of the future. Another difficulty in stabilizing the population is that our standard of living and our economy cannot survive in a static state.

Limiting Size of Families

We can no longer be prophets and philosophers; we must act. The biomagnification of births must be brought to an abrupt halt. Procreation must come under governmental control if no other way can be found. Perhaps what is needed is a system of permits for the privilege of conceiving, or compulsory vasectomies of all men and sterilization of all women who have been responsible for two births.

Since the taboo against birth control is inviolable to some, regardless of the dire consequences of overpopulation, laws must be passed to regulate conceptions and births. Each individual needs to have the right to produce or adopt only a replacement for himself or herself.

The general public must be made to realize that from now on, for a married couple to have more than two children or three at most, is a very socially irresponsible act. We must advocate small families. When business is good and living has quality, marriages will naturally tend to be earlier and births more numerous; therefore, only through the development of new nonfamilial rewards can later marriages be made to appear attractive to people. Taxes now subsidize children, whereas we should be taxed for the privilege of having children.

A rising age at marriage is an effective way of reducing births, and, sociologically and economically, it gives women more time to become better educated, acquire nonfamily sorts of interests, and develop greater cautions toward pregnancy.

Up to now, only death has been of public concern; procreation has remained an individual and highly cherished private matter. But this privilege cannot continue, and regulation of the number of conceptions, or at least births, must also become a government function.

Population Control or Premature Deaths

Man must decide whether the future growth of populations will be governed by famine, pestilence, and war, on whether he will use his intellect to control birth rates artificially. If the population growth is not controlled by lower birth rates, hundreds of millions of people must soon die prematurely each year.

Man must use his intellect to counteract his excessive fertility, for all species have been endowed by nature to be overfecund. If he does not, the extra individuals will be eliminated by the natural process of "struggle for existence—survival of the fittest," which causes all surplus individuals to die prematurely as a result of nature's ruthless laws of involuntary "self-limitation" whenever the carrying capacity has been exceeded. That territoriality and aggression are life-preserving functions of the social order of animals is frightening when man applies these same principles to his own species.

There have always been hungry people in the world, but both the total number of individuals and the percentage of the total population that are destined to go hungry in the future will be dramatically increased if birth rates are not drastically checked. Many like to think that nature will somehow take care of things. They fail to remember how nature has taken care of many species that were no longer adaptable to existence on this earth—they are now preserved as fossils.

Modern public-health methods and medical technology have lessened the chronic hunger, general economic misery, and other vicissitudes that once caused high mortality rates. But, sooner or later, any increase in births over deaths will be balanced by an increase in the rate of premature deaths.

Human Husbandry and Quality Living

Human husbandry implies that we reg-

218

ulate the population density before the natural self-limiting demographic and societal stress factors do it for us. But human motivation will always work against good human husbandry, because to each individual who has quality living, a large family will seem desirable.

The population of the world is so great that what used to be a ripple when it doubled now means catastrophic effects because of the great numbers involved and the lack of this earth's ability to support them. Man is not practicing good husbandy when he lets his population density expand beyond the carrying capacity.

The most important thesis regarding the need for human husbandry is that human beings will not voluntarily restrict their number of children to just two when economic, social, and political conditions appear to be personally favorable. A quality society with quality existence is now unattainable in many parts of the world, and may soon be unattainable any place in the world. The "economic" struggle of overpopulation is the world's greatest threat to quality living, enriched leisure, and even man's ultimate existence.

Conclusion

The ultimate goal must be a zero population growth. To achieve "quality living" instead of nature's "survival of the fittest," as has persisted throughout the history of mankind, the birth rate must not continue to exceed the death rate. If the birth rate of nations and the world are not greatly reduced, an ever-increasing amount of starvation and other types of premature deaths are inevitable. There is a prodigious need for mankind to practice human husbandry (Human Husbandry, a guest editorial in *BioScience*, **18**: 372-373, 1968, by Walter E. Howard).

A conscientious regulation of fertility is needed, or a calamitous rise in premature mortality rates is inevitable. Without this tremendous voluntary restraint or the development of a strong social stigma against bearing more than two or three children, the rate of conception must come under some form of governmental control. It can no longer be a basic human right to have as many children as one wants, especially if such action dooms others to a premature death.

Even though the above picture is bleak, the world is not going to come to an end. In fact, none of the people who read this article are going to starve, but their very existence is going to cause others who are less well off to perish. As overpopulation becomes worse, the percentage of the people who will fall into this nonsurviving unfit category must obviously increase. If babies of the future are to live, there must be fewer of them now.

Biomedical Aspects of Population Control

William D. McElroy

The population of the world is now growing at an unparalleled rate of 2% per annum. Translated into a head count, this means that 132 persons are added per minute to the present population; as time passes this figure will increase in magnitude. It took us over one million years — from the emergence of man from a primate stock to 1830 — to reach one billion individuals.

In 1930, 100 years later, we had increased to 2×10^9 and only 30 years later, 1960, we added a third billion. The Population Reference Bureau sets the world population as of January 1, 1968 at 3.44 billion individuals. The 4.5 billion mark is expected to be reached by about 1976.

The current 2% per year may not sound like an unusual rate of growth. However, a few calculations can demonstrate what exponentials really mean. Markert (1966) has shown that if this rate had existed from the time of Christ until the present time, the increase would be about 7×10^{16}. There would be over 20 million individuals in place of each person now alive or 100 persons for each square foot. At our present rate of 2% per year there would be over 150 billion pople within two centuries.

We are on the logarithmic phase of a typical growth curve after a long lag period. In nature no animal, plant, or bacterial population has ever maintained a logarithmic phase of growth for very long. The major factors that slow this rate of growth are exhaustion

The author is head of the Biology Department, Johns Hopkins University, Baltimore, Maryland. This paper and the two following by Drs. Robinson and Thurston were presented at the Plenary Session, 19th Annual AIBS Meeting, Ohio State University, Columbus, on September 1968.

of food supply, accumulation of toxic products, decimation through disease, or the effects of some outside lethal agent which kills a high proportion of the population. Any one or all of these factors will force the population back into a lag phase. I leave it to your imagination which of these factors might apply to the human population. Of course, you will say that humans have intelligence and can intentionally modify some of these factors whereas a bacterial population cannot. I wonder if the present evidence does not support arguments to the contrary.

Some feel that the battle to feed the world population is now lost, and that it is a foregone conclusion that by 1985 we will have world-wide famines in which hundreds of millions of people will starve to death. I must admit that at this time I see no major crash program which would lead me to disagree with this conclusion.

If the world were divided into two groups, the so-called "have" and the "have not" countries, only about one-third of the total population would be found to live in the "have" nations where per capita income is high, food supplies ample, and literacy nearly universal. How to feed, educate, house, and find meaningful employment for the remaining two-thirds of the world population is the number two problem of the world. It might even replace the search for peace as the number one problem if we do not act soon.

We can no longer wait to deal with this set of problems even though the population growth may presently seem unimportant to some here in the United States. We must depress and actually reverse this logarithmic phase of growth

Bioscience, January, 1969, Vol.19, No.1, pp. 19-23.

before our problems become completely insurmountable. It is up to the United States and other developed countries to take the leadership. I suggest the following:

1) The appointment of a special assistant to the President of the United States whose sole responsibility would be to identify ways and means of solving the growth of world population and increasing the world food supply.

2) Set up world-wide institutions in which family planning and population control advice is intimately coupled with maternal care services.

3) Change completely our farm policy so that the farmer can move toward maximum production. This will allow us to extend our Food for Freedom program in order to provide emergency food assistance to stave off disaster while hungry countries build up their own food production capability. At a time when people all over the world are starving it will be decidedly un-American for the United States to do nothing in the way of supplying some food. We must insist, however, that countries receiving food aid from the United States make vigorous efforts to improve their own food production.

4) We must make an all-out effort to supplement traditional land-based agriculture by the development and manufacture of a low cost protein from fish. It has been recommended on several occasions that we must develop the technology of farming the oceans, but little seems to be happening. This will take time, and the need for urgency is great if we are not to destroy this natural resource before we learn to manage it effectively.

5) Instruction in family planning and the principles of population dynamics should be an essential part of the curriculum of all secondary schools.

6) Finally, we must start a general discussion now, in the community, in the states, in the nation, and throughout the world on the merits of famliy planning versus population control. The possible consequences of the decision between these two alternatives must be carefully spelled out to the world at large.

The Present Position of the United States

We must soon reach a satisfactory ending of our struggles in Southeast Asia. We must continue our efforts to work out cooperative solutions of international problems relative to thermonuclear devices. We must work for a stable economic situation and continue our drive to solve the major domestic problems, particularly those in large urban centers. But the population and food problems of the world will not wait for a solution — they can only get worse, and, in the not too distant future, will make our other problems look insignificant by comparison.

Recently, the President made the following statement in his health message to Congress: "Two vital fields long neglected by research are population and human reproduction. Thousands of parents want help in determining how to plan their families. Thousands of others are unable to have the children they desire. Our lack of knowledge impedes our effort to provide the help they need. Far too little is known about the physiology of reproduction and its effect on all aspects of human life. Searching studies are needed to determine the complex, emotional, sociological, physiological, and economic factors involved. A wide range of scientists must bring to these problems their specialized disciplines — biologists, behavioral scientists, biochemists, pharmacologists, demographers, experts in population dynamics.

"To launch this effort I have directed the Secretary of Health, Education and Welfare to establish a center for population studies and human reproduction in the National Institute of Child Health and Human Development. The center will serve to give new energy and direction to the research activities of all federal departments and agencies in these fields.

"I am asking the Congress to appropriate $12 million to support the research activities of the center during its first year of operation.

"As we move to expand our knowledge of population and human reproduction, we must make that knowledge available to those who want it. Last year the federal government helped to bring information and counseling on a voluntary basis to more than 500,-000 women. But there are millions more who want help.

"I recommend that the Congress provide for an increase in funds from $25 million in fiscal 1968 to $61 million in fiscal 1969 so that 3 million women can have access to family planning help if they so desire."

Although these proposals are major steps forward for family planning and the medical health of the nation, they will do little to slow the growth of the U.S. population and will have little or no effect on the total world population. I am not arguing, however, against these recommendations and as chairman of the Population Committee of the National Academy of Sciences I have always supported recommendations concerning additional research. However, we cannot wait for new solutions. We must start now with what knowledge we already possess and continue to find better ways to approach an ultimate solution as we move into the future. The appropriation and distribution of funds for population control in the United States or developing countries has not kept pace with the superlative statements made by national and responsible individuals on the importance of this problem.

AID Population Policy

Recently, Mr. William S. Gaud, the administrator of the U.S. Agency for International Development, made the following statement relative to the U.S. position concerning population policy. ". . . the government of every nation with a population problem, whether developed or developing, should do its utmost to increase the knowledge and practice of family planning among its citizens. Our role is to encourage and help the developing nations with this task." He went on to say that the United States must "respect the sovereignty and sensibilities of the nations we assist. The population question is as delicate as it is urgent. Over half the people in the developing world now live under governments that have policies of reducing birth rates. But some countries, even though they are aware of the seriousness of the problem and are working on it, either do not welcome outside help in this field or do not want it on a large scale. Our work in the population field must be carried on in such a way as not to raise political problems. The family planning programs we assist must be the host nation's programs — not our programs. They should avoid labels marked "Made in the United States." Mr. Gaud went on to say that "AID will support no family planning or population program unless it is voluntary. . . . We will assist only those programs in which individuals are free to participate or not as they see fit and where they have a choice of means. . . . We want no part of either international coercion or individual coercion. We do not make family planning a condition of aid."

It may be that we have reached a point where our policies, although admirable as first glance, must give way to a more vigorous program. It is quite clear that during the past 10 years our indirect efforts have had very little effect in slowing down the growth of world population. Furthermore, if the problem of population growth and food supply is the number two problem of the world, then it most certainly must be placed alongside the number one problem, namely, the search for lasting peace. It needs the same status and it needs the same amount of money. Most of all, it needs the leadership of the

United States in convincing the world that something must be done, and done now, to decrease the growth of the world population and to increase food production dramatically and immediately. It is for these reasons that I encourage the President to appoint a special assistant who would be concerned exclusively with population and food problems.

Family Planning Programs

In 1963, the Committee on Science and Public Policy of the National Academy of Sciences issued a report on the "Growth of World Population" which emphasized in part that the governments of the world can no longer ignore the population problem. For the first time, a president of the United States made a positive statement concerning government programs and support for family planning programs. Until that time all government agencies were careful to avoid discussing this matter in open meetings. Both President Kennedy and President Johnson have repeatedly indicated that they recognized the seriousness of the problem and the need for intelligent and forthright action.

Much has been done in a number of areas and in a number of countries to deliver family planning services to individual families, but it is quite clear that only a minimal start has been made. A number of steps can be taken, but one area of particular promise is that which concerns family planning and maternity care.

Family Planning and Maternity Care

Much recent work has been done to couple family planning with maternity care. Drs. Howard Taylor and Bernard Berelson (1968) have summarized the effectiveness of providing family planning instruction in association with other aspects of maternity care. The results of the collaborative trial of the postpartem approach to family planning in 25 hospitals throughout the world have been reported by Dr. Gerald

Zatuchni. Even in the underdeveloped countries, the data from these trials have been most encouraging. As Taylor and Berelson point out, there are some very compelling advantages of the association of family planning with maternity services. These may be indicated as follows: (1) *Physiological*. the use of the event of child birth for the identification of the physiologically most fertile women is especially important in countries where facilities are limited and efforts must be concentrated at points where they will have the most effect. Thus, the effort in India should be directed not to the 500 million people or to the 250 million females, but rather to the 20 million females who bear their first child in a given year and who have the greatest residual potential for adding to the population. It is well known that in the absence of birth control information, a second pregnancy is likely to occur very soon after delivery of the first child. In any case, an early decision has to be made with regard to family planning, and the delivery room or one close to it is an excellent classroom for transmitting this information. (2) *Educational*. The educational impact of a supervised obstetrical experience will be relatively greater where school systems are lacking and illiteracy is widespread. The education needed to convince people to reduce their family size is extremely difficult where literacy is low, Unfortunately, solution of the population problem cannot wait for the development of a general program of education. Thus one starts the educational process at the time of the first delivery. (3) *Accessibility*. Taylor and Berelson emphasize that a national program based on maternity care can in theory reach every eligible woman. In other words, it is much easier and more feasible to detect cases of pregnancy and to see to it that all pregnant women are provided with information about family planning than to educate the total female population.

(4) *Acceptability*. It is felt, in general, that the pregnant population would accept family planning principles if these are presented at the time of the first birth. In this way family planning is built into the concept of maternal and infant care.

This whole concept of uniting family planning with maternity services, depends, of course, upon an organized effort to identify institutions where child delivery takes place. Unfortunately, in many underdeveloped countries, delivery of children is not concentrated in a few well-defined clinics or hospitals. In the United States, on the other hand, the proportion of all births that are professionally supervised is very large. However, much still needs to be done, particularly in the large cities, to educate the individual obstetricians in the techniques of providing adequate family planning advice. The amount of information on family planning given to the parent on delivery of the first child is less than adequate. This is particularly true in the poverty areas of large urban centers.

Taylor and Berelson have arrived at some approximate figures for cost of construction and of annual operation of a maternal help and associated family planning facility in a typical unit of 100,000 people involving 4000 annual deliveries. Construction costs would be about $100,000 and an annual operating budget of $40,000 or $10 for each delivery would be needed. To service completely a country like India, they estimate that at least $500 million would be needed for constructing hospital units for obstetrical and gynecological practice, and approximately $200 million for annual operation. For all of Latin America the figures would be approximately $250 million for construction and $100 million for annual operation. In a country of 5 million population it would cost approximately $2 million a year for operation and for a country of 25 million it would cost $10 million for operation. Using such calculations for the entire developing world, they estimate, with a population of about 2.2 billion, that the operating cost would be of the order of $880 million annually. It is of interest that the value of the foods which were shipped by the United States over the past few years to other countries has been about 1.5 billion dollars annually. Thus, to do the most effective job of trying to control the population growth in the underdeveloped world would cost approximately only one-half as much as we are currently spending in a stopgap manner to supply only food.

The Taylor-Berelson approach possesses, therefore, the great merit of reaching the most significant elements in a large population, and of dealing with them effectively and with dignity. Furthermore, the plan merits very serious consideration since it appears to be the one approach that could bring about a coordinated world effort.

I have emphasized this program for the developing countries because of the immediate and pressing need; however, much remains to be done in the United States along this same line. As Jaffe has pointed out "despite the vastly improved climate of the last decade, it remains true that in terms of systematic knowledge we know more about programing to meet community family planning needs in the developing countries than in the United States. In the U.S. many physicians, health officers, and researchers continue to be somewhat indifferent to the implementation of family planning services, although this is a field of health care with both immediate and long term medical, social and economic consequences of significance." Therefore we need the Taylor-Berelson plan even in the United States. In addition, we need to reach the nonpregnant but potentially fertile population. This means establishing family planning services in locations geographically accessible to the population in need. These services in most cases must be free or very heavily subsidized. Jaffe points out that "in most urban and suburban communities, this means establishment of a network of active, visible clinics in hospitals, health centers and other principal medical institutions, complemented by satellite clinics in poverty areas." We have ignored the needs of the poor too long. They want smaller families and therefore should be supplied with the necessary information to achieve a reduction in the number of offspring.

Education on the Problems of Family Planning and Population

The need for education at all levels is great; the earlier it is begun the more effective it will be. I believe that instruction in family planning and the principles of population dynamics should be an essential part of the curriculum of secondary schools. A successful program can lead to a lower incidence of unwanted pregnancies in the United States among both married and unmarried couples. In addition, it would greatly enhance America's sense of public urgency about helping nations everywhere that want and need to solve their problems of population growth.

A number of school systems have made an initial attack on this important problem and have worked up detailed outlines and supplied materials to the appropriate teachers for their use. In Baltimore we start the instruction in the elementary grades and give detailed information on family planning and population growth to the high school student. By placing the discussion of population growth and birth control in the same matter-of-fact setting as the teaching of social studies and biology, schools can help greatly to educate not only the students but also their parents as well. Someone must take the leadership to work with national organizations who are concerned with curriculum development. It is clear that a way must be found where this kind of information can be introduced systematically into the curriculum, either in social studies during the early stages of training or the biology courses at the high school level. One of the major problems is the identification of personnel who can present adequately these concepts to the students. It may well be necessary to establish summer institutes, with the appropriate fellowship support, for the training of teachers on the various topics that should be discussed in relation to family planning, population growth, and birth control. It is evident that secondary schools also face problems of community relations which tend to limit the extent to which they can deal with these so-called sensitive issues, and it may well be that initially other kinds of institutional frameworks must be provided where birth control education can be given to unmarried students.

There are many other important matters that might be discussed under this heading, but probably one of the most important is that of *motivation*. Even though contraceptive technology has greatly improved, which makes it possible for families to lower their family size, the fact remains that there are many large *planned* families. Reduction of family size from 4 to 3 to 2 is essential if we are going to solve our population problem in the long run. At the present time there is some disagreement on the long range effectiveness of the family planning program and population control.

Population Control versus Family Planning

Some time in the not too distant future it is, of course, essential that the growth of the world population approach zero, i.e., where the deaths equal the births. Multiplication of the human population cannot be allowed to increase to a point where it would be greater than the mass of the earth. We can, to be sure, slow down on our medical research and let the natural epidemiological controls take over, or we can limit our food production and thus limit the population through famines and starvation. Wars provide another way of reducing the size of the population. It is evident that both morally and psychologically most people in the world would like to think that sometime in the not too distant future we will have peace, that sometime in the not too distant future we would be able to control disease and famine throughout the world so that all would live a meaningful, humane existence to a ripe old age. Under these circumstances, however, a large number of people will be capable of multiple births, and this would inevitably lead to an astronomical world population. It is under these conditions that we must gradually approach the population growth rate of approximately zero.

Recently, Kingsley Davis (1967) has criticized the family planning concept of population control because the basis of population planning has always been that of giving the family the "right to have the number of children that they want when they want them." Although he is perfectly correct in indicating that this is not population control but really population planning, it is the feeling of many of us that at least this is where one has to start.

Family Planning Is Not Population Control

I do not believe that anyone I know who has thought about the problems carefully would claim that family planning programs will, by themselves, achieve population control. Furthermore, Dr. Davis feels that the very existence of family planning programs creates "the illusion that it is solving the population problem" and "obscures potentially effective methods." On this basic point I disagree. What other *effective methods* can Dr. Davis suggest *at this time*? It seems to me that most governments that have considered this problem have been doing a part-time job in trying to stabilize the population by spreading the knowledge of the pill and other contraceptive devices. An inadequate job is being done in promoting the reduction of the birth rate. We need an all-out effort from all countries concerned to see if we can solve this problem. We have not had this effort to date.

Family planning, as I understand it, is not a program just for the distribution of contraceptive devices. Where knowledgeable personnel are available, they try to point out the broad social problems resulting from large families. They try to influence the *behavior* of the individual couples with regard to the size of the family. Unfortunately, even in the United States we have inadequate personnel to carry out this large educational program. But it could be done if adequate funds were available and family planning was intimately associated with maternal care. Therefore, I say we have not given family planning and the social education associated with it a fair chance in the United States.

Davis may be correct in emphasizing that this is not a *long-range* solution, The real question, then, is what can be done, and what should we be discussing and researching in terms of the long-range problems and true popula-. tion control.

I agree with Dr. Davis that one of the first things that could be initiated immediately is alteration of the abortion laws state by state or even nationally so as to liberalize and promote free abortions. It is perfectly true that even in families that practice family planning through the use of current contraceptive technology mistakes are made, and the wife becomes pregnant even though she had no desire to be. The logical extension of the concept of a baby "only when you want it and if you want it" would allow the person to make the decision to have an abortion. It is not possible to determine the exact figure on how many abortions would be sought if they were legalized. But one

226

can comment on the fact that Japan has effectively used this as a method of lowering its population growth. In some states it is now possible to obtain a legalized abortion for mental reasons and in cases of rape, but unfortunately this is not true in most of our states.

A type of research which would have a great effect on population control would be that related to the discovery of methods for sex determination. It has been suggested that if one could predetermine that the first offspring would be a male, it would have a great effect on the size of the family. In some, if not most societies, male babies are more desirable than females, and if the male was the first offspring, the motivation for having additional offspring would be reduced.

There have been a number of interesting incentive suggestions that might be made part of a national policy which would encourage a reduction in the size of the family group. In a positive way the federal government, for example, could pay a fee to a couple if they delayed their marriage beyond a given age. For example, if they did not marry until they were 24, they would receive a $500 fee from the government; if they waited until they were 30, they might even get a $4000 or $5000 fee. In this way one would tend to reduce the size of the family. It is evident that in the countries where late marriage is usual, the rate of population growth is considerably lessened. Unfortunately, this may not work in underdeveloped countries where education is at a low level and early marriage is customary. Even if marriage occurred early, it has been suggested that if pregnancy is delayed for 3 years, the couple would receive a government fee. If there is an additional 5-year delay between the first and second baby, the fee might be higher. All of these suggestions are interesting ones and should be further discussed by competent groups.

In the negative way, it has been suggested that the tax burden should be increased when a family has gone beyond a certain size. For example, there might be a tax exemption for the first two children, none for the third, and with the tax actually increased for any number above three. One might even add educational benefits for the first child, but decrease these for the second and eliminate them for the third, etc.

It has also been suggested that marriage fees be greatly increased, and that low cost public housing not be related to family size. In addition, a number of investigators have stimulated us to think about the possibilities of increasing female participation in the labor force and of promoting equal treatment for male and female. Of course, this trend has been greatly increased in recent years, but if it were fostered to an even greater extent for jobs that were most appropriate for females, it could be a decisive factor in delaying a marriage. It has also been suggested that when we are in a peace-time economy, we might promote a domestic peace corps program for all men between the ages of 18 and 20 which, in effect, would delay the age of marriage and inculcate changes of attitudes of family size.

Whatever the circumstances, however, it is clear that we must agree with Davis that the zero growth-rate concept must be explored, and that we must try to find ways to make it acceptable as one of our national goals.

It is possible that the U.S. Government itself could set some national goals and try to educate the people to accept them; but this would be no more than a certification of a *good* family planning program. It is one thing to idealize about policies which would bring about zero growth rate in the population but it is another thing to find a way to achieve this. Certainly broad-based family planning can reduce family sizes from 10, 8, 6 down to 4. This is the problem in many if not in most of the developing countries and in part of our own society. Having achieved this, then one is in a much better position to educate the population about the long-range desirability of having smaller families.

What Can a Biologist Do?

There is a lot that biologists can do individually and collectively. Probably the most important is to educate the public with regard to the urgency of the problem. We seem to be talking to ourselves. For example, during the summer of 1968 the Gallup poll asked a national sample of adults the following question: "What do you think is the most important problem facing this country today?" Less than 1% mentioned population. If the population problem is not too important in the minds of the public, there will not be an all-out effort by elected officials to institute new programs and support existing ones aimed at a solution.

Biologists understand what a logarithmic growth phase is and the consequences if it is allowed to continue for long periods of time. I urge you therefore to take every opportunity offered to speak about this subject. The undergraduate premedical students should be thoroughly trained in the subject before they get to medical school because they will not get this information in our present medical curriculum. Every course in biology, including biochemistry and molecular biology, should devote at least one lecture to the subject. Every college, university, and high school should organize at least one public session on this subject every year. The biologists must take the leadership — now is the time to stop talking to ourselves and "speak out" to the rest of the population. An informed public will demand action.

References

Davis, Kingsley. 1967. Population policy: Will current programs succeed? *Science,* **158**: 730.

Markert, C. L. 1966. Biological limits on population growth. *BioScience,* **12**: 859-863.

Taylor, Howard C., Jr., and Bernard Berelson. 1968. Maternity care and family planning as a world problem. *Am. J. Obstet. Gyn.,* **100**: 885.

A review of the world population problems and references to "teaching projects, new curriculum ideas, resources and materials, program tools, books, articles, seminars and conferences and other important educational developments" can be obtained from *Intercom,* Vol. 10, July-August 1968. Single issue is $1.00 from Foreign Policy Association, Inc., 345 E. 46th Street, New York, N.Y. 10017.

Health, Population, and Economic Development

Carl E. Taylor and Marie-Francoise Hall

No problem in international health is as important or as poorly understood as the complex interrelationship between health, population growth, and general economic development. Most traditional dogmas dealing with these interactions have proved to be oversimplifications. Causal relationships are not straightforward. Instead, they are buried in a complex matrix of multiple causes and feedback interactions. Findings and interpretations which are valid under certain conditions and at specific times may be totally reversed in somewhat changed situations and at other periods. A more valid and consistent conceptualization will become possible only as the interacting forces in the three-dimensional matrix formed by health, population growth, and general economic development are viewed as a whole.

The basic thesis of this analysis is that, in the dynamic equilibrium between the three major components of this matrix, optimum progress occurs when all elements move forward together, the general objective being improvement in the quality of life. Neither economic development nor health of itself is a sufficient goal. Economic improvement or better health can be measured in quantitative terms, such as growth in per capita income or lowered mortality rates. The general concept of an improved quality of life obviously cannot be readily measured. The social components of a better quality of life are benefits in themselves, but, more importantly, they can be used as instruments of change or as means of in-

creasing productivity. Better health is both an objective of and an instrument for development. In this process population growth is an intermediary force of increasing relevance.

In the first section of this article the influences of health programs on population growth are analyzed in terms both of effects on mortality and effects on fertility. For comparison, the influences of other development activities on population growth are also summarized. The next section deals with the influence of health on socioeconomic development through effects on both material and human resources. The third section deals with the reverse effects of population growth on both health and socioeconomic development. The data here are so well known and so generally accepted that a detailed analysis seemed unnecessary. A simple conceptual model is, however, presented. The remaining relationship, the effects of socioeconomic change on health, is, again, not discussed in detail because this has, for so long, been a primary area of concern of public health workers. The final section deals with practical aspects of present planning for population control.

Influence of Health and Economic Development on Population

Until recently, health workers used their ability to reduce mortality as a major criterion of success. Old texts in public health described with pride instances in which health programs contributed to population growth [1]. Since the hazards of rapid population growth have been recognized, health workers no longer seem proud of their

Dr. Taylor is professor and director and Dr. Hall is research associate in the Division of International Health, Johns Hopkins University School of Hygiene and Public Health, Baltimore, Maryland.

Science, August, 1967, Vol.157, No.3789, pp. 651-657.

achievements in reducing mortality. Many international health specialists welcomed with considerable relief reports which showed that other socioeconomic factors were primarily responsible for past reductions in mortality and that the effectiveness of mass disease-control efforts had been overrated (2).

In the early industrialization of Europe, mortality declined before specific health measures were effectively applied. Today, statistical analysis of data from many countries shows a strong correlation between per capita income per se and decreased mortality. In fact, most programs leading to any kind of development directly produce population growth. Improved agriculture, by providing more and better food, decreases mortality. Better transportation, by reducing the loss of food and decreasing isolation and ignorance, leads to the same result. Improved housing decreases crowding, and the more favorable home environment reduces the spread of communicable diseases. Improved water supply for agricultural, industrial, or other uses not primarily associated with health also reduces the spread of disease. Basic education increases understanding of personal hygiene and of the causes of disease. Mass media help diffuse knowledge and ideas. In some Asian countries child mortality for females is considerably higher than for males, largely because mothers and families take more conscientious care of sons than of daughters (3). The quality of a mother's care has been shown to be the most important identifiable factor influencing child health (4). Equal rights for women may substantially improve the health of girls and, secondarily, may lead to population growth by increasing the number reaching childbearing age. In Ceylon, after World War I, mortality rates fell approximately equally in the nonmalarious third of the island and in the much-publicized malarious area where mosquito control was dramatically effective (5, 6). In both cases general economic and nutritional improvement were probably the dominant forces.

Even if it were politically possible to discontinue major disease-control activities, mortality would continue its downward trend, though perhaps more slowly. Writers on economic development have questioned whether the slower mortality-rate decline which would occur in the absence of modern health measures would be more conducive to economic development than the present rapid shift (7). Data have been accumulated which indicate that net population increase will be lower if maximum efforts to reduce death rates and birth rates are made simultaneously. A somewhat higher rate of natural population increase for a few years is better than a lower one for the much longer period that action of spontaneous balancing mechanisms would require.

Attention has been directed mainly to mortality. It must be recognized that the increase in population associated with general development may also be due to an increase in fertility. Such an increase has been described for the more-developed countries (8), and a similar increase in fertility is being recorded in several of the developing countries (9). Public health programs probably directly contribute to such trends. By decreasing female mortality and the incidence of widowhood, they increase the number of reproductive years in marriage. By reducing the prevalence of diseases which limit reproduction they increase reproductive capacity. The depressant effect on fertility of venereal disease (10) and malaria (11) is documented. Again, however, it is an oversimplification to ignore other factors in the development process which increase fertility (12). Better nutrition increases reproductive capacity by shortening postpartum amenorrhea (13) and lengthening the reproductive span (14). A community development project in Peru (15) and irrigation schemes in the Sudan (16) were associated with increases in fertility. The very optimism about the future which is engendered by an increase in per capita income may have the immediate effect of increasing fertility before slower retarding forces, such as education, have a chance to act (17).

Numerous and complex cultural values and norms developed as traditional ways of controlling fertility. Any modernizing influence which weakens these norms may increase fertility. Greater participation of women in industry, for example, may encourage bottle-feeding of infants, thus decreasing the prolonged period of lactation which is a major mechanism for child spacing (18). The weakening of local customs may diminish the force of taboos on sexual intercourse at specified times. In India, such taboos include almost one-third of the days of the year (19). Acceptance of the pattern of stable marriages in Latin America, where unstable temporary unions have been common, may make a woman's exposure to the risk of pregnancy more constant and increase fertility (20). The increased fertility observed in several developing countries can only partially be accounted for by improved statistical reporting.

We have made an attempt (Fig. 1) to summarize graphically our impressions of the net effect of individual development sectors on population growth. Each arrow in Fig. 1 represents, by its length, a summation of forces leading to increased or to decreased population growth, or to both. Under special circumstances different results will obviously ensue. The net effect indicated is purely impressionistic and is meant to indicate roughly the quantitative relationships in spontaneous situations where no organized efforts have been made to control population growth. The net effect of better health is to increase population growth markedly, while education contributes the most important net effect toward reducing population growth. As indicated later in this article, quite different results may be expected when these forces are deliberately used to control population growth.

Influence of Health on Socioeconomic Development

It has become fashionable to try to justify health programs in economic terms. This exercise is salutary for health workers in that it leads to more careful efforts to measure cost-versus-benefit returns from health services. The recent tendency of health workers to undertake economic analyses does not, however, mean that there is decreased recognition of the importance of better health for its own sake in improving the quality of human life. Much has been written about the relative importance of health as a consumption item versus its value as an investment. The argument is artificial. The major reason for health programs will continue to be the fact that people insist on, and are willing to pay for, better health as a basic right. Both officials and the public will continue to derive satisfaction from the many quantitative measures of lowered mortality and morbidity which have constituted the bulk of health statistics.

More sophisticated measures will permit definition of additional social and economic benefits of health programs. In the above consideration of the effect of health programs on population growth, attention is directed toward mortality and fertility. In this section, dealing with ways in which better health influences socioeconomic development, attention is directed to lowered morbidity. The fact that morbidity is harder to measure than mortality or fertility adds to the complexity of the analysis. Techniques will be needed for measuring improved health as a positive socioeconomic force (21).

An immediate effect of some health programs has been the release of previously unusable material resources for purposes of development. Reduction of a disease which had made settlement of a given area impossible directly increases access to material resources. Some data on malaria have been collected to help justify eradication programs. Because malaria has a clearly recognizable clinical picture and may be distributed throughout a community, it lends itself to the gross analyses which are so satisfying to economists. In Nepal a malaria barrier in the Terai along the southern border had for centuries reinforced the country's isolation. Control measures in the late 1950's initiated a wave of local migration from the overpopulated hillsides, leading to economic and social development of the country as a whole (22). In Ceylon, eradication of malaria was accompanied by migration from the crowded third of the island to what had been the malarious two-thirds, and to development of that fertile part of the country (5, 23). Sardinia was once described as "the hell hole of the Mediterranean" because of the almost universal prevalence of malaria. Since dramatically effective control started, in 1946, it has enjoyed agricultural development, economic growth, and a booming tourist trade (24). In the Mexican state of Tabasco, it was only after malaria had been eliminated that major agricultural development could occur (25). Similar examples could be given for other geographically defined diseases such as trypanosomiasis and schistosomiasis.

For maximum contribution to economic development, particular attention should be paid to conserving the health of economically active age groups. Increased productivity of the labor force augments returns on other investments. There have been many historical observations, such as those reported by Winslow (26), of the effect of health programs on the quality of the labor force. In the Philippines in 1946 a survey of large enterprises revealed a daily absenteeism of 35 percent, attributed largely to malaria. After initiation of an antimalaria program, absenteeism due to the infection was reduced to between 2 and 4 percent, and 20 to 25 percent fewer laborers were required for any given task than had previously been needed (26, p. 22). In the Transvaal and in Natal, malaria control programs decreased worker absenteeism by at least 30 percent (26, p. 24). In Southern Rhodesia, an antimalaria campaign reduced absenteeism during the harvest season in the Mazoe Valley from 25 percent to almost negligible levels (26, p. 25). In Haiti, where yaws was widely prevalent among the rural population, 35,000 to 55,000 persons were treated monthly in a joint World Health Organization–UNICEF campaign. It was estimated that 100,000 incapacitated persons returned to work (26, p. 30).

It has become apparent that, where health conditions are worst, relatively simple and low-cost health programs can produce dramatic lessening of debility and disability of the labor force. In these situations major increments in productivity are most readily seen. It is precisely such programs, however, that cause the dramatic reductions in mortality which precipitate population growth. Whereas lowered morbidity is usually most evident in the increased productivity of working adults, the concomitant lowered mortality effect is more apparent in infants. There is no common standard of measurement which permits comparison of the essentially qualitative morbidity effects with the more quantitative mortality effects, from which a cost-benefit ratio may be derived. The mortality changes are more dramatic and easier to measure, and they now receive primary attention because of concern about population growth. However, in programs such as those against malaria, schistosomiasis, hookworm, malnutrition, yaws, trachoma, leprosy, tuberculosis, filariasis, and onchocerciasis, the net economic impact of lowered morbidity —through potential increase in productivity—almost certainly outweighs the demographic impact of reduced mortality.

Is there any way of determining quantitatively the increased productivity required to outweigh the negative economic effect of population increase? So far no actual data have been gathered, but preliminary estimates have been made on the basis of econometric models. Mushkin has estimated (27) the probability of occurrence of a gain in gross national product as a result of eradication of disease. She assumed (i) that a disease, such as malaria, affected 80 percent of the population of an agricultural area, prevalence being uniform among adults and children and among men and women, and (ii) that disability and debility reduced the productivity of agricultural workers by 30 percent during a 3-month period when the disease was at its peak. The output loss would be 6 percent for the agricultural sector. If agriculture accounted for one-third of the total output, elimination of the productivity loss attributable to this specific disease would increase the gross national product by 1.0 percent.

If the disease exerted its debilitating effect for the whole year rather than for 3 months, as would be the case, for instance, for schistosomiasis, the increase in national output which would result from its elimination could be as great as 4.0 percent. (Measures for controlling schistosomiasis are, unfortunately, not yet as effective as those for controlling malaria.) Enterline and Stewart estimated (28) that an increase in life expectancy at birth from 30 to 32.5 years would require an increase of 0.8 percent in output per worker to maintain per capita income, a marginal capital-output ratio of 3 to 1 being assumed. Using this estimate Mushkin concluded that, where eradication of a disease increased life expectancy at birth in the country by 2.5 years, gains in output due to reductions in morbidity would exceed the 0.8 percent increased productivity required to maintain living levels.

The economic value of reductions in morbidity depends mainly on other considerations (29). Most important is the extent to which expanding economic opportunities put to use the increased productive capacity of workers. As already noted, the same programs which decrease mortality and morbidity often also make previously unusable material resources available. Where such a synergistic effect occurs, the economic benefit is usually great. In postwar Ceylon, for example, the opening up of fertile areas for cultivation, in combination with increases in manpower resulting from decreased morbidity more than balanced any negative effect of population increase (6).

According to classical economic theory, however, in agrarian societies such increased productivity and expanded labor force will not be readily absorbed because unemployment and underemployment are already at high levels. Recent work has all but demolished this dogma. It is currently estimated that disguised unemployment probably does not exceed 5 percent of the labor force (30). What is more, recent comprehensive surveys of Indian agriculture show no labor surplus (31). The small land holdings are the most productive, a major factor in output being maximum utilization of family labor. Most surprising was the inability to demonstrate seasonal unemployment; the work-year of farmers in several states ranged from 266 to 329 days per year. Even where seasonal underemployment does exist, special climatic conditions tend to cause diseases such as malaria to strike most severely during the planting and harvest seasons. Even though unemployment may be high during the rest of the year, a severe labor shortage may occur during these critical seasons. The reports of apparent labor surpluses in agrarian regions appear to be spurious, since idleness during slack seasons has little bearing on total annual productivity (32). In British Guiana it was the Sugar Producers Association, not the government, which started malaria control in the 1940's, because a seasonal shortage of labor meant that many estates were having to close down (25). The malaria program in this case increased the ratio of the *effective* labor force to the population. An even more clear-cut example comes from the impact of the 1918–19 influenza epidemic on Indian agriculture. A more isolated and intensive single episode that would hit only human resources can scarcely be imagined. Nine percent of the total labor force died. This was followed by a 3.8-percent decline in the acreage sown, a decline which would scarcely have occurred had there been in fact a labor surplus. Furthermore, the decline in acreage was clearly highest in provinces which had the highest death rates (33).

Another important consideration is the fact that a healthier population is more likely to include individuals capable of growth-contributing activities—in Leibenstein's terminology (34), "growth agents": the entrepreneur who originates new investment opportunities, the inventor of new production processes and techniques, the discoverer of new resources and commodities, the teacher of new skills, the learner of new skills, the disseminator of useful ideas, the saver. The factors which lead to attitudes favorable for the creation and spreading of knowledge, for accepting innovations, for acquiring new skills and for developing entrepreneurial perceptiveness are elusive and usually ignored in economics. Yet they are essential to the development process (35, 36). The required personal qualities are certainly multiple and probably have a synergistic action (37). Whatever the other conditions are, however, a minimum level of health must be essential. Galenson and Pyatt (38) of the International Labour Office analyzed some factors contributing to the quality of the labor force. Noting great variations among countries in the degree to which a given investment increased economic growth, they analyzed qualitative differences in the labor force. The relationships of four factors were measured: education, health, housing, and social security. Health, and more specifically per capita caloric consumption, proved to be the single factor most closely related to the observed differences in economic growth.

Innovative thinking is required in order to make use of labor to stimulate economic growth. Labor can be imaginatively used as an investment for social benefit rather than as a drag on progress. An example is seen in Ceylon (39), where social services, including health services, have for many years been at a higher level than in many other countries at comparable stages of development. Per capita income in Ceylon is approximately $150 per year; the gross national income increased each year by about 2.5 to 3 percent, essentially the same as the 2.8 percent annual increase in population. The level of unemployment and disguised unemployment has been seasonally high, especially in rural areas. Since 1948, the work potential of the healthy unemployed has been tapped by the Rural Development Department of the Ceylonese Government by means of the donation of labor and services for the common good, or "Shramadana" movement. Voluntary contributions of free labor have substantially helped community projects such as the construction of village roads, schools, textile centers, latrines, rural housing, and minor irrigation works. Particularly since 1960, the movement has systematically harnessed under-utilized manpower and has provided an inexpensive source of new capital formation. The psychological attitudes favorable to development which volunteer work promotes are an added benefit.

Influence of Population Growth on Socioeconomic Development

Economists generally have concluded that a moderate rate of population growth has been almost a precondition for development. Likewise, too rapid a rate of population growth is known to be damaging to the economy (40).

The well-known negative relationships between excessive increments in population and the various indices of development, ranging from percentage increase in per-capita gross national product through the ratios relating population to such items as schools, hospitals, and doctors, are so familiar as to require only the briefest mention. When the population denominator grows too rapidly, progress in all the social numerators falls behind. The great lack, which economists and social scientists can presumably do most to fill, is a scale indicating, for each social and economic situation, the threshhold beyond which favorable effects of population growth shift to increasingly negative influences, and progress is overwhelmed by people.

Potential Use of Health Services in Modifying Population Growth

Population control has become too critical an issue to wait for the chance operation of spontaneous, self-adjusting mechanisms. In the past, population size was responsive to the wide range of social forces shown in Fig. 1. Most of these self-correcting mechanisms were indirect and therefore acted only after a significant lag. As is so often true in biological and social phenomena, an excessive lag in response tended to lead to overcorrection and damaging cyclic fluctuations. In planned change, adjustments should be made early enough to prevent excessive cyclic shifts.

Population control can be made more effective through better understanding and planned use of relevant social forces. In the spontaneous and uncontrolled situation (Fig. 1), better health contributed more than any other factor to increasing population growth. The balance is completely different when the same development sectors are impressionistically charted according to their potential usefulness in population control (Fig. 2). Health now makes the maximum contribution. Let us con-

sider some of the reasons for this dramatic change in net effect.

Parents will not stop having babies until they have some assurance that children they already have will survive. Social and cultural norms are adjusted to produce the minimum replacement number of two children per family when allowance is made for the mortality patterns of past generations. Religious beliefs tend to reinforce such cultural norms. Hindu families expect to have at least one son survive longer than his parents, to assume important responsibilities pertaining to their funerals (41). In most agrarian societies security in old age depends on one's having surviving children, especially sons. Econometric models have shown the high number of births necessary to assure survivorship of sons either to age 65 (42) or until after the death of the father (43) under conditions of high infant and child mortality.

Fertility and infant mortality have always been highly correlated. Increasing evidence indicates that a lowered infant mortality must antedate lowered fertility (44). Parents will be encouraged to accept family planning if they are satisfied that health measures will provide the number of surviving children they want (45).

There is little prospect of fertility control being accepted where high mortality and morbidity make life so uncertain that the only faith in the future the individual can have is faith in an afterlife. Only as reduced mortality and morbidity provide some physical security can concepts such as planning, saving, or investing for the future have meaning, whether they are applied to one's own family or to the whole society. Improved levels of health encourage an orientation toward the future which is as essential for family planning as for planning other daily activities (46). The fatalism which slows the whole modernization process also delays acceptance of birth control. Mass disease-control programs have unique ability to provide rapid and dramatic demonstrations that change is possible and desirable. Spraying for mosquitoes rapidly reduces the prevalence of malaria. A few drops of an antibiotic in children's eyes promptly give tangible evidence that trachoma and conjunctivitis need not be part of growing up. The disfiguring lesions of yaws seem to melt away after injections of penicillin. Vaccinations convincingly prevent several dreaded diseases. Health programs can start the process of social education and increase people's willingness to take their destiny into their own hands, thus encouraging an orientation which is as necessary for control of fertility as for deciding to use a new type of seed, improving one's own house, or seeking to learn any new skill.

Many newly independent countries still associate a rapidly growing population with power and national prestige. Fertility control is then regarded as a device by which developed countries attempt to emasculate less-developed countries. The inevitability of demographic trends will eventually convince even the most nationalistic leaders. Until countries spontaneously ask for help with population control efforts, pressure from outside can only have a negative effect. Better statistics may, of course, accelerate such spontaneous recognition of the need for help.

For the individual, strong traditional associations continue between notions of adulthood, virility, proving one's worth in the world, and having many children. Marked geographic variations in readiness to accept family planning can often be related to intrinsic features of particular political traditions and cultural heritages. Where a combination of social and economic pressures has already led to some modernization of attitudes, the demand for control of fertility tends to be greater.

As pointed out by Taeuber (47), the dramatic decline in population growth in Japan can be attributed to appropriate preconditions. Fertility control programs in Taiwan and South Korea also developed within the context of a

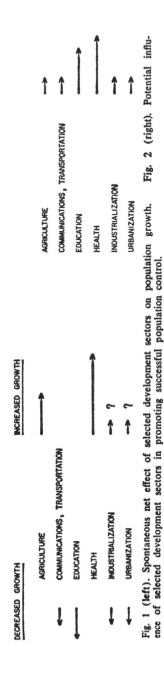

Fig. 1 (left). Spontaneous net effect of selected development sectors on population growth. Fig. 2 (right). Potential influence of selected development sectors in promoting successful population control.

fair degree of literacy, some urbanization, a higher-than-subsistence living standard, and political events which had shaken faith in traditional ways of life. Most important, the health services were relatively highly organized. Even in these countries, initial successes in family planning are reaching a plateau and further activities will have to be even more health-centered than has been the case in the past.

Where modernizing influences are weak, the strong cultural support for high fertility continues to prolong the demographic lag after general socioeconomic improvement and health measures have produced a significant decline in mortality. In these societies, the limited demand for birth control services comes from the women already burdened by a "too large" family, who can be found in any society. These women are nearing the end of their reproductive years and have already made more than an average contribution to population growth. They are ready to do anything to stop having children, and their future fertility probably would not be high even in the absence of birth control services. The deceptively rapid initial acceptance of contraceptives in any program is due to these women switching eagerly to any new method that is offered.

How can family planning be introduced where it is among the first modern-day influences in a traditional rural culture? Missionaries, when faced with a similar problem, often chose medical services as a means of gaining acceptance. The fact that curative services win almost immediate acceptance suggests that an activity which is as little understood by villagers as family planning will be most readily accepted if it is included in a larger health program. Various field trials support this view.

The Singur project is an example. In this small rural town north of Calcutta the teaching health center of the All India Institute of Hygiene and Public Health is located. A family-planning program was superimposed on a local health services program which had been running more or less successfully for 20 years. Continued contact over this period had progressively built confidence and rapport between the inhabitants and health personnel. Acceptance of innovation was cumulative. Even though the only methods presented were the rhythm method, coitus interruptus, and the use of foam tablets, the birth rate was lowered from 45 per 1000 population in 1956, before the study, to 37 per 1000 in 1961, while in the control areas the decrease was only to 43 per 1000 (48). The fact that this difference then disappeared, due to decline in the birth rate in the control villages, probably indicates that the long-term effect on birth rate of the general health program was equal to that of the intensive family-planning program.

The experience of a family-planning pilot project in rural Ceylon was similar. The program was built around Family Welfare Centers where prenatal, postnatal, and child welfare clinics had been operating for many years. Practically all pregnant women attended the prenatal clinic, which provided an opportunity for preliminary discussion of family planning. Supplies and further information were given at the postnatal clinic. The birth rate dropped from 31 per 1000 in 1959 to 20.4 per 1000 in 1964 (49). Because the most notable decline in age-specific rates was among women between the ages of 25 and 35, it is probable that the lowered rate resulted directly from the project. The methods presented were diaphragm, foam tablets, rhythm, and condom.

In contrast to these two studies, the Khanna Study in the Punjab, India (50), is an example of an attempt to introduce family planning without the preexisting base of a well-established general health program. A large staff made a real effort to gain the confidence of village people. The contraceptive method presented was use of foam tablets. There was much verbal acceptance, and the results at first were encouraging, with up to 40 percent of the eligible wives accepting contraception. Yet after 2½ years of sustained effort, only 17 percent of the couples were actually using the tablets. Whether because effective use of contraception was minimal or because the women using the method were only substituting foam tablets for methods previously used, there was no effect on the birth rate.

Other examples could be cited to show that with the relatively inefficient traditional contraceptive methods, which require a high level of continuing motivation, birth control has a better chance of acceptance when it is part of a general health program which people trust. We make this statement despite recognition of the fact that, once utilization is established, use of such methods as foam tablets and condoms does not require medical examination or supervision and the needed materials can be sold through regular marketing channels.

With development of the oral pill and the intrauterine device (IUD), methods have become available which promise to reduce the birth rate more rapidly. The IUD is particularly promising for mass use because it does not require repetitive use. These pills and devices cannot be obtained through regular commercial channels and require at least minimum medical services. The intrauterine devices have to be inserted by a physician or perhaps by a trained nurse or midwife, and the pill should be taken under medical supervision. Thus, the doctor, nurse, or midwife who can gain the people's confidence by helping in moments of physical need can also talk with them about preventing pregnancies and can personally provide the service. The major limitation on wide acceptance of IUD's is the fact that the small fraction of women who have complications tend to talk more than the women who don't; this negative publicity can be countered only through adequate follow-up and care.

Basic health services will probably continue to be important in family planning because the several most promising new contraceptive methods being studied in research laboratories also will require at least minimum medical supervision. Further research on hormones offers hope because controlled interference with the sequence of hormones required for the reproductive process offers multiple possibilities. Estrogen antagonists may interfere with normal passage of the zygote or with priming of the endometrium. Compounds which interfere with progestational changes may lead to methods which are effective until about the time of the first missed menstruation, when motivation to avoid pregnancy is probably particularly high. Research in immunology is directed toward inactivation of gonadotrophins and active immunization with sperm or testicular antigens (51). Such methods will probably require continuing medical supervision, which may have to be even more sophisticated than that now required for the pill and the IUD.

Health education has a unique role as a vehicle for family-planning information and can be directed at important target segments of the population. For female methods of contraception, women in the reproductive ages are the obvious target group. Especially where birth rates are high, the great majority of women are either pregnant, in the postpartum period, or the mothers of young children. Women before, during, or after pregnancy constitute the largest single group visiting local health units (52). As they come seeking medical care, they are a willingly captive family-centered audience. The high cultural value placed on children in their society can be turned into an asset for fertility control. Child-spacing can be presented as part of a comprehensive child health program. This process should begin during pregnancy and continue up to the postpartum period, when contraception can be started.

Proof that spaced children are healthier children can be based on simple demonstrations from their own and their neighbors' experiences. To make this type of approach applicable on a national scale, more research is needed to determine what minimum level of maternal and child care will have the greatest impact in promoting acceptance of birth control.

In male-dominated societies men must also be reached. In many countries family planning can be included in the army's program of health education, as is being done in Turkey (53). Most countries have workers' insurance programs through which the labor force can be reached. In Chile, the employees' medical insurance program includes contraceptive services for the stated purpose of preventing induced abortions (54).

Lastly, if fertility control is to become an accepted social ideal in balance with death control, the subject must be discussed in schools. Appropriate health education must be introduced at this crucial level.

The various social and economic aspects of life can scarcely be separated. While a minimum health level in the community and minimum medical services are probably necessary preconditions for acceptance of present methods of family planning, the most successful programs are likely to include advances on many fronts. Research is needed to delineate which advances are most necessary, together with more projects of the type developed in Comilla, East Pakistan (55). With community development as a point of departure, the concept of family planning is introduced to women as one of many modernizing influences—along with instruction in reading and writing, home sanitation, child and maternity care, gardening, and the prevention of accidents. Local indigenous practitioners and midwives distribute foam tablets and condoms. Such measures will help us learn the balance between health care and general development activities which is appropriate to specific types of communities and likely to produce a favorable response to fertility-control efforts.

Summary

Health as a basic human value is particularly important to people in the developing world. Rates of economic development lower than had been hoped for and ever more steeply rising population growth have precipitated a reaction against public health programs. Among economists, agriculturalists, and even health professionals the philosophy arose that one should "hold back" on using modern weapons against disease because they are "too effective." To satisfy the recognized popular demand, simple and relatively ineffective measures of curative medicine could be substituted. It was said that the emphasis should be, instead, on agriculture, community development, education, and industrialization and that family planning should be pushed as a separate program. Documentation presented here sharply challenges such a point of view. No segment of the total development process can be effective without the other sectors.

Among the major activities essential to socioeconomic development, the large-scale, effective, and relatively cheap public health programs have contributed and can continue to contribute substantially to human resources. Dramatic thrusts of economic development have occurred when the amount of land available for cultivation or the size of the labor force has been sharply increased by removal of a health bottleneck through a program such as malaria eradication. Even where there is seasonal underemployment, improvements in health and other social and economic changes can be synergistic, so that increased human resources and opportunities for employing these resources can develop together. Successful health programs tend to produce qualitative improvements in general attitudes, such as recognition that change is possible, and the innovative thinking and action that cannot be expected of the sick and debilitated. Such attitudes tend to generate the conditions necessary for economic growth. In many instances, these positive effects of health programs on development have outweighed the much-publicized negative influence of population increase.

Population growth results from the whole complex of modernizing influences. In the past it was caused more by general economic development than by health services. The great advantage of modern health programs is the fact that demographic effects are becoming direct, selective, and measurable rather than being secondary, uncontrollable, and cyclic.

Increasing evidence shows that health service may be indispensable for reducing population growth. A minimum level of health seems to be necessary for acceptance of the idea and practice of limiting or spacing births. Parents need assurance that children already born will have a reasonable chance for survival. In addition, readily accessible minimum health facilities are probably essential for providing modern contraceptive information and materials.

Maintenance of health activities at a high level in developing countries should not be justified only on humanitarian grounds. Sound demographic, economic, and scientific evidence indicates that health programs promote economic development and directly stimulate the demand for, and practice of, family planning.

References

1. J. Broadhurst and M. Lerrigo, *Health Horizons* (Silver Burdett, New York, 1931), pp. 147, 499; L. Dublin and A. Lotka, *Twenty-Five Years of Health Progress* (Metropolitan Life Insurance Company, New York, 1937), p. 3.
2. T. McKeown and R. Brown, *Population Studies* 9, 119 (1955); T. McKeown and R. Record, *ibid.* 16, 94 (1962).
3. J. Gordon, S. Singh, J. Wyon, *Indian J. Med. Res.* 51, 304 (1963).
4. J. Spence, W. Walton, F. Miller, S. Court, *A Thousand Families in Newcastle upon Tyne* (Oxford Univ. Press, New York, 1954), p. 168.
5. P. Newman, *Malaria Eradication and Population Growth* (Braun-Brumfield, Ann Arbor, 1965).
6. H. Frederiksen, *Indian J. Malariol.* 16, 379 (1962).
7. G. Winfield, *China: The Land and the People* (Sloane, New York, 1948), pp. 343–359; C. Clark, *Intern. Labour Rev.* 68, 1 (1953); W. Paddock and P. Paddock, *Hungry Nations* (Little, Brown, Boston, 1964), pp. 128—139.
8. H. Habakkuk, *Econ. Hist. Rev.* 6, 117 (1953).
9. J. Ridley, in *Public Health and Population Change*, M. Sheps and J. Ridley, Eds. (Univ. of Pittsburgh Press, Pittsburgh, 1965), pp. 143–173.
10. R. Scragg, *Depopulation in New Ireland, A Study of Demography and Fertility* (Administration of Papua and New Guinea, Port Moresby, Papua, 1957), p. 115.
11. R. Indra, in *Proc. U.N. World Population Conf. 1st* (1954), pp. 889, 900; "Pakistan: The Medical Social Research Project at Lulliani," *Studies in Family Planning No. 4* (1964), pp. 5—9.
12. J. Stycos, *Milbank Mem. Fund Quart.* 43, 299 (1965); C. E. Taylor, *Foreign Affairs* 43, 475 (1965).
13. M. Kamat and R. G. Kamat, in *Proc. Intern. Conf. Planned Parenthood, 6th* (International Planned Parenthood Federation, London, England, 1959); United Nations and Government of India, "The Mysore Population Study," *U.N. Pub. ST/SOA Ser. A34* (1961), p. 124.
14. S. Chennatamby, *J. Reprod. Fertility* 3, 342 (1962).
15. J. Alers, *J. Inter-Amer. Studies* 7, 423 (1965).
16. R. A. Henin, *Develop. Digest* 3, 6 (1966).
17. D. Heer, *Demography* 3 (1967); C. E. Taylor, in *Population Dynamics*, M. Muramatsu and P. Harper, Eds. (Johns Hopkins Press, Baltimore, 1965), p. 55.
18. R. Potter, M. New, J. Wyon, J. Gordon, in *Public Health and Population Change*, M. Sheps and J. Ridley, Eds. (Univ. of Pittsburgh Press, Pittsburgh, 1965), pp. 377–399.
19. K. Mathen, in *Research in Family Planning*, C. V. Kiser, Ed. (Princeton Univ. Press, Princeton, N.J., 1962), pp. 33–49.
20. J. Stycos, *Population Studies* 16, 257 (1963).
21. J. Gordon, *Amer. J. Med. Sci.* 235, 337 (1958); S. Mushkin, *J. Polit. Econ.* 70, Suppl., 129 (1962); H. Singer, *Intern. Develop. Rev.* 7, 3 (1965).
22. C. E. Taylor, *Foreign Affairs* 43, 475 (1965).
23. H. Frederiksen, *Public Health Rep.* 75, 865 (1960).
24. J. Logan, *The Sardinian Project* (Johns Hopkins Press, Baltimore, 1953), pp. vii–xi.
25. P. Ruderman, in "Economic Benefits from Public Health Services," *Public Health Serv. Pub. No. 1178* (1964), p. 16.
26. C. Winslow, *The Cost of Sickness and the Price of Health* (World Health Organization, Geneva, 1951).
27. S. Mushkin, *Intern. Develop. Rev.* 6, 10 (1964).
28. P. Enterline and W. Stewart, "Health improvements, worker productivity and levels of living in rapidly growing countries," paper presented before the AAAS, 1960.
29. R. Fein, in *Proceedings of the Conference on the Economics of Health and Medical Care* (Univ. of Michigan, Ann Arbor, 1962), pp. 271–85.
30. C. Kao, K. Anschel, C. Eicher, in *Agriculture in Economic Development*, C. Eicher and L. Witt, Eds. (McGraw-Hill, New York, 1964).

31. M. Paglin, *Amer. Econ. Rev.* **55**, 815 (1965).
32. B. Kenadjian, *Z. Nationalokonomie* **21**, 216 (1961).
33. T. Schultz, *Transforming Traditional Agriculture* (Yale Univ. Press, New Haven, 1964).
34. H. Leibenstein, *Economic Backwardness and Economic Growth* (Wiley, New York, 1957), pp. 113–243.
35. H. Keenleyside, *Dynamics of Development* (Praeger, New York, 1964), pp. 1–87.
36. D. McClelland, *The Achieving Society* (Van Nostrand, Princeton, N.J., 1961), pp. 391–438; ———, *Econ. Develop. Cultural Change* **14**, 257 (1966).
37. G. Myrdal, *World Health Organ. Chron.* **6**, 203 (1952); B. Weisbrod, *Ann. Amer. Acad. Polit. Soc. Sci.* **337**, 137 (1961).
38. W. Galenson and G. Pyatt, *The Quality of Labour and Economic Development in Certain Countries* (International Labour Office, Geneva, 1964), pp. 5–23.
39. C. de Fonseka, *Intern. Develop. Rev.* **7**, 14 (1965).
40. J. Spengler, *Amer. Econ. Rev.* **41**, 344 (1951); *ibid.* **56**, 1 (1966).
41. "Observations on Factors Related to Family Planning in West Bengal," *Family Planning Commun. Res. Conf. Mem. No. 12*, pp. 1–11; C. E. Taylor, *Atlantic Monthly* **190**, 51 (1952); ———, J. Wyon, J. Gordon, *Milbank Mem. Fund Quart.* **36**, 107 (1958).
42. D. Heer, "Births necessary to assure desired survivorship of sons under differing mortality conditions," paper presented before the Population Association of America, New York, 1966.
43. G. Immerwahr, "Survivorship of sons under conditions of improving mortality," paper presented before the Population Association of America, Cincinnati, 1967.
44. D. Heer, *Demography* **3**, 423 (1966); H. Frederiksen, *Econ. Develop. Cultural Change* **16**, 316 (1966); S. Hassan, "Influence of child mortality on fertility," paper presented before the Population Association of America, New York, 1966.
45. C. E. Taylor, *Foreign Affairs* **43**, 475 (1965); H. Frederiksen, *Public Health Rep.* **81**, 715 (1966).
46. R. Hill, J. Stycos, K. Back, *The Family and Population Control, A Puerto Rican Experiment in Social Change* (Univ. of North Carolina Press, Chapel Hill, 1959), p. 225; L. Rainwater, *And the Poor Get Children* (Quadrangle Books, Chicago, 1960); T. Herlihy, *Amer. J. Public Health* **53**, 1770 (1963).
47. I. Taeuber, in *The Population Crisis and the Use of World Resources*, S. Mudd, Ed. (Indiana Univ. Press, Bloomington, 1964), pp. 188–196.
48. "India: The Singur Study," *Studies in Family Planning No. 1* (Population Council, New York) (1963), pp. 1–4.
49. "Ceylon: The Sweden-Ceylon Family Planning Pilot Project," *Studies in Family Planning No. 2* (1963), pp. 9–12; A. Kinch, in *Family Planning and Population Programs*, B. Berelson, Ed. (Univ. of Chicago Press, Chicago, 1966), p. 109.
50. J. Wyon and J. Gordon, in *Research in Family Planning*, C. Kiser, Ed. (Princeton Univ. Press, Princeton, N.J., 1962), pp. 17–32.
51. S. Segal, in *Advances in Planned Parenthood*, A. Sobrero and S. Lewit, Eds. (Schenkman, Cambridge, Mass., 1965), pp. 29–37.
52. G. Leiby, *Amer. J. Public Health* **54**, 1207 (1964).
53. T. Metiner, in *Family Planning and Population Programs*, B. Berelson, Ed. (Univ. of Chicago Press, Chicago, 1966), p. 137.
54. W. Bustamente, "Breve Resena de lo que es la 'Planificacion Familiar'," *Pub. Employees Med. Serv. Santiago, Chile* (1963).
55. "Pakistan: The Rural Pilot Family Planning Action Programme at Comilla," *Studies in Family Planning No. 3* (1964), pp. 9, 10.

241

The Inexorable Problem of Space

Paul B. Sears

Dr. Sears, retiring president of the AAAS, is chairman of the Conservation Program at Yale University, New Haven, Conn. This article is based on his AAAS presidential address, which was given 28 December 1957, during the Indianapolis meeting.

Discovery and communication are the two prime obligations of the scientist. On occasions such as this, however, the scientist has the added opportunity to examine broad issues in the light of his peculiar knowledge and experience. This I propose to do with respect to that limited segment of space in which we live, move, and have our being. For my subject was chosen long before man's most recent and dramatic invasion of outer space.

Science and Perspective

My thesis is that, among the practical problems of humanity today, our relation to immediate space is of critical importance. In developing this idea, I shall try to show that our applications of science have been both restricted and shortsighted. In terms of moral choice, we have looked upon science as an expedient rather than as a source of enlightenment.

To be specific, our very proper concern with the applications of mathematics, physics, and chemistry may be clouding the fact that we need biology in general and ecology in particular to illuminate man's relation to his environment. At present the biological sciences are largely sustained as utilities in medicine and agriculture, the social sciences for dealing with immediate ills. But we must not forget that all science is needed to guide the process of future evolution —cultural and physical—now so largely in our own hands. The nest of anti-intellectualism is being warmed by the ignorant, but some of the eggs in it may have been placed there by those who should know better.

Science and Policy

I have no quarrel with the exploration of outer space. It is a legitimate and challenging subject for scientific inquiry and bold experiment. Our optical and mathematical studies of it have long since given us that basic confidence in order without which there could be no science. But, as we extend our astronomy by whatever celestial acrobatics we can get away with, I should like to see some consideration given to relative values. We have a vast amount of unfinished business at our feet. The golden moment for the pickpocket comes when everyone at the county fair is craning his neck at the balloon ascension.

So far as the skies are concerned, we are feeling the natural soreness that comes from losing a sporting event we thought was in the bag. Actually, if my information is correct, the Russians had explained that they intended to launch a satellite, had indicated its probable size, and have promised to share the knowledge so gained. Since any ray of light should be welcomed in an atmosphere of gloom, it may help to recall that our Olympic athletes, in the face of leading questions from their interviewers, had nothing but respect to offer for the conduct of their Russian rivals.

Of course our present concern is much more than simple chagrin at losing a contest. What has happened in outer

Science, January, 1958, Vol.127, No.3288, pp. 9-16.

242

space raises a question about how outer space will be allocated and controlled. We fear, not unreasonably, that whoever controls the space around the earth can impose his will upon all who live on the earth's surface.

Though we grant freely the military significance of space experiments, our present hysteria seems to me to indicate an even deeper source of insecurity. We are beginning to sense that the elaborate technology to which we are so thoroughly committed makes us peculiarly vulnerable. And we are not wholly confident that the ideals of our civilization —so reasonable to us—will really stand up to free competition with other systems of thought. To the extent that this is true, we suffer from an initial handicap of morale.

The pattern of conflict is much the same, regardless of scale. Whether one is watching small boys in the school yard or great powers in the world arena, the preliminaries are marked by bad manners and vituperation on both sides. Missiles are piled up and seconds are assembled, the advantage going to the cooler, less hysterical side. The contestant who gets rattled is asking for trouble.

I do not envy our public servants charged with the delicate business of managing international relations. But I am firmly convinced that unless one is determined on war, there is merit in self-restraint and good manners, as well as in prudent measures of self-protection. I am also convinced that the choice of policy is not limited to boasting and belligerence on the one hand or craven appeasement on the other. We have no monopoly on self-respect and other human virtues, nor is there any merit in debasing the original meaning of the word *compromise* as we have done. We should deplore every display, whether by statesman or journalist, of dunghill courage that lessens the hope of mutual understanding, good-will, and ultimate collaboration among human beings.

So far as purely domestic problems go, our almost hypnotic concern with outer space comes at a bad time. Outer space is one more item that diverts attention and energy from the prosaic business of setting our terrestrial space in order. And it has fostered an incredible type of escapism that must be experienced to be believed. One hears too frequently for comfort the sober assertion that we need not worry about depletion of natural resources, now that interplanetary travel is just around the corner! If such a comment came from jesters or cranks, it could be disregarded. But we hear it uttered with the solemnity and assurance of the true believer. No doubt we shall continue to hear it, despite the chilling analysis by Arthur Clarke, the British astronomer, in the November 1957 issue of *Harper's* magazine.

Actually this obsession is not a detached phenomenon. Rather it is the culmination of a new faith—the belief that technology will solve any problems that may confront humanity. Curiously, it comes at a time when the scientist is more suspect than he has been since the days of witchcraft and alchemy, as recent opinion studies show. A high proportion of people consider scientists to be queer fish, if not inhuman and immoral. For a parallel we would have to think of a religion which wants the favor of its gods but does not trust them for a moment.

Opportunistic Application of Science

I do not question the tremendous accomplishments and future possibilities of technology. I yield to no one in my admiration for the cleverness, manual and intellectual, of those who apply science to meet the needs of mankind. But faith in technology is not faith in science or sympathy with the creative impulse of the scientist. The direction in which science is applied depends upon the values of the culture applying it even while science is in turn modifying the culture.

Our present applications of science are selective and opportunistic, neither wholehearted nor balanced. We are applying it out of all proportion to the elaboration of consumer goods, often to such an extent that vast sums must go into persuading people to desire what they have not instinctively wanted. The making of things has become so facile that their sale creates major problems in advertising and credit. As Max Beerbohm once put it, "Buy advertised goods and help pay the cost of advertising." Some of the keenest satire on advertising has come from advertising men themselves. Raymond Loewy, the famous automobile designer, has protested the corruption in car design that has resulted from too great facility—traditionally the death of any sound art. The current models waste space, materials, and fuel, violate good taste, and impose needless economic burdens on the public. And while we are applying science in this manner, we are blandly ignoring its highest function, which is to give us perspective and inform us about what we are doing to ourselves. Even the scientist, as Kubie has so ably shown, suffers from his lack of self-analysis.

On the whole, a man's actions are a response to his idea of the kind of world he thinks he is living in and to his concept of his own nature. That this is true is shown very practically in the history of human thought: No great religion is content merely to lay down maxims of conduct; it also develops its own cosmogony, its own pattern of the universe, to justify those maxims.

Our present attitude toward terrestrial space exemplifies with peculiar clarity our selective use of science. For living space, if we consider both its extent and quality, subsumes all other resources, being in that respect equivalent to the economist's technical concept of land. Yet the power of applied science has been overwhelmingly employed to exploit space, while those aspects of science which could illuminate its wise and lasting use are still largely ignored.

I am assuming at the outset that the human adventure on this planet is worth our best efforts to keep it going as long as possible. I am also assuming that man is capable of responsible judgment and conduct and that he has at hand much of the important basic information he needs. Finally, I am assuming that it is not enough for man to live by bread alone but that intangible, as well as tangible values are necessary to justify his persistence. If this be true, the question is, not how many people can exist on earth, but what kind of a life will be possible for those who do.

Limiting Factors

From New Jersey to Oregon one sees great egg factories, where highly selected strains of poultry are confined at maximum density and with maximum efficiency. Every need—nutritive, environmental, and psychological—is taken care of. These gentle, stupid birds have no responsibility but to stay alive and do their stuff. Yet they are at the mercy of any break in an elaborate technological mesh that keeps them going. And should a stranger burst abruptly into their quarters, the ensuing panic would pile them up in smothering heaps in the far corners of their ultramodern apartment. The underprivileged, pretechnological hen ran many hazards, but at least she had the freedom to scratch around for food and a sporting chance to dodge under a bush to evade the swooping hawk.

People, of course, are not poultry, but they are living organisms, subject to the limitations inherent in that condition. I am unmoved by any protest against applying biological analogies to human society. Analogy is one of the most powerful tools of the scientist. From physics to physiology, and notably in the latter, analogies suggest our models which we must then test and either accept or reject as the evidence may dictate. And besides, man is a living organism, as I have said.

Fortunately, in considering man's relation to terrestrial space, our models do not all come from observing other forms of life. We have some impressive ones furnished by our own species. Let us reserve them, however, for the present, and look at the other living things. Here from students of bacteria, trees, insects, or any of the sundry groups of vertebrate animals—fish, fowl, or mammal—we get the same story. No known form of life has been observed to multiply indefinitely without bumping up against the limitations imposed by the space it occupies. These limitations involve not only quantity but quality. And quality rests upon the pattern of that complex of factors, whether known or unknown, that are necessary to sustain the species in question. So far as environment is concerned, an ancient bit of wisdom sums up the situation: "A chain is no stronger than its weakest link."

This principle was recognized by Liebig in his famous law of the minimum: the growth of a crop is determined by the essential nutrient available in least quantity. It was restated more precisely by Blackman in his law of limiting factors: physiological processes are limited by the least favorable factor in the system of essential conditions. These statements rest upon controlled experiment. They are independent of the circum-

stance that an English political economist and parson, Malthus by name, had suggested that human populations did not, in fact, increase indefinitely beyond certain limitations of environment.

It should be emphasized, however, that the writings of Malthus did give the necessary clue that enabled Charles Darwin to formulate a reasonable explanation of the mechanism involved in the origin of species. Since there remain many misconceptions with regard to both Malthus and Darwin, it may be well to review the thesis of the latter. This thesis has never been successfully controverted, although there are perennial headlines "Darwin Refuted" whenever some detail of his work is brought into question. Briefly, Darwin had noted the universal tendency of organisms to vary and to transmit these variations to their offspring. Our knowledge with respect to these matters is now being applied daily by plant and animal breeders with the same effectiveness with which the phase rule is used in chemical engineering.

Darwin's second point was that organisms tend to reproduce far beyond their capacity to survive. This again in fact occurs, and is a matter of household knowledge among those who, as scientists, observe living organisms. The tagging of fish that return to the place where they began migration reveals that, despite the thousands of eggs laid by each female, not more than a few adults from each batch survive to make the return journey.

Anyone who has observed, year after year, the nesting of robins in his yard has noted the consistent toll—from cats, jays, crows, and accidents—that serves to keep numbers down. And though the clutch of eggs is fairly uniform from year to year—implying a potential doubling of the robin population—the number of nests does not increase significantly, nor do these birds spread beyond a well-defined territorial range. Even though predators might fail to control their numbers, competition within the species would establish a threshold of limitation, as it did for deer when wolves were eliminated.

The final point made by Darwin was that the relatively small proportion of individuals surviving did so, not merely by random chance, but largely because they were those best fitted to cope with their environment. The less favorably endowed tended to be eliminated. Thus the better adapted lived to transmit their favorable variations. In this way he accounted for two great riddles of living nature—the immense variety of living things and the remarkable adjustments they show.

It is not my object here to justify Darwinian theory. It is enough to say that the theory coordinates more information than any alternative that has been proposed. This is all we have a right to ask in science. We need emphasize only one corollary—that the pattern of environment is built solidly into that of life. Survival rests upon this relationship. No organism known to biologists has ever, so to speak, had things completely its own way. Some, of course, are more "successful" than others, as the late L. O. Howard indicated in his famous dictum that the last survivor on earth would be a living insect on a dead weed.

Extension to Man

The rub comes when we attempt to extend these principles to our own species. As life has advanced from simple beginnings, it has played an increasing role in geological processes. Man is no exception. He is a world-wide dominant, the first such species in earth history. And through advancing technology he is producing tremendous changes. That this should confer a sense of power is understandable. But power is not the same thing as control. Only when power is balanced by responsibility is there control, as the record of our highway accidents attests. The corrupting effect of irresponsible power is an axiom in human history.

Is there any reason to believe that man is exempt from the rules that apply to living organisms in general? Or does the difference lie in his ability to learn those rules and profit by respecting them? Can we make use of known physical and biological principles in discussing problems that involve man? Can we view psychological and sociological considerations in the light of simpler and more obvious ones, or must we rely solely upon a higher level of discourse when we speak of man? These are not idle questions. I have mentioned the indignant protests against applying "biological analogies" to sociological problems. But it is one thing to hold that man is *merely* a physicochemical system, or *merely* an animal, and quite another to insist, as I must, that he is a physical phenomenon, and a biological one too, whatever else he may be.

Man's physical body occupies space, somewhere between two and four cubic feet of it. At his present rate of increase in the United States, he is set to double the aggregate volume occupied by human bodies in about 41 years. Continuing at this rate, it would be less than 700 years—say 22 generations—until there is standing room only, with each space of 3 by 2 feet, or 6 square feet, occupied. On this basis there is room for exactly 4,646,400 people in each square mile. I have perhaps been overgenerous in estimating the per capita area, but I did wish to leave space enough to permit each individual to reach in his pocket for the rent money when it falls due. A little after this the hypothetical human population would weigh more than the planet.

In thus giving rein to imagination I have in mind sundry pronouncements regarding the potential capacity of the earth, some of them to the effect that by proper scientific management it can take care of any conceivable increase in population. The numbers I have mentioned are both conceivable and begettable. The question is, are they supportable?

Some Examples

The most densely populated continent is Europe, with 142 people per square mile, as against Asia with 78, although the most densely populated areas are as yet on that continent. Australia follows with 31, then North America, including great areas of desert and tundra, with 23, while Africa and South America are nearly tied, with 17 and 16, respectively. The figure for the United States is 51, intermediate between that of Australia and Asia. Evidently cold fact, as so often happens, has not kept pace with theory. Either people do not breed as fast as they might, or survival rates are not what they could be. Actually both of these things happen, and in curious combinations. We may, I think, allow the battered bones of the Reverend Malthus to rest in peace as we examine a few case histories quite briefly.

First, however, let us retrace our steps for a glimpse at what we pleasantly call the lower orders of life. Abstracting an item from the valuable studies of Thomas Park, we learn that when populations of flour beetles reach certain densities, their rates of increase drop sharply. Among other things, these animals begin to eat their own eggs and pupae, a very effective way of slowing down the operation of the compound interest law. Whether this practice is due to a craving for food and water or simply to the fact that hungry beetles bump into eggs oftener than before, we do not know.

The lemmings in Alaska are likewise instructive. These small rodents, living and breeding under the snow, have a kind of pulsating population record, abundance alternating with low density in fairly regular fashion. With summer melting, they are preyed upon by a variety of animals, including the Arctic fox and snowy owl. A third predator, the jaeger, a kind of sea hawk somewhat resembling a gull, has been studied by Frank Pitelka, who reported on it at the Berkeley meeting of the AAAS. When the lemming population is low or average, the jaegers space their nests and consume their prey in an orderly manner. But when the lemmings are at a peak, so that food should be no problem, the jaegers spend so much energy quarreling over nesting space and food that relatively few of them raise normal broods. So their numbers decline, but not primarily from lack of food. They do not urbanize well—or shall we say that when they attempt to urbanize they pay the usual penalty of a greatly lowered reproductive efficiency? For it is, I believe, an open secret that few cities of major size have heretofore maintained their population by their own birth rate—a situation that is probably changing through the rapid development of suburban life. Perhaps it is time for some modern Aesop to instruct us on manners and morals, using for that purpose the verified behavior of animals instead of their imagined words. Certainly we learn that for the jaegers plenty is not an inevitable road to biological success.

Yet the idea of plenty—in food in particular, in energy and minerals to a lesser degree—dominates the discussion by scientists of man's future. Some of this material is excellent, notably that by Harrison Brown, who not only understands the physical sciences but has biological sense and a conscience to boot. Too few, however, bother to read the fine print and observe the *if*'s in such analyses as his. Those who, like Osborn, Cook, Sax, and Vogt, concern themselves with space and numbers are written off as "pessimists," as though the fixing of a label adjudicates the issue and solves the problem.

It is the merit of the men named, including Brown, that they have raised not only a material but a moral issue that is too often neglected by those who proudly label themselves "optimists." The question is not only how much but what kind of life will be possible if humanity continues to hurtle along its present course. Russell, the Huxleys, and Berrill have all warned us of the inevitable loss of freedom and personal dignity that must follow the multiplication of numbers and the depletion of resources.

Physical Limitations and Cultural Influences

The findings of archeology are in agreement with recorded observations of prefarming cultures about the space requirements of hunters, fishers, and gatherers. For such folk the space requirements are great, by modern standards, being no less than three to five square miles per person where conditions are most favorable. The best estimates for pre-Columbian United States, even with such agriculture as it possessed, do not reach three million in about the same number of square miles. Specifically, the state of Ohio, some 40,000 square miles, mostly fertile and well-watered, does not appear to have supported more than about 15,000 Indians at the time of European discovery. Even the Basin of Mexico, with a highly efficient system of horticulture and an im-

posing array of domesticated plants, did not have numbers exceeding a million— one-third the population of the present Mexico City, which occupies only a fraction of the modern basin.

Yet we know that this rather moderately concentrated population experienced pressures of various kinds during the centuries preceding 1519. However the situation might be rationalized, the limitations of space, with regard to both extent and quality, were stern and tangible within the Basin of Mexico. The ancient chronicles are a record of floods, drouths, volcanism, and hunger. Toward the end of the Aztec Empire, in a desperate attempt to placate the angry gods, human sacrifice was stepped up until it reached scores of thousands—suggesting the rate of emigration that today serves to stabilize the population of Ireland, whose chief export is people.

Our judgment of the whole history of agriculture has been revamped since the 1930's. Dale and Carter have done this brilliantly, showing that every great center of power and civilization has been based squarely upon fertile space, and tracing the parallel decline of culture and the nutrient capacity of the soil.

Certainly human communities have, as a matter of record, more than once run hard into the physical limitations of their environment. Often they have intensified these limitations by their own activities. That man can preserve and even enhance the potential of his environment, I do not question. But I see no warrant for asserting that he has often done it or can do so indefinitely under his present pattern of behavior.

Limiting factors are not necessarily physical in the strict sense. Cultural disruption and spiritual discouragement may likewise act as restraints. This is believed to explain the well-known decrease of the native Indian population during the century following the Spanish conquest of Mexico. With little to live for, people may simply not have families, whatever the physiological facts and urges may be. Another instance is that of the slave population in Jamaica prior to 1842. The white population, numbering less than one-tenth that of the slaves, vigorously discouraged breeding among the slaves, since it was cheaper to buy new slaves than to propagate them. Nevertheless, the apathy toward life, attested by the high suicide rate among victims of the slave trade, is believed by competent authority to have been an important factor in the low effective reproduction rate among these pathetic humans.

If we come closer home, we have the significant drop in family size during our own depression of the 1930's. In this instance, the slow-down cannot be attributed to pressure from the physical environment, for the depression preceded the great drouth. Even then there was no real scarcity of food, merely a breakdown in the mechanism for its economic distribution. Presumably the direct pressure came from cultural anxiety, or what is sometimes called "social shock." Even the "recession" of 1949–50 produced a measurable effect, total births in 1950 numbering 17,000 less than in 1949.

We have, too, the earlier decrease in the British birthrate about 1921. This was the year in which Marie Stopes, already famous as a paleobotanist, enlightened the public on responsible parenthood. It was also a time of high postwar prices, and subsequently a time of flaming individualism. But it was not, so far as I know, a period of physical pressure from environmental forces. Having myself reared a family during the 20's and 30's, I can testify that in our own country there were many cultural pressures, neither physical nor economic, that encouraged one-child or at most two-child families. Not least among these

pressures was increasing focus upon the personality and development of the individual child, at times to the point of morbid sentimentality.

Cultural influences can also act in the opposite direction, the classical instance being in the scriptural injunction to be fruitful and multiply and replenish the earth. Today, despite the staggering cost of education and the increasing cost of food—unchecked by our continuing agricultural surplus—the four-child family is in vogue. Incredible though it may sound, it is through the influence of fashion (call it example or prevailing custom if you prefer) that many modern families work out their response to the problem of population and space.

Certainly the record suggests that population density is influenced both by the physical and the cultural environment. However these may operate, either singly or in conjunction, they find expression in the behavior of individuals, and individuals differ greatly. Indeed, one of the most difficult of problems is to sort out the strands—cultural, physiological, intuitive, and rational—that are interwoven into the fabric of individual values and conduct. As Russell has pointed out, and as those who style themselves "human engineers" know only too well, the new psychology has little comfort to offer about the importance of reason in human conduct. This would be especially true among those least capable of using it, yet I, for one, would not give up what confidence we have in it.

Coming now more specifically to the problem of space, we find that the grim facts in certain countries which we euphemistically call "underdeveloped" speak for themselves, as anyone who has visited the Orient, the West Indies, or certain portions of Latin America must honestly admit. Humane and successful efforts to improve health conditions in such areas have, to date, merely intensified the problem, while equally high-minded efforts to improve food production and distribution have only deferred a solution. Ceylon, where disease control has resulted in doubling the population in less than a score of years, is a classical example. Meanwhile, food production has not kept pace, and the usable area of the island has been increased only very slightly through drainage of malarial swamps.

Technological Vulnerability

Perhaps the one bright spot in this gloomy picture is that many of the leaders in these crowded countries are now frankly recognizing the problem and trying, according to their various lights, to face it. But while I would not suggest for a moment that we allow them to stew in their own juice, I do suggest that our own problem deserves more attention than it is getting. The very fact that we have a margin of safety not enjoyed in many parts of the world is both a challenge and an opportunity. Let me recite a few facts, even though they may be familiar.

That the productivity of our agriculture can be increased far beyond the limits of the present surplus is not questioned. But each increment in production calls for increasing capital outlays. The investment in machinery, to say nothing of that in fertilizers, feed supplements, maintenance, taxes, and insurance, frequently approaches the value of the land. The knowledge, skill, and competence of the successful farmer today rivals that tolerated in the practice of medicine fifty years ago. In that interval our farm population has diminished by more than a half, being now less than 20 percent of our total population. The pressure to keep costly machinery earning its way often results in extensive operations at the cost of personal attention to those details which prevent deterioration of the whole enterprise, and which, in the end, may make the difference between profit and loss. So meager is the margin that a significant and growing number of model farms are now owned by industrialists and other people of means to permit legitimate losses on their tax returns. So far as our ultimate food and fiber supply is concerned, we need not expect something for nothing. The late Robert Salter, surely a very conservative individual, pointed out that the high yields from hybrid corn were definitely being obtained at the expense of soil fertility. In the corn belt, yields of 100 bushels per acre are now about one-third as frequent as they once were. My guess is that farm surpluses will be only a memory within two decades.

Alternative methods of production are, of course, being proposed and investigated. Most of these involve increasing dependence upon elaborate technological devices, hence increasing energy, capital, and maintenance costs. Equally serious is the increasing vulnerability that comes from utter dependence upon elaborate technological systems. This can be illustrated by what has occurred when a brave and competent army, trained to rely solely upon mechanical transport, has faced in difficult terrain an enemy hardened to simpler and more primitive methods. It was illustrated by the comparative ease with which the Ozark hill people adjusted to a depression while their highly dependent urban neighbors were thrown completely out of gear for a long period of time.

I forbear to recite what would happen to some of our great urban centers in the event of certain entirely possible technological failures. This is information which ought to be classified if it could be. In October I observed the confusion following a two-hour power failure in the Grand Central area in New York City. Four days later an accident to a single car on the Merritt Parkway in Connecticut delayed traffic for an hour, during which time seven miles of motor cars were halted bumper to bumper. The analogy between extreme urbanites and the denizens of the egg factories mentioned earlier is too close to be comfortable. No doubt the subconscious realization of this accounts to some degree for the difference between our present mood and that of the Turks and Finns. These sturdy people proceed phlegmatically about their simple way of life in spite of their hazardous geographical position.

We too are a brave and peace-loving people. It is entirely possible that we are not so much moved by fear of an enemy as by lack of confidence in the structure of a system in which we are so deeply committed and involved. What I am saying is inspired by those who see in technology the complete answer to the world's problems. For I do not doubt that technology, like a human being, has the defects inherent in its own virtues. If, as I believe, it should be our servant and not our master, its advancement should be in the light of all scientific knowledge and not merely of those facets which are of immediate use. The biologist who attempted to apply his knowledge in defiance of known physical principles would be laughed out of court. Yet we seem singularly trustful of engineering projects carried out in disregard of ecological principles.

The Urban Sprawl

The most obvious and acute pressure upon space is in our great cities and surrounding metropolitan areas, whose existence and expansion depend upon technology. They and the associated industries and highways that connect them are absorbing agricultural land in the United States at the rate of some million acres a year. This means fewer orange and walnut groves in California, dairy farms in Georgia, truck and tobacco land in Connecticut, and less of the proverbially fertile valley land along the Miami in Ohio. All of these instances I have seen, as I have seen 15,000-acre tracts of the best farm land condemned for military installations when less productive sites could have been chosen.

There are some 500 major cities of over 25,000 population in the United States. Assuming that they could be evenly distributed, and neglecting smaller towns and cities, each would be in the center of a rectangle roughly 80 miles square. I have seen a fair number of them in recent years and recall very few that were not sprawling out into suburbs with little heed to open space, recreation, agriculture, beauty, or even the protection of future values. An exception, as a taxi driver profanely informed me, was not growing because the local university had everything sewed up!

Since this problem of urban sprawl is now receiving intelligent attention in a series of articles in *Fortune* magazine, I shall note only that it is serious, immediate, and far from simple. Municipalities generally have powers of expansion and taxation against which the rural landscape is without defense.

And between cities, across the land, highway departments are busily freezing the nation into a permanent interurban geometry. Often, in fact if not in theory, they are responsible to no one but themselves and their Euclidean rule that the shortest distance between two points is a straight line. Only through leaders who will devise and citizens who will support better use of urban and highway space can growing blight be checked. Professional planners, who, by the way, are seldom summoned until it is too late for them to be of real use, now frankly regard the entire strip from Washington to Boston as one great metropolitan area. Any lingering doubts on this score should fade at the sight of a new throughway blasting its course among rocks and homes, across land and water.

At Washington, southern end of the megalopolitan strip, fateful decisions regarding the future allocation of American space are made. One of the cabinet members who has much to do with such decisions told a recent visitor, "For one individual who, like yourself, comes here to protest the exploitation of wilderness areas, parks, and other public lands, there are a dozen who come here to press the opposing view." No matter what the sympathies of such a public official, these are elementary facts of political life with which he must reckon.

There are, moreover, numerous agencies of government, not always in close harmony, that are charged to administer space and its resources. What happens is the resultant of many forces, including the pressure put upon Congress and the advice it receives from appropriate bureaus.

The late Colonel Greeley used to relate how much of our national forest space was reserved. Congress, alarmed at the rate at which Theodore Roosevelt was setting aside forest reserves, lowered the boom on him, but the law could not become effective until he signed it. During the few weeks of grace Roosevelt, Pinchot, and Greeley spent evenings sprawled on a White House floor with maps, for all the world like kids with a comic supplement, marking out forests while the President still had power to do so.

District of Columbia

Unlike most cities, Washington was built on a definite plan and is still under close supervision. But the unremitting pressure of housing, traffic, and waste-disposal problems is a constant threat to the space required for recreation, let alone for esthetic values, traditionally a matter of concern. Among other things, the Potomac is notoriously polluted, and the pressure for schools and other public facilities in the overflow region outside the district is a headache to all concerned. In these environs, as around growing cities all over the country, one sees a wilderness of houses built to sell. And the buyer is usually more concerned with pushbuttons and gadgets than with sound construction. It takes no prophet to visualize what the condition of these potential slums will be in less than a generation.

New York Area

Not quite midway to Boston is Jersey City and the whole complex of sleeping towns for New York. As of October 25th of this year the authorities of Jersey City were weighing the relative merits of pails versus paper milk bottles to dispense drinking water. The reserve for Jersey City and nearby places was then enough for about one month. Not even that flower of technology, the modern city, is exempt from the pressure of natural forces. Nor should this be surprising. While the per capita demand for water rises, so does the area that is waterproofed and designed to get rid of rain as fast as it falls.

Even the air is a problem. One approaches the Hudson through one of the most unsavory mixtures of gases on earth. What smells bad, with such noble exceptions as Limburger and Liederkranz, is seldom good. New York City, whose canyons full of fumes are no bed of roses, is within the same general zone of turbulence. The resulting uproar reminds one of the classical dispute as to which stank worse, a goat or a tramp.

252

New York City illustrates what might be called a space paradox. As its population has grown, so has the per capita space, except possibly in some very congested areas. At the same time, the rural areas, whose emigration supplies the growth of nearly all major cities, have fewer people. Farms are increasing in size; fewer men are farming larger farms. Everyone is getting more space while the population rises. The answer is, of course, that the rural man who becomes urban is not getting more space than he had—simply more than he would have had had he moved into the city a generation ago.

New England

Further north, in New England, we encounter other interesting problems of space. Most of them involve conflicts of interest, often elements of minor tragedy. I have in mind the annihilation of homes for which money cannot compensate. One such, whose sturdy hand-made beauty, books, pictures, and furnishings represent the slow accretion of high cultural influence—not mere personal luxury—is now untenable because no better way has been found to dispose of the garbage of an expanding dormitory population than to burn it nearby. In southern Massachusetts I saw the occupants of a group of new homes trying to repair the damage of flood in a site which was notoriously subject to high water. The unwary newcomers who bought these houses did not know this, and no one warned them.

It was, in fact, the floods of 1955 that revealed most dramatically what can happen when important fields of science are neglected while others are being applied to the limit in technological development. Manufacturers of electronic equipment, optical instruments, and precision tools certainly keep abreast of scientific developments. Yet in locating their plants they took risks which no geologist, or competent botanist, would have sanctioned had his opinion been sought. Not only did they expand their activities upon the hazardous flood plain, but in many instances they intruded upon the channel itself, thus making bad matters worse. The old water-mill builders took no such chances. Their homes were on high land, for they knew and respected the power of water.

New England, northern end of the great metropolitan strip, offers many other examples of the pressure of humanity upon space, although it has no monopoly in this respect. The West Coast, the most rapidly growing area in the nation, may be more graphic, for it lacks any protection from past cultural inertia. But in New England one may see a losing struggle to preserve esthetic and recreational values in the face of an insistent desire to expand industry, cater to the automobile, mine for gravel and rock, convert the rivers into free sewers, and in divers other ways capture the nimble dollar.

In these respects New England is no worse—and no better—than other parts of the nation. Two-thirds of its hinterland are now covered with forest, largely of poor quality, occupying land that was once farmed and later grazed during a booming wool industry. Yet this two-thirds of the area produces not more than ten percent of the rural income. In contrast to this, I know a Danish forest of 2000 acres that furnishes year-round employment to 50 men and 20 additional during the winter months, all at a profit. True, the New England soils are often thin and not highly fertile, but the chief trouble seems to be that we have consistently used up the finest trees, while the Danes since 1800 have been saving them for seed stock. Even though one cannot increase space, proper measures will greatly increase its yield. Inferior races of trees are just as wasteful of space as inferior breeds of livestock on pasture and farm. While New England forests even in their present poor condition add vastly to the beauty of the countryside, the time is not too far distant when their products will be needed. European experience shows that good yield is quite consistent with esthetic value.

Pressures upon Space

Across the continent, with infinite variations due to local conditions, the problem of space is growing in urgency. Ultimately we shall have to face the purely physical fact of increasing numbers on a finite area containing finite resources. Of these resources, water is now getting some of the attention it deserves. But we should keep other substances in mind, recalling that we, with less than 7 percent of the world's population, are now absorbing more than 60 percent of the world's mineral production, or ten times our quota.

Meanwhile, the general pressure is complicated by conflicts of interest. Different groups and individuals see different possibilities in the same area, and all alike wish to secure the most from it. As great cities grow they become more, rather than less, dependent upon widening circles of rural land—for water, milk and other food, transport, recreation, housing, labor, and income. It is interesting to consider the sources of support for the four world territories that have more than 10,000 people to the square mile. They are, in order, Macao, a shipping and commercial center, Monaco, a gambling resort, the District of Columbia, where taxes are collected and spent, and Gibraltar, a military post! No great concentration of people is ever self-sustaining. The Valley of the Nile, which has had perhaps 1000 people to the square mile for millenia, depends upon the vast headwater areas reaching south to Lake Victoria for its water and fertility. The same principle applies to the crowded downstream river margins of China and India.

The time must come when we shall have to deal openly, honestly, and realistically with the basic biological fact that numbers of organisms cannot multiply indefinitely within a finite area. And since our own species is under discussion, we must face the unparalleled conditions of increasing numbers and biological dominance combined with accelerating mobility, power, speed, and consumption on the part of the individual. Eventually we must come to grips with these fundamentals. Meanwhile we can, in my judgment, help matters greatly by admitting that conflicts of interest do exist, identifying them, and establishing some order of priority for conflicting claims.

I have no easy solutions to suggest. The first step in dealing with a scientific problem is to make it clear. This I have tried to do, aware of the fact that in our society solutions must be worked out by common consent—generally a painful process. There is a maxim among medical men that more mistakes come from not looking than from not knowing. So far as space is concerned, both looking and knowing are involved.

Training in Science

Much concern is now being expressed for better science training. Here at least we can make a sound, if modest, beginning. Training in the rudiments of science—asking, observing, and reasoning—should begin along with training in the mother tongue and be a part of the same process. College science, training as it does both scientist and citizen, should

254

be taught in context with the rest of human knowledge and experience. It should certainly be a convincing and challenging aspect of education. How far it falls short of these ideals one can discover by asking those who have been exposed to it. Always excepting those who have an innate taste for science, the average college graduate, in my experience, does not retain enough for literate conversation upon the subject, let alone enough understanding to use it in civic affairs. Too often his mood is one of active distaste.

As a rule he has been required to take *a* course in *a* science weighted too often for the benefit of those who must go on in the particular field. How many times I have been told by colleagues: "We must teach it this way, or our students will not be ready for the next course." Such a philosophy misses the fact that by sacrificing insight to detail, fine intellects that might be potential candidates for further work may be lost.

Nor does the mischief stop there. No one science by itself can give that balanced view of the world of nature so essential to the citizen in our modern culture. A peep-show, no matter how good, is no substitute for a panorama. Until citizens, administrators, engineers, and businessmen become aware of the broad sweep of science, we may expect to see it applied, as it has been so largely, for immediate return rather than ultimate and lasting benefit.

Education and Self-Discipline

Let us, therefore, avoid the folly of thinking that science can be separated from the broader problem of education and self-discipline. The present hue and cry for more and better science education could easily lead us into the trap that caught the Germans in 1914. More and better science teaching we must

have, not merely to produce needed scientists, but to create an atmosphere of scientific literacy among citizens at large. Only by general understanding and consent can truly creative science be sustained within our system of society and its results applied for the ultimate welfare of mankind.

Liberal education today should require not less than two years of college science, based on a skilfully planned and interwoven sequence dealing with time, space, motion, matter, and the earth and its inhabitants. Nothing less than this is adequate for a proper appraisal of the natural world and our role as a part of it. This experience should be obtained at the hands of men who believe in it, who have status with their colleagues, and who are in intellectual communication with each other. There is no place for loose ends or superficial business in such an enterprise. Nor can it be carried on without the actual contact with phenomena in laboratory and field. Science that is merely verbalized is dead stuff.

But to this end it is equally essential that the educated individual must acquire such experience in the context of history, the arts, and an understanding of his own species. As a rough objective, I would propose turning out a product aware of what is going on around him in the world of nature and of man, able and willing to relate the present to the past and to the future in both thought and action.

To do this we must recognize with greater frankness than we have that there are vast differences among individuals. Let us learn to look upon these differences with respect, as a source of enrichment rather than discrimination, training each, honoring each, and expecting service from each according to his gifts. Let not the slow impede the fast, nor the fast bewilder and condemn the slow.

With a population set to double in

less than half a century, with a national space which, though vast, is finite both in area and quality, with each individual making growing demands, moving faster and further by a factor of at least ten, we have on our hands a problem without precedent in geological history. But if we sense the problem and believe it worth solving, we can solve it.

Our future security may depend less upon priority in exploring outer space than upon our wisdom in managing the space in which we live.